Judging Mohammed

Judging Mohammed

JUVENILE DELINQUENCY, IMMIGRATION, AND
EXCLUSION AT THE PARIS PALACE OF JUSTICE

Susan J. Terrio

Stanford University Press
Stanford, California

Stanford University Press
Stanford, California

Printed in the United States of America on acid-free, archival-quality paper

Library of Congress Cataloging-in-Publication Data

Terrio, Susan J. (Susan Jane), 1950–
    Judging Mohammed : juvenile delinquency, immigration, and exclusion at the Paris Palace of Justice / Susan J. Terrio.
        p.   cm.
    Includes bibliographical references and index.
    ISBN 978-0-8047-5959-5 (cloth : alk. paper)—ISBN 978-0-8047-5960-1 (pbk. : alk. paper)
    1. Juvenile justice, Administration of—France—Paris.   2. Juvenile delinquency—France—Paris.   3. Juvenile courts—France—Paris.   4. Minority youth—France—Paris.   5. Children of immigrants—France—Paris.   I. Title.
    HV9156.P37T47   2009
    364.36089'00944—dc22   2008040715

Typeset by Westchester Book Composition in 10/14 Minion

For Sydney, Gabe, Noah, and Ben

In memory of Scott Macpherson Stapleton

CONTENTS

ACKNOWLEDGMENTS

COMPLETION OF A SEVEN-YEAR BOOK PROJECT necessarily involves the accumulation of numerous debts in France and the United States. It began with a summer of preliminary research in Paris in 2000, where I made initial contact with key figures at the juvenile court and with French academics studying delinquency. Jocelyne Kanner, a court caseworker in Paris, introduced me to Hervé Hamon, the president of the Paris juvenile court, and to Yvon Tallec, Hamon's counterpart in the juvenile prosecutor's office. Yvon Tallec's persistence in negotiating the labyrinth of the Justice Ministry was critical in obtaining the necessary approvals for me to conduct extended ethnographic research. Sylvie Perdriolle, director of the Office of Judicial Protection of Youth, provided the research clearance and opened other doors. Hervé Hamon was always generous with his time and put me in touch with Alain Bruel, Antoine Garapon, Madeleine Sabatini, and Denis Salas, eminent jurists and judges who granted interviews. I thank sociologist Eric Fassin for persuading Antoine Garapon to take time out of his always busy schedule to speak with me. Sociologists Francis Bailleau, Joëlle Bordet, and Nadine Lefaucheur and political scientist Sophie Body-Gendrot generously shared their work and made invaluable suggestions as I defined my project in its early stages. Discussions with sociologist Dana Diminescu in 2003 were also enormously helpful. Numerous magistrates, caseworkers, and researchers at the Office of Judicial Protection of Youth, including Marie-Anne Baulon, Dominique Cazier, Madeleine Chami, Dominique Dray, Marie-Colette Lalire, and Anne-Sylvie Soudoplatoff, took time to answer questions. Archivist Marie-France Barut graciously arranged for me to do research at the Justice Ministry library. Delphine Bergère, Françoise Cataneo, Bertrand

de Villeneuve, Manuela Néagu, Andrée Pometan, and Nicole Van Loyen, direc-
tors and caseworkers at the Paris Social Service and Probation Office and affiliated service providers, permitted me access to staff briefings and/or gave
extended interviews. A number of cultural psychiatrists, including Yolande
Govindama, Botimela Loteteka, and Chérif Slimane, spoke at length about
their work, and, thanks to Jocelyn Kanner, Director Lucien Hounkpatin of the
Centre Georges Devereux permitted me to attend a therapy session he led there
in June 2003.

My deepest thanks go to the juvenile judges serving at the Paris court between 2000 and 2005, who granted me interviews, opened their courtrooms
and case files, and welcomed me in various venues, such as their regular meetings and professional conferences. To preserve their confidentiality, along with
that of the minors at court, I had to change the names of all but two—Thierry
Baranger and Martine de Maximy—whose public visibility made it impossible
to disguise their identities. One of the judges, whom I cannot identify, not only
arranged for me to attend a trial at the juvenile Assizes Court and sessions of an
adult criminal trial, but instructed me patiently in the finer points of French
law and judicial process. She also provided materials from the judges' professional association and internal court documents. I also express my appreciation to the prosecutors, court clerks, caseworkers, and defense attorneys who
granted formal or informal interviews. I met former juvenile judge Elisabeth
Catta in 2005, and she arranged for me to attend hearings of the Paris appellate
court. The dynamic head of the Juvenile Defense Bureau, Marie-France
Ponelle, saw me twice, and both she and Martine de Maximy facilitated my access to attorneys specializing in juvenile justice or family law, including Dominique Attias, Martine Blanc, Laurence Gottscheck, Etienne Lesage, Pascale
Louvigné, Cécile Maréchal, Brigitte Ponroy, and Christophe Renay. I thank
them for their time. I am grateful to Viviane Martial for her assistance in ar-
ranging my first visit to the Youth Detention Center at the Fleury-Mérogis
prison. I also want to thank Maude Dayet, the head of the Youth Detention
Center, for hosting me in April 2001 and for allowing me to observe a debriefing session with her and the Youth Center guards.

I was able to conduct my research thanks to extraordinary institutional
support from Georgetown University in the form of a 2001 sabbatical leave;
Graduate School Summer Research fellowships in 2000, 2001, and 2002; summer travel grants in 2003 and 2005 from the School of Foreign Service at
Georgetown; a 2003 Senior Faculty Fellowship for the fall semester; and a fall

2006 fellowship from the Georgetown Center for Democracy and the Third Sector. Outside funding was also provided by a 2001 National Endowment for the Humanities Summer Fellowship. The award of a 2005–2006 Radcliffe Residential Fellowship at Harvard University provided me with one of the most wonderful years of my academic life. The generous support, collegial atmosphere, and intellectual stimulation, and the Radcliffe Institute leadership of Director Judy Vichniac and Dean Drew Gilpin Faust, now president of Harvard, provided the perfect alchemy for the write-up phase. I left Harvard with warm memories and new friends. For their companionship and support I thank fellows Vince Brown, Tera Hunter, Vyvyane Loh, Salem Mekuria, Kathy Peiss, Betty Shamieh, and Eve Trout-Powell. As I wrote and rewrote the manuscript, I was often reminded of the hilarious imitation of academic jargon that Tony Horwitz performed more than a few times during our Radcliffe year. I have tried to follow his advice and example by writing clearly and staying on point.

For their critical insights on the project at various stages and their thorough reading of evolving work, I am deeply grateful to colleagues in many places, including Andy Bickford, Denise Brennan, Susan Coutin, Melissa Fisher, Elzbieta Gozdziak, Cymene Howe, Mary Lewis, Susan Ossman, Joanne Rappaport, Andrew Sobanet, and David Vine. I am particularly indebted to Melissa Fisher, who read four key chapters several times and gave me invaluable comments. My work also benefited enormously from participation in a fall 2003 interdisciplinary Social Science Research Council workshop on Youth, Law, and Globalization organized by Ron Kassimir and Sudhir Venkatesh. I also acknowledge the talented students, both undergraduate and graduate students, whose research assistance was indispensable to me. At Georgetown I thank Ian Bourland, Holly Beardow, Chloe Asselin, and Laura Anne Thompson, and I am grateful to Sabrina Peric and Neesha Maria Rao at Harvard. Finally, my deepest appreciation goes to Kate Wahl for her exemplary editorial support, and to the three reviewers of the manuscript for Stanford, John Bowen, Debbie Durham, and Miriam Ticktin, whose thoughtful, thorough, and judicious commentary helped me to clarify my argument and tighten the whole book.

Research agendas and individual lives intersect in strange ways. Many people asked how, after writing a first book on French chocolatiers, I chose the topic of delinquency. My initial response was that I was attracted by media coverage of delinquent youth who were all assumed to be of immigrant ancestry. Although this was partly true, it took me five years and a move to Harvard to realize that the choice had much to do with my own childhood and the repressed trauma of growing up with an older brother who was labeled a delinquent by the time he was twelve. Because of the age difference between us and because of his chaotic adolescence, we grew up apart and never had a real relationship. I came to see this book as a partial attempt to understand his early entanglement in the juvenile justice system and to account for the divergent paths our lives took. The project itself had curious bookends: It began with rowdy teenagers I encountered on a Paris subway en route from the juvenile court, and it ended with a death in the family. The same day I got the news that Stanford accepted my book for publication, my brother died of a massive heart attack.

There were other happier bookends to this project. Over the seven years it took me to research and write the book, my husband and I became grandparents. Our first grandchild, a girl, was conceived in 2000, the summer I began research, and our fourth, a boy, was born just before Christmas in 2007 as I was completing the final book revisions. Grandchildren are precious for many reasons. They are part of families we choose and inherit and so link us to the past and the future. They are a source of constant renewal, with the attendant joys and unexpected turns that implies. I dedicate this book to my grandchildren and bless them, and their parents, for so enriching my life.

Susan Terrio
Bald Head Island, North Carolina
February 2008

Judging Mohammed

PROLOGUE

THE FIRST FULL DAY I spent in a juvenile courtroom at the Paris Palace of Justice was a shock because all of the "suspects" were at-risk minors, and all but one were foreigners or minorities. Their offenses constituted less of a risk to public order or municipal security than to themselves and their future. Violence figured in only one of the infractions, and it involved grabbing a cell phone from a tourist who was making a call. It was a raw day in January 2001, but I decided to walk to the Ile de la Cité from my tiny studio apartment on the Left Bank. En route I passed many of the venerable state institutions that produce the nation's elite. In this part of the Latin Quarter, the monumental paeans to France's civilizational grandeur are everywhere—prestigious preparatory schools, elite public universities, research centers, ancient churches, and the national mausoleum itself. My destination, the Palace of Justice, is flanked by the imposing Conciergerie prison (where Marie Antoinette was held briefly before her execution) and encompasses within its walls the magnificent twelfth-century Sainte-Chapelle. The medieval gated fortress housing the Palace of Justice is where I came to know the "other" Paris—"the hoodlums, delinquents, recidivists, and marginal families" at court, which was one judge's parody of the public perception of the juvenile justice system.[1]

I was scheduled to attend penal hearings in the Eighteenth District South courtroom. When I arrived at the public entrance, I was unprepared for the large crowd of tense people waiting to enter the Palace of Justice, in contrast to the few intrepid tourists who had come to visit the Sainte-Chapelle. The police had divided the line in two. I soon found myself caught in the press of mostly brown and black people clutching court summonses and jostling for position to pass through the metal detector. When one man on the Palace of Justice side set off the alarm by passing through with change in his pocket, everything stopped. People looked anxiously at one another or at their watches, and a young man behind me swore softly. An infant in the arms of his African mother began to whimper. It was close to 2:00 P.M. and the start of the afternoon hearings. I did not know then that if a person is absent when his or her case is called, it usually means an even longer wait or a rescheduled hearing. For the working-class and poor families who constitute the majority of the court's clientele, this is not an inconvenience but a hardship involving lost time and wages and the ordeal of dealing with the legal system.

Court proceedings in the Eighteenth South rarely started on time. This was fortunate, because after entering the court I was stopped by the policeman on duty. I had made eye contact and looked uncertain, two moves that attracted his attention. When I could produce only a Maryland driver's license as identification—not the summons or passport he requested—he had the excuse he needed to ask me to leave. When I insisted that he contact the judge or even the court president, he relented and allowed me to pass. I found the door to the chambers of the presiding judge around the next corner. Although judges normally supervise the cases of children and families who live in their districts, on this afternoon, in addition to normally scheduled hearings, the juvenile judge was on call (*de permanence*) and required to conduct hearings for all the minors who had been arrested during the preceding twenty-four-hour period, as well as urgent child endangerment cases, which required immediate investigation.

Because juvenile proceedings are closed to the public, the only outsiders ever permitted inside are judicial interns (*auditeurs de justice*) in their last year of training at the Ecole Nationale de la Magistrature (also called ENM, the elite public graduate school in Bordeaux that trains all French judges) or their counterparts from foreign institutions. After approval of a required research plan by the French Ministry of Justice, I was permitted to observe court proceedings and to interview court personnel. My ability to maneuver within a highly policed space and to make my presence understood not only to court personnel but to the children and families under supervision was contingent upon the adoption of a socioprofessional category that made sense to everyone concerned. After preliminary research the preceding summer and consultation with the president of the juvenile court, the head of the juvenile prosecutor's section, and the director of the Protection Judiciaire de la Jeunesse (Office of

Judicial Protection of Youth), I had the approval I needed to become an intern. This gave me unprecedented access to hearings and trials, even as it constrained me in other ways.

On this day I arrived just a few minutes before the court-affiliated caseworkers (*éducateurs*), also on duty, who conduct intake interviews with the teenagers in the juvenile quarter of the Paris jail, brief the judge on their backgrounds, and assess their physical and psychological states. The presiding judge, a senior magistrate with many years of experience in the juvenile court system, described her jurisdiction. The Eighteenth South is a district of approximately 100,000 residents unevenly divided between two groups: a large, poor multiethnic population dominated by African immigrants living in overcrowded apartments and makeshift public housing, and a smaller, affluent group in gentrified neighborhoods in the Montmartre area. Delinquency consists largely of public order violations, thefts, muggings, and petty extortion.

I did not know it then, but that afternoon's proceedings were largely representative of the civil and penal cases tried in the five courtrooms where I conducted my research. They involved parental abuse or neglect of minor children, or penal infractions of simple theft or theft aggravated by the circumstance of assault (*violence*) and/or in a group (*en réunion*). The overwhelming majority of the accused were Maghrebi, African, and Antillean males from working-class and underprivileged backgrounds, or eastern European (primarily Romanian) males and females who were unaccompanied, irregular migrants and lived in squats outside the city, then earning large sums of cash from the theft of parking meter receipts.

The éducateurs' briefing began with the case of a fifteen-year-old Ethiopian girl who had been arrested for an immigration violation. She was carrying a false passport on a train bound for London, where she hoped to study English and to get an education. She had come to Paris from Greece, where her widowed mother worked as a domestic, and had left with her mother's approval. She spoke fluent Amharic and Greek but knew no French, and she had learned English from watching American TV sitcoms. She had spent a night at a local police station before her transfer to the Palace jail, where a formal twenty-four-hour detention began. When questioned by the éducateurs, she indicated that she had not eaten or slept in two days and had "been treated like a criminal by the police." She wanted to get to Great Britain "because," she claimed, "immigrants were welcome there."

The second case involved an emotionally fragile young man from a mainstream working-class French family in northern France, who was arrested for a first-time theft in the Paris metro. He had been tracked as an at-risk case after an unsuccessful attempt at suicide but had had no regular contact with French social services since that episode. His father told the caseworker that the boy was under the influence of a local "gang" and had "violent rages." In his intake interview the teenager complained that the police had tightened the handcuffs to the point of causing him pain.

The third case told the story of the abuse and neglect of a fifteen-year-old girl of Antillean ancestry, who became a mother at twelve and had just given birth to a second child, a boy. The teenager revealed for the first time that the father of both children was her mother's "companion," a single man from Guadeloupe who lived one floor down in the same makeshift facility housing welfare recipients, formerly a hotel. Next, the police brought in a French teenager of Algerian descent, a drug abuser with a long police record who was arrested for aggravated theft against an American tourist. Under French law, snatching a cell phone qualified as such an offense. He insisted that "this time" he wanted help for his drug problem. There was a brief break, after which the caseworker arrived to describe the last two cases as Romanian boys, aged twelve and fifteen, who were apprehended for the "umpteenth time for stealing from Paris parking meters." Turning to me, she added, "the little one escaped from an orphanage eight months ago. He met an adult who brought him to France via Italy. They live in an abandoned building outside the city and look like they have been beaten. They are caught in a criminal network, treated like slaves, and forced to work for adults." Later in the day more cases arrived in court—specifically, two French teenagers of North African ancestry, for arrests following an altercation with the police in which the charges were "insulting and resisting public authorities."

The hearings did not end until nearly 7:00 P.M. The pace was rushed, the attorneys took no active role in the defense of the accused, the caseworkers seemed overburdened, and the accumulated suffering to which we were exposed weighed heavily on me. The judge arranged for judicial protection orders and temporary placements for the Ethiopian migrant and the teenage mother. The judge was clearly concerned that the teenage girl had spent almost forty-eight hours in custody because of a "technical mishap." Nothing illegal had occurred, because the police had never officially extended the twenty-four-hour limit for police custody. Despite the teenager's allegations of abuse, the judge declined to elicit any further details about the girl's time in police custody from the minor. The judge transferred one penal case back to the Compiègne court in the north but indicted all the other suspects.[2]

When the judge questioned the two youths, they explained they were on a street corner talking when the police arrived in response to a neighbor's call about noise. The police demanded to see identification, using the condescending, familiar *tu* form of address with the teenagers. When one of the youths protested that it was the second identity check of the night, the police "got rough, I lost my temper, he slammed me up against the wall and put on the handcuffs." After finding out that the teenagers lived in the Eleventh District, the judge set a hearing date in that court for them.

Although the judge was inclined to offer protection to the Romanian teenagers, the Romanian interpreter and a defense attorney argued that they "did not want help" and would not benefit from state assistance. The caseworker commented that "they couldn't care less that they were arrested." The Romanian translator stepped out of her legally neutral role and offered insider knowledge on the irregular migration of the unaccompanied minors as well as the criminal networks that exploited them. She used her privileged perspective to refute the caseworker's portrayal of systematic abuse. The translator insisted that "torture was rare, that the Romanian rings that bring them to France usually include a family member, an uncle who plays the role of banker. They split the money from crime and pressure the families to keep their children here." When the case of the Algerian teenager was heard, the caseworker summarized his family background. His father was uneducated and had given up on his son. Given the boy's delinquent career and drug addiction, the attorney offered advice that seemed completely inconsistent with her role as his defense counsel. She was pessimistic about rehabilitation and implied that because he was out of school and unsupervised, his only "productivity seemed to be robbing tourists." The judge agreed, saying to him, "You'll surely end up in prison." The caseworker suggested giving custody to the teenager's paternal aunt, who had agreed to take him "on the condition that he return to Algeria." This was something the teenager adamantly opposed, because he was French. The judge exercised her prerogative to schedule hearings in chambers or the full juvenile court. She referred all three cases to the full juvenile court, which hears the cases of serious misdemeanors and crimes of thirteen- to sixteen-year-olds and can render prison sentences.

By the time these hearings ended I had more questions than answers. How did these cases square with the reputation of the French juvenile justice system? The French legal code governing minors has been widely viewed as a progressive welfare approach because it privileges prevention and rehabilitation and does not distinguish between delinquent and at-risk youth. First legislated in 1945, this ordinance is celebrated as "famous" because it represented a shift away from a repressive prewar system that relied on punitive confinement in state institutions for both delinquent and endangered children to one that emphasized assistance and integration within the family setting. Its moniker as "famous" is partly ironic because it has been the subject of recurrent controversy and continuous reform since 1945. Although the 1945 law remains in effect, in the 1990s a punitive model attracted attention and resuscitated acrimonious debates among proponents of repression and defenders of rehabilitation. Since the 1990s there has been a marked shift from prevention and assistance to accountability, restitution, and retribution in the treatment of youth offenders. This occurred in response to what many viewed as a new, more threatening type of delinquency—a delinquency of exclusion. When I began my research in 2000, "a delinquency of exclusion" was a coded reference to the children of predominantly marginalized Muslim families from North and West Africa.

What did these hearings suggest about the individual-centered welfare approach still enshrined in French juvenile law? Was this the intrusive therapy and preventive protection widely associated with court supervision? Could one argue that this system still made no distinction between delinquent and at-risk children? Given increased attention to juvenile defense rights internationally, these hearings beg the question of what due process protections were extended to minor defendants in the French juvenile justice system. Were they accorded the presumption of innocence? What are we to make of a system that has an arsenal of antidiscrimination laws but recognizes no minority groups and permits only individuals to seek legal redress? How are we to understand a system that records only nationality in court documents but whose clientele in both civil and penal cases in the Paris court are overwhelmingly minors of immigrant and foreign ancestry from disadvantaged and working-class families? Court proceedings have much to teach us about evolving conceptions of childhood and the boundaries separating it from adulthood. Does the consensus on childhood as a malleable and perfectible stage extending to the late teens apply only to certain children and adolescents? Who is considered amenable to rehabilitation and, therefore, eligible for scarce therapeutic resources and educational opportunities in a stagnant labor market for young people?

.   .   .

When I left the court that evening, it was pouring rain and I was too exhausted to walk, so I took the metro. I ran across the bridge spanning the Seine to take line seven at Châtelet. This is a line that runs along an axis from north to south as it wends its way through the multiethnic, mixed neighborhoods in the northeast arrondissements inhabited by working-class families, students, new immigrants, and young couples. It then moves through the city's wealthy commercial center and past the Opera, paralleling the river with stops at the Palais Royal and at points in the financial and fashion districts and the now upscale Marais neighborhood on the Right Bank before crossing under the Seine to the Left Bank and the Latin Quarter. At its terminus points on the city periphery, line seven connects suburbs in the red belt around Paris, Aubervilliers in the north, and Kremlin-Bicêtre in the south. Once known primarily as working-class strongholds of the Communist Party, the *banlieues* (suburbs) have come to be associated with youth crime and to signify the danger posed for the nation by high concentrations of immigrant "Others"—whether Maghrebi (North African), African (Sub-Saharan), or Antillean. That night I did not anticipate any unusual encounters on the subway and was not thinking about what Marc Augé describes as the numerous signs of alterity, "often provocative and even aggressive," in the Paris metro that function "as a magnifying glass, inviting us to consider a phenomenon we might otherwise not see or try to ignore."[3]

I boarded the train and collapsed in a seat near the end of a car. At first I did not see the three teenagers in the seats at the back, one of African ancestry and the two others of Arab descent. A few seconds later I was punched in the back. When I turned around, assuming it was a mistake and expecting an apology, they made a magnificent and uniform show of pleading ignorance. Although no one else was within three seats of us, they exchanged exaggerated, outraged looks suggesting, "Who, me?" and "What?" I turned back around, supremely annoyed and shocked out of my stupor. I decided to ignore them and bent over my newspaper until I noticed that a blunt metal hook had suddenly appeared, suspended over my head from behind. I could not think of how to respond so I just swung around and mustered my most professorial glare. This convulsed them with laughter but they promptly removed the offending hook.

What happened next could have been their response to the questions buzzing inside my head. They began a rap on who they were, in obvious counterpoint to me, the white, middle-aged woman with the supercilious manner and bourgeois demeanor whom they no doubt assumed to be French. I had descended to the level of their expectations by not seeing them and refusing to engage them verbally. They initiated what I interpreted as a call-and-response parody of the mainstream discourse on the problematic cultural difference and identities of so-called immigrant youth born in France but not of France. "So who are you . . . are you French?" one of the boys sang out. "Oh no, I'm not French, I'm Algerian," was the rapid rejoinder followed immediately by the question, "So if you are Algerian and not French, are you an atheist (*athé*)?" That is, if you are not white and Christian and part of the unmarked majority category, but you are Arab and Muslim, does that assign you a marked and lesser status? Does that put you in the category of the unbeliever? The boys pressed on in their wordplay on French attitudes regarding Islam: "Are you an atheist or a Christian?" "No, not me, I'm just a cretin (*crétin*)." Here the boys used a play on the French words *crétin* and *chrétien*, which are pronounced the same with the exception of one syllable. He is not *chrétien* (Christian), so he is, therefore, an idiot.

The boys soon forgot about me and their conversation turned to other subjects. I overheard only bits and pieces about school, homework, and teachers. They rose to leave at the stop before mine and gave me a final knock on the head. As the train door opened, an elderly lady used a cane to steady herself as she entered. As they passed her, one of the boys grabbed the end and tugged gently on it as if to take it. She leveled an indignant stare at him, saying loudly, "*Et alors?*" ("What's this?") He immediately released the cane and the three friends jumped off the train, howling with laughter.

How could I not be struck by the timing of this encounter at the beginning of a fieldwork project on delinquency at the Paris court? I have lived and traveled in France periodically over a period of twenty-five years, much of that time in Paris, and I have never had a problem on the subway, even late at night during a year when I lived in a working-class neighborhood in the eleventh arrondissement. I was reminded of the writings of Azouz Begag, the Algerian novelist, sociologist, and former minister of the center-right government of Dominique de Villepin who grew up in a Lyonnais shantytown and experienced racism in French schools firsthand. Begag has repeatedly discussed the charged topic of juvenile delinquency. For him, youth crime is a phenomenon intimately linked to spatial configurations of power and the interactions among unequal groups, not the social origin of specific populations. The teenagers' stop and my stop were located in the fifth arrondissement, a trendy area popular with Parisians and tourists not only for civilizational landmarks, but for colorful open-air markets, shops, arthouse cinemas, and ethnic restaurants. In a 1999 newspaper editorial, Begag argued that the public visibility of youth of immigrant origin beyond the boundaries of the projects "provokes discomfort, rejection, and relentless identity checks [by police]" and "fuels a powder keg of frustration."[4]

My encounter was illustrative of the type of incivilities that figure prominently in French talk about the cultural difference and delinquent potential of "immigrant" youth. The deterioration of inner-city neighborhoods is said to begin with incivilities such as offensive comments and rude behavior and to degenerate rapidly into criminal offenses. I described it to the senior judge of the Eighteenth South courtroom and shared my view that it was a plea for visibility on their part that revealed entrenched relations of inequality. She dismissed that theory as nonsense and insisted that it was a diversionary tactic; the boys were after my purse. Based on the scores of cases I had observed and the files I had read in which young men of immigrant or foreign ancestry were targeted for public order violations, such as attempted theft or aggravated theft; riot or incitement to riot; insulting, assaulting, or refusing to obey public authorities; or physical assault, I was certain that if the police had seen the youth hit me or hassle the elderly woman, I had no doubt they would have ended up in handcuffs and under arrest.

Between the summer of 2000, when I conducted preliminary research, and June 2007, when I finished the book, global attention focused on France's youth violence and bleak ghettos. The anger and frustration of the rioters in 2005, and the government's failure to deliver on the promises made that year (see Chapter 1), produced incidents in the fall of 2006, on the first anniversary of the unrest, that were considerably more violent than the property destruction of 2005 and included, for the first time, deadly assaults on French police and the torching of occupied buses in Marseille. Youth in the blighted and segregated regions of the public housing projects (*cités*) do not see themselves fully reflected in the promises or entitlements of the liberal democratic republic. The economic polarization wrought by deindustrialization and a shrinking welfare state have left them with few viable choices outside of the underground economy. Their sources of revenue—from the provision of illicit services, the fencing of stolen property, or participation at the low end of the drug trade—all hold risks and engender social alienation. Moreover, the meager educational opportunities offered them are premised on their own fraught social reproduction within marginal cités through low-level credentials in counseling for at-risk teenagers and positions in underprivileged areas.[5] Their isolation and disaffection are fueled by the stigma and discrimination they face, based on their social origin and cultural difference.

Silhouetted against burning cars, sporting hooded jackets and turning exuberant faces to the camera, the 2005 rioters, like offenders at court, are signified in the popular and scholarly French imagination by the collective noun *les jeunes issus de l'immigration*. "Youth of immigrant ancestry" indexes a physically powerful and threatening mass of underclass, violent male Others. Most often they are Arab or black, but the elasticity of the category means it can expand to incorporate new Others, such as vagrant foreigners from eastern Europe. My encounter on the metro in central Paris may be an ominous harbinger of things to come. These are youth who refuse to be invisible and to stay in the degraded internal colonies of the cités or in the miserable squatter settlements of the periphery, where they suffer the daily indignity of intensified surveillance and police intervention coupled with worsening social inequality and economic polarization. In November 2005 one young teenager of Arab descent, a certain Mohammed, brandished his French identity card in front of a TV camera with burning cars and buildings as a backdrop and insisted: "We are already French. We were born in French hospitals. Why do they talk about integration? We are French."

1 ARE THEY ALL DELINQUENTS?

ON 9 NOVEMBER 2005, when France 3 TV broadcast programming devoted to the French riots called the *Banlieues: The Big Scare*, it asked viewers to consider the nature of the events unfolding around them: "Is it guerrilla warfare? Barbarism? Civil war? Intifada?" Speaking over close-ups of young men of non-European ancestry against a backdrop of burning cars and smoky ruin, the hosts asked: "Are they all delinquents?" Urban violence in the impoverished Paris suburb of Clichy-sous-Bois, where 50 percent of the population are under twenty-five, one-third are foreign, and 25 percent are unemployed, focused unwelcome international attention on France's "immigrant" problem and youth crime.[1] It was here that three boys fleeing the police risked hiding in a power substation—where two died accidentally by electrocution and a third was severely burned—rather then face the likely ordeal of arrest, detention in police custody, and a hearing in court. When Interior Minister Nicolas Sarkozy insisted that the teenagers were possible suspects running from the crime scene, not from the police, rioting broke out.[2] The violence escalated rapidly when he promised to rid the suburbs of the "gangs of delinquent scum" (*bandes de racaille*) responsible for crime.[3]

The riots that spread across urban peripheries throughout France prompted Prime Minister Dominique de Villepin to declare a state of emergency for only the third time in half a century.[4] He justified his proposed policy of mass arrests and deportation orders for foreigners convicted of rioting by referring to "structured gangs and organized crime," despite any conclusive evidence that they were the main perpetrators.[5] Taking a cue from Interior Minister Sarkozy, conservative legislators blamed the violence on insufficient controls over illegal immigration and on youth from polygamous families.[6] A quarter of those legislators signed a petition circulated by Deputy François Grosdidier denouncing seven rap artists for lyrics that endorsed "hatred for France" and "anti-white racism." Justice Minister Pascal Clément responded by initiating prosecution against them in November 2005 for promoting "incivility if not terrorism."[7] These events show the state resorting to the use of, in David Cole's felicitous phrase, "anticipatory coercion" against internal Others and foreign nationals to reinforce national security and lessen public fears linked to youth crime.[8] On one hand, issues of national sovereignty and public order were foregrounded; on the other, a specific category of person was debated. It is the relationship between these two lines of questioning that is at the heart of this book.

The FR3 journalists' rhetorical blurring of all young males in the projects speaks to a dramatic shift concerning juvenile delinquency, not only in French public and scholarly opinion but in the courts. In that one broadcast, the journalists naturalized the link between the juvenile delinquents who were burning cars and all young people of non-European ancestry living in the projects, whether in the suburban areas or in "bad" inner-city neighborhoods. By suggesting that the riots might represent a French intifada, the journalists evoked the threatening Muslim or the violent Jihadi whose alienation from mainstream society made him a ripe convert for terrorist plots. The reference to "barbarians" echoed colonial categorizations that separated the civilized from the uncivilized in the empire and at home mapped the "barbarians" onto groups of menacing Others, understood historically as the dangerous classes. The allusion to "civil war" played to postcolonial anxiety over the problem of "integrating" the children and grandchildren of the immigrants whose labor in French factories, construction, and agriculture was critical to the unparalleled economic growth of the "thirty glorious years" following World War II. These generations "born of immigration," as the phrase goes, did not enjoy the benefits of full employment in semi- or unskilled jobs or realize the promise of social mobility through French public education. Rather, by 2005 extended periods of low economic growth, deindustrialization, limited blue-collar work, and a difficult job market demanding greater professional credentials and longer schooling had combined to produce high youth unemployment and underemployment, particularly for those of working-class, "immigrant," and foreign backgrounds.[9]

A "DELINQUENCY OF EXCLUSION"

How did this new definition of France's non-European immigrant youth come about? In the 1990s, as juvenile arrest rates rose while overall crime declined, public attention centered on what was identified as a newly threatening social category, a "delinquency of exclusion." Some influential magistrates began to collaborate with a group of new sociologists who were studying urban violence and, drawing on their work, linked the foreign or immigrant delinquent to inherited cultural pathologies and dangerous social milieus. In a conference held to commemorate the fiftieth anniversary of the passage of modern juvenile law, it was eminent jurist and former juvenile judge Denis Salas—a judge with close ties to the Paris court—who coined the term *delinquency of exclusion*.[10] This was a category conflated with disadvantaged Muslim youth, both French citizens and immigrants, spatially rooted in stigmatized urban and suburban spaces. Many experts in the media, law enforcement, the bar, the magistracy, the academy, and the government depicted the "new" delinquents as younger, more violent, and irredeemable. These experts came to view an offender "from an immigrant background" through the lens of a cultural ecology model and as the product of deficient social milieus shaped by cultural pathologies and economic deprivation. The offender became associated with the 150,000 young people who leave French schools each year without degrees of any kind or with those who try to find work but fail because they have the wrong skills and worthless diplomas. Unlike his father or grandfather, this young man was no longer seen as part of a potential labor reserve but was viewed as permanently excluded from the fabric of mainstream society and condemned to resort to the informal economy for his survival. In a short time, this delinquent figure assumed monstrous proportions and his deviance was portrayed as unprecedented.[11] His offenses were depicted as a crisis of public order and as an assault on French values. The representation of youth crime gave rise to moral panics and created a collective amnesia regarding other historical episodes of juvenile delinquency that were understood by contemporaries in identically menacing terms—the hoards of Parisian vagrants in nineteenth-century Paris, the urban Apaches from southern Europe in the 1910s, the fatherless thieves during the German occupation of France of the 1940s, and the "black jackets" of the 1950s.[12]

As a result of extensive media coverage of short-term spikes in the rates of certain youth crimes, the topic of *insécurité*, or fear for public safety, became a highly politicized public issue in the 1990s. It resuscitated acrimonious debates on the nature and causes of juvenile delinquency as well as the relative merits of punishment versus rehabilitation. It dominated opinion polls, shaped public policy agendas, produced legal reform, and helped to determine electoral outcomes, eliminating Prime Minister Lionel Jospin from the second round of the 2002 presidential elections and pitting far-right extremist candidate Jean-Marie Le Pen against incumbent president Jacques Chirac. In 2007 Nicolas Sarkozy's embrace of a leaner welfare state coupled with tough anticrime initiatives targeting minors contributed to his election as president. In a pivotal January 2007 speech he declared that "if we excuse violence we must expect barbarism."[13]

Jurists, politicians, academics, and public intellectuals on the left and the right reached a consensus on the new delinquents as being radically different from juvenile offenders of the past. They differentiated the new delinquency from earlier understandings of delinquency, prevalent until recently, that viewed it as the product of coming-of-age risk-taking and immaturity, individual pathology, or flawed parenting. As these minors came to be overrepresented in police custody, the courts, and in prison, the consensus on childhood as a malleable and perfectible stage extending to the late teens was shaken. The dispensations and protections normally granted to young teenagers for exposure to bad influences at an impressionable age or for the developmental immaturity that leads to risky behavior came under attack for this population. Formal penal reforms and informal judicial practices worked to separate French children from those born to immigrant and foreign parents and radically narrowed the boundary of the child for the latter group. In a campaign to protect public order, politicians, police, and court personnel began to "adultify" even young children from these families, ascribing conscious intention, bad character, or even total responsibility to them for offending.[14]

During the years from 2000 to 2005, the preventive welfare approach legislated in 1945 was challenged by critics on the left and the right and the legal codes governing minors were rapidly amended. This critique focused explicitly on the juvenile court, its judges, and the nationally uniform legal codes that have earned France its international reputation as a rehabilitative system. From the mid-1990s, an uneasy political consensus arose on the imperative to emphasize accountability, restitution, and more punitive retribution in the treatment of youth offenders. This change was supported by governments and politicians who drew selectively on the expert opinion of jurists, judges, social scientists, and security analysts.

Successive governments continued a long-standing territorialized approach to urban crime in state-classified or locally identified "bad" areas with high concentrations of "immigrant" and foreign populations and instituted aggressive modes of policing and control of minors who were deemed dangerous based on their origin. They constructed a new category of violent youth crime through systematic reform of penal codes that created new public order violations and heavier penalties for existing infractions. They extended the coercive force and reach of the state through the justice system by enhancing prosecutorial and police power and by accelerating the adjudication process to permit swifter prosecutions, investigations, and trials for juveniles. They reexamined the very notion of penal irresponsibility for minors and, in a dramatic reversal of postwar philosophy, they lowered the age at which children could be held accountable and given "rehabilitative" punishments from thirteen to ten.[15] Legislators also changed the rules for preventive detention, permitting a new "flexible incarceration" regime for minors aged thirteen to sixteen.[16] In early August 2007 a new law on adult and minor recidivists went into effect. This law created minimum sentences for the first time in modern French law, suspended the automatic application of the excuse of minority for sixteen- to eighteen-year-olds,[17] and mandated prison for a range of offenses.[18] By treating sixteen- to eighteen-year-olds as adults, this law effectively lowered the age of penal majority to sixteen years of age and returned France to the 1810 penal code.

Because the juvenile court's preventive and rehabilitative mandate is subject to constant challenge, it has become a site of competing discourses about the best way to deal with first-time and repeat offenders. Given the rapid increase in the proportion of penal to civil cases (from 50 percent to 75 percent of the total between 1998 and 2001) and in the numbers of endangerment warnings transmitted to the prosecutor's office by school and municipal authorities, the court is now discussed in terms of its many problems. The problems that are commonly cited include heavy caseloads, staff shortages, and hearing backlogs; a lack of specialized clinics in adolescent psychiatry; a scarcity of state-licensed emergency and long-term residential facilities and service providers for court-ordered measures; the increased power of prosecutors and judicial police; the creation of a new magistrate with no specialized training to preside over detention decisions for minors; the use of diversionary measures for first-time offenders presided over by prosecutorial representatives and not career magistrates; the insufficient guarantee of the presumption of innocence or a full adversarial debate in hearings; deliberate profiling and intimidation or abuse of ethnic minorities by police; and the high percentage of court judgments and sentences rendered in the absence of irregular foreign defendants. The fact that there is some agreement on problems at court does not mean that there is any consensus on why they are problematic or how they should be resolved.[19]

RECONCEPTUALIZING CHILDREN AND ADOLESCENTS

Youth and childhood are social categories that signal important relations within and between generations. As such, they are often the object of intense debates on authority, obligation, and maturity.[20] In the 1990s, the category of the child became a highly contested domain of public policy and cultural politics.[21] This occurred in a global context marked by advancing neoliberalism, radical transitions to democracy, the transnational pursuit of human rights, and the specific recognition of children's rights in universal charters such as the International Convention for the Rights of the Child (CRC). The convention stipulated increased rights such as the freedom from discrimination, exploitation, and abuse. It also specified the right to special treatment in juvenile justice systems, notably the imperative to treat minors differently from adults, to limit the use of restrictive custody, and, building on earlier human rights conventions, the right to due process provisions and fairness in trial proceedings.

France's ratification of this law was consistent with the nation's historical status as a champion of human rights and as an enthusiastic signatory of international conventions advancing children's rights. Nonetheless, its ratification had the unintended consequence of highlighting the significant gap between new international norms and French legal codes and practices, particularly in the areas of policing, prisons, and trials of both juveniles and adults. The European Court of Human Rights has condemned France many times for violations that reveal systemic failures of the criminal justice system, such as police brutality, a lack of respect for defendants' rights, and the excessive length of pretrial detention.[22] In 1999 France became only the second country after Turkey to be condemned by the European Court of Human Rights for violation of article 3 on the grounds of inhuman treatment and torture.[23] After inspections of French prisons and police jails in 1991, 1996, and 2000, reports to the European Committee for the Prevention of Torture noted severe overcrowding and filthy conditions and strongly criticized France for its treatment of prisoners.[24]

Legal review of the lack of due process protections at juvenile courts prompted debate and pressure from within successive governments, professional groups, and nongovernmental organizations (NGOs) to mobilize to effect reforms. These included the legislation in 1991 to provide legal counsel to indigent clients, the 1994 creation of a Juvenile Defense Bureau at the Paris court (and other tribunals) to train and remunerate attorneys for juvenile defendants, legislation in 2000 to reinforce the presumption of innocence and due process protections, and the 2000 appointment of a children's rights commissioner with a mandate to criminalize human trafficking.

These gains obscure the fact that although the CRC is the most ratified of all human rights directives, it is also the most violated. It is possible to claim compliance with the human rights agendas while pursuing policies that exacerbate structural inequalities and punitive institutional regimes. International legal instruments such as the CRC construct children not only as vulnerable and developing beings but as rational and accountable agents. They engender new conceptions of childhood that emphasize children's decision-making abilities and justify harsher punishment for offending. Children are simultaneously celebrated through the new claims to rights and entitlements and hollowed out through the attendant expectations of enhanced moral and legal responsibility for their actions. The modern model of the protected and innocent child conceptualized by Ariès increasingly applies to the affluent classes alone.[25] In contrast, the shantytown notion of youth has wide currency. It evokes the premodern notion of the child as a miniature adult endowed with intentionality and malice.[26]

Reconceptions of childhood dovetail all too well with changes initiated in the United States and exported globally in criminal and youth justice systems, which place less emphasis on the social contexts of crime and the state provision of protection and more importance on punitive accountability.[27] The shift from state welfare–based approaches to privatized neoliberal modes of governance has decisive and unforeseen consequences for young people. The global spread of universal rights has bolstered Western notions of individualism and perpetuated postcolonial notions "of a barbaric and authoritarian 'global east' or 'global south.' "[28] As states lose control over global labor, capital, and culture flows, they struggle to reassert their power and authority over borders, identities, and legal codes through the criminalization of internal Others and undesirable outsiders. Many states have moved to enforce parental authority, institutionalize national norms through citizenship workshops or pro-marriage legislation, punish "bad" parents, and criminalize antisocial behavior.

This trend was evident in the decisions to open penal rather than civil cases for teenagers who acted out in French schools, as well as the treatment reserved for the unaccompanied, irregular minors who broke the law on Paris streets. In a pattern that began in the 1990s and rapidly accelerated in the twenty-first century, the legislature voted stiffer penalties for existing offenses, such as threatening or insulting the police, and created new infractions, such as anti-loitering laws.[29] Those most vulnerable were foreigners without legal status, verifiable identities, or adults to protect them. Unaccompanied, irregular migrants from poorer regions to the east and the south whose survival strategies in Paris included stealing, sex work, pimping, and burglary exemplified the principle of categorical mixture that produced higher anxiety and led to public rejection and legal sanction.[30] They were increasingly placed within the anomalous category of the child-adult, putting them at risk for more severe punishment.

A recent press report described an unaccompanied minor from eastern Europe who was arrested for theft without identity papers and detained in prison pending trial on the strength of a widely used but controversial test of skeletal development determining her age to be over sixteen (see Chapter 8). Although her correct age was finally established as eleven, the case was striking because the controversy centered on the age of the defendant, not her incarceration for theft. Based on her police record as a "recidivist," all involved assumed that she was a delinquent rather than an endangered teenager. These assumptions were a repudiation of the central tenet of French juvenile law, which theoretically makes no distinction between endangered and delinquent minors, considering them all at risk and eligible for rehabilitation on the optimistic belief that they are all redeemable. Despite the fact that violent juvenile crime targets mostly property, not people,[31] and crime rates remain low compared to other industrial nations such as the United States, new understandings of delinquency created a crisis of the rehabilitative ideal and generated public support for a punitive model. How did long-standing public support for prevention erode in just a decade? How did it translate into punitive policies at court?

MEDIA HEADLINES AND THE JUVENILE JUSTICE SYSTEM

Sensationalist sound bites and headlines have been a staple of the coverage on youth crime since the urban unrest of the early 1980s. Current coverage of juvenile delinquency tends to focus on particularly egregious and largely unrepresentative acts of physical violence committed by "immigrant" youth in public housing projects. It relies discursively and visually on the trope of the "time bomb" and of violent outsiders. The moniker "youth" (*les jeunes*), preferred by the media, is a complex signifier and is used interchangeably with "foreigner" (*étranger*), "immigrant" (*immigré*), of foreign origin (*d'origine étrangère*), of North African origin (*d'origine maghrébine*), or non-European foreigner (*étranger non-européen*), sometimes in the same sentence, when the topic is crime.[32] Those so signified are often represented as an internal threat that attacks the social body like an infectious "contagion," spreading without warning through the cités or public housing projects. Rather than center on increases in youth crime that resulted from aggressive policing, such as drug violations, insults, threats and assaults on public authorities, and physical assaults, the media reported on gang rapes, honor killings, revenge murders, or savage attacks.[33]

Journalists interviewed professional criminologists and quantitative sociologists as authoritative sources but ignored or silenced those analyses that contradicted the newly emerging visions of the ghetto predator.[34] Even tough law-and-order politicians, such as the former Interior Minister and now French president Nicolas Sarkozy, could spout incendiary rhetoric about the threat to public order from the constant increases in physical violence and in the next breath cite official statistics that belied this bleak image.[35]

Disputes over the "facts" regarding the severity of youth crime and the brandishing of warring statistics become weapons in a divisive topic. Accusations of both subjectivity and political bias are used to attack the credibility of different authorities with conflicting accounts. Inconsistent public talk surrounds juvenile delinquency, suggesting both knowledge and misrecognition, and has the power to shape public policy. Talk about juvenile offenders has the capacity to mesmerize and to frighten because it poses clear-cut distinctions and radically simplifies good and evil as well as danger and threat. Teresa Caldeira argues that it relies on stereotype and generalization to bring order to the disorder of crime by locating the offender outside of the social order. This category elides nuances, masks complexity, and downplays events that contradict the dominant narrative. As a distortion of reality, the category of the violent offender is necessary to make sense of a terrifying experience—for example, only fifteen minutes away from Paris, cars may be burning and schools destroyed, and within the city, people are mugged and homes are burglarized, or worse. Talk based on categories of deviance is important because it assumes the language of political contests over crime and conditions legal debates concerning the capacity of the juvenile justice system to deter crime and to protect victims. It frames larger discussions about the shifting boundaries between the child and adult, the origin of the problem, and the nature of solutions to treat it. It works to facilitate new alliances between political elites and expert consultants whose specialized knowledge of the problem will be deemed authoritative.[36]

FRANCE AS A REHABILITATIVE MODEL

Modern juvenile law was legislated in a 1945 ordinance after the political upheaval and economic crisis of World War II. In contrast to the United States, France never adopted the model of the blameless child and moved haltingly toward a rehabilitative approach. Although many scholars depict France's move toward a rehabilitative model as a unilinear process that was definitely achieved with passage of the 1945 ordinance,[37] I argue instead that juvenile law has always remained firmly grounded in French penal law and has remained more or less punitive, depending on the period. Although most French scholars treat the justice system as an autonomously functioning system or transcendent, disembodied apparatus—the preferred term is *regalian*—I connect it not only to its twentieth-century history but also to politicized notions of the family and the child, reigning therapeutic models, legal debates, and state immigration and labor policies. The juvenile justice system has displayed both continuity and change since the legislation of an embryonic juvenile court system in 1912. Despite the 1945 reformist attempts to reduce the punitive aspects of the law and recent reforms to enhance due process protections, French penal codes still privilege the protection of the social order over individual rights and parental authority over children's rights and give enormous power to judicial police, *procureurs* (prosecutors), *juges d'instruction* (JIs, or investigating magistrates), and trial judges versus lawyers.

Given this larger pattern, the period after 1945 may be viewed less as a permanent paradigm shift than as an exceptional period in which adherence to a rehabilitative model gained support for a variety of reasons. These include sustained and expansive economic growth, full employment, demographic vitality, and social optimism. With the beginning of deindustrialization, the rapid rise of youth unemployment, the reconception of immigrant populations as social problems and labor liabilities, and the failures of a public education system ill prepared to convert to a mass education model, the consensus on assistance and rehabilitation began to unravel in the 1980s. This process accelerated in the 1990s. In the sections that follow, the debates over juvenile law, sociological models, and judicial practice constitute an integral part of the data. I examine them critically to explain how powerful actors have positioned themselves on a contested issue and shaped the debate in a highly charged political context.

It should come as no surprise to those familiar with French elites that judges who were all trained at the highly selective Ecole Nationale de la Magistrature (ENM) were conversant with sociological theory on crime, prisons, and social control. In short, they were all familiar with Foucault.

Contesting a Rehabilitative Model

Even before a "delinquency of exclusion" began to dominate debates on youth crime, the juvenile justice system was subjected to a withering critique from the Left for its therapeutic paternalism. This critique was launched in the late 1970s and early 1980s by Michel Foucault and those influenced by his writings. Foucault was one of the first influential intellectuals to reject the view that the modern juvenile justice system constituted a more humane alternative than its predecessors. He described the nineteenth-century agricultural penal colony for boys at Mettray as the embodiment of the more efficient and pervasive techniques of social control heralded by the modern prison. Foucault dismissed depictions of Mettray as an enlightened model of penal reform, noting that the inmates included not only boys who were judged to be delinquent but also boys who were merely rebellious, homeless, unwanted, abused, and even boys whom the court had acquitted of penal responsibility for wrongdoing. Nonetheless, they were all subjected to a regimen of uninterrupted surveillance, relentless regulation, and punitive correction. This was intended to produce docile subjects who internalized the institutional norms and supervised themselves.[38]

Foucault's critique of disciplinary institutions powerfully influenced sociologists who studied the treatment of children and the policing of families in twentieth-century institutions as well as the contemporary juvenile court. They published their findings in the late 1970s and early 1980s, a period dominated in France and elsewhere by Foucauldian critiques of penal systems and disciplinary knowledge regimes. Jacques Donzelot and Philippe Meyer documented the existence of a new intrusive sphere of state intervention directed at families. Born in the nineteenth century, this new sphere of the social—what Donzelot termed the *tutelary complex*—designated a specific scientific field of knowledge and new modes of social control.[39] It relied on a corpus of law, medicine, psychology, psychiatry, and social professionals, from child psychiatrists and social workers to juvenile judges, whose primary function was to assign labels, assess risks, construct norms, and sanction deviance.

Donzelot linked the creation of the first juvenile courts in France in 1912 to urgent demands created by a growing market in incorrigible and maladjusted children and by public scandals surrounding the brutality of children's prisons. He charted the shift from the routine confinement in prisons, penal colonies, and houses of correction notorious for their brutal disciplinary regimes to the supervision and treatment of children within their families in open settings.[40] Systematic incarceration at penal colonies was largely replaced by new normalizing instruments such as clinical observations, psychiatric tests, personality evaluations, family counseling, social worker visits, and court hearings. Like Foucault before him, Donzelot rejected received wisdom on the juvenile court as a progressive alternative to the more repressive systems in the past. He argued that rehabilitative measures were modeled on penal sanctions and that social inquiry reports into family backgrounds merely empowered social services and juvenile courts by indicting parents' child-rearing abilities. He noted that a substantive shift from nature to nurture in French child psychiatry after 1945 supported rehabilitation but saw it as a more pervasive means of social control.[41] Scientific psychiatric tests became normative instruments that justified long-term court supervision through recurring demands to assess abnormality and impose treatment. Philippe Meyer has also studied social reformers, criticizing them as agents of state paternalism and coercive intrusion into private spheres.[42]

Legal and Sociological Debates

The crisis of the rehabilitative model has been accompanied by legal and sociological debates among the proponents of penal versus rehabilitative approaches. International pressure following ratification of the CRC put renewed attention on the impartiality of juvenile judges, the fairness of sentences, their sovereign and arbitrary powers, and the adequacy of due process protections for the accused. Beginning in the late 1980s when a punitive trend was gathering attention, legal experts elaborated a critique of the therapeutic paternalism, arbitrary powers, and personalized justice dispensed at juvenile court. As we shall see, juvenile judges gained public legitimacy after 1945, if not recognition by their legal peers, because of their commitment to child advocacy and social justice. They were viewed less as rigorous jurists than as social workers. Their embrace of their work as a vocation resulted in their marginalization within the legal establishment. This critique of juvenile law and courtroom practice occurred at a time when the feminization of the profession came to be constructed as a problem. It coincided with a turn to legalism and a challenge to social activism among both new and older judges. By the 1990s many were eager to erase the stigma of juvenile justice as a lesser justice and willing to assume the penalizing function that has always been implicit in the 1945 ordinance.

Debates about the unprecedented nature of the new delinquency generated two opposing but by no means uniform groups of experts. The majority demands more restitution and repression in contrast to a minority, who defend, to varying degrees, prevention and rehabilitation. Both groups include public intellectuals and media-savvy activists with privileged access to national print and visual outlets as well as to prestigious Parisian publishing houses as a means to shape public opinion and government policy. The pro-penal group includes police commissioners, juvenile judges, and new crime and security experts, some with close ties to the private corporate security sector as well as to French police unions, prosecutors, JIs, and conservative public institutes on domestic security. Their alarmist newspaper editorials, crime forecasts, testimony before state commissions, and book publications—some in eminent French university presses—draw public attention to the issue and build political support for more accountability for offenders. Social scientific opinion is solicited and informs public policy in governments on the left and the right. Since 2002, security experts in particular have gained legitimacy at the highest levels of the center-right governments of Prime Ministers Raffarin and de Villepin. They have secured an institutional base in the French public university system, where they direct graduate programs on criminology and organized crime. One such security analyst, Alain Bauer, now heads the National Observatory of Delinquency within the conservative Institut National des Hautes Etudes de Sécurité, created in 2003 by Interior Minister Nicolas Sarkozy. The Institut publishes monthly crime statistics that are defined in terms of public order and police control. Security experts have advocated for more prosecutorial power, more police, faster adjudication procedures, and the increased penalization of juvenile justice. The containment of "lawless zones" and the management of the enemy within—by implication, the disaffected "immigrant" delinquent—are at the top of their agenda. The most extreme writings link disadvantaged youth of Muslim heritage to the menacing global specter of Islamic terrorism and organized crime.[43]

In contrast, pro-prevention advocates include a loose and shifting coalition of juvenile and family court judges, jurists, attorneys, public caseworkers, child psychologists, human rights activists, and social service providers. Through their writings, professional organizations, collaborations with NGOs such as the League of the Rights of Man, media appearances, and street demonstrations, they are vocal critics of the new punitive trend. Their critique focuses on the defense of the rehabilitative ideal and the goal of socioprofessional integration within French society. They criticize the new powers of prosecutors, aggressive policing, lack of institutional resources, and legal reforms that created new categories of violent juvenile crime and public order violations. This group also includes leftist academics who denounce institutional injustices and who are suspicious of the rehabilitative intent of the current system. Once again, sociologists, influenced by Marx, draw attention to structural inequality and pervasive class bias in the courts and social service agencies that work against the interests of working-class and disadvantaged youth, making them more vulnerable to state control and punitive correction. They are distrustful of specialized child professionals and judicial authorities with the power to define deviance. In their view, the personalized sentences, consensus building, and negotiated agreements that characterize the court proceedings serve to mask, legitimatize, and reproduce unequal and exploitative relations of power.[44]

RACE AND ETHNICITY AT COURT

Although both sociologists and jurists have argued that the force of law is grounded in ideologies that support and reproduce unequal class structures, most conspicuously ignore the question of ethnic or racial discrimination in the justice system. Although the gap between abstract principles guaranteeing equality under the law and the reality of the criminal prosecution of disproportionate numbers of disadvantaged minorities is hardly new, what is distinctive about the French case is the silencing of race and ethnicity in the law and the constitution. This remains true despite the historical significance of race and ethnicity as salient social categories and their current importance to the sociopolitical construction of deviance. The question of racism in the court and the overrepresentation of minority and foreign defendants there is impossible to know from official sources. Beginning with the 1789 revolution, nationality, in contrast to birthright and rank, became the only legal category of difference as a means to bind individual citizens within the nascent Republic. French law thus recognizes no collective versus individual rights and the constitution rejects the very notion of minority status. The issue of whether one should infer the rule of color-blindness from the principle of equality was incorporated into article 1 of the 1958 Constitution rather than being left to the courts. Since the end of the racist policies of the World War II Vichy period, it has been illegal in France to collect data on ethnic, racial, religious, or cultural origin or to track racial or ethnic distributions in jobs or institutions. With the goal of rejecting racial categorization and institutionalized discrimination, public bodies have refused to permit any official recognition of racial or ethnic difference.[45]

The legal void on race must be interpreted within the still dominant narrative of the French nation that is actively and continuously reproduced in the juvenile court and other public and private institutions. France represents itself as the original color-blind Republic as well as an exemplar and champion of universal human rights. The universalist, egalitarian rhetoric on equality and the inclusive logic informing the "one and indivisible" Republic nonetheless perpetuates the official myth that because France recognizes no legal minorities, it has no minority problem or ghettos segregated by race and ethnicity. In a logic mirroring French antiracist law, racism is viewed primarily as overt individual behavior, not indirect action or institutional discrimination. Because only individuals can seek redress under current law, proving discrimination based on race is extremely difficult, in part because it signifies origin and belonging in an unofficial legal category.[46]

As Laurent Dubois argues, "there is ultimately no language or method" with which to confront and seek redress for systemic racism in French institutions such as schools or the courts because the discrimination that people of color experience is a result of color-blindness inscribed in French law.[47] The critique of color-blind policies articulated by American critical race theorists in the wake of attacks on U.S. affirmative action is particularly useful as a means to unsettle enduring myths and political consensus on the topic of French racism. In the 1980s American conservative legal scholars rejected affirmative action law, arguing that a race-neutral view of civil rights was the surest way to avoid future discrimination, end judicial activism, prevent collective conflict, and ensure sociopolitical stability. In a vivid critique that speaks directly to the

French situation, Kimberlé Crenshaw and others suggest that color-blind policies offer less protection for civil rights than promised, for a number of reasons. First, the focus on present wrongdoing ignores past injustices as well as the racist stereotypes, "Othering" devices, and unequal conditions that created and continue to sustain them. Second, under race-neutral laws, discrimination is seen as isolated actions against individuals rather than social policies aimed at entire groups. These laws effectively remove the courts from playing an active role in redressing past racism rather than merely policing and eliminating narrowly proscribed discriminatory practices.[48]

Crenshaw warns that the adoption of race-neutral law and the embrace of color-blindness entails neither a commitment nor an ability to end racial inequality. In fact, race-neutral law may constitute a formidable obstacle to the alleviation of inequality based on white dominance and, in the case of France, on unacknowledged ethnoracial hierarchies. A color-blind society built on the subordination of persons of color—in this case, ethnoracial minorities from former colonies—cannot correct that subordination because it cannot recognize it.[49] Although difference in France is framed primarily in terms of culture, phenotype as a marker of difference is also part of the ideology defining belonging and foreignness. Although racism begins with discussions of cultural differences judged to be qualitatively different, it also draws on racial stereotypes. It substitutes the rhetoric of racial inferiority in popular consciousness for the presumed cultural deficits and pathologies of Arabs and Africans.[50] This has serious consequences for those who "hang" together as racial crews within public housing projects or are identified in police reports on the basis of phenotype, as in the common description of the accused as "an individual of African or North African descent." This is all the more significant in that the "new" Frenchness is marked by the increasing visibility of groups who self-identify in multiracial and multicultural ways. The fact that no social scientific literature exists on race or race relations, and that groups are identified discursively in national cultural terms as ethnicities rather than as "generic black people," should not imply an absence of racism based on race-based characteristics.[51]

The constitutional ban on statistics other than nationality means that there are no de jure mechanisms in place to assess and address the treatment of French minors of immigrant ancestry within the justice system.[52] As French nationals, they disappear from figures on arrest, prosecution, conviction, and incarceration rates. The only way to know who gets prosecuted, for what offenses, and in what proportion is to get inside the courts and, through ethnographic observation, to see who arrives for a hearing from jail; who will be issued a warning and returned to his parents after an offense; or whether, and under what circumstances, the judge will revoke a probation (*contrôle judiciaire*) and send a teenager to prison.

Some note a new phenomenon in French political rhetoric, namely the explicit racialization of the 2005 conflict. They argue, for example, that the racialized language used by legislators to denounce rap lyrics represents a denial of long-standing understandings of France as "race-less" and the beginnings of a national reimagining in terms of "racialized political actors." They note that this shift can be seen in public policies that draw on an American-style model of social management combining elements of affirmative action, neoliberal privatization, and domestic militarization.[53] I argue that from the viewpoint of French courts, and in contrast to political rhetoric, the appropriation and acceptance of such an American model, a subject of considerable debate, are premised on an explicit rejection of racialized understandings of social personhood and political activism and on the preservation of certain legal fictions. These fictions are that France recognizes only individual citizens and in this way ensures those citizens' equal treatment under the law.[54]

During my time at the French court, the only times I provoked outright defensiveness and charges of inability to see beyond American racial categories were times when I raised the issue of racism within the justice system. One French colleague was shocked and angry that I even suggested it. She retorted hotly, "they [defendants including youth of immigrant ancestry] are all treated the same in the French system." Other jurists and judges saw racism in the courts as a much more pervasive problem in the United States than in France. Although I eventually learned to censor myself, when French court personnel (rarely) asked how I viewed the system, I did point out the glaring reality that the overwhelming majority, if not all, of the defendants awaiting trial outside the juvenile correctional court on any given day were teenagers of color or foreigners. Some court personnel responded that the discussion was misplaced because "it is not about races or ethnic groups but individuals who get arrested." Others insisted that if youths got arrested "it was for a reason." Some judges naturalized the links between delinquency, immigration, and foreigners. They mirrored public discourses that racialized crime, saying, "of course they constitute the majority of the court's clientele." Some readily agreed that discrimination was a problem and even cited examples of colleagues whose aversion to Maghrebis or Africans was notorious but situated the origin of the problem outside the court, within other institutions or among misguided individuals.

This silence on race and ethnicity belies the persistent use of ethnoracial categories to discriminate against populations of immigrant and foreign ancestry in housing, in education, and at work.[55] State authorities in employment agencies have long facilitated and/or engaged in systematic discrimination against minority groups based not only on addresses and last names but also on skin color. Public housing representatives have used unofficial quotas, imposed limits on ethnic minorities based on a putative "threshold of tolerance" for difference among native French residents, and relegated them to poorer-quality properties. Racially motivated incidents of police brutality and intentionally provocative tactics such as excessive force, racist slurs, recurrent identity checks for youths who are known, and unwarranted arrest have been denounced by human rights organizations, the leftist union of magistrates, and its counterpart among French lawyers as factors that reinforce hatred for public authorities and produce violent unrest.[56]

CULTURE AND DELINQUENCY: A CULTURE OF POVERTY?

If race was absent from discussions at court, culture was not. Politicians on the left and the right attributed the causes of the new delinquency of exclusion to culture. Two variants of this culturalist argument emerged in the 1990s. The first views youth violence as the result of an inevitable culture clash between mainstream French values and backward immigrant traditions magnified by poverty and exclusion. The second variant blames a total lack of culture within immigrant families whose children are said to lack moral values, social norms, and grounded identities.[57] The French social scientists who support this explanation borrowed liberally from a cultural ecology model originating with the Chicago School of Sociology. French analysts appropriated the concept of a culture of poverty to link the "new" delinquency to negative environmental influences in closed, ethnic neighborhoods.

Some delinquency studies were commissioned by governments on the left and the right seeking to document the rise of youth crime, others were written by academics anxious to provide the insider ethnographic view of street culture in an effort to counter media stereotypes, and still others were produced by a pro-penal group of security experts and police motivated to influence public policy. In their role as newly visible public intellectuals and legal authorities on a highly charged public issue, Parisian jurists and magistrates were familiar with and drew on this work in diverse ways to interpret the cases they saw in court as instances of aberrant cultural norms and dangerous social milieus. Judges attended to the role played by cultural difference in one of two ways, particularly when it involved non-Western values and practices such as arranged marriages, family honor, control over sexuality, polygamous arrangements, and belief in witchcraft. Either they stigmatized and neutralized it through the standard interventions at their disposal or they medicalized and treated it through the specialized services of university-affiliated ethnopsychiatrists whose consultations were reimbursed by the state. In either event, culture was an obstacle to be surmounted.

Court personnel draw not only on social theory and cultural psychiatry but also on folk ideologies that conceive of culture as an internally homogeneous and geographically bounded system. In this understanding, a mosaic of ethnic or national groups under court supervision, such as Antilleans, Algerians, Moroccans, Bamberas, Soninkés, or Romanians, are hierarchically ordered into discrete, qualitatively different systems regardless of the nationality they hold. These cultural hierarchies function like race to ascribe certain immutable traits to the peoples born within them. Because culture, like biology, is understood to determine the practices of the people born into it, particularly in what many French people see as less evolved non-Western cultures, it is thought to be resistant to adaptation or change and, thus, even rehabilitative intervention. Such cultural hierarchies are a direct legacy of colonialism. The imperative of the civilizing mission that the French imposed on their African, Asian, and Caribbean subjects borrowed from dominant understandings of them as culturally inferior. The contemporary corollary of the need to civilize colonial subjects is the punishing expectation that their postcolonial descendants who are now settled in France must forget their parents' languages and cultures in order to integrate fully within French society.

THIS PROJECT TAKES SHAPE

I was initially attracted to the study of French juvenile delinquency for personal reasons and because of my advocacy of rehabilitative approaches. The French media focus on "youth as trouble" rather than "youth as risk" resonated with me, especially because of my own experiences with my family. I grew up with a sibling who was labeled a delinquent by the time he was in middle school; thus I have intimate, long-term experience with a complex reality and a personal investment in the debates surrounding the issue. I had been personally hurt by the stigmas school authorities consciously or unconsciously assign to the younger siblings of troubled children. I could understand the responses of parents who felt guilt, shame, anger, or bewilderment when social professionals scrutinized the family background and the child's upbringing in a search for answers. In my family's case, the origin of the "bad" behaviors that got my sibling into serious trouble—attention deficit hyperactivity disorder (ADHD), mild dyslexia, and disruptive behavioral disorders such as oppositional defiant disorder (ODD)—were not recognized psychiatric conditions or cognitive handicaps in the 1950s. The result was a misrecognition of the problems by many authorities that produced misguided solutions, and also, at least for a time, a certain leniency based on the reigning developmental model in the American juvenile justice system of that period.[58] Much later, I recognized that this initial indulgence was also premised on the white, middle-class respectability of my parents—my father was a civil engineer and my mother taught elementary school.

I should point out that my position as an objective observer of the juvenile court proceedings was compromised by the fact that, given my family background, I am a strong proponent of prevention and rehabilitation. I have watched with growing dismay as federal and state laws in the United States have progressively dismantled a system that was once viewed internationally as a model of rehabilitative justice. Human Rights Watch and Amnesty International report the horrifying statistic that in 2004 there were at least (and probably many more than) 2,225 juvenile offenders serving life sentences in U.S. prisons without the possibility of parole.[59] I had watched the rhetoric heat up in France and tracked French politicians, judges, and legislators who traveled to the United States in the 1990s because of what I viewed as a misguided interest in the purported success of a "broken windows" crime prevention initiative, and zero-tolerance policing in American cities (see Chapter 2). It seemed imperative to understand why and in what ways American punitive trends were being adopted in the land of the Rights of Man.

Given the centralization and dominance of public institutions in France, I thought that it was logical to begin with Paris, the site of the largest and most influential juvenile court in the nation. I began preliminary fieldwork in Paris in the summer of 2000 with only two names—those of a caseworker and a judge. My contacts with both opened many doors, initially to the refined and urbane head of the juvenile prosecutor's section, Yvon Tallec, whose persistence in negotiating the labyrinth of the French Chancellery bureaucracy was invaluable to me in designing a research project they would approve, and to the genteel and intellectual president of the minor court, Hervé Hamon, who, during our first meeting, gave me a stack of reading materials so I could become fluent in the language, concepts, and norms of the institution I would later describe.

SUBJECT POSITION

Given my unusual access to the court and tolerance of my presence by most court personnel, I did not anticipate that the space of the court as a technology of power and an architecture of control would constrain me to the extent that it did. Paradoxically, these limitations resulted from my spatial contiguity to a vulnerable population and my social proximity to the judges who enforce legal norms. When I arrived in the courtroom of Judge de Maximy in January 2001, the first problem that presented itself was what to do with me. The question of where to put me was significant because of what my placement would signify to court personnel, children, and families. The demarcation of space and the movement within it are directly linked to judicial power and professional function. Juvenile judges sit at desks in the center of their chambers and control all communicative exchanges. An invisible but rigid line separates them from the children and families who sit directly in front of them and the attorneys and court social workers who flank them. When minors arrived disheveled and dirty from lockup, they were accompanied by armed police who stood at the back of chambers. In some cases where the quarters were close and the families were large, my proximity to the accused risked blurring crucial boundaries. Judges always instructed me to move nearer to them, even if it placed us so close that movement of our arms was difficult.

Most judges were careful, as least at first, to introduce me as a visiting researcher from the United States, to ask the families' permission to have me attend, and to assure them that strict confidentiality would be observed. All of the judges I observed gave me permission to write about the cases provided that I changed minors' names and distinguishing characteristics. Nonetheless, because I looked like the judges—similarly educated women from the mainstream majority population—and spoke French without an American accent, given the fraught circumstances of the hearing, I am sure that few actually heard any of these details. Most were ready to believe I was a judge or affiliated with the court. As time went on, court personnel also saw me this way. One bailiff, whose job is to announce the cases being tried and to escort defendants into court, saw me sitting with the defendants and their families during a recess. She insisted that I move to a different area of the hallway where the attorneys normally examined case files. When I attempted to resist, she authoritatively motioned me away insisting, "No, you will be more comfortable here." The issue had less to do with my comfort and more to do with my "proper" place and proximity to those waiting for the verdicts.

This posed the question of my subject position in anthropological research and presented ethical and methodological dilemmas. As a novice to the French legal system, I was expected to listen and to observe. As a judicial intern, my subject position was assimilated to that of the judge and my role was to learn how judges applied the specialized law governing juveniles. At the same time, I was observing in courtrooms governed by extraordinary time and labor constraints. As an anthropologist, I wanted to participate in the lives of the judges and the judged. Despite my access to unfolding proceedings and active case files, I could not interview the children and families with open cases at court. It was out of the question for me to conduct interviews outside of the courtroom or in homes on cases involving allegations of illegal activity by minors or child endangerment by parents before judgment. Since I was so closely associated with the judicial apparatus and the court, how could families speak freely? Why would they? The fact that I was older, a foreigner, and had no clearly defined status beyond that of trainee was also a problem. They were constrained to appear in court but under no such obligation to me.

The rules of interaction in a court of law shape how people produce speech and have enormous implications for justice in the sense of who controls language, who assigns labels, who can contest charges, and who, in the end, has the power to assign blame and punish. There are serious implications for minor defendants from families of foreign and immigrant ancestry when interacting with judges and prosecutors from middle and upper-class social milieus. They can be intimidated by their ignorance of the law and judicial protocols, the emphasis that judges place on middle-class social norms such as correct linguistic usage and proper demeanor, and the social distance between them and court personnel. Many minors and families nourished a hearty distrust and disdain of the court and its motives. In the end, this produced many silences in court but, at times, it also produced strident resistance. Too often, they did not have the language to explain or defend themselves. I had the language but not the opportunity to use my voice in court, except with the powerful. Over the years that I observed court proceedings in the Paris court, I did see some young people and their families use their voices in court to attempt to resist and reframe hegemonic constructions of juvenile delinquency.

LEGAL SUBJECTS

The growing violent unrest of young people who feel excluded and the increasing role of punitive sanction in the French legal system lead us to consider Gramsci's notion of hegemony. The political authority of any state relies on the consent of the governed and on the willingness of the dominated to accept their subordination. A state's capacity to legitimize its political authority, to rationalize its use of force, and to maintain the consent of the dominated within an unequal social order finds its limits, particularly when it engages in or tolerates discrimination against that group. The French state has been successful in asserting its political hegemony through the power and prestige of national public institutions, the civil service, and the legal system itself. It has been far less successful in ensuring its ideological hegemony among disadvantaged minority youth in the face of unequal opportunity, socioeconomic polarization, and institutional racism within public and private institutions.[60] Those who suffer discrimination have little reason to accord legitimacy to French institutions, whether in the public schools or the juvenile court, because, despite vigorous official denials, many know they have been tracked on the basis of collective origin and their rights have been denied or restricted. The ways in which French authorities have used the law and the legal system to control and contain politically disaffected minorities have in turn shaped the ways youth in "lawless zones" see themselves as legal subjects, make sense of the choices they have, and view (or not) the law as a counter-hegemonic tool available to protect and advance their interests.

The growing French interest in repression begs the question of what the late Paul Ricoeur has called "the just" in the process of accusation, the act of judging, the application of sanctions, and the meaning of rehabilitation. His queries in *The Just*[61] speak directly to the question of rights when he asks who is assigned blame, held accountable, and recognized as the subject of both rights and obligations. He argues that claims to rights are grounded in individual notions of agency and responsibility that allow political subjects to recognize, trust, and respect one another. These are not abstract rights merely encoded in the law. Entitlements are created and reproduced as individuals claim them in personal interactions and through recourse to institutions such as the courts. He implies that the legitimacy of democratic systems is underwritten by able subjects whose responsibility to one another is enhanced by mutual recognition of shared rules. As we move into the juvenile court, we must ask if the judges, victims, defendants, and their families in these cases recognized themselves and one another as political subjects with the same rights and obligations before the law. How did the accused and their parents position themselves with regard to the law? Did they view the justice system as a site where they enjoyed equal treatment under the law? As defendants in penal cases, how well were they able to refute charges and mount a credible defense? Did their accusers—police, prosecutors, and victims—see them, as so many allege, not only as above the law but outside it, the products of lawless zones? At a time when victims enjoy greater rights in French law, it bears reminding that the French police are the ones increasingly constituting themselves as civil plaintiffs and claiming restitution for offenses that involve minor physical injuries or merely symbolic insults. Their status as victims and demands for damages rest on their very power to accuse and arrest, begging the salient question of who would hold them accountable. Finally, the increase in warnings involving endangered children, the majority concerning lower-class or disadvantaged families, raises further questions. How did the legal mandate for protection, based on mainstream middle-class norms of family and childhood, affect their ability to contest expert opinion and deflect accusations of abuse or neglect even as they sought assistance?

AN ETHNOGRAPHIC AND ARCHIVAL STUDY OF THE COURT

This book is based on both ethnographic and archival research conducted at the Paris juvenile court. I routinely observed proceedings in four regular courtrooms, including three serving densely populated and multiethnic northeastern districts of the city (the Eighteenth South, Nineteenth East, and Twentieth North), the Eleventh, as well as the special court (Court L) created for unaccompanied, undocumented foreigners. I limited my observations to select courtrooms to which I was permitted access, preferring to concentrate on a long-term and in-depth investigation of court cases and judicial practices in fewer courts rather than attempt to cover all courts more superficially. Nonetheless, the choice of cases is representative of the tenor and substance of hearings in other courtrooms as reported in judges' meetings, interviews with them and attorneys, the head juvenile prosecutor, the president of the minor court, and the 2004 Justice Ministry Inspection Report of the juvenile court.

I attended mediation sessions, evidentiary hearings, trials, judgments, and sentencing procedures. I accompanied caseworkers to the Paris jail for intake interviews and rode with them to visit teenagers serving time at the Fleury-Mérogis prison outside Paris, one of the largest prisons in Europe. I observed the nonpublic deliberations of the juvenile judge and her assessors that produced the verdict and the sentence and also waited outside the court with anxious families. Mediation sessions—especially those pitting illiterate Algerian parents against their French-educated daughters, an appeal of a custody decision by a Soninké mother on the grounds that sorcery poisoned the process, and a civil case in which a French middle-class convert to fundamentalist Islam was accused of child abuse by her own mother—have much to teach us.

Although I conducted many interviews, both formal and informal, with the main participants within the system, such as judges, prosecutors, attorneys, court caseworkers, and social workers, the richest data came from my observation of court proceedings as well as the dense texture of my interactions there, including informal conversations before and after hearings or over meals with judges. I found it essential to concentrate on the court as an institution in order to understand how it works, why various participants perceive it as they do, and how they came to view one another in a process that is designed to elicit the active participation of the people under supervision. Furthermore, the court provided an excellent angle from which to view salient tensions at the core of French society, an insight provided to me by a Paris juvenile judge. These are tensions involving national sovereignty and immigration; race, ethnicity, and culture; gender and sexuality; secularism and religious expression; changing parental models and a shrinking welfare state; social class and professional mobility; and the newly porous boundary between the child, the adolescent, and the adult.

In this book I focus on how newly dominant notions of a delinquency of exclusion are produced and reproduced within civil and penal hearings at court. I center on the language of judging and its relationship to the written file—social worker evaluations, police reports, criminal records, and previous judgments—and the more dynamic, face-to-face interactions among minors, their families, and court personnel that involve complex negotiations, contestations, and accommodations concerning the law, legality, and legitimacy.

These interactions produce new intertextual relations among written and spoken material and differing interpretations of both the law and the social.[62]

Many people asked why I chose the provocative title of *Judging Mohammed*. The present participle indexes the hidden discrimination within the justice system that officially recognizes only individuals but prosecutes certain groups such as marginalized Muslims and unaccompanied minors in disproportionate numbers. The use of Mohammed suggests that what is at issue now is a dangerous conflation of Islam, violence, and youth crime that builds on negative stereotypes. Many of those who land in court are not delinquents but at-risk minors. One additional layer of meaning invites a rethinking of the judgment of these young people and an admonishment for all law courts to live up to higher ideals of justice. The title does not imply that large numbers of the accused were actually named Mohammed, although many young men, particularly first-generation immigrants, had this name.

The progression of this book mirrors the historical evolution of juvenile delinquency, its contemporary construction as an urgent public policy issue, and the treatment of both delinquent and at-risk children at the largest and most influential court in the nation. Chapter 2 provides an overview of the French criminal and juvenile justice systems. Chapter 3 charts the shift from a focus on the individual-centered model legislated in 1945 back to the current cultural ecology model, centering on the social milieu, and it traces evolving conceptions of childhood and shifting psychoanalytic models. It also examines public discourses and media coverage that ethnicize delinquency, pathologize culture, and produce consensus across the political spectrum. Chapter 4 focuses on judges as a professional group and considers their ambiguous position within the legal establishment. It examines how judges frame their work experientially, cope with its demands, and endow it with meaning, even as they strive to manage the twin constraints imposed on the court by increased retribution and scarce resources. Chapter 5 takes readers into the court the same way young people experience it: arrest, detention in the Paris jail, and a court hearing before a judge. In Chapter 6 I center first on hearings held within the chambers, site of the informal justice that has fueled debates on the quality of judgments and the impartiality of judges, before examining the trials within the formal correctional juvenile court in Chapter 7. This latter is the scene of flamboyant and highly ritualized confrontations between prosecutors, judges, defense attorneys, victims, and the accused. Chapter 8 is devoted exclusively to the identification and treatment of undocumented, unaccompanied minors within the Paris court. The chapter compares the situation before and after the 2001 creation of a special court and centers on the gaps between the official state rhetoric depicting them as victims in need of protection and the judicial practices treating these minors as delinquents deserving punishment. The concluding chapter considers the dangerous effects of the new penology in France and the United States.

2 THE FRENCH CRIMINAL JUSTICE SYSTEM

THROUGHOUT HISTORY, criminal proceedings in French courts have been marked by an inquisitorial heritage, nineteenth-century Napoleonic codification, and the primacy of abstract legal doctrine over empirical case precedent. This history has been marked by French ambivalence toward the power of judges as royal magistrates in the past and career functionaries in the present. This chapter looks at that history and examines to what extent the French juvenile justice system bears the imprint of French penal codes that differ so markedly from Common Law systems such as that in the United States.

THE REPUBLICAN LEGACY

Under the Old Regime, before the revolution of 1789, French criminal law was a complex mix of Roman law, canon law, and customary law. There was no centralized justice system. Laws differed by region and were applied to individuals based on their social rank. Criminal justice was governed by inquisitorial procedures characterized by secrecy, the investigation of crimes by one all-powerful judge, and the conducting of trials without witnesses based on confessions obtained beforehand, often through torture.[1] The result was justice that was unequal and authoritarian.[2] Punishment was fierce, judgments were arbitrary, and death was the penalty for a large number of infractions that would be considered minor offenses today. Until 1789, children were subject to torture, imprisonment, exile, and even execution.[3]

After 1789, revolutionary assemblies established criminal codes that swept away the old system of privilege and inequality. They reacted against an inquisitorial system in which there had been no adversarial oral debate, the accused had little possibility of a defense, and royal magistrates were free to apply whatever punishments they deemed fit. Revolutionary legislators were influenced by eighteenth-century philosophies of natural law as an expression of the sovereign will of the people. French republican tradition made the people sovereign but stipulated that such sovereignty be exercised by the state as the legitimate representative of the nation.

Revolutionary legislators replaced some inquisitorial procedures with elements of an adversarial system modeled on English law, whereby judges were elected, indictments were handled before a grand jury, and an individual was guaranteed a trial by a jury of his peers.[4] These legislators espoused a doctrine of law as a minimum constraint, particularly after their bitter experience with arbitrary detention and the criminal trial as political tools of monarchical despotism. They legislated the principle that still governs French criminal justice today, setting standard punishments for each crime based on an ascending hierarchy of penalties corresponding to the seriousness of the offense and establishing maximum, not minimum, penalties.[5]

Despite adopting certain aspects of the English system, revolutionary legislators retained an inquisitorial emphasis on the protection of the social order over individual rights and a lack of attention to the victims of crimes. Crime of all sorts was deemed an offense against society that demanded the reestablishment of common values, punishment for an attack on public order, and, as a low priority, reparation of the wrong done to individuals. The 1791 penal code made many references to the general interest and public safety, but the protection of individual rights and interests was subordinate to the demands of the social order.[6]

Napoleonic penal law marked both a dramatic departure from revolutionary innovation and a return to some Old Regime inquisitorial principles.[7] Napoleon's republican vision relied on strong centralized national institutions and a cadre of loyal public functionaries, including career judges (*magistrats*) appointed by the state. Napoleon ended judicial elections and created a professional judiciary with limited autonomy. The 1808 *Code d'instruction criminelle* and the 1810 penal code established the first public ministry and replaced the grand jury with a single judge enjoying vast powers, the juge d'instruction (JI), whose task was to gather evidence in support of a criminal indictment. Working under the authority of the public prosecutor, this judge enjoyed policing and investigative powers and could operate secretly to issue warrants; order and conduct searches, seizures, and arrests; and detain suspects at will without informing them of the charges or the nature of the evidence. Concerns over the enormous power of the JI led to reforms such as the Constans Law of 8 December 1897,[8] permitting the accused's attorney to be present during questioning by the JI and to consult the case file beforehand. This reform had the unforeseen consequence of prompting the police and procureur to begin their own process of investigation that incorporated the detention of suspects by the police (*garde à vue*), a process that kept suspects outside of a legal framework until the 1958 code of criminal procedure established formal procedures for dealing with individuals held in police custody.

Debates about judicial power and the rights of the accused speak to an unresolved tension in criminal trials between France's inquisitorial legacy and adversarial influences borrowed from English courts. In 1789 revolutionaries disagreed on how to resolve the dilemma of combining a secret and written criminal investigation before trial with the new democratic imperative of an open and adversarial debate during trial. On one side, some revolutionaries considered it dangerous to conduct trials through written depositions and transcribed interrogatories. In contrast, Robespierre was suspicious of the exorbitant powers of the English jury and declared that written procedures "were a precaution against ignorance, weakness or judicial laxity."[9] Jurists have argued that the dilemma was never resolved and that an enduring legacy of the revolutionary period was to produce a hybrid legal system combining elements of inquisitorial and adversarial procedures that is in force to this day.[10] The French criminal trial remains divided between an investigative phase that is secret and written and is less concerned with the rights of the accused, material witnesses, or victims than those of society as a whole, and a judgment phase that is, oral, public, and, to a very limited degree, adversarial, because it accords primacy to a written archive of evidence, collected beforehand, over the oral testimony heard in court.[11]

AN INDEPENDENT JUDICIARY?

Because of bitter memories associated with powerful royal magistrates, early republican state officials mandated that judges be subordinate to their political masters and limited judges to declaring and applying the law in a literal way. At the same time, revolutionary legislators viewed the law as the basic guarantor of the liberties of individual citizens.[12] Thus, they moved to codify national legal statutes and initially accorded judges an important role in this process. The codification of statutes inhibited the development of case law jurisprudence in

France and cast the legislature and Justice Ministry, rather than individual magistrates, in the role of the sole guardians of public liberties. Today in France, the executive claims to protect the people from the excesses of powerful nonelected judges, in contrast to the United States and the United Kingdom, where judges are understood to play a role in protecting citizens from executive power.[13] An enduring distrust of the judiciary and of the "rule by judges" (*le gouvernement des juges*) still exists in France. In a recent interview a judge commented bitterly, "In France you have an executive and legislative power but no judiciary power. We must not forget that it is the head of state who presides over the Conseil Supérieur de la Magistrature [the advisory body for all judicial appointments, which is composed of magistrates and state functionaries]."[14]

In reality, judges had little say over the direction of their careers until the first reforms protecting the judiciary from political interference were enacted in 1946 (reforms continued through 1993).[15] Before that time appointments were imposed on judges; the results were published directly in a government publication, the *Journal Officiel*; and judges had no right to contest or appeal Chancellery (Ministry of Justice) decisions. Currently, judges make requests for particular posts to both the Chancellery and the Conseil Supérieur de la Magistrature, but the Ministry of Justice retains the power to appoint and promote. Chancellery decisions are now posted on the Internet and judges have a right to appeal. Despite 1993 reforms intended to provide judges with limited self-determination through their majority representation on the Conseil Supérieur de la Magistrature, this body is limited to approving or rejecting Justice Ministry decisions. Typically, it rejects only 2 percent of the Chancellery selections.[16]

Today the system is more transparent, although no less organized around upward advancement through a multi-tiered hierarchy. Promotion from the lowest-grade magistrat to "middle grade" and "highest" requires regular performance evaluations by superiors and movement among courts on average every three years. The day in April when the Chancellery decisions about the next year's appointments are announced is, in the words of one judge, a time of "serious upset" and frayed nerves. It is a testament to the serious contests over professional rank and judicial status that the Chancellery either confirms or denies in its appointments.

A CAREER JUDICIARY

Like other European judicial systems, France has a career judiciary, known collectively as the *magistrature*, the members of which are recruited and appointed by the state. All magistrats prepare advanced degrees in law before taking a competitive entrance examination and obtaining intensive training at the Ecole Nationale de la Magistrature (ENM) in Bordeaux, modeled on the most selective national institutions, the Grandes Ecoles. The common curriculum at the ENM prepares future magistrats to perform a range of judicial functions from prosecuting cases to conducting trials, and most move among different jurisdictions over the course of a lifelong career. The shared experience at ENM also imparts a distinctive professional ethos. Magistrats see themselves, in contrast to lawyers, as professional public servants entrusted with the protection of the general interest and the application of the law.

The judiciary in France is not a unified whole but is divided into different judiciaries. One of the major divisions in terms of judicial tasks and professional trajectory is between civil and criminal judges on the one hand and administrative judges on the other. The most prestigious route to a judicial career is external selection by the rigorous ENM entrance examination at an early age, generally between twenty-four and twenty-six. Entry to the ENM is also possible based on years of experience in public sector positions. The decision of who is appointed to which courts depends on the candidate's competitive ranking on the exit examination at the ENM, available openings, and the desirability of a position. In the hierarchy of appointments the juvenile court ranks near the bottom and is associated with novice judges just out of training who stay for an average of two years before moving up and out to other jurisdictions. Those who request positions as juvenile judges are often assigned to provincial or suburban courts. Then, depending on their performance, seniority, and overall image within the Chancellery and the Conseil Supérieur de la Magistrature, an assessment that for many remains tinged with mystery, they may advance to larger and more prestigious jurisdictions closer to urban areas. The jewel, of course, is an appointment to Paris.

THE ORGANIZATION OF THE FRENCH CRIMINAL JUSTICE SYSTEM

The Magistrats, the Procureurs, and the JIs

In France the judicial function is defined more broadly than in the United States and encompasses three types of magistrats: the procureur, the JI, and the trial judge (*juge*). Although there is a historical overlap with the range of tasks performed by judicial officers, the French criminal justice system does distinguish between adjudicatory and investigative functions. Within the magistrature the standing judges (or *parquet,* the collective noun for all procureurs) prosecute cases on behalf of the state, in contrast to the "sitting" judges (*siège*), who gather and review evidence outside of court or rule from the bench. The pretrial investigation of a case is supervised by a procureur or a JI but dominated by the police. The procureur decides whether to prosecute cases after consideration of the evidence gathered by the police. As part of the parquet, a procureur is embedded within a centralized hierarchy that demands strict accountability to superiors within the Ministry of Justice, in contrast to sitting judges, who are not subject to this form of state control. Among procureurs, the law tends to be presented as fixed and uniformly applied, with an emphasis on technical competence rather than individual discretion.[17] The procureur's goal is to protect and represent the public interest and to neutralize the threats to the legal and social orders that crime poses. The public interest justifies concentrating vast powers in the hands of one person, an orientation that contrasts sharply with adversarial systems in the United States and United Kingdom, where functions are divided between different actors.

The JI is charged with investigating the most serious and complex criminal cases. This judge reviews and evaluates cases during the pretrial phase to determine if the evidence and charges are well-founded. Magistrats with broad investigative and adjudicative powers have no equivalent in the United States and United Kingdom, where judges do not gather or present evidence and only rarely question the defendant or witnesses at trial. This judge's wide powers— in particular, to order searches and seizures, to authorize telephone taps, and until legislation in 2000, to detain suspects and material witnesses in custody— has earned him or her the moniker of the most powerful judicial figure in France.[18] Debates over these powers have prompted repeated attempts to redefine the JI's authority and to limit the power of this position.[19] They have centered on the contradictions inherent in inquisitorial systems and the "ambiguous position" of the JI: "He must be both the grand jury and the judge, he presides over the judicial investigation, draws conclusions [regarding prosecution], and sends the case to trial."[20] In the recent past the power and role of procureurs have expanded as those of the JI have decreased. It is estimated that the JI is currently involved in investigating only 5 percent of the cases referred for prosecution, with the remainder handled by the police in conjunction with prosecutors.

Trial Judges and the Legal Facts

Antoine Garapon has remarked that France finally got a new penal code in 1994 but never managed to change the code of criminal procedure.[21] This commentary speaks to strong historical continuities in the legal system in the establishment of facts, the concept of legal truth, the rights of suspects following arrest as well as the accused after indictment, and the power and status of magistrats in contrast to lawyers. In adversarial systems such as that of the United States, the facts of the case emerge from a strategic confrontation between the prosecution and defense attorneys in which the presiding judge is primarily a neutral arbiter. Such systems assume broad equality between the prosecution and the defense. Each side gathers evidence and presents arguments in oral proceedings intended to establish the facts of the case. In the French system, no such equality is presumed between the parties. The facts are established by the JI or the procureur and presented by the state in the person of the trial judge, not by the individual parties to the case. They are premised on a conception of the truth that is established independently of the prosecution and the defense and puts the onus on the accused to prove his or her innocence.

Although the presumption of innocence is guaranteed in article 9 of the Rights of Man, in article 9-1 of the Civil Code, article 11-1 of the Universal Declaration of the Rights of Man, and in the 15 June 2000 legislation, the process of discovery in the French system cannot in practice presume innocence. The state has a monopoly on the facts and the "objective truth" that provide the basis for the decision to prosecute as well as on the act of accusation itself.[22] Public prosecutors initiate and control criminal proceedings, although victims may join criminal prosecutions as civil plaintiffs (*parties civiles*).[23]

Discussions of the public good and the protection of the social order lead logically to what counts as legal truth in a criminal trial. The French understanding of legal truth explains the concentration of power in the hands of the trial judge as well as the unequal exchanges between the judge and the accused. The French judge, in contrast to his or her American and English peers, takes an expansive role in the trial. This judge presides over and controls the exchanges in court and all parties address him or her, not one another. His or her function is to conduct inquiries into the case, not simply to judge the evidence as presented. The trial judge actively questions the accused, witnesses, and victims and will request more information if needed.

Because the French trial is understood as the symbolic affirmation of legal order over social disorder and of the collective will over individual transgression, defendants must be ritually isolated and stripped of their individuality. They stand alone at the bar and respond directly, without advice from counsel, to an aggressive stream of questions controlled by the presiding judge. French courts intrude authoritatively into the personality and private life of the accused because one of the paramount goals is to reintegrate the "bad" citizen through the internalization of legal norms. The active participation of defendants, both before and during the French trial, is central to this process. In inquisitorial systems the accused is expected to contribute to the process of finding the truth, in contrast to adversarial systems in which guilt or innocence must be established objectively and on the basis of evidence external to the defendant.[24] The confession reigns supreme as proof of guilt, creating a culture of confession in the French legal system. French law is not interested in external behavior alone; rather, it has a pedagogical role and a structuring dimension. Close behind the confession as proof of guilt is the police statement taken after arrest. Unless other evidence is presented, the police statement plays a determining role in the establishment of the facts of a case.[25]

The ideology of the French criminal justice system relies on the image of the impartial magistrat who applies the law in a consistently uniform manner because he or she is bound by fixed rules and codified statutes. This representation of the law and its application suggest a "homogeneous model of French society and values, where all citizens are equal and equally bound by the law."[26] It masks the true power relations that exist as well as the reality in French courtrooms where magistrats do exercise discretion and interpret the law. As Daniel Soulez-Larivière has argued, the presumed obligation to apply the law as written allows judges to mete out even severe punishments without pangs of conscience because they can blame it on legal requirements rather than personal choice.[27]

The dominance of trial judges and public prosecutors in criminal trials as opposed to the popular jury and defense attorney reinforces the power of the former to formulate the facts and assign guilt. In contrast to adversarial systems in which citizens participate in all aspects of criminal proceedings from grand juries to criminal juries, professional magistrats control deliberations behind closed doors in police and correctional courts, where they work alone, with colleagues, or with nonjudicial assessors. The popular jury exists only in felony courts (Cour d'Assise) in France, where the outcome of cases is rarely in doubt, acquittals are rare, and, until 2000, there was no possibility to appeal the verdict.

In contrast to the power and status of sitting and standing magistrats, French attorneys suffer (see Chapter 7). Antoine Garapon, who was trained as a judge and not as a lawyer, gives examples of the negative images surrounding attorneys in French cinema. He shows how lawyers are depicted as relying less on rational argumentation and professionalism than on rhetorical verbosity and showmanship. Their very capacity for objectivity is made suspect by their identification with (and receipt of payment by) their individual clients as well as their presumed devotion to private interests over the protection of the public good.[28]

In France the function of the trial is to neutralize the crime and to protect the social order by reaffirming the supremacy of the law. The justice system shows little concern for the consent of the accused who pleads guilty, allows frequent preemptive detention pending trial, and until the 2007 law establishing minimum sentences, granted judges great discretion in deciding which infractions—even simple theft—warrant such deprivation of freedom. French law only belatedly accorded enhanced due process protections for adult and minor suspects, material witnesses, and victims. In 1993 international pressure, notably condemnation by the European Court of Human Rights, prompted France to enhance due process protections. Until the laws of 4 January and 24 August 1993, suspects in police custody (*garde à vue*) had no access to legal counsel and no knowledge of their rights.[29] In the past, material witnesses could be detained, but since the 2000 reform was enacted, only those accused of criminal activity can be detained. This law mandated that the accused be advised of the right to remain silent,[30] to see an attorney at the outset of a twenty-four-hour detention, to use the telephone to contact family members or an employer, to receive medical attention, and to have rest periods (although not necessarily sleep or a bed).[31]

The Juvenile Court

French jurists and legislators have always been keen observers and imitators of international trends in criminal justice and penal reform, most famously with the 1833 study of American prisons undertaken by Gustave de Beaumont and Alexis de Tocqueville.[32] In the early twentieth century French reformers closely studied the Chicago court as they began to craft their own system of juvenile justice. They saw Chicago as a pioneering experiment in prevention and rehabilitation, but not one they could adopt whole-cloth, in part because they considered it to be too progressive and too divergent from French "traditions and customs."[33]

In 1912 French legislators recognized the "need for a new treatment system for guilty children" as well as "the excellent results obtained in the United States." Nonetheless, they balked at the implications of adopting a therapeutic system and were suspicious of the potential erosion of paternal authority such intrusive state intervention would represent.[34] The 1912 legislation establishing an embryonic juvenile court system rejected the American model of the blameless child and retained the Napoleonic statutes, articles 66 and 69 of the 1810 penal code. These statutes premised leniency for children aged thirteen to twenty-one on the judge's determination of their penal responsibility (*discernement*). Regardless of this determination, the outcomes remained largely punitive. Those judged to have acted with an understanding of wrongdoing could be brought before the new correctional juvenile court and receive penal sentences that included prison terms or confinement in state-run institutions. Under article 66 those who were acquitted or judged to have acted without understanding could be returned to their parents, placed in private institutions, or sent to state penitentiary colonies until their majority, which was at that time age twenty-one. Between World Wars I and II, these institutions became infamous for their brutal disciplinary regimes, harsh living conditions, and exacting work rules.[35]

Although legislators in 1912 hailed the creation of a specialized juvenile court as "a true instrument of moral correction," that would end "the [systematic] use of prison sentences for minors" through the newly created measures such as probation, the reality was quite different.[36] Judges did not hesitate to confine, in state-run houses of correction (*maisons de correction*) and reform camps (*colonies de rééducation*), children who were indigent, abandoned, abused, truly delinquent, merely rebellious, or those deemed endangered because they lived with a widowed, separated, or unmarried parent. This was a period during which the bureaucracy that ran French prisons also controlled state institutions for juveniles.[37]

The modern juvenile justice system dates back only to 1945. Demographic stagnation, political upheaval, economic crisis, and abortive legislative reforms under the Vichy government during World War II coalesced with demands for truly separate chambers to hear minor cases, for specially trained judges, and for a system that abandoned repression in favor of rehabilitation.[38] The 1945 penal statutes eliminated article 66 of the penal code and the requirement that judges first determine a minor's discernement. This ordinance created for the first time a specialized corps of juvenile judges and éducateurs and put the latter under their own administrative unit separate from the department of prisons. It established penal irresponsibility for minors under thirteen, a focus on the child rather than the act, deferred judgments, individualized sentences, a separation between minor and adult jurisdictions regardless of the severity of the offense, and national sentencing guidelines that automatically reduced penalties by half for minors.

It is instructive to review some provisions of the original 1945 ordinance because this will allow us to understand the extensive powers given to juvenile judges (*juges pour enfants*), the JI, and the procureur. Article 5 of the law gave only prosecutors the right to initiate legal proceedings and to designate either a JI or a juvenile judge to handle the investigation. Juvenile judges who were so designated were authorized to examine charges and to undertake investigations as well as to conduct trials and to render judgments. In this way they combine the functions of investigation and judgment that are normally separated in the French system. Article 9 of the ordinance specified that the investigation of cases involving serious misdemeanors or crimes led by the JI must follow the general rules of criminal procedure. Articles 10 and 11 gave juvenile judges and JI wide powers pending an investigation to return children home, to place them in state residential institutions for treatment or education, or to incarcerate them. Article 11 further permitted judges to take any of these measures for children under thirteen if it would prevent a crime and was properly justified. As we shall see, although judicial practices differed, the relegation of "simple" penal offenses to juvenile judges and more serious infractions to the JI had serious consequences for troubled youth. In the 1990s, when legislators defended a turn to repression and amended juvenile law, they noted the provisions for punishment that had always existed in the original 1945 ordinance.

THE REHABILITATIVE IDEAL

Many in the legal establishment still accept that a minor's criminal misbehavior is symptomatic of factors beyond his or her control—such as bad parenting, nefarious influences, and underprivileged living conditions—rather than a conscious and deliberate will to break the law.[39] When juvenile judges elect to hear penal cases in chambers as opposed to the juvenile correctional court, they do so in order to prioritize the rehabilitative process. This decision is grounded in a progressive philosophy that makes no rigid distinctions between endangered and delinquent children. Elisabeth Catta defined the approach enshrined in the original 1945 ordinance this way: "the endangered child is a delin-

quent . . . or victim of a disadvantaged upbringing or systematic abuse, someone who runs away, seeks refuge in a gang, sniffs glue, shoots heroine, prostitutes himself, skips school or misses work—all are in danger" and in need of
protection.[40] According to this philosophy, the notion of a child's best interest
implies a perfectible age of life, belief in the minor as a social and psychological
work in progress, and support for slow, prolonged justice (*justice dans le
temps*). Court-ordered interventions are understood to evolve and adapt along
with the emotional and social maturation of the child. This approach accepts
the view that children can be resocialized much more easily than adults. It
reserves punishment for confirmed recidivists but only as a last resort.[41] It is
premised on deferred judgments, individualized sentences, the primacy of civil
over penal law, and a future with viable economic possibilities.

The rehabilitative ideal and individual-centered penology of the past are increasingly challenged by the new penology that emphasizes restitution and retribution. It is reshaping judicial practice and weakening the commitment of
court personnel to the social goals of judgment. Under existing court conditions, the intrusive supervisory gaze of the court is conspicuous for its selective
and differential focus on the disadvantaged children of immigrant and foreign
ancestry.

A HEARING IN JUVENILE COURT

After arrest, the decision to prosecute an offense, and the designation of the
minor as a formal suspect under investigation (*mis en examen*), the next step is
the penal hearing before a juvenile judge. Hearings for minor infractions may
be scheduled in the judge's chambers or be referred to the formal juvenile court
in cases involving more serious offenses and/or repeat offenders.[42] Once she is
in possession of the case, the juvenile judge reviews the evidence and examines
the charges in light of the minor's family background and personal history.
Only one word in French, *les faits*, indexes both the charges alleged during the
investigation as well as the facts established during the trial. The presumption
that the charges are synonymous with the facts of the case speaks to a justice
system that has always privileged the protection of the social order over individual rights.

Hearings begin when the suspect hears, confronts, and responds to the
charges against him or her. Beyond this, normal legal procedures are routinely
suspended in the juvenile court. For example, the right to remain silent is never
invoked. Rather, it is deemed antithetical to the establishment of a rehabilitative

bond between the youth and "his" or "her" judge. Significantly, in cases where the infraction is a first-time offense or a minor infraction, the judge may suspend the waiting period that is legally required between the investigation, the judgment, and the sentencing.[43]

The substance and conduct of hearings within chambers have been the subject of virulent debates within the legal establishment. These debates began in the 1960s and intensified in the 1990s as juvenile law became a charged public policy issue. French law schools tended to embrace a pervasive critique of the role of the juvenile judge and maintained a "scornful silence" on the court's special jurisprudence, generally deeming it unworthy of more than a passing mention in their curricula and texts.[44] This hostility derives in part from the suspicion with which some jurists view the exceptional powers granted to juvenile judges who examine charges and issue indictments as well as conduct trials and render judgment.[45]

In the hearings I observed, juvenile judges began by establishing the facts and usually addressed the teenagers with the formal *vous* form of address, unless they knew the accused well or he or she was under twelve years of age. The use of the second-person plural (vous) registered the solemnity of the proceedings, created the necessary distance between the judge and the youth, and also signaled the court's disapproval of the disruption to the social order that the infraction represented. The basis of the charges and, thus, the facts of the case greatly depended on statements obtained by the police during questioning in police custody. Judges relied heavily on statements signed by the accused, victims, and witnesses and referred to them repeatedly. They resisted attempts by the youth to reframe or retract these statements, even when the youth complained that they were handed statements and urged to sign their names without reading them. The common retort to such protests from a youth was, "You signed it, didn't you?" Judges likewise refused attempts to undermine police credibility or integrity. They tended to reject youth accounts of police malfeasance as this constituted an unacceptable attack on the moral authority of the legal system. In confronting the word of victims to that of the accused and lacking other elements of proof, judges prioritized the testimony of victims over the accused. This is all the more significant in the wake of legislation in 2004 mandating that penal convictions may no longer be erased automatically from the police records of minors who turn eighteen.[46]

The minor standing in front of the judge, flanked by his or her attorney, social worker, and family, was subject to the power asymmetries that structure the relations between court personnel and children. Before the hearings even began, judges already had extensive knowledge of the child's background from the court file, knowledge that defense attorneys often lacked. The briefings I attended before court hearings suggested that judges had already formed opinions about the nature of the child accused of wrongdoing. Myriad social professionals, such as school counselors, nurses, social workers, and child psychologists, had assessed risks and classified children on the basis of their academic performance, psychological screening, social conformity, and their parents' origin, lifestyle, and educational levels.

Although judges emphasized to me that their role was to focus on children rather than parents and to avoid judging parents' lifestyles, it was clear that the disciplinary system of the court included not only penal infractions but also unwritten class-based norms of social interaction that govern the relationships between adults and children. Children who did not master the mainstream codes of politeness, demeanor, responsiveness, or oral expression were corrected in court. They were admonished to sit up, to speak clearly, to not interrupt their parents, to control their feelings, to be courteous, and to use the proper salutations. At the conclusion of one hearing that resulted in the imposition of probation, the angry and disappointed youth turned to leave the judge's chambers. He had been accused of attacking a policeman but insisted on his innocence; and witness depositions suggested that he was the victim not the assailant. In addition, he had a visible scar that he (and several witnesses) claimed resulted from the blow of a policeman's nightstick during his arrest. The presiding judge rebuked him for forgetting his manners and not saying good-bye.

The hearing consisted of two unequal parts. The first was a confrontation of the version preserved in the written depositions with the oral testimony produced in court. As in the adult criminal court, juvenile judges controlled the questioning and were the center of all communication. All parties, even attorneys, addressed their pleas to the judge. Judges directed a series of rapid and direct questions at the accused. These involved the skeptical query regarding disputed circumstances, the incredulous probe related to previously undisclosed or new facts, and the vigorous challenge to any inconsistencies that emerged in the questioning. Although delivered in a neutral tone, judges frequently interspersed sarcastic comments and moralizing questions, such as "So when the police found you behind the wheel of the car, you were just passing the time of day?"; "And you are telling the court that this Tunisian guy from the neighborhood forced you to steal the cell phone? So if he told you to commit murder would you do that?"; and "Did I really hear you say that? Is this a bad dream?" Their rhetorical style of questioning was premised on the individual responsibility of the youth and his acknowledgment of the wrong done. They viewed claims of innocence, implausible excuses, and the disavowal of responsibility negatively, and they considered the accused's acceptance of culpability a precondition of clemency and rehabilitation. Cases that resulted in verdicts of not guilty or acquittals were relatively rare in the courtrooms I observed. The longest hearings were typically those in which two parties disputed the facts and confronted one another in chambers. In these proceedings there was pressure to produce a result in which one of the parties would accept guilt and underwrite an authoritative account of the facts.

In the confrontation between the written statement and oral testimony, the inchoate utterances, involuntary interjections, monosyllabic responses, emotional outbursts, vernacular and slang expressions, and even the pauses and hesitations of teenage suspects or defendants disappeared. They were refashioned into a truncated version of the facts that the judge dictated verbatim to the court clerk and that became part of the permanent court record. Delivered in standard French and in the first-person singular as if spoken by the accused, this version provided an authoritative narrative of events that was intended to reinforce the account already presented by the state. In cases in which the accused disrupted the ideal scenario, insisted on his or her innocence, and forced an alternative account of the judicial facts, the resulting narratives often included slang and vernacular terms to highlight the recalcitrant and outsider status of the youth.

The second part of the hearing began after the facts were clearly established and the minor admitted his or her guilt and showed remorse. Some judges declared minors guilty even in the total absence of proof, justifying such an action for the "rehabilitative benefit" it would have. One juvenile judge, François Touret-de-Coucy, noted that a defense attorney requested a rehabilitative measure for his minor client even after the judge had acquitted the minor.[47] A French legal anthropologist who observed several Paris juvenile judges described the linguistic practice of systematically switching from the formal *vous* to the familiar *tu* form in addressing minors during this phase of the hearing.[48] She inferred that this shift signaled the beginning of the redemptive work of the court. She argued that in this phase the judge moved away from the legal facts of the act to center on the personal circumstances of the youth. These included family relations, scholastic performance, and career plans. She claimed that the use of *tu* was strategic because it symbolized the integrative and assistance functions of the court and suggested that improvement was possible. The phase associated with the *tu* form of address, like the phase allotted for rehabilitative measures to bear fruit, was linked to a notion of time as long-term and reversible time (*temps long*). She contrasted the preference for the *tu* form of address in this phase of the penal hearing and in social assistance or civil hearings with the rule of the *vous* form in the judgment phase of the formal juvenile court trial.

Although I did observe the same division of the hearing into two unequal parts, none of the judges I observed in chambers marked the beginning of the second phase linguistically. Some judges used the *tu* form in penal hearings, but sporadically and in different ways, to signal asymmetrical authority relations, to maintain distance, to register empathy, to create complicity, and to foster cooperation. But the preference for the *vous* form of address throughout the penal hearing was striking. This may have had to do with a complex mix of gender, class, and power. A majority of the juvenile judges in Paris were middle- and upper-middle-class women. Their preference for the formal form of address with the poor and disadvantaged males who made up 90 percent of juvenile defendants in court reflected the gaping social distance separating them as well as linguistic practice in a bourgeois social milieu where the familiar *tu* is used relatively less frequently than the formal *vous*.

Hearings ended with the pronouncement of guilt or innocence and a sentence that could range from a benign return of the minor to his parents' home without court supervision to a revocation of pretrial probation and an incarceration order.

CONCLUSION

Judicial police and prosecutors enjoy enhanced powers and tend to dominate the pretrial investigation and the construction of written evidence within the criminal justice system. Police interrogate suspects in custody without defense attorneys or magistrats being present. Procureurs supervise this process from a distance and see suspects only at the end of custody, a period that can extend from twenty-four hours to four days, depending on the nature of the charges. Suspects consult with counsel for only thirty minutes and their attorneys have no access to the case file. The same rules apply to minors in custody, except that since 2000 police interrogations of legal juveniles must be videotaped and attached to the file.

This process has enormous implications for the rights of suspects, the presumption of innocence, and the types of cases that are prosecuted. Despite international pressure to reinforce the individual rights of suspects in France and to align them with legal instruments such as the European Convention on Human Rights, successive governments on the left and the right have reaffirmed their commitment to a state-centered approach to crime and time-honored inquisitorial procedures. Justice ministers have consistently resisted a movement to adopt adversarial procedures, denouncing them as unfair because they favor the strong over the weak and reinforce inequality.[49]

The ideological representation of transcendent justice grounded in legal requirements and fixed statutes ignores the social categories and judicial practices that form the culture of the French criminal justice system. The tensions between adversarial and inquisitorial approaches in the adult system are evident in the juvenile courts. These are emblematic of larger shifts in the understanding of what constitutes justice for minors. In the next chapter we will consider the historical and contemporary representations of juvenile delinquency by state officials and new experts on urban violence, including journalists, jurists, sociologists, and ethnopsychiatrists. We will examine recurring media coverage of "bad" areas, such as public housing projects, and the ways in which moral panics surrounding delinquency have shaped public perceptions and prompted legislative amendments to French juvenile law.

3 NEW SAVAGES IN THE CITY? HISTORICAL AND CONTEMPORARY REPRESENTATIONS OF JUVENILE DELINQUENCY

IN 1998 THE INTERIOR MINISTER of the leftist government, Jean-Pierre Chevènement, sent a confidential memo to Prime Minister Lionel Jospin, which was leaked to the leftist daily *Libération*.[1] He urged a major overhaul of the ordinance of 1945. His recommendations foreshadowed legislation enacted since 2002, namely, the reopening of juvenile detention centers, the transfer of the trials of recidivists to adult court, and the pretrial imprisonment of thirteen- to sixteen-year-olds accused of misdemeanors.[2] In early January 1999, Chevènement appeared on national television to declare that it was high time for a "republican conquest of the suburbs" when confronting those "little savages" (*petits sauvageons*).[3] Two years later, in 2001, the French Senate created a commission to organize public hearings on juvenile delinquency. Commissioners agreed that the problem of youth crime had worsened since 1997, when legislative elections returned the Socialists to power and Prime Minister Jospin made insécurité a major policy priority. One year later, in 2002, commissioners began hearings in the midst of an acrimonious presidential election campaign dominated by the topic of youth crime. Jospin, incumbent center-right President Jacques Chirac, and political figures on the far right and far left were all presidential hopefuls. The Socialists' perceived failures to manage escalating violence were instrumental in eliminating Jospin from the second round of national voting and forcing a runoff election between President Jacques Chirac and a far-right extremist candidate, Jean-Marie le Pen. A stunned French electorate, forced to choose between the center-right and the far right, reelected Chirac in a landslide.

Although the theme of insécurité dominated the 2002 presidential campaign, French fears of violence emerged in 1977 when the first state report on crime was published. Between 1977 and 2002, governments on the right and the left commissioned five reports on delinquency. These reports were all produced after the oil shocks of 1973, the close of legal immigration in 1974, the end of full employment, the advance of deindustrialization, and the coming of age of the second and third generations of children of immigrants in a climate of reduced economic opportunity, particularly for those unprepared for work in the new service economy. These reports shifted from a focus on violence as a national phenomenon afflicting rapidly urbanizing areas to an emphasis on the crime of the immigrant (that is, non-European) delinquent endangering the social fabric in specific territories. In the years between 1993 and 2003, the topic of insécurité, or fear for public safety, narrowed in meaning to convey not just urban crime but juvenile delinquency.

The five state reports were commissioned in the context of relentless and sensational media coverage of violent youth unrest in the suburban projects. They perpetuated a collective amnesia by suggesting that the car chases, vandalism, and violent confrontations with police were totally unprecedented and could only be understood by comparison with events outside metropolitan France, such as race riots in Brixton, apartheid in South Africa, or intifada in the Palestinian territories. They were written during a period when adolescents of North African ancestry became visible in new ways to the French public. Sociologist Michèle Tribalat describes this collective encounter, beginning in the early 1980s, as a culture shock because it lessened the "symbolic distance separating the French from the world of immigration." It made " 'foreigners' seem strangely similar" while simultaneously linking different parenting models in the North African family with rising urban violence and the specter of wild immigrant youth.[4]

Anxiety surrounding the generations born after their families' immigration to France generated intensive debate on their capacity to be educated, rehabilitated, and integrated within French society. Legal, psychiatric, social scientific, and political attention centered on the causes of youth violence and the identification of youth offenders. New specialists on urban and youth crime, juvenile justice, and child psychiatry appeared and published books in prominent French presses. French psychiatrists have argued since the nineteenth century over the question of heredity versus environment as risk factors for "defective" children. Despite a significant shift in medical discourse after 1945 emphasizing individual psychology and environmental factors such as parenting, the social milieu theory inherited from the nineteenth century never entirely disappeared.[5] Rather, the emphasis on biological determinism and social milieu that were important factors in earlier formulations of delinquency were largely replaced in the 1990s by cultural determinism based on origin. As the explanations shifted from economics and individual psychology to culture and collective origin, the cultural group itself became an object of scrutiny, as evidenced by the courts' increasing use of ethnopsychiatrists to deal with what court personnel saw as the cultural disorders resulting from migration to France.

In this chapter, I chart the shifts in juvenile law and the discourses on delinquency that have taken place since the 1970s. I argue that the rehabilitative ideal legislated in 1945 never entirely materialized, particularly for older adolescents aged sixteen to eighteen and for those from immigrant families. This explains the rapid consensus in French public opinion that emerged in the 1990s on the need for more accountability and retribution to manage the threat of a "delinquency of exclusion." This consensus relied on the construction and dissemination of key tropes in popular and scholarly discourse, such as the "suburb," "ghetto," "culture of poverty," and "delinquent youth cultures." This discourse was informed in part by punitive models imported from the United States, which I will now examine.

TRANSATLANTIC DIALOGUES: CHANGING MODELS IN THE UNITED STATES AND FRANCE

By 1912, when the French Assembly enacted the law creating an embryonic juvenile justice system, twenty-six of the then forty-six U.S. states had established juvenile courts on an excuse-based model in which offenders were considered blameless children in need of treatment and rehabilitation. Although racial and ethnic bias was always present in the U.S. juvenile and criminal justice systems, judges and caseworkers were inclined to suspend the blameworthiness of all youthful offenders on the basis of mitigating factors such as abusive childhoods, malevolent influences at an impressionable age, or the developmental immaturity that gives rise to risky behavior and bad choices.[6]

By the time I began my research on France in the late 1990s, the U.S. juvenile justice system—which French reformers had scrutinized as a potential model a century earlier—had been substantially dismantled in favor of a full-responsibility approach. Since the late 1980s a wave of punitive legal reform lowered the age and broadened the range of crimes for which American youth could be tried and punished as adults, imposed mandatory sentencing guide-lines, and moved many juveniles into the adult criminal justice system.[7] In the 1970s and 1980s state legislatures instituted punitive reforms that were driven by moral panics surrounding superpredators. There was a radical reconceptualization of youth offenders as capable of forming criminal intent and as morally responsible. The pervasive dispensations for adolescents—as well as the paternalistic social attitudes and legal policies that existed for minors in other contexts from school, employment, voting, and the military—were readily set aside for teenage "criminals." The punitive legislation was shaped by distorted perceptions of the threat arising largely from minority delinquents, both African American and Latino. These youths came to be viewed by the media, the public, politicians, and personnel in the justice system as more dangerous, more mature, and more deserving of punishment than whites because their offenses expressed bad character and malicious intent rather than the effects of structural inequalities and poverty. Critics within and beyond the United States documented the disproportionate representation of minorities in the justice system and the prisons as well as sentencing disparities for similar offenses. Other evidence shows that court personnel attributed the offenses of black juveniles to internal, character-related factors and those of white juveniles to external, environmental elements.[8]

French jurists, including juvenile judges, who visited the United States in the 1990s were uniformly critical of the emerging American penal state, its warehousing of minority populations in expanding prison populations, and the get-tough approach to juvenile defendants.[9] One judge, Denis Salas, even invoked Hannah Arendt's conception of totalitarian regimes marked by punitive retribution and rapid legal reform as a cautionary tale for French reformers too intent on imitating a bad American model.[10] Despite political challenges to the French juvenile justice system, many judges, even those who favored more repression at home, still viewed it as a superior and progressive alternative to the "backward" and "overly repressive Anglo-Saxon [that is, British and American] systems," widely described in the French media and in legal publications. Many of the French magistrates I knew believed that there was no juvenile justice system in the United States. What were their reactions to an American anthropologist who had come to study the French juvenile justice system? Most found it interesting, others were impressed, but a few were skeptical, hostile, or frankly bewildered that with so many problems at home I should have chosen to study France. One thought that, like a latter-day

Tocqueville, I had come to study their penal system as a model to take back with me.

In order to understand how the French juvenile justice system came to be viewed as a problem, it is necessary to revisit its beginnings in the 1940s and to review the writings of its principal architects and defenders.

LESSONS FROM FRENCH CHILD PSYCHIATRY:
SOCIAL MILIEU AND CULTURAL DISORDER

Despite its representation as an innovative law, the 1945 ordinance establishing modern juvenile justice relied on older theories of delinquency. This section traces the roots of psychological and psychiatric theories that center on social origin and continue to inform judicial practice.

The principal architect of the 1945 legislation, Jean Chazal, was a prominent judge and child advocate during and after World War II. He defended the special powers newly accorded to juvenile judges because, in his view, they provided a "continuity of judicial action" between the investigation of a case and its hearing during trial. These powers also facilitated the contact between the judge and the child, allowing him to "acquire a thorough knowledge of the child's personality and family milieu," which became basic elements of the court decision after 1945.[11] For Chazal and fellow advocates, it was imperative that juvenile judges be psychologists in dealing with the "irregular" children within their purview, because the child is "unable to resist his nature and his milieu" and must, therefore, "be protected, cared for, rehabilitated, and not convicted."[12] Chazal claimed that "delinquency, vagrancy, and lack of discipline" were merely the outward signs of youth maladjustment. His discussion of the "medico-psychological" causes of juvenile misbehavior reveals the influence of nineteenth-century neo-Lamarckian theory positing the interaction of a bad social milieu with inherited personality traits. Despite significant permutations in postwar child psychiatry, the social milieu theory still prevailed in the late 1940s when he wrote and never entirely disappeared. It reemerged in the 1990s as cultural origin in the appraisal of deficient families based on immigrant and foreign descent.

Chazal referred to the two opposing theories of crime causation involving "constitutions" or biological heredity versus social milieu. Based on consultation of "thousands of penal case files," his classification of the primary causes of juvenile delinquency suggests that he, like his contemporaries, was deeply influenced by both schools of thought. He viewed children as "defective" based on character problems that revealed the "deep inter-penetration of hereditary or somatic factors and those that were 'acquired' from the environment."[13] He constructed three categories: the first included minors who were apathetic, suggestible, unstable, and hedonistic; the second, less numerous than the first, was comprised of children who were impulsive, instinctual, given to lying, and paranoid; and the third included those who were emotional and perverted. His insistence on the "ravages of the hereditary influences of alcoholism, syphilis, tuberculosis, and nervous disorders" on the development of the juvenile personality is a direct reference to the work of the most influential French child psychiatrist of the twentieth century, Georges Heuyer.[14]

Although Heuyer admitted that social conditions such as poverty and bad influences were important, his early work focused on heredity as the primary cause of juvenile delinquency.[15] Like most early twentieth-century psychiatrists, Heuyer sought the causes of abnormal children and juvenile delinquency in the theories of hereditary degeneracy, which then dominated the profession.[16] Heuyer and his students focused on degenerates who inherited the predisposition for diseases including alcoholism, tuberculosis, syphilis, epilepsy, mental retardation, or psychopathological disorders. They could be recognized by their "perverse personalities" and unbalanced behavior," labels that were broad enough to accommodate Chazal's arbitrary classificatory system.

In addition to heredity, Jean Chazal also adhered to the nineteenth-century Lyon school of criminology, which privileged the social milieu in the etiology of juvenile delinquency. He attributed delinquency to "children whose nature is corrupted or altered by a deficient family milieu" in which the parents "deprive the child of care, abuse him and give a pernicious example of bad behavior and immorality."[17] Chazal criticized the nefarious influence of "broken homes," whether they resulted from death, divorce, or separation, and of family models that deviated from the norm of married biological parents. He claimed that more than 70 percent of delinquents and 90 percent of vagrants had lived in broken homes.[18]

The head of the Lyon school, Alexandre Lacassagne, asserted that the "social milieu was the cultural breeding ground of criminality: the germ is an element which only becomes important the day it finds the liquid which gives it life."[19] The delinquent was not an atavistic primitive, as Italian criminologist Lombroso claimed, but a professional type created by bad examples and bad associations. Emile Raux, a member of the Lyon group, published a sociological study of incarcerated minors in an adult prison in Lyonnais—a study that remained the major reference linking family breakdown to delinquency until the 1950s. Raux noticed the high percentage of juvenile prisoners from broken and blended families. He concluded that widowhood, remarriage, or unions outside marriage favored the development of bad instincts. Living with a lone parent or an indifferent stepparent risked turning children into vagrants, thieves, and street youth.[20]

Despite Heuyer's reliance on heredity factors, he too was struck by the predominance of abnormal family milieus in the case histories of the juvenile delinquents he examined.[21] Later in his career Heuyer conceded the importance of the environment but explained it by turning to psychoanalysis—not sociology—and to notions of family conflict, specifically the Oedipus complex. For example, when the natural mother or father were replaced by lovers or stepparents whom the child rejected, the Oedipus complex could cause the child to run away or to commit any other delinquent act. It seems clear that Chazal read Heuyer because he viewed Freudian psychoanalysis as essential to understanding family conflicts resulting from broken homes. He was particularly eloquent on the dangers of single mothers, a risk factor still prioritized by the Paris court in cases involving large immigrant families with absent fathers: "If the child lives [alone] with his mother, his attachment can become exclusive, tyrannical, and ferocious. He will sometimes show a true hatred of his stepfather because of jealousy. . . . It is the Oedipal complex which manifests itself. . . . The child becomes unstable, rebellious, cruel, a runaway, a thief to exact vengeance."[22]

Freudian analyses have persisted in French psychoanalytic models along with virulent debates about the deleterious effects on children of bad marriages versus divorce and remarriage or single parenthood.[23] In 1983, one of Heuyer's successors, Didier-Jacques Duché, concluded that children raised by single parents generally turned out well, but he also warned that, when a boy was raised alone by his mother, they risked becoming a "virtually incestuous couple."[24] Ten years later, in 1993, Serge Lebovici, another student of Heuyer, declared, in an echo of both the Lyon school and of Heuyer, that blended families, even more than single parents, were the source of "numerous forms of social and mental pathology" in children.[25]

As immigrant children increasingly came to the attention of juvenile courts for psychological problems and abnormal behavior in school or in the neighborhood, the inadequacy of Western diagnostic labels and psychoanalytic treatment models became apparent to some court personnel. They looked outside the national health system to the influential work of Georges Devereux, who had trained in anthropology and psychoanalysis, and combined scientific psychiatric nosologies with culturally specific categories of normality and abnormality.[26] His pupil, Tobie Nathan, a professor of clinical psychology and psychopathology, created the Georges Devereux Center at the University of Paris VIII, which specializes in clinical psychology and the treatment of mental disorders among people from non-Western cultures. Nathan and his successor, Lucien Hounkpatin, incorporated Devereux's insistence on recentering power relations in the therapeutic encounter by including patients as active participants. Indigenous psychologists who were trained and credentialed in France but fluent in the patient's native language and culture participate along with other cultural specialists in group consultations. The patients can speak in their native languages and, with the help of a native healer, understand the nature of their problems by repositioning them within their cultural context.[27]

When I arrived at the Paris court in 2000, the Devereux Center was ten years old and Tobie Nathan's work in clinical psychology was both influential and controversial. Ethnopsychiatry and its avatars came to be dominant in the psychological and political treatment of Otherness, despite the absence of solid epidemiological data on the needs of immigrant and refugee groups. The triumph of ethnopsychiatry was the culmination of what began as a clinical encounter in the French colonies of Africa where psychiatry and psychology played a crucial role in "culturalizing racial representations and at the same time naturalizing cultural specificities."[28] Ethnopsychiatry provided the basic building block for the reification of cultural difference embodied by "the African."[29] Nathan and his colleagues published widely and were frequent expert witnesses in criminal trials dealing with drug addiction and female genital excisions involving immigrant populations. Their conception of cultural tradition as an irresistible force with the weight of biology has been used as a defense in the trials of West African women accused of performing genital excisions on minor girls or of parents who arranged excisions.[30]

Professionals trained by Nathan or his successor and/or affiliated with the Center regularly do court-ordered consultations for the minors and families supervised by Parisian judges. By drawing on the expert knowledge of ethnopsychiatrists, some judges at the Paris court seek to reframe cultural pathologies for which minors can be held accountable and punished. They elicit the medical intervention of cultural psychiatrists who diagnose culturally based psychological disorders that require treatment and prescribe "traditional" talk therapies to address aberrant behaviors (see Chapter 6).

In his study of nineteenth-century debates on criminality, Nye argues that medicalized understandings of deviance developed as a result of the collaboration of doctors, jurists, psychiatrists, and social theorists. This produced a mix of sociological and biological determinism in claims surrounding scientific "facts" about crime that allowed for widely diverging ideological approaches, alternating between appeals for rehabilitative intervention and calls for punitive correction.[31] In the late twentieth century social milieu theories of crime causation reemerged in the appraisal of deficient families. The cultural determinism that came to inform understandings of a delinquency of exclusion involved the collaboration of jurists, sociologists, anthropologists, and ethnopsychiatrists. The populations associated with cultural disorders were large poor or working-class families of immigrant origin in rundown neighborhoods.

RECURRING MEDIA THEMES ON THE SUBURBS AND VIOLENCE

Even before there were media outlets as we know them today, many Europeans and the French in particular conceived of outlying suburban areas as stigmatized and violent spaces. The term *banlieue* itself dates back to the thirteenth century when it referred to a perimeter of one league around the city. In medieval usage the term signified a liminal space associated with social marginality, uncontrolled movement, and spatialized poverty. To be *au ban* meant to be excluded by royal edict, and to be banished from a city was to be relegated to the margins of what then constituted social life and moral order.[32] In the nineteenth century emerging industrialization provoked by a rural exodus added a new class of unruly factory workers to what was perceived to be an already unstable population living outside the city. The demolition of inner-city slums— in the interests of public order—produced new, dangerous classes in areas associated with criminality, disease, and disorder. The nineteenth-century popular press reported salacious detail and illicit activity in the "zone," as the suburbs came to be known. This created the first moral panics among Parisian elites and further intensified the demand for spatial demarcation from the city's suspect peripheries.[33]

In the early twentieth century, working-class youth in eastern Parisian suburbs termed the *Apaches* became resonant signifiers of random violence. Journalist Arthur Dupin, who wrote for the mass circulation paper *Le Journal*, compared these suburban "gangs" to Apache Indians. Europeans, fascinated by fictional accounts of the American West in the 1890s, viewed the Apaches as "the bloodiest, the cruelest, and the most terrifying" of all the American Indian tribes.[34] The French Apaches captured national attention during a period of industrial expansion in working-class districts in the northern and eastern parts of Paris as well as in the ring of suburban villages outside the city. This expansion brought waves of immigrants from the French provinces and southern Europe, particularly Spain, Italy, and Corsica, producing population density, a severe housing crisis, and dismal living conditions. Dupin and other belle époque journalists attributed gang warfare, ritual vendettas, and violent mores to the southern European culture of young male immigrants who were relatively poor, underemployed, and housed in insalubrious and overcrowded conditions.[35] The Parisian press contrasted newly visible Others in suburban "zones" with stable bourgeois populations in central city neighborhoods. In an uncanny echo of contemporary rhetoric, the *Petit Parisien*, then the world's largest newspaper, exploited the theme of insécurité to demand more police and containment strategies for "Apache-infested" areas, accusing them of being in an "insurrectional state against society" because they "repudiate work of all kinds."[36] Parisian media emphasized the need to manage the Apaches with harsh corporal punishment. Their deviance was even used as an argument to keep the death penalty.[37] The creation of suburban zones near metropolitan centers paralleled the spatial differentiation under way in the French colonies. European neighborhoods of colonial cities were clearly distinguished from those relegated to the *indigènes* (native populations colonized by the French), a practice enacted out of similar concerns for security, hygiene, and historical preservation.[38]

In 1990, when riots exploded in the Lyon suburb of Vaux-en-Velin, media coverage relied discursively and visually on the tropes of conflagration and pathology associated with the "new dangerous classes." Although leftist publications such as *Le Monde*, *Libération*, *l'Humanité*, and *Témoignage Chrétien* had earlier insisted on the economic marginality and social vulnerability of disadvantaged youth in the projects, these media outlets came to interpret the urban violence as an unresolved immigration issue and a failure of integration. Media on the left and the right converged to focus on delinquency as a cultural lack rather than a socioeconomic problem.[39] This was a period marked by intensified anxiety concerning the perceived increase in youth crime as well as its troubling displacement from outside the city in suburban peripheries to inside the city limits. The "savages," according to the rightist daily *Le Figaro*, "were younger and more violent."[40] They were infiltrating social spaces historically immune to violence, such as schools, transportation systems, and public parks—in short, daily life in the city. Journalists introduced the French public to specialized slang on deviance borrowed or coined from English, Arabic, and youth vernaculars. Curious readers learned that the projects were the privileged arenas for *le racket* (extortion), *les rodéos* (high-speed chases with stolen cars), *le joint* (marijuana) and *le shit* (hash), *la tchoure* (shoplifting), *les gumgums* (assault weapons), and the reemergence of *les gangs d'Apache* (violent youth gangs).

Media outlets were instrumental in reformulating and disseminating what counted as authoritative knowledge about juvenile delinquency. The expert commentary of social scientists and political journalists based on "objective," quantitative data on crime gleaned from state ministries was preferred over local sources of knowledge on youth protests and urban poverty. Political journalists with degrees in political science from elite public universities, such as the Institut des Sciences Politiques, came to specialize in urban violence. They used fewer on-site interviews with local residents, elected officials, and social workers and relied more on the criteria of evaluation used by their similarly educated colleagues in high political office or government service.[41]

This reformulation occurred, paradoxically, from 1997 to 2002, when Socialists were in power, and largely through the influential national daily, *Le Monde*. News media concentrated on the debates among officials from the Interior Ministry, who focused on arrests, and those from the Justice Ministry, who centered on convictions. This legitimated the role of state functionaries from two law enforcement institutions to define delinquency as a phenomenon knowable through crime statistics and, therefore, containable through sanctions. This positivist vision of the delinquent saw the publication of new "scientific" typologies as well as opinion polls, which were deemed objective measures of the gravity of the problem. The dissemination of alarmist findings in state-commissioned studies on the suburbs established delinquency as both an objective social fact and a fearsome evil to be eliminated.

In late 1998 the media visibility and role of the police commissioner, Lucienne Bui Trong, in the construction and naturalization of a typology of violence were emblematic in this regard. Bui Trong was an unusual police commissioner, as both a woman and a *Normalien* (a graduate of one of the most prestigious public graduate schools) of immigrant ancestry. Those scholarly credentials and erudite commentary gave her a unique authority in terms of both the police hierarchy and political elites. As the head of the Department of Cities and Neighborhoods at the Central Service of General Intelligence, she had, in the fashion of former New York City Police Chief William Bratton, collected daily police data all over the country and compiled a graduated scale of urban violence, described as collective, emotional, expressive, provocative, and always juvenile.[42] The lowest-intensity violence included vandalism, shoplifting, extortion, and car chases, gradually escalating to hostile crowds hindering, threatening, or stoning police to culminate in assaults on law enforcement, guerrilla warfare, and full-blown riots. It was a typology made to order for internal colonies of immobile populations who were marked as racial and ethnic Others, both French and foreign. The scale completely elided the economic marginality and geographic isolation of residents in poorly served public housing projects, conditions that have worsened since France entered the Europe Monetary Union and the government made deep cuts in social welfare budgets for these areas. It likewise ignored the reality of police harassment in the forms of arbitrary identity checks, unwarranted arrests, repeated detention for both petty delinquents and suspected terrorists, and deportation of scores of illegal immigrants to which residents are subjected.

It is instructive to compare the coverage of the November 2005 riots by marginalized "immigrant" youth with those in Paris by middle-class "French" youth during March 2006. Journalists readily recognized the March demonstrators as autonomous political actors forming part of a legitimate protest movement over labor contracts even as they denied that very status to the November rioters. The erasure of all but violent forms of protest in the suburbs stands in marked contrast to the tolerance for violence elsewhere in France by farmers, middle-class high-school and university students, and antiglobalization activists.

In the 9 November 2005 broadcast on France 3, which was devoted to the riots, the only representatives of suburban youth invited to participate in the roundtable discussion were members of the French rap group Tandem. After viewing footage of angry rioters burning cars and wrecking businesses, one of the white female French journalists turned to the two black members of Tandem, insisting that such youth "could not be engaged in any kind of protest." Rapper Grégor disagreed, saying it was "a cry of alarm against unemployment and bad housing." The journalist's rejoinder was telling: "But the French don't understand this recourse to violence on their part. There are also French people who are unemployed and have housing problems." Grégor retorted evenly:

"These young people are French. They are children of France, of immigrant ancestry. They want the same rights as other French people. Young people who study for years and then end up as sewer workers. That is what they are protesting against."[43]

GHETTOS IN FRANCE?

When the riots erupted across France, some U.S. newspapers reported on them through the lens of the American inner-city ghetto, a fertile site since 9/11 onto which anxieties about a violent underclass of Muslim radicals can be projected. The *Boston Globe* was among the most hyperbolic in its rhetoric, conflating the riots and the youth into an amalgam of "criminal gangs, Islamist radicalism, de facto apartheid, and crucibles of alienation."[44] When the French gaze has focused on American inner cities, the concentration of extreme poverty, joblessness, and violent racial domination in black enclaves has inspired a mixture of fascination and horror. Even the term *cité-ghetto* (ghetto-projects) was until recently considered to be foreign to the French political lexicon.

Despite high youth unemployment (particularly among working-class youth of non-European ancestry), their relegation to the most marginal segments of the formal job market, increasing reliance on a burgeoning informal market, and the spatial concentration of poverty, many analysts, particularly on the left, continue to resist the very idea that full-fledged ghettos exist in France. They argue that a state ethos of solidarity in the form of social welfare policies, housing subsidies, and urban renewal initiatives rejects "a policy of abandonment" with regard to suburban problems similar to large American cities.[45] Despite ample documentation of high spatial concentrations of extremely disadvantaged families of immigrant and foreign ancestry, Loïc Wacquant, one of the leading experts on American ghettos and urban poverty, argues that such areas do not constitute ghettos because they are based on class, not ethnicity; exhibit no racial or ethnic uniformity; and are not constituted by force. Rather, he asserts that the suburbs are "anti-ghettos" because of their cultural, ethnic, and national heterogeneity.[46]

With the emergence of the "immigrant" delinquent, the strong trope of the ghetto has become a pervasive part of the public rhetoric that links the threat of violence in the projects with calls for anticipatory coercion in policing or radical policies in urban renewal to maintain public order. This was true of a series of Interior ministers in governments on the Left and the Right. It began with

Pierre Jox under Socialist president François Mitterrand, who declared after the 1990 riots that "we will not tolerate a Bronx in France" and continued with Charles Pasqua, head of the center-right government from 1993 to 1995, who feared that the Paris region might become a ghetto "with tribal quarrels and an ethnic impulse."[47] Following a 10 percent increase in juvenile arrests in 2001, Prime Minister Lionel Jospin, a Socialist, announced a costly plan to raze "urban ghettos."[48] Security experts close to the former center-right government of de Villepin, Alain Bauer, and Xavier Raufer, declared that the "ghetto" in its American sense could no longer be denied because of the "ethnic nature of violence," involving "guns, rival gangs, and drug trafficking."[49]

Prosecutors and attorneys representing victims used the ghetto to naturalize the link between immigration and delinquency, to justify demands for harsher punitive sanctions, or to obtain higher compensatory damage awards. The ghetto is a complex signifier and a powerful courtroom device to marshal sympathy for innocent victims and to plead for retribution for pitiless attackers. It plays on deep-seated French fears of dangerous liminal zones depicted as outside French national culture. By recycling media references to the "law of the jungle" and "the survival of the fittest," magistrates and lawyers evoked a Hobbesian state of nature in the ghetto and underscored its distance from mainstream, law-abiding French society. The categorical oppositions it establishes mask structural inequities and the history of state housing policies. The "relegation" of poor ethnoracial populations to rundown and overcrowded areas poorly served by public transportation, commercial infrastructure, and social services is not merely a question of economic restructuring. It involves political choice within state ministries as well as institutional discrimination within public schools, employment agencies, and housing offices. Communist mayors of red suburban towns outside Paris and the local managers of public housing units collaborated to prevent ethnoracial uniformity and to maintain the proper ratios among native French families and immigrant newcomers. Local managers of public housing blocks allowed some apartments to go empty rather than rent to certain immigrant groups and upset the ethnic balance they deemed necessary to social harmony.[50]

In a series of state-commissioned reports published between 1977 and 2002, a new and more menacing category of delinquent youth was constructed. The ensuing moral panics shaped not only state policy and legislative reform of juvenile law but also influenced judicial practices at court.

THE HISTORICAL EMERGENCE OF A
DELINQUENCY OF EXCLUSION: INSÉCURITÉ
AND THE FEAR OF CRIME, 1977–1981

Beginning in 1977, French politicians distinguished between crime and the fear of crime, labeling the latter *insécurité*. In 1977, the Peyrefitte Commission, created under the center-right government of Valéry Giscard d'Estaing, began its report on violence by describing "a feeling of *insécurité*... which can itself engender violence in a society where the rule of law is no longer upheld."[51] Commissioners blamed large urban concentrations, the faster pace of life, commercialized social relations, and industrial work for contributing to violence that was both more brutal and anonymous. The Commission's report became the standard format for subsequent state reports. It relied on a highly selective chronology of events that depended on political agendas and economic exigencies for its content.

In 1977 questions about crime, deindustrialization, and a surfeit of immigrant workers were compelling in the wake of the 1973 oil crisis, the economic slowdown, and the end to full employment. Relying on 1974 state statistics, the Commission reported that foreigners were overrepresented in crime and committed proportionally more violent offenses than French offenders.[52] This was the first in the series of state reports to flag "cultural deprivation" within immigrant families as one of the causes of violence: "The immigrant accumulates all the major handicaps dispersed through the entire French population. The phenomenon of cultural uprooting, family rupture, linguistic and educational breakdown, segregation in housing or work, isolation, geographical and professional instability, and the impossibility to participate in local life through the vote. We are surprised that violence did not exceed current levels."[53]

Of particular concern in all the state reports on delinquency was (and is) the proportion of crimes committed by minors compared to adults. Minors, then defined as youths under age 21, were proportionately much more involved than their adult counterparts in violent offenses against people (homicides, assault and battery, rapes, insults and attacks on public authorities such as the police, and possession of weapons) and property (aggravated theft, arson, and vandalism). Commissioners blamed escalating violence on the ecology of public housing projects marked by social anomie and class segregation, deploring the immense bleak towers and lack of green spaces. In a cautionary note they warned, "the city today has its Indians and its reservations."[54]

Specialists from juvenile courts provided detail that appeared only in an annex to the general commission report. Although they never specifically mentioned the problem of ethnic discrimination, they detailed the harassment of young people by the police, who in the 1970s were already using aggressive identity checks against "problem" youth:

> The young person who is sent away from common areas that he is accused of ruining, chased away from sports areas where he interferes with organized activities, told to leave parking areas where he might damage cars, forbidden from frequenting shopping centers where he is suspected of shoplifting . . . so he stays too long in the street without any parental supervision because of the condition of the family apartment and becomes the object of a social stigma by the neighbors and the police.[55]

The commissioners' report was issued after legislators reinforced the protective provisions of juvenile law with passage of the 23 December 1958 ordinance and the law of 4 June 1970. This legislation gave juvenile judges the authority to open separate civil or social assistance cases for children whose "health, security, morality or education" were imperiled by "recalcitrant, negligent or abusive families." It empowered judges to remove endangered children from the custody of one or both parents and to place them with willing relatives, foster families, or state residential facilities. As a result of this legislation, judges could order an educational measure in an open setting (*Assistance En Milieu Ouvert*) for the children and families under their purview.[56] This legislation produced a marked deinstitutionalization of at-risk and delinquent minors. The percentage of minors sent to public institutions declined from 19 percent in 1959 to 3 percent in 1973. At the same time, state officials dismantled large public residential institutions prevalent in the 1940s, 1950s, and 1960s in favor of smaller facilities designed to house no more than twenty to thirty teenagers.

Commissioners reported that penal sentences for juvenile offenders doubled between 1959 and 1975, rising from 15 percent to 32 percent, despite the 1958 legislation that reinforced the protective provisions of juvenile law and ended closed detention centers in 1970.[57] Although the report is said to emphasize repression, it is impossible to conclude this even after a careful reading. The commissioners stressed the need to combine prevention with punishment, urged the government to create more positions for juvenile judges—whose numbers had doubled since 1945, whereas their caseloads had quintupled—

and, tellingly, requested that the number of incarceration orders for minors be reduced. Both this report and recent research suggest that even after 1945 the French juvenile justice system continued to emphasize penal sanctions for older minors and to reserve rehabilitation only for the youngest children.

Sociologist Francis Bailleau examined case files of teenagers placed in a closed observation center for the most serious offenders in the Paris region from 1970 to 1976 prior to the 1977 Peyrefitte Commission Report. His study showed both the class and ethnic bias in the system and the punitive orientation of certain jurisdictions as well as the role played by institutional malfunctions in producing delinquent careers.[58] Arbitrary and disproportionately punitive sentences were meted out to an underprivileged population of minors from immigrant and working-class backgrounds who had no skills or jobs. In one emblematic case, a fifteen-year-old who was arrested for a first-time offense, a simple theft, was sent to a JI rather than a juvenile judge. He was incarcerated in the adult Fleury-Mérogis prison for a week before being placed in a closed observation center in the Paris region. This was the beginning of a delinquent career that earned him fourteen prison sentences by the age of twenty-one and half of his adolescence spent behind bars.[59]

The same year the Peyrefitte Commission released its report, Jacques Donzelot and Philippe Meyer published two important studies on the policing of children and families at the court based on courtroom observations, interviews, and archival research. In their view, social professionals "colonized" families, predicating state welfare benefits and juvenile protection on intrusive supervision and perpetual evaluation, including home visits, psychological assessments, counseling sessions, and judicial hearings. Meyer noted one case in which a young dropout, who balked at factory work and refused to accept blame for his problems, was diagnosed with "obsessional tendencies, an obvious failure complex," and "an unresolved Oedipal complex."[60] Donzelot was particularly dismissive of the formal juvenile correctional court which, in his view, mimicked adult penal law in its coercive aspects without being encumbered by the "democratic principles" that guarantee a fair trial, such as public proceedings, an adversarial debate, and the genuine possibility of appeal.[61]

THE LEFT IN POWER: 1981–1993

In 1981, the same year the suburbs outside Lyon exploded, François Mitterrand was elected on a pro-immigrant platform. Recognizing that the riots provided an impetus to direct political action in the form of a multicultural movement of Beurs, the children of immigrant guest workers, Mitterrand defended the "right to difference" as a universal human right, a claim that was echoed in a task force report on delinquency released under the aegis of his government in 1982. The National Assembly, which was controlled by parties on the left, enacted legislation that expanded protection for abused and neglected children, decentralized state control in the administration of child welfare services, abolished the death penalty, and, in 1987, passed a law making pretrial detention illegal for thirteen- to sixteen-year-olds who were accused of misdemeanors, the largest category of offenses.

The task force on delinquency was commissioned by a Socialist, Prime Minister Pierre Mauroy, and headed by a Socialist mayor of a Parisian suburb, Gilles Bonnemaison. Supported by 800 city mayors, the task force was committed to bring more flexible, rapid, and appropriate responses to urban crime. It advocated a positive approach to street crime that emphasized social prevention and vociferously debated including even the word *repression* in the report's final title. In a tone typical of the Left, commissioners revealed a distrust of police tactics and punitive approaches and emphasized attacking the root causes of crime through local initiatives. The report signaled the beginning of a trend that gained wide currency in the late 1990s by admonishing local officials to fight against welfare dependency through political action, to encourage the underprivileged to take responsibility for their own integration within French society, and to provide assistance to crime victims.[62]

Like the Peyrefitte Commission report, the task force linked delinquency to chaotic state housing policies, which had produced "overcrowding, problems with social and professional insertion, and the poverty and marginalization of certain categories of the population."[63] Commissioners echoed deep historical preoccupations with the problem of vagrancy and "travelers" from outside France, such as Roma or Gypsies. This was a worry that resurfaced in the late 1990s with the arrival of unaccompanied minors from Eastern Europe. At a time when the state was creating incentives for home ownership as a means to foster stability and attachment to local community, the high percentage of public housing units in the rental sector (30 percent) in which immigrant families were overrepresented spelled trouble. It signaled "the accumulation of welfare cases in these projects, school failure for children and teenagers which leads directly to professional under-qualification, and therefore, unemployment—which explain the rise of petty delinquency creating a fear of crime [insécurité]."[64] They noted cultural uprooting as a source of conflict between French residents and their Others, a category that encompassed not only "immigrants but French citizens from overseas departments such as Martinique and Guadeloupe, whose life styles aggravated problems for them and their neighbors."[65] Even as commissioners recognized the right to cultural difference, they explicitly identified certain practices that were incompatible with mainstream French norms, such as the isolation and subordination of "spouses and mothers."

The emphasis on prevention through new local-level initiatives such as community policing and collaboration among state and municipal representatives provoked strong jurisdictional conflicts over control of resources. Police commissioners and unions saw prevention as a direct challenge to two primary law enforcement functions in a highly centralized national force: the maintenance of public order and the fight against organized crime. Police viewed community policing as an impediment to career advancement because it was not controlled by the Interior Ministry and did not fit union rules that limited the work week to three days during daylight hours. They were trained to confront crime, not petty delinquency. Interacting with youth in bad neighborhoods was not "real police work" but the province of "janitors or nannies."[66]

Criminologists and jurists have argued that juvenile courts maintained an emphasis on rehabilitation through the judicial practice of routinely opening civil and penal cases simultaneously for troubled children.[67] Bailleau's study of juvenile courts supported this finding but revealed that different criteria were applied to minors, depending on their age, family background, and scholastic ability. After prosecutors referred cases for investigation and prosecution to juvenile judges, they had the option to open both penal and civil case files for the same minor. In this way, they could elect to pursue prevention and assistance measures. They could emphasize rehabilitation by extending the investigation of the case and by deferring judgment for extended periods—months or even years—to allow court-ordered interventions to bear fruit. Judges were inclined to do this most often for those under sixteen they deemed already amenable to rehabilitation. Bailleau also showed that, between 1958 and 1990, there was an increasing tendency to contrast penal cases with civil cases and to reserve the latter for the youngest children, whose hearings were held in chambers where judgments were limited to rehabilitative sanctions.[68]

Bailleau's quantitative survey of civil and penal case files and judgments from child welfare services in two different French departments over the period from 1980 to 1990, when Socialist governments emphasized social prevention, is revealing. Court personnel constructed distinct categories that differentiated between endangered children in civil cases and delinquent children in penal procedures. In his survey, he argues that the differences in the treatment of the cases were so substantial as to constitute two distinct populations on separate tracks within the juvenile justice system. Movement between the tracks was limited, one-directional (from civil to penal), and irreversible. The penal track included males over the age of sixteen, an overwhelming majority (80 percent) of whom were unemployed or out of school and had no skills or trade. Among the oldest minors in the penal track, youth of foreign ancestry born within France and abroad were overrepresented (15.1 percent). Those with penal cases open at sixteen were less likely to benefit from rehabilitative measures and more apt to receive penal sanctions than their counterparts in civil cases. In contrast, children in civil cases were younger, included both boys and girls, and were more often enrolled in school or professional training or were already working.[69]

THE RIGHT RETURNS: THE IMMIGRANT DELINQUENT
AND PENAL REFORM, 1993–1997

The Interior Ministry's report of rising juvenile delinquency arrest rates focused renewed attention on the merits of punishment versus rehabilitation and posed questions about the efficacy of existing juvenile law. Beginning in 1993, when legislative elections returned a center-right government to power, lawmakers collaborated with experts and policy makers to make substantive amendments to the 1945 ordinance. They also initiated the first complete revision of the French penal code since 1810. In the new penal model that gained legitimacy, the meaning of imprisonment and probation served more as a means to control at-risk populations than as a possibility for the transformation of vulnerable ones. This model delegated new powers to prosecutors and police, was preoccupied with recidivism, emphasized immediate responses to first-time offenses, and focused on restitution for victims. This model also relied heavily on new modes of policing in targeted neighborhoods, the systematic repression of petty crime and public order violations, and a continuum of judicial control extending from pretrial detention to conditional probation. Although it appears new, in its rhetoric and internal logic, it is reminiscent of the nineteenth-century campaigns for social defense against deviant Others.[70]

In 1993 legislators enacted a law to permit preventive identity checks in the absence of probable cause as well as a penal mediation reparation law, which allowed prosecutors to target first-time offenders and to repair the offense to victims with victims' approval. It was intended to silence critics of excessive leniency shown to minors. Similarly, article 309 of the new penal code recategorized a physical assault without injury as a correctional offense if it was accompanied by any one of a number of aggravating circumstances. One year later, in 1994, the most common infraction, simple theft, was transformed by adding six new aggravating circumstances. Any one of these circumstances substantially increased the accused's sentence if he or she were convicted.[71] Whereas the numbers of minors in prison dropped dramatically between 1982 and 1992, that trend reversed between 1993 and 1996, when there was a 45 percent increase in the number of minors sent to prison.[72] Most of that increase could be attributed to juvenile judges ordering minors to go for short stays of preventive detention pending trial. This was remarkable, because JIs had a history of issuing incarceration orders "much more frequently than juvenile judges."[73]

In 1995 center-right candidate Jacques Chirac won election as president after a campaign dominated by the themes of social fragmentation and economic polarization. His prime minister, Alain Juppé, assumed office faced with the threat of fundamentalist Islamic movements in France, their infiltration into the basement prayer rooms of subsidized housing blocks, and their recruitment of impoverished youth as soldiers for global jihad.[74] These fears played out live on national television when French police shot and killed Khaled Kelkal, a youth of Algerian ancestry from Vaux-en-Velin who was accused of playing a role in the summer 1995 bombings attributed to the Algerian Islamic group (GIA). In response to this threat, Juppé unveiled a Marshall Plan for the banlieues, modeled on the plan initiated by the U.S. government to rebuild postwar Europe. It was designed to draw young residents from the street economy into the formal economy through the creation of 744 "sensitive" urban zones earmarked for state-subsidized youth internships. The plan established 44 trade zones in state-classified "bad" areas to stimulate the return of commercial businesses driven out by petty crime. In addition, the plan included funding for heightened police surveillance and round-ups of suspected Islamists, as well as increased deportations of undocumented immigrants.

Faced with a shortage of residential facilities for delinquents and no possibility for incarceration other than prison, center-right politicians sought to resurrect closed detention centers. In light of the perceived Socialist failure to institute community policing and local crime prevention councils, and given the demand for detention facilities, Prime Minister Alain Juppé commissioned another report on delinquency even as the National Assembly voted amendments to the 1945 ordinance permitting accelerated adjudications. In contrast to the Peyrefitte Commission and Bonnemaison reports, which were critical of sensationalist media coverage of youth violence, the 1996 Rufin report reinforced the media depictions of delinquents as younger and more violent by using the Interior Ministry's higher figures of arrests versus the Justice Ministry's lower numbers of convictions.

Unlike the previous commissions, the Rufin report centered squarely on juvenile law and the institutions directly responsible for the supervision of troubled youth. Rufin, a conservative senator, noted approvingly the "innovative" legislative amendments to the 1945 ordinance voted in 1995 and 1996. The amendments were designed to reinforce accountability, such as accelerated indictment hearings as well as immediate judgment proceedings.[75] The Rufin report drew on extensive data documenting the crisis within the Protection Judiciaire de la Jeunesse (PJJ), the agency that monitors delinquent and at-risk minors. It noted the shortage of emergency and long-term residence facilities for delinquents, the high turnover among and lack of experienced counselors and éducateurs to staff them, the "troubling" feminization of the profession, and, "most worrisome of all" given the public consensus on violent youth crime, a leftist profession of éducateurs that viewed imprisonment for minors as a disavowal of its basic rehabilitative mission. Rufin selectively quoted those professionals who focused on the cultural deficiencies of families in bad neighborhoods. Poverty had bred not only literal contagion in the reappearance of "illnesses that were thought to have disappeared" but in the spread of a culture of dependency. Rufin catalogued intergenerational unemployment, bad parenting, and weak authority structures at home and in school where "children enjoy more rights than obligations." He cited social workers (*assistants sociaux*) who described families in which "children were the only ones in the family to get out of bed in the morning for school or work and where money is no longer associated with employment."[76]

Although Rufin did advocate increased resources for staff, facilities, and professional reinsertion, he subordinated the rehabilitative logic focused on prevention, diagnosis, and treatment to a punitive principle based on surveillance, control, and containment. He recommended more reliable statistics on juvenile court activity; reinforced coordination among police, prosecutors,

National Education, and the courts; a swift and immediate response to all deviance, particularly for first-time offenses; additional efforts to make negligent parents assume their responsibilities; the creation of specialized juvenile police brigades to deal with urban offenses; more residential facilities to house hardcore delinquents; and, given the problem of "poorly controlled immigration and the obvious failure of integration,"[77] renewed "educational services" prepared to support the "return home" of undocumented immigrants.[78]

THE SOCIALISTS REGAIN CONTROL: PUBLIC ORDER, YOUTH CRIME, AND INDIVIDUAL ACCOUNTABILITY, 1997–2002

Jacques Chirac's 1997 plan to reinforce his center-right majority in the National Assembly backfired. Legislative elections held that year produced a victory for his Socialist rivals and forced him to name Lionel Jospin as prime minister of a center-left government. While that legislative defeat thwarted Chirac's political agenda, it obligated the Left to deal with juvenile delinquency in a very different context than in the 1980s when it had controlled the French presidency and the National Assembly. Five months after assuming office, then–Interior Minister Jean-Pierre Chevènement organized a highly publicized conference, held at Villepinte, on the theme of "Safe Cities for Free Citizens," in which legislators, magistrates, mayors, police, and gendarmes were invited to reflect on two national threats: unemployment and insécurité. Denis Salas, the eminent jurist and former juvenile judge who coined the term "delinquency of exclusion," was among them.

The center-left government, like its center-right predecessor, turned to new experts on youth crime. One such expert, sociologist Sébastien Roché, was well regarded across the political spectrum and was one of only two social scientists invited to attend the Villepinte conference. Roché had published a book on insécurité in 1993 and another on incivility in 1996. These books decisively shaped public opinion by clearly identifying a threat that was eroding the fabric of urban life.[79] Roché was instrumental in importing and popularizing J. Q. Wilson and G. L. Kelling's theory of "broken windows" crime prevention, which they outlined in 1982.[80] In 1994, with Roché's imprimatur, the editors of the Institut des Hautes Etudes de la Sécurité Intérieure's journal on internal security, Les Cahiers de la Sécurité Intérieure, translated and published Wilson and Kelling's famous 1982 Atlantic Monthly article in a 1994 issue.

Roché defined incivility in the French context as any and all breaks in normal appearances and basic codes of social life that unfold in public spaces, provide no substantial economic benefit, and are not considered dangerous.[81] Defining incivility as a social, not a legal, category with multiple, overlapping components was compelling politically. It included actions that were offensive, although not illegal, because they violated middle-class social conventions. Public forms of incivility included obscenities, intimidation, loud music, spitting, and public urination. It also encompassed acts that were both offensive and illegal, such as insults and threats to public officials, thefts, graffiti, vandalism, and physical assaults. The very elasticity and ambiguity of the term tended to conflate the social with the penal.[82] This concept was useful to legislators as they criminalized behaviors that had once been offensive but were recategorized as illegal between 1994 and 2004, such as playing loud music and loitering in public housing buildings.

The published proceedings from the Villepinte conference represent an important turning point in the political understandings of juvenile delinquency. In contrast to the past, when governments solicited psychologists and clinicians to explain delinquency, the Socialists turned to social scientists, law enforcement, and cabinet ministers. We hear Socialist ministers and conservative prosecutors attribute a delinquency of exclusion to cultural difference, a claim echoed more forcefully in the 2002 Carle and Schosteck Commission Report on Delinquency. Two variants of the culturalist argument can be heard in the discourses of conference participants. The first variant blamed delinquency on a pathologized culture of alienation and confusion within foreign and immigrant families who were said to lack moral values, social norms, and grounded identities. Martine Aubry, then minister of Labor and Solidarity, paradigmatic Socialist militant, and champion of the French working classes, described the newest and most violent delinquents as

> poorly or not at all socialized. Without any mental or emotional structure, these teenagers have only one reflex, violence. No longer having any bearings or norms, they are ignorant of what a crime means. . . . They are sometimes even incapable of telling us what relationship they have to the adults with whom they live. Is it their mother or stepmother, their father or stepfather that they call by his first name? It is clear that the emotional and social destructuring of these children is the principal cause of violence.[83]

The second version viewed youth violence as the result of an inevitable culture clash between mainstream French values and "backward" immigrant traditions magnified by poverty and isolation. The extreme version heard on the far right linked most delinquency to immigrant youth whose "culture" was structured by violence and decried as barbaric. The less extreme version, evident on the center-left and on the right, ostensibly condemned racism even as it affirmed French republican values and the respect for democratic institutions. Interior Minister Chevènement reminded his listeners that no "policed, that is civilized, society exists without common values." He blamed rising crime on violence in blighted neighborhoods and repeatedly invoked pervasive incivility as evidence of "certain categories of the population whose cultural origin does not recognize basic republican concepts such as secular values and the primacy of the individual."[84]

In the drive to restore safe cities, public schools were deemed crucial. They became the locus of the debate over the question of republican values and citizen subjects. There was little talk of the challenges of attending lesser schools in state-classified priority zones, which were underfunded and staffed by teachers with little experience and no knowledge of multiethnic populations. One educator lamented "pathogenic urbanism," and Minister of Education Claude Allègre recommended an apprenticeship of civility. This reproduced a colonial discourse that foregrounds the renewed imperative of a civilizing mission in the internal colonies of the French projects where the grandchildren of immigrants must be integrated so they can be fully French.[85]

Although government ministers ostensibly supported notions of the collective good, favored civic education, and promised professional insertion through the creation of new jobs, the real focus of the conference was on the criminalization of social policy, the policing of urban space, the prosecution of all juvenile offenses, and the search for more appropriate sanctions for delinquent youth.

The 1998 Lazerges/Balduyck Commission

One year later, in 1998, Prime Minister Lionel Jospin commissioned a report on juvenile delinquency from two Socialist deputies in the National Assembly, one of whom, Christine Lazerges, was a jurist. Jospin began his charge to the commission by noting that "delinquency had reached worrisome proportions."[86] In the months between his charge to the commission and the publication of its report in December 1998, the topic of delinquency took center stage. In May, the publication of the Body-Gendrot and Le Guennec Report commissioned by the Interior Ministry centered on domestic increases in youth crime.

Also in May, Interior Minister Chevènement's memo advocating a harder line on juvenile offenders was leaked to and published by the leftist daily *Libération*. In June, the new Council on Domestic Security, a Socialist creation, announced a harder line on youth crime. In September, eight well-known intellectuals, including philosopher Régis Debray and historian Mona Ozouf, published an open letter in *Le Monde* in which they lamented the widening gap between "law-abiding, legitimate Parisian France" and "suburban, lawless, and demoralized France." "Is it racism," they wondered, "to say that the most violent neighborhoods are those where illegal immigration is the highest" or "to demand that parents take responsibility for their children in return for the social welfare assistance they receive?"[87]

Both the prime minister's charge and the larger national mood set the tone for the Commission on Delinquency, headed by two Socialist deputies in the newly elected National Assembly: Christine Lazerges and Jean-Pierre Balduyck. Despite the authors' stated aims to refute sensationalist media coverage, they highlighted short-term trends in delinquency, stressing in bold type a temporary spike in the juvenile delinquency rate and the severity of youth violence.[88] They disregarded the detailed quantitative analysis in an annex to their own report by eminent French criminologist Bruno Aubusson de Cavarlay, who concluded that there was "no way to confirm or deny" the emergence of a new, more violent type of juvenile delinquency, a "so-called delinquency of exclusion."[89] They repeated the same alarmist themes centering on a crisis of the French assimilation model and the emergence of identities inextricably tied to ethnic origin.

The Commission report centered on the possibilities for punishment inherent in the original 1945 ordinance. The authors insisted that cases of extreme deviance justified the suspension of total penal irresponsibility for those as young as seven years of age (the age of reason). Thirteen-year-olds could be sentenced to prison and those sixteen and older could get a life term.[90] They justified enhanced accountability, paradoxically through a turn to human rights and social justice. They selectively highlighted legal statutes centering on parental authority, couples' responsibility, child protection, and filial obedience. They argued that the systematic prosecution of all acts of delinquency would restore the foundation of the social contract that was guaranteed in article 2 of the Rights of Man. Although article 2 speaks to the preservation of property rights, security, and freedom from oppression, the commissioners focused exclusively on security. Their appeal to human rights rather than humanitarian concerns was strategic because, as Miriam Ticktin has argued, human rights appeals are grounded in the law and are intended to further individual accountability rather than to foster sympathy for suffering.[91] The commissioners' recommendations also argued that political recognition was a contingent, two-step process based on individual behavior and cultural citizenship. Minors had to internalize the law and their families had to assimilate the putatively French middle-class mainstream norms associated with two-parent nuclear families, domestic power-sharing arrangements, egalitarian gender relations, and tolerance for adolescent sexuality.

Despite a large literature on the transformation of the French family, the proliferation and legal recognition of single-parent households, the decline in or postponement of marriage, and the exponential rise in the number of children born out of wedlock, the commissioners focused exclusively on "aberrant" patterns within "immigrant" (that is, North and West African) families.[92] They noted the importance of "aunts and uncles," an indirect reference to the patrilineal kinship systems in parts of Sub-Saharan Africa, the widespread practice of fosterage in which children are raised by members of the extended family, and the role played by "brothers and sisters" as opposed to parents in the disciplining of younger children in North African families. Citing the French civil code, they admonished parents, not siblings, to raise children. They recalled the law of 1970, which established legal obligations such as monitoring a child's movements and forbidding bad associations to prevent school truancy. Despite an enduring French preoccupation with the presumed subordination of women and a distrust of patriarchy in North African families, the commissioners centered on the dangers associated with the devaluing of the father, the loss of paternal authority, and a matrifocal organization of immigrant families given the absence of fathers due to death, divorce, separation, or disability.[93] This situation allowed older children to serve as authority figures, created unhealthy attachments between mothers and children, and deprived children of a normally structured upbringing.

The commissioners issued lengthy recommendations to support, make accountable, and punish the parents. They emphasized that abdication of parental responsibility through neglect, abandonment, or abuse was punishable by the loss of child welfare payments and/or child custody and the imposition of fines and/or imprisonment. Here they catalogued the criminal penalties awaiting families who shielded, ignored, or facilitated their children's involvement in a parallel economy. Despite the abundant evidence of delinquency in middle-class milieus, commissioners targeted the families of drug lords and gang leaders, who represented a small percentage of hard-core delinquents. They cited the sanctions for complicity when a minor commits a crime (article 121-7 of the penal code); for hiding, holding, or transmitting property acquired illegally (article 321-6 of the penal code); and for being unable to justify a particular lifestyle (article 222-39-1). Although they urged more child care workers, day care centers, and flexible work schedules for working mothers, the tenor of their recommendations was punitive. They demanded civil fines for parents who failed to answer court summonses, the legal recognition of children born to unwed parents at a formal ceremony in the town hall, systematic prosecutions of deficient parents, and a parent's obligation to pay child support even after he or she has lost custody of that child. Noting that the numbers of minors in prison had increased as well as the average length of the sentence for those convicted of crimes (between 1987 and 1995, the average sentence increased from four to five years), the commissioners declared that prison conditions for minors were generally "bad" and did not permit long-term rehabilitation. Nonetheless, they deemed prison necessary and urged reform rather than rejecting incarceration, quoting Jean-Louis Daumas, a former warden of the Youth Detention Center at Fleury-Mérogis, who insisted that it "was prison conditions, more than prison itself, that created recidivism."[94]

The criminalization of parallel economies and the enhanced accountability aimed at poor parents ignores the French state's complicity in creating the conditions that encourage these economies: closing French and European borders when there is increased demand for low-wage workers in the agricultural, garment, and construction industries, and restricting the conditions for the legalization of undocumented immigrants already in France.[95]

Considering the "New York Miracle"

It is no accident that the moral panics created by juvenile crime led Socialist Party members to revise their thinking on the efficacy of rehabilitation and to claim that the primary causes of delinquency were no longer economic marginality or social isolation but the criminals themselves. Prominent Socialists declared that crime was not social in nature but individual in choice.[96] In a search for new crime-fighting methods, Socialists were curious to examine firsthand the widely reported "New York miracle" produced by Mayor Rudy Giuliani and his law-and-order police commissioner William Bratton. In 1998 Julien Dray, a prominent Socialist deputy and antiracist militant turned security expert, led a French delegation to New York. Despite reservations about police brutality, racism, and the escalating U.S. prison population, Dray was deeply impressed with zero-tolerance policing and "broken windows" crime prevention that involved an immediate and coordinated response to all offenses, even petty delinquency, in targeted neighborhoods. He returned to France advocating zero-tolerance approaches for what he termed the emergence of a new generation of wild children, "with no collective values beyond a defense of their territory, a code of honor," and "violent, aggressive, and brutal exchanges."[97]

The following year, in 1999, during policy debates about the appropriate response to youth crime, Prime Minister Lionel Jospin explicitly affirmed that juvenile delinquents had to be accountable as individual subjects before French law. He was unequivocal on the topic of extenuating circumstances: "[Poverty, unemployment, and cultural handicaps] do not in any way constitute a valid excuse for individual criminal behaviors. We must not confuse sociology and the law. Each person is responsible for his actions."[98]

What exactly did sociology conclude about youth crime? What were the explanations for a delinquency of exclusion?

SOCIAL SCIENCE AND A CULTURE OF POVERTY

In contrast to the black jackets of the 1950s and the hoodlums of the 1960s who were of French working-class ancestry, the "immigrant" delinquent of the 1980s and 1990s was viewed as a new phenomenon. The selection of research sites, subjects, and theory were said to pose epistemological and methodological dilemmas for researchers given the unequal power separating these research subjects from sociologists in the middle-class, mainstream French population.[99] Until the 1980s, American sociological theory was largely absent from a French sociology of delinquency for several reasons. Psychological and structural models dominated French youth studies in earlier periods. French sociologists strongly resisted American cultural explanations of violence as well as the American sociology on race relations, ethnic gangs, and minority subcultures as phenomena foreign to France. This perception still contributes to the relative lack of ethnographic field studies and the prevalence of quantitative studies centering on violence.

One of the first influential sociological studies of exclusion, *La Galère*, was published in 1987 by François Dubet. The study was based on extensive interviews drawn from constructed subject groups that combined equal numbers of youth who were French and of immigrant ancestry as well as adults from different French and Belgian cities. Dubet allowed subjects to participate on the condition that they didn't belong to naturally occurring groups such as gangs. After studying these contrived groupings, Dubet concluded that delinquency was not part of a uniform, normative system in which youths were socialized but instead resulted from the random logic of struggle and exclusion in impoverished cités. Devoting an entire chapter to refuting the Chicago School analyses of delinquent subcultures, he argued that violence was not culturally constituted or politically motivated but was explosive, gratuitous, and unpredictable.[100]

Dubet's work lent scientific credibility to a category of youth focused on crisis and stimulated both qualitative, ethnographic-based work and quantitative, survey-derived research in marginal areas. Given the economic restructuring and concentrations of poverty that extended the transition into adulthood, some French sociologists and anthropologists appropriated a cultural ecology model and the notion of youth subcultures drawn from the Chicago School of Sociology. Although relying on different methodologies and ideological orientations, this research theorized youth subcultures as the product of the economic marginality, social disorganization, and cultural deprivation of populations in enclaved (that is, ethnic) neighborhoods. The structural functional emphasis of the Chicago School served as a perfect model to depict the youth subcultures in French cités as bounded, internally homogenous, self-referential, and largely alien systems of norms and values. A standard trope implicit in this work is the culture of poverty concept popularized by Oscar Lewis in the 1960s. Although the culture of poverty concept was the subject of virulent polemics and has been largely discredited in the United States, it was imported to France as a largely unproblematic device to explain how the ecology of state-classified bad zones trapped residents in intergenerational cycles of violent familial dysfunction and culturally deficient value systems.[101]

As the concept of the culture of poverty migrated into political and public discourse, state officials used it selectively to center on cultural explanations rather than on structural inequities as the reason for the plight of the poor and the violence of the young. State-commissioned reports in the late 1990s drew on this work, noting the central role gender relations and family dynamics played in the bundle of traits associated with a culture of poverty in bad neighborhoods. These traits were strikingly similar to those given thirty years earlier by Lewis: identity disorders, unstable families, negligent parents, psychological pathology, chronic unemployment, present-time orientation, and school truancy. The breakdown of patriarchal authority and the loss of status, notably in the arenas of family and employment, led to a focus on masculinities in crisis, first among immigrant fathers and then among their sons and grandsons. The ethnicization and racialization of masculine identities in situations of poverty and distress was presented as synonymous with volatile hypermasculinity and violence. Sociological accounts of youth subculture in all its expressive forms—from vernacular language, verbal jousting, and dress codes to pitched street battles—drew on American studies of ethnic gangs and delinquent boys.[102]

A number of well-received ethnographies of impoverished projects outside Paris were published in the 1990s and reviewed in national newspapers.[103] They emphasized the self-reflexive nature of fieldwork, were alert to issues of power and subjectivity, and documented naturally occurring behaviors and speech. Their authors explicitly intended to counter negative public stereotypes of youth culture by providing the insider perspective and by insisting that it be judged on its own terms, not in relation to dominant sociolinguistic norms. Despite efforts to ascribe agency to social actors, to emphasize diversity among peer groups, to focus on attachments to stigmatized places, and to accentuate the resilience of North African and West African family systems after immigration, these studies presented peer group formation as apart from and in opposition to dominant French society.

A core element in all these ethnographic accounts was the fascination with and positive view of violence, both verbal and physical, among young residents. In contrast to Dubet's emphasis on spontaneous rage, these authors argued for cultural patterns of violence designed to enhance male honor, inspire fear, and augment respect for the family and peers. They depicted violence as integral to a transgressive street culture based on the defense of territory and male virility.

The structure of the North African family figured prominently in these studies. In one 1995 monograph set in the suburban projects, the focus was the role of the big brother, who served as a family cop, neighborhood advisor, and valued mediator between children (both their own siblings and neighborhood youth), their parents, and state representatives.[104] In the authority vacuum left by fathers, big brothers were the linchpins of an urban ecology dominated by the young. They drew their legitimacy from the neighborhood youth, not adult personalities or municipal leaders, a fact not lost on French politicians.

Although big brothers strove to instill responsible behavior in neighborhood children, their pasts too often belied their admonishments to children to stay in school. Most were school dropouts, ex-convicts, or recovering addicts. The riveting ethnographic examples made it easy to forget that Duret's research sample consisted of just fourteen "big brothers." The "threat" posed by the big brother was expressed in the 2002 report on delinquency. Commissioners concluded that big brothers were bad role models because of their inability to leave home and find permanent jobs that paid a living wage.[105]

In 1997, the same year that the Socialists returned to power, anthropologist David Lepoutre published a book based on his two years of fieldwork in the Parisian suburb of La Courneuve, where he taught in the local middle school and lived in one of the now infamous 4,000 public housing projects. Lepoutre depicted the functional integration of all aspects of adolescent street culture, from scatological humor, verbal jousts, and ritualized insults aimed at mothers to agonistic public displays of physical force. In his account, youth culture reinforced the central values of reputation and honor linked to ethnic origin and shared territory. Here, too, violence was a constituent component of youth culture. Deviance brought recognition at an age when adolescence was experienced as both constraint and obligation. Shared marginality in the projects produced a greater tolerance for illicit activity. This experience enhanced peer solidarity against the police and earned heightened prestige from the ostentatious display of goods obtained illegally.[106] Gérard Mauger's influential work draws on the sociology of American Robert Merton to depict the "warrior logic" of masculinity and force that structure French street gangs. These were the only assets of a youth underclass who are excluded from legal work.[107]

In a book published in 1999 and based on six years of research in the projects of Grigny outside Paris, Joëlle Bordet argued that the enlistment in youth gangs and involvement in the parallel economy, both stolen goods and drug sales, was unavoidable given the limited availability of legal work. Nonetheless, her description of a criminal Maghrebi family, whose profits from drug trafficking financed the purchase of a single-family home, was recycled into other sociological accounts on delinquency, notably by Hugues Lagrange. Paris judges were familiar with this work. It also shaped the alarmist view of parallel economies depicted in the 2002 Carle and Schosteck Commission Report on Delinquency.

In contrast to this qualitative research, the new studies commissioned by the Socialists in power between 1997 and 2002 and their center-right successors were based on quantitative, survey-driven data gathered during short-term site visits and interviews.[108] Newly established public university programs on organized crime and terrorism, research groups, and policy institutes contributed studies. Institutes included those that were university affiliated or those that were state aligned and specialized in criminology, justice, and security issues, including the Institut des Hautes Etudes de Justice, associated with the Ministry of Justice; the Ecole Nationale de la Magistrature; and a conservative institute on domestic security, the Institut des Hautes Etudes de la Sécurité Intérieure (IHESI),[109] created in 1989 and financed by the Ministry of the Interior. The IHESI was particularly influential in shaping national understandings of youth crime through the seminars and conferences it organizes as well as the journal and books it publishes. A number of academics, independent researchers, and law enforcement personnel who have enjoyed prestige among governments on the left and the right are regularly invited to speak there and to testify before state commissions.

Sociologist Hugues Lagrange was one of the social scientists, along with Sébastien Roché, whose work was influential in political and judicial circles. Lagrange participated in a study group with judges such as Denis Salas. Lagrange's books used quantitative data and drew extensively on data conducted by other social scientists (including sociologists, political scientists, criminologists, police commissioners, jurists, and selected anthropologists such as Lepoutre) on poor neighborhoods, delinquent youth, juvenile justice, and immigrant families. Lagrange employed Robert Merton's structural functional analysis to argue that delinquent subcultures filled the gap between the unfulfilled aspirations of disadvantaged young men for both recognition and plenty and their inability to achieve those goals legally. Although he insisted that their delinquency had a political dimension and ostensibly rejected Oscar Lewis's "cultural" explanations, he systematically undercut this assertion by arguing that delinquents were mired within a cultural ecology of poverty, unemployment, discrimination, and little access to legal status that offered no choice but violence. Their frustration and rage at systematic exclusions led them to seek honor and regain self-esteem through brawls with rival gangs, confrontations with police, the fencing of stolen goods, and drug dealing.[110]

Lagrange also argued that high rates of school failure and low economic prospects among working-class and immigrant men compared to their female counterparts made them less attractive as marriage partners and increased sexual tension, producing a crisis of masculinity. He centered on young men from the poorest backgrounds and identified a cultural trait that juvenile court personnel also viewed as a significant risk factor in "immigrant" families, namely that sons were too attached to their mothers because of the social stigmatization of their fathers.[111] As we shall see, this had immediate and sometimes devastating consequences for the children and mothers at the juvenile court. The problem here as with the preceding work was the failure to identify or distinguish among "immigrant" groups. Were the "Islamic norms" of polygamous Soninké from Sub-Saharan Africa similar to those of urbanized Algerian Arabs? Of third-generation Kabyle Berbers? Did this apply to Turkish and Lebanese Muslims?

In 2001, the same year that Lagrange published his book, Sébastien Roché produced a study, the conclusions of which also figured prominently in the 2002 Carle and Schosteck Commission's Report on Delinquency. Roché's study was one of the first French studies based on the self-reporting of delinquent behavior by teenagers aged thirteen to nineteen years old. He rejected economic marginality or unemployment, class discrimination in public schools, and ethnic concentration in neighborhoods as causal factors. Roché argued that delinquency was rampant because society had done nothing to stop it. Reviving a classic teleological argument from the Far Right, he argued that the only solution to the crisis of civil society, deterioration of authority, outdated penal code statutes, and lack of collective norms was more punishment. He proposed to shatter the hypocritical silence on race and ethnicity by dealing openly with the question of youth of foreign ancestry and their role in crime. Roché defended a new criminology of ethnic origin in France for several reasons. First, given the concentrations of youth of foreign ancestry in neighborhoods with "distinctive music, communication, religious symbols (the Islamic veil) in public space, it was imperative to ask if they form communities." Second, he insisted that like criminologists elsewhere, notably in the United States, it was necessary to consider ethnicity (that is, race). He declared that the overrepresentation of foreigners (24 percent) in European prisons and the disproportionate number of youth of foreign origin under court supervision (43 percent, without specifying if they were supervised in penal or civil cases) required it. Since current debates deal with integration and discrimination, and Maghrebi youth are the most numerous immigrant population, he asked: Don't we need to look at them and ask how conflicts and hatred are organized?[112]

The crux of his argument was that a significant risk factor for minor and serious delinquency, across social classes and regardless of residence, was one's origin or parentage. Having two parents born outside of France, particularly from Algeria, Tunisia, and Morocco, was more frequently associated with serious delinquency. Roché used quantitative data culled from interviews conducted in Grenoble and St. Etienne to create a typology in which he mapped the propensity for delinquency onto the degree of foreignness determined by the birthplace of one's parents.[113] His conclusion was an alarming echo, with a scientific gloss, of the depiction of Apaches at the turn of the previous century. Maghrebi and foreign youth were more often deviant than their French counterparts because of the cultural gap that had its roots in ethnic difference and "in a colonial history in which one people takes revenge on the other."

CONCLUSION

I end this chapter where I began with the 2002 Carle and Schosteck Commission Report on Delinquency. Its conclusions, published after the return of the center-right government to power, were grim. After hearing from seventy-three experts on delinquency in fifty-one hours of testimony, the commissioners concluded that delinquency was not new in France, as many alleged, but radically different in kind. Delinquents were "younger, more violent" and, according to clinical psychologist Philippe Jeammet, "beyond reform" because the delinquents' deviance was motivated by an "absence of being [human]."[114] The severity of the problem had been understated rather than exaggerated. Who was to blame? What had happened? Marginalized families no longer socialized their children, schools ignored violence, the courts were too erratic in their treatment of offenders, and the Protection Judiciaire de la Jeunesse refused to accept the principle of punishment, even incarceration, as an integral part of rehabilitation and integration. Who were these offenders? Borrowing Roché's new "scientific" typology linking the predilection for serious youth crime to foreign origin and drawing on selective portions of testimony from court and law enforcement personnel, commissioners identified the "immigrant" delinquent as the source of insécurité in French cities. They drew on the testimony of two long-standing youth advocates who appeared to endorse this conclusion: a priest, Christian Delorme, who had worked in the Lyon suburbs of Les Minguettes; and Thierry Baranger, a senior juvenile judge, child advocate, and then-president of the French Association of Juvenile and Family Court Judges. In a 2001 interview reproduced in the report, Delorme said, "on the pretext of not stigmatizing young people, we have for too long denied the over-representation of immigrant youth in delinquency."[115] In a similar vein,

Baranger's long and nuanced Senate testimony, excerpted in an appendix to the report, included only a small section on cultural handicaps: "It is no accident if a significant proportion of the young people we have to treat and who end up in prison are of immigrant ancestry." They borrowed expert opinion from advocates and critics of the present penal welfare approach enshrined in French juvenile law to blame a culture of poverty in public housing projects and bad neighborhoods marked by the "survival of the fittest," "a climate of unrelenting violence," and "families where aggression was the only medium of communication" because of their debilitating "cultural deficiencies."[116] No ethnopsychiatrists were called to testify to relativize the delinquency of immigrant youth by medicalizing cultural difference and identifying the psychological disorders that result from migration and displacement.

It is telling that a Marxist sociologist highly critical of the juvenile justice system should echo widespread fears about handling a delinquency of exclusion linked to cultural difference. When I spoke to Francis Bailleau in 2000, he argued that the individualized interventions designed for a troubled youth were no longer tenable. The courts now dealt with groups, not individuals, from "balkanized neighborhoods," who had few skills, no viable diplomas, or access to legal work. He quoted Oscar Lewis's 1961 definition of a culture of poverty to describe the "collective responses" and forms of resistance such as illicit activity among poor youth that "prevent participation in a national culture and become a subculture."[117]

In the next chapter we move into the court to meet the judges whose individual trajectories and understandings of work in a fraught context are central to the functioning of the institution and the delivery of justice.

4 JUSTICE FOR MINORS: A MINOR JUSTICE?

WHAT DO YOU JUDGE?

I met Elisabeth Catta late in my fieldwork through her friend, Judge Chaland.[1] They graduated the same year from the Ecole Nationale de la Magistrature and were posted to neighboring juvenile courts in rural France. In contrast to Judge Chaland, who spent most of her career at the Paris juvenile court, Catta spent only six years in juvenile justice before leaving to pursue a career in civil law in Paris. She moved from various ministries between 1979 and 2002 before accepting a position as a public prosecutor (*avocat général*). In the late 1980s she published her book, *What Do You Judge?*, a moving memoir of her first years as a juvenile judge in a court in Brittany. The book appeared at a time when a punitive trend in juvenile justice was reemerging. At that time long-standing and largely positive views of juvenile judges as child advocates still predominated. Her memoir is exceptional in two regards. It was one of only two I found that had been written by a woman, despite the fact that in 1988 women made up 59 percent of juvenile judges. Rather than depict the juvenile judge's work through the accepted convention of case studies in the style of "a day in the life of a magistrate," Catta offers a penetrating analysis of the legal debates and systemic contradictions surrounding the court, its judges, and the specialized jurisprudence governing minor children.[2] She documents the ambiguous and stigmatized position of judges within the legal establishment, both historically and currently. It is the only memoir that raises the issue of gender and questions the naturalized link between women and juvenile justice. In contrast to memoirs written by male judges, it deals explicitly with the ramifications of class in hearings and illustrates these with material from her own experience.

One of the central contradictions Catta identifies is the statute creating a specialized corps of juvenile judges in 1945. It specifies that the "juvenile judge will be chosen according to the interest he has in questions of childhood." Given that all judges receive identical training at the Ecole Nationale de la Magistrature to prepare them to fulfill any legal function, Catta finds this "specification on the qualities required of a juvenile judge" to be a complete anomaly. "Nowhere in other texts do we find similar indications concerning judges, who serve on the bench [siège] or the state [parquet]"[3] This begs larger questions. What are the "natural" predispositions for judging children? How are judges appointed to the court and how is appointment viewed by the legal establishment? Is it a calling to save troubled youth and intervene in the tragic lives of damaged families? What kind of law is practiced in the juvenile court and how does it differ from civil law or penal law for adults? It invites us to ask how juvenile judges perceive their position at court, frame their work experientially, cope with its daily demands, and manage their relations with more powerful interlocutors such as juges d'instruction and prosecutors. Many of the challenges identified by Catta not only persist in juvenile courts but have been exacerbated by the punitive trend and, in Paris, by the explosion of penal cases with which some court personnel feel unprepared to deal. Although Catta discusses the social homogeneity of judges and the power asymmetries between judges and families in their courtrooms, she is largely silent on the questions of bias that result from cultural and ethnic difference. These are questions at the center of this book, questions that pose dilemmas for judges whose courtrooms are peopled predominantly with children of immigrant and foreign ancestry.

At a time when juvenile delinquency has been politicized, some juvenile judges, particularly male magistrates from the Paris region, have become more visible as public intellectuals. Their commentaries on a volatile urban phenomenon are published in print media and broadcast on radio and television, providing a potential forum for reframing critical social issues and shaping public policy. Here I examine internal divisions among career magistrates on the issue of the punitive trend. A reconceptualization of judges as jurists rather than social activists, along with disagreements regarding the new penology, have worked to increase rather than diminish public ambivalence concerning them and to undercut their potential influence.

The contradictions that emerge in the juvenile court arise in part from the workings of neoliberal capitalism. The rhetoric of enfranchisement, the opportunity for employment, and the promises of full inclusion within society are undercut by the reality of deindustrialization, the shrinking welfare state, and the specter of permanent exclusion. Neoliberal governance regimes increasingly devolve risk and responsibility onto individuals, families, and entire communities. They demand more individual accountability even as the state limits its regulatory purview, reduces public expenditures, and privatizes both social services and the security apparatus. Under neoliberal pressures less is reserved for preventive rehabilitation and more for public order threats to be addressed by police, prisons, and antiterrorism initiatives. Like the children in their courtrooms who face limited resources for therapy, work, or training, juvenile judges perform in reduced and often demoralizing circumstances. These include judgeships left vacant or filled temporarily, too few certified clerks, case backlogs, and a chronic shortage of state-licensed residential facilities and available service providers and the personnel to staff them.

BECOMING A JUVENILE JUDGE

How do French magistrates become juvenile judges and what specifically attracts them to the juvenile court? Why do some judges make it a lifelong career? I answer these questions in the next three sections. When I interviewed Judge Boyer in early February 2001 and asked her to describe her career, she replied by invoking "a relatively standard trajectory" involving several advanced university degrees in law, admittance as an external candidate to the Ecole Nationale de la Magistrature (ENM), and the fulfillment of her childhood ambition to be a juvenile judge: "I must have been ten or twelve and imagined being the savior of humanity, that was the idea, and once I realized that dream, you know it is true, this feeling is very strong, it is very exciting." Judge Boyer was part of the graduating ENM class of 1988 and spent her first seven years at two juvenile courts, one in the north and the other in suburban Paris. In an effort "to deepen and reflect theoretically on my experience as a practitioner," she taught juvenile law for four years at the ENM before returning to the courtroom when she accepted an appointment in Paris in 2000. Despite her mention of a "standard trajectory," my interviews with current and retired judges in Paris and elsewhere suggest that this motivation and career path are more exceptional than routine despite its presentation as a career ideal (see the next section).

Promotion through the ranks of the magistrature requires regular performance evaluations by superiors and movement among courts on an average of every three years. Because of limited openings in juvenile courts, those who are committed to juvenile justice but motivated to advance their careers must sometimes move out of the function, becoming JIs, family court judges, sentencing judges (*juges de l'application des peines*), or, less frequently, prosecutors. In the spring, judges anxiously await the announcement of Chancellery decisions regarding transfers and promotions. In April 2001, some Paris magistrates had their requests for promotion denied and were visibly disturbed. Only one judge was promoted from junior to senior juvenile judge, but his happiness was tempered by an obligatory move to the suburban juvenile court in Bobigny. This was a court headed by a president, Jean-Pierre Rosenczveig, whose "revolutionary" reforms were premised on what many viewed as less impunity and more accountability for young offenders (see the "Public Debates" section of this chapter).

"I NEVER WANTED TO BE A JUVENILE JUDGE"

In her book Elisabeth Catta explains that she had never had any affinity for working with troubled youth, describing her arrival at the juvenile court as purely accidental. A memoir published a year later by Philippe Chaillou, a magistrate who now serves on the Paris appellate court but who spent fifteen years as a juvenile judge and authored many books on his experiences, is another case in point. He began his career as a deputy prosecutor before moving into fiscal crime where, despite achieving "respectable professional success" by the age of twenty-eight, he said he was "dying of boredom" and longed to deal with "social questions." So he "decided to be a juvenile judge."[4] When I met Judge Martine de Maximy in 2001, she described her return to the Paris juvenile court in 2000 as her "first love" after a three-year appointment as an investigating magistrate in Bobigny. Later I discovered that her dream had been to become a doctor but her family was opposed to the idea: "I didn't dare defy their refusal. I studied law and only later did ENM."

Of the four male judges I was able to interview in 2001, only two had intended to be juvenile judges: the president of the Association of Juvenile and Family Court Judges, Thierry Baranger, and the president of the Paris juvenile court, Hervé Hamon.[5] Hamon began and remained in juvenile justice, gaining the crown jewel in 1999, the presidency of the Paris court. Baranger gave up his initial plan to be a journalist after a fascinating rotation with a former juvenile court president. One of his two male colleagues, Judge Marchais, a native of the

Island of Reunion, spent four years studying law in Madagascar and Paris and a year in a doctoral program in psychiatry before ENM. He requested an appointment at a lower court but explained what happened this way: "In the 1970s when I finished, it wasn't the ranking [on the exit exam], it was [the perceived] merit that was the main factor [implying that he was the subject of discrimination, since he received a high ranking but still did not obtain a desirable posting]. I chose to take the only position that no one else wanted. I did not want a fight, so I took the position of juvenile judge and it pleased me . . . you see I began with my first position in French Guyana. I spent a year there, then two years in rural France and five years in Versailles, before coming to Paris. I have personally lived the problem of exile, of immigration, of the Mayflower." The other male magistrat, Judge Franconi, like several of his female colleagues, was an "internal" candidate to the ENM, a less prestigious avenue to admittance. He qualified to enter the judiciary by virtue of his experience in other public sector positions. In contrast to those women colleagues who had experience in teaching or social work, he worked in the Finance Ministry and for the Customs Service. He spent six years at a small court in Beauvais before being appointed to Paris. It was common knowledge among court personnel that he wanted to be a prosecutor.

Four other female judges—one who was a prosecutor before becoming a juvenile judge, and five other judges appointed to Paris between 2001 and 2003—described taking up juvenile law accidentally or reluctantly. Judge Dinard, who was from an upper middle-class family "that included a long line of magistrates," stated that she had no desire to become a juvenile judge: "In my mind the image of the profession required being a middle-aged man so that what we said was respected and respectable. The position I wanted was taken by someone else and so I became a juvenile judge. To my surprise I really liked it." Three judges at the Paris court—Judge Boyer, her successor Judge Bondy, and Judge Chaland—went to the ENM knowing they wanted to be juvenile judges. Judge Boyer hesitated discussing her plans at the school (because it was frowned upon), while Judge Bondy hesitated acting on her plans. Judge Bondy remembered being strongly discouraged by one of her mentors, who told her, "You won't have the maturity or authority." Thierry Baranger described his arrival at a tiny juvenile court near Metz in eastern France and the obligatory ritual visit to the president of the appellate court there, who sneered, "You are a juvenile judge? Don't you mean a social worker?" Baranger instructed his own judicial intern in 2001 never to mention her ambition to be a juvenile judge when she took the entrance exam to the ENM because "if she does she'll take it on the chin from the examiners." After her first year at the juvenile court, Elisabeth Catta's superior recognized her talent in law by advising her to leave juvenile justice, saying, "I hope you won't stay in this function too long. You have better things to do than child care."[6] Judge Franconi is reported to have conflated juvenile judges' marginality with their disadvantaged clientele when he exclaimed, "So what are we? We are judges of shit!"[7]

In 2000 I interviewed Alain Bruel, who had just retired as president of the Paris juvenile court.[8] Bruel spent his entire career within the juvenile justice system, published extensively, and as former president of the Paris court, was frequently solicited by the media as a recognized public authority on minors. He nonetheless felt compelled to defend his career choice: "Some say that it is stupid to do this and not to aspire to a higher position, not to finish one's career at the top of the judicial hierarchy at the Cassation Court."[9] He termed it a "specialization of generalists" that took years to master because it required knowledge of the specialized statutes that comprise juvenile law, extensive experience on the bench, and a dose of "pragmatic humanism," as well as familiarity with sociology, psychology, and psychiatry. Despite these exacting requirements, he added, "We are a profession of beginners." Becoming a juvenile judge is something one does at the beginning of one's career. Making a career of it is considered an "unfortunate" choice because it suggests insufficient talent or ambition. Bruel continued: "Most leave as soon as possible to pursue a 'normal path' with the excuse that they cannot get stuck dealing with children for their entire careers. So they stay two or three years before moving on to other functions, notably civil law. This gives them just enough time to limit the damage they do."[10]

A GLORIFIED SOCIAL WORKER

The negative image of juvenile justice as lesser is linked paradoxically to the profile of the first generations of juvenile judges who gained public legitimacy, if not legal respect, because of their strong commitment to child advocacy and social justice. As Judge Boyer put it, "they were militants and pioneers in community justice, who developed very close relations with families and minors." Their willingness to forego professional promotion and to specialize in juvenile justice marginalized them within the legal establishment, where career advancement then demanded and still requires rapid movement among different functions and/or jurisdictions. In the immediate postwar years they could choose to remain within one function. As a result of their willingness to collaborate with social professionals, to eschew the legal norm of impartiality, and to conduct a personalized justice, juvenile judges came to embody a model of practice grounded in the social sphere. They came to be viewed more as "doctors of the soul" and "social workers" and less as accomplished jurists. This legacy still shapes the current view of the profession, according to Bruel, who suggested that juvenile judges gained a reputation as being "too nice, too understanding, [having] insufficient juridical knowledge, and [being] second-rate magistrates."

In contrast to the abstract, transcendental model of law that predominates in the practice of French law, juvenile law became synonymous with an empirical, interpretive model applied by a new corps of judges. In the dominant model, judges apply the law and reinforce legal norms through a close adherence to written codes. In juvenile court, judges not only apply the law but interpret it by drawing on the social sciences, particularly psychology, psychiatry and sociology, their own experiences, and "intuitive wisdom."[11] Defenders of this model insist that the juvenile judge's competence cannot be reduced to knowledge of legislative statutes, respect for procedural rules, or the extent of her judicial powers. Rather, the measure of a juvenile judge is the quality of her personal relationship with the child and ability to adapt the legal norm to each case. Judge Marie-Anne Baulon argues for a humanist justice in which equitable judgments are grounded in an empathetic understanding of individual cases. She insists that we cannot really understand case histories if "we don't feel them."[12] Judge Suchard, who was appointed to the Paris court in 2003, echoed this view, "I am very much a jurist. Obviously, the law exists and I apply it but always with the concern to understand why and in what circumstances the minor did what he did."

The social vision of justice cannot be separated from the ways some juvenile judges framed their profession experientially. Judges who chose to spend their professional careers at the juvenile court described a set of evolving practices and shifting motivations through time. Judges who are admitted as external candidates to the ENM and finish thirty months later get their first position at the young age of twenty-five. They spend long careers on the bench. In these testimonies judges spoke to their professional maturation, a process mirroring that of the children under their supervision, which is fraught with obstacles and uncertainty, and must be weighed against the potential for failure. This does not mean the loss of employment as a judicial appointment is a guarantee of lifetime employment. Rather, failure is measured in social terms, by the incalculable cost of a ruined child, a discredited parent, or a shattered family. Many juvenile judges felt ill prepared to assume their duties after completing only one short six- to twelve-week rotation in the juvenile court during their final year at the ENM. The first years of practice were a crucial period in which the vast majority left the juvenile court. Those who were "smitten" stayed. They described their first position as an initiation by blood and fire, sometimes with humor, other times with incredulity when remembering the enormous challenges and the inevitable mistakes. This was a time when judges took hold, earned their stripes, and learned the profession. This was when internalized professional norms and institutional silences on class, race, and gender did battle with evolving subjectivities, moral imperatives, and social responsibility.

The French magistracy recruits its 7,000 judges largely from the mainstream middle and upper-middle classes, so many juvenile judges first confronted both social marginality and cultural Others as they began work in the juvenile court system. In the northern city of Douai, where Judge Boyer began her duties, there were families who requested court summons dated before the fifteenth of the month because they received social welfare checks on the first. When she left the north and was assigned to one of the "difficult" multiethnic suburban courts of Paris, she described it as "completely different, less social welfare cases but families who have another defensive posture." When I asked her to elaborate, she said, "You know what I mean, it was something else completely in terms of the clientele [disadvantaged families of immigrant and foreign ancestry]." Judge Bondy was appointed to a jurisdiction that included the entire western half of the rural department of the Charente-Maritime in 1979. She described how difficult it was to deal with a "backward, insular social milieu where there were many cases of incest, intermarrying family clans, areas where they were quick to get out the hunting rifle, oyster cultivators who insisted that their children work instead of attending school." Judge Rabinovitch explained that it was a relief to accept an appointment at a "difficult" suburban court outside Paris after her experience with the "absolutely desperate poverty" she witnessed in the northwest between 1975 and 1979, "where children were eating out of garbage cans" and little social assistance was available.

Most of the judges at the Paris court between 2000 and 2005 were at the midpoint or height of their careers, and a number had between fifteen and twenty-five years of experience in juvenile justice. Judge Boyer explained: "The motivations, those mature and change [like we do]. The reasons I wanted to be a juvenile judge at fourteen are not at all the reasons I became a judge at twenty-four; they are not the reasons I remain a judge. It is not static." A common theme was that they "had grown up with their function" learning the measure of a good judge and the pitfalls to avoid, in the courtroom, by trial and error, as in life. If, at the beginning of a career, they had no parental experience and little experience with suffering, loss, or even life, they all had, in the words of Judge Baranger, "a personal history and accounts to render." Looking back, some recognized that they initially identified more with the children than with the parents. Judge Bondy explained that at first she favored minors' perspective over that of parents, systematically speaking with minors first and earning the moniker "leftist judge." As those judges grew older and became parents themselves, they tended to view problems more from the parents' perspective. Judge Marchais explained that "from the moment I had children, it was the son of his parents, now a parent, who came to court and spoke."

Yet most judges insisted that taking one side over the other was "extremely dangerous" because one needed to maintain an impartial perspective to be just. On the one hand, they practice a social profession where one of the basic requirements is, in the words of Judge Binet, "to create (or recreate) relationships and to make connections." It demands a core optimism in the resilience of the human spirit. With twenty-five years of experience in the profession, Judge Rabinovitch shared the "poem" inspiring her courtroom praxis: "I believe in man, this pile of garbage." Judge Binet described it as a profession based on "speech, exchange, and permanent negotiation." It offers the possibility for initiative and creative solutions. Because it requires enormous energy and skill to persuade angry teenagers and distrustful parents, it also demands "a certain passion." This, on the other hand, is a quality that inspires fear because it threatens the proper detachment deemed essential for all judges. Speaking to me and his judicial intern who was present for the interview, Judge Baranger warned, "You cannot do this job if you need to be flattered. It is the beginning of the end if you need to be loved as a judge."

The juvenile court is often a site where children, siblings, parents, and grandparents purge ugly disputes and powerful emotions. It is a stage on which multiple human dramas unfold and verbal violence is routine. Many judges explained that little in their legal training or social background—a reference to the class differences separating them from their "clientele"—prepared them for the explosive demonstrations of emotion—blaming, self-pity, hurt—that attend to emergency custody proceedings or hearings after arrest. Faced with a husband who called his wife a "bitch" or a "tramp" in front of their children, a wife who accused her husband of sexually molesting their five-year-old daughter, parents who rejected their child, or a runaway who shut down, the judge must keep her subjective opinions in check. She must hear all parties knowing it would be worse if the explanations did not surface in court. But the enduring challenge, according to Judge Chaland, has been to encourage "certain" (that is, Maghrebi and African) groups to discuss "culturally sensitive" topics such as sexuality in an "open and objective" fashion.

Most judges agreed that they should never fall into the trap of supposing they could repair broken families by taking on the role of failed parents. In a telling remark that speaks to the social distance and power differentials at court, one judge asserted, "although it would be simpler and more satisfying to disqualify" many of the families in court, the judge must act to avoid "replacing cultural violence with legal violence."[13] Whatever the circumstances, judges hesitated to sever parental authority and cut the bonds between parents and children. French law posits them as primordial and permanent, favoring blood ties over social ones and posing adoption and fosterage as difficult, if sometimes necessary, enterprises.

Judges applied the law but explained the meaning of their rulings. They saw their punitive and rehabilitative measures as part of the unique pedagogical role afforded them within the special statutes that govern juvenile law. It demanded a proper balance, an ability to adapt, and the patience to adopt a long-term view. According to Judge Baranger, "This is the richness of the profession, the only magistrate whose work continues beyond the hearing. At the beginning of our careers, we don't realize. It is only with time that we see it. We have to accomplish our own personal work, one transfer for another." This social vision and personalized trajectory is distinctly at odds with the prevailing juridical model. Catta describes the tension between the competing models this way: "[When I entered the magistracy] I wanted justice to be absolute, a search for total and transcendent truth, erasing all approximation and human confusion . . . by becoming a juvenile judge I met a prosaic, ordinary justice: that of the everyday family event with a lasting impact, the justice of the black eye, the end of the month, the failed abortion, the empty bed. Reversible, changing, it raised doubt and confusion in the mind of the judge—a challenging and consuming justice but alive, so alive."[14]

The social vision of juvenile justice was under siege, both from within and outside the profession. As new generations of judges began to redefine themselves as jurists rather than social activists, they became less committed to the purely social goals of sentences. Rather, their view of child advocacy has been reconceived as contingent on a reform of juvenile law that provides for legal rights and due process protections to children. This view recognizes them as agents with choice and intention but demands enhanced judicial accountability and individual responsibility.

TOO MANY WOMEN

Catta suggests that the image of the judge as social worker is linked not only to the empiricist model associated with the juvenile court but to the female judges who are the majority there.[15] Legislation in 1946 authorized women to enter the bar and the magistracy, but a feminization of the profession did not begin until the 1960s. Since then, their ranks have increased steadily, and they now constitute the majority of ENM graduates and the profession. Although women constitute the majority of the profession, they are concentrated at the l ower levels, whereas in 2004 they made up 64 percent of the bottom-grade judges, 48 percent of the middle grade, and only 20 percent of the highest grade. The numbers were even worse among senior management positions, where women comprised only 9 percent of heads of courts or chief prosecutors.[16]

In 1960, just two years after the founding of the ENM, Madeleine Sabatini became a judge and later was the first woman to serve as president of the Paris juvenile court. The previous year, when she was studying law, only nine of the thirty-eight candidates (23 percent) who passed the entrance exam to the judiciary were women. By 1982, when Sabatini was appointed president of the Paris juvenile court, women represented 28 percent of "ordinary" judges in France.[17] Her trajectory has much to teach us about the career options and status of women. She entered the magistracy too late to train in the newly inaugurated ENM. Under the old system she prepared an advanced law degree, was assigned to a prosecutor's office to gain experience, took the state examination for the magistracy, and began her career in Algeria, then an overseas department of France. She explained:

> At the time the examination was open to women but in reality they were never named to any positions. In Algeria, given the bloodshed and war for independence, they had fewer and fewer male candidates so they sent women there. That is how I was admitted as a judge in a lower court. I stayed there two

years and then was appointed at the same level to a court in Boulogne, advancing to the higher court in Lille before requesting a transfer to the South where I was raised. It wasn't until 1971 that I was finally appointed as a juvenile judge in Marseille, something I had always wanted.[18]

Sabatini eventually moved to Paris, where she stayed from 1976 to 1988. The recognition she earned in this position was her passport to greater distinction and professional capital through her appointment as first president of the Court of Appeals in Reims.

A number of eminent jurists—such as Antoine Garapon, Denis Salas, and Philippe Chaillou, to name only a few—began their careers as juvenile judges but became known as public authorities on the law and the judiciary only after they left the minor court. They thereafter assumed positions at higher courts or as research fellows at public research institutes, such as the Institut des Hautes Etudes sur la Justice. The logic of advancement is premised on the primacy of civil tribunals over penal courts; higher courts over lower ones; Paris over the provinces; and adult jurisdictions over juvenile and family courts, which deal in the "messy" disputes of troubled children and broken families. The small number of juvenile judges relative to the judiciary as a whole is eloquent testimony to the function's low status. In 2003 there were only 262 junior juvenile judges and 125 senior juvenile judges in the country, and in 2004 there were 245 and 155, respectively.[19]

Elisabeth Catta suggests that the niche of childhood and family predisposed the juvenile court to become the naturalized province of female judges, because the 1945 statute creating specialized juvenile judges simultaneously mandated that they be chosen, not exclusively on the basis of merit, but for their subjective interest in children. When she told people she was a juvenile judge, the typical reply was, "what a wonderful position for a woman." If someone is troubled, disadvantaged, unloved, or abandoned, who better to do "the work of emotional repair and to fill a maternal absence" than a woman?[20] When I asked Alain Bruel about the feminization of the profession, he insisted that women had achieved parity in this area but he also related a revealing story. Bruel began his career at a juvenile court in Lille. When he and his wife, also a judge, requested a transfer together from Northern France to Toulouse in the south, Chancellery officials mistakenly assumed *she* was the juvenile judge. It is also significant that Bruel and others saw the overrepresentation of women at the juvenile court and in the magistracy as a problem. Judge Boyer explained it this way: "More women take the entrance examination [of the ENM] despite the fact that the oral component [compared to the written part] has become much more difficult for them than for men. Examiners have more of a tendency to favor men." "Why?" I asked. She replied, "It is the image of the profession that is at stake. We now have a situation where more women study law and prefer the career of a magistrate over that of a lawyer. It offers more flexibility for those with a family."

How are we to understand the acceptance of state officials' seemingly discriminatory behavior presented as gender balance? As Joan Scott has argued, in the post-1945 period there were competing visions for the attainment of political enfranchisement and professional parity for women. On the one side was the presumed equality that followed from the legal possession of universal rights, and on the other was the inequality that followed from the presumed natural facts of sexual difference. Both visions could be applied to the experience of women as juvenile judges. Women belatedly earned the right to become judges only two years after they became full political subjects with the right to vote (in 1944). They henceforth enjoyed equal opportunity to professional appointments in the judiciary through state examinations that supposedly recognized only merit. In a view favored by feminists such as Elisabeth Badinter, who has been influential within the legal establishment, women judges, like their male counterparts, were constituted as abstract individuals before the law. They share human rights recognized by universal principles of liberal democratic law.[21] In practice this was far from the case, not only for women but for candidates from lower status groups. Personal testimonies undercut the claim that republican universalism guarantees equal rights by suppressing sexual difference.[22]

These testimonials support Luce Irigaray's critique of equality based on the abstract individual that is enshrined in French law. The experience of both men and women chronicled here suggests that juvenile judges became assimilated to their presumed sexual difference and natural predisposition as nurturing professionals when more women joined their ranks and the profession embraced social justice and interpretive law as goals. The juvenile court became the repository for judges perceived within the legal establishment as second rate, women as well as men, because of the community justice they practiced and because their anomalous powers put them in a liminal category (see "A Critique of the Juvenile Judge and Her Court"). When an exceptional "minority" candidate such as Judge Marchais appeared—he is a secular Muslim from an overseas French territory who has no upper-middle-class social connections—the juvenile court may have seemed a "natural" placement for him. Similarly, Judge Chaland, an outspoken proponent of social justice, suggested that because of her politics she was "not well viewed by senior Chancellery officials." By the 1980s, when a majority of judges were women, the stigma was well established. In this context, mentors and Chancellery officials discouraged (and still discourage) future judges, both men and women, from choosing juvenile justice as a career. In fact, the refusal to move judges out of the juvenile court—recall the frustrated Judge Franconi—may have been intended to send them a direct message about their professional performance, social capital, or both within the Chancellery. Conversely, when juvenile judges manifested exceptional talent in their function, they were rewarded with prestigious appointments to higher courts or research positions. When Judge Boyer acknowledged the Chancellery's concern about the feminization of the magistracy and revealed the gender bias exercised against women by state examiners in the name of the balanced representation of the sexes, she inadvertently voiced one of the inherent contradictions of republican individualism. Abstract notions of equality "repress a difference based on gender that can never be overcome and perpetuate the oppression of women by making masculinity the norm."[23]

WORKING AS A JUDGE

The juvenile court is the province of troubled children and vulnerable families who are poor, working-class, and socially and economically disadvantaged. Although these families have no monopoly on misfortune or offending, middle- and upper-class children and families rarely appeared in court because they could mobilize resources in order to resolve or camouflage family disputes, deflect accusations of criminality, seek private treatment for illnesses, and protect their children from legal sanctions. Disadvantaged children and families were more vulnerable to both intrusive supervision and punitive correction.[24] The cases that came before the court exemplified the complications of economic marginality. They also provided in a particularly concentrated form a glimpse into what problems and conflicts the society at large deems serious enough to warrant judicial review. The overrepresentation of a clientele linked in the public eye with "hoodlums, delinquents, recidivists, and marginal families sprawled in a disturbing closeness on benches outside chambers" stands in contrast to the "serenity and nobility of the proceedings in civil chambers."[25]

The poor image of the court's clientele and the stigma associated with juvenile justice are mirrored in the location and resources allocated to the juvenile court within French Palaces of Justice. The justice of minors is first and foremost a lesser justice in its means. In his 1989 memoir, Chaillou identified the "shabby quarters, lack of court personnel, absence of any consideration in judicial milieus for the function of the juvenile judge, [and] no or few defense attorneys, who have absolutely no interest in a sector that pays so little."[26] Little has changed with the exception of the presence of defense attorneys. The juvenile justice system is notable for its failure to deliver promptly the services many of the underprivileged children and families under its supervision desperately needed. This is due in part to heavy caseloads and persistent staff shortages at the court—judges, éducateurs, and clerks. In a number of large French cities, the number of judges has not changed since 1912, when the first juvenile courts were created. In Paris the courtrooms with the heaviest caseloads, those serving the twentieth and nineteenth arrondissements, respectively, remained without judges for extended periods (between July 2002 and March 2003). All but one of the fourteen Paris courtrooms experienced delays in scheduling hearings that exceeded six months. In the Twentieth East courtroom the average delay was 8.5 months.[27] Moreover, a lack of specialized facilities in adolescent psychiatry and a scarcity of state-licensed emergency and long-term social service providers sharply increased the implementation—in some cases up to six months—of therapy and rehabilitation measures ordered by judges. This was also the case in suburban courts outside Paris, notably at Bobigny.[28] One member of the Paris Appellate Court admitted to me in 2005 that she had been a juvenile judge but quit because she "was sick of prostituting herself" to garner scarce resources.

Within the otherwise imposing locale of the Palace of Justice, the juvenile court is notable for its peripheral location compared to other tribunals. The gilded gate and grand staircase that tourists admire at the main entrance to the Paris Palace of Justice on the Ile de la Cité do not lead to the juvenile court. Rather, after passing through the metal detectors one continues beyond the Sainte-Chapelle and enters under a sign marked Staircase Y. Inside the *Tribunal pour enfants*, there are drab walls, metal benches screwed to the wall, three cubicles for attorneys to consult case files, and a tiny desk for a policeman on duty. The judges' chambers are merely cramped offices in which the judge and her clerk work in close proximity. Outside are the bare wooden benches where children and families wait for their hearings. The *dépôt* or jail within the Palace of Justice, which houses suspects after arrest who await hearings, has been described as the worst of prisons because of the bare, windowless enclosure reserved for minors.

The mandate of the juvenile judge is to deal with the exceptional circumstances involving children who are endangered or in trouble.[29] Juvenile judges schedule civil and penal hearings in advance, frequently months ahead, but their best-laid plans are often undermined by the press of events. Such events may include a minor under pretrial supervision who has violated his or her probation by offending again; a warning from the prosecutor's office of child abuse that demands immediate attention; or a fourteen-year-old who has run away a fifth time, getting arrested for theft with a "weapon," listed as his German shepherd dog. Although the judge scheduled to be on duty (de permanence) handles the mandatory hearings of minors following arrest, in cases where minors put themselves at risk by running away and stealing or are endangered by adults through neglect and abuse, the prosecutor's office contacts the supervising judge. A typical day then involves not only regularly scheduled hearings and meetings but unexpected calls; impromptu visits from caseworkers, psychologists, lawyers, or colleagues; stacks of mail waiting to be read, and a never-ending avalanche of case files requiring attention. It is an atmosphere of ordered chaos.

The enormous stakes involved in judging can give pause to both novice and experienced magistrates. Deciding to revoke parental custody and to place a child with the state or to send a fourteen-year-old to prison are acts that have permanent consequences. In a number of particularly difficult cases, the judges I knew hesitated before deciding and, even after judgment, remained unsure. I well remember a case involving a drug addict who had two children by different fathers and was pregnant with a third. She was high when she arrived for her hearing. The judge hesitated between awarding custody to the mother's sister or placing the children with a foster family. After interviewing the children's aunt, the judge decided to award custody to the mother's family, in spite of reservations voiced by social workers. Afterward she turned to me, as a middle-aged woman and parent with life experience, asking if she had done the right thing. This happened a number of times with other judges. As I got to know judges and socialized with them, I was struck by their reluctance to make everyday decisions—such as where to have dinner or what film to see—given the weighty professional obligations they bore every day.

Although judges enjoy undeniable status and professional privileges—such as lifetime employment in the public sector, the freedom to set their work schedules, a monthly salary calculated on the basis of 140 work hours, and ten weeks of annual paid vacation—the work is stressful, time-intensive, and emotionally draining. Despite the necessity to keep emotions at bay, some described their anger and outrage at certain parents and institutions as well as their relief and joy at seeing "life and progress win out over unhappiness and misery."[30] Only a few judges dealt at any length with the psychological stress, physical fatigue, and emotional labor that I observed, and few mentioned these when I specifically asked about professional problems. Yet the oblique references to difficult labor conditions were eloquent testimony to the demands of their work. These included complicated psychosocial problems evident in children and families; hearing delays; staff shortages and the burdens posed by sharing a court clerk if someone became disabled or seriously ill or went on maternity leave; complaints about scarce office supplies and old machines; the pull and tug between the large caseloads at court and the need to meet with service providers, municipal officials, and the precinct police outside court; the constant struggle to find emergency and long-term service providers, to locate housing, schedule psychiatric consultations, and conduct social investigations; and the very nature of the cases themselves—specifically, the increasing proportion of penal to civil cases.

As an observer at court, I found the substance, length, and intensity of hearings to be an emotional ordeal and was impressed with the professionalism and stamina of the judges whose proceedings I observed. After hearings that stretched from six to eight hours, I sometimes could not summon the resolve to revise my notes the same evening; instead, I sought refuge at the cinema or with friends for late-night dinners. A typical day of regularly scheduled social assistance hearings might include a case of child abuse at 10:00 A.M., truancy at 11:00 A.M., disruptive school behavior with a threat of expulsion at 2:00 P.M., intrafamilial incest at 3:00 P.M., and the attempted forced marriage of an underage minor at 4:00 P.M.

Recall that on my first full day in court, I observed Judge de Maximy, who was on duty and had five penal cases, each more complicated than the next. At one point she received a call involving a child endangerment case from her own jurisdiction that was so horrific as to strain credibility. It concerned the neglect and abuse of a fifteen-year-old girl who became a mother at twelve and had just delivered a second child. Although allegedly supervised by a caseworker, the case had acquired renewed urgency when the teenager revealed for the first time that the father of both children was her mother's partner, a man who lived in the same Paris welfare hotel. He had pursued the mother and daughter simultaneously and they each bore him daughters spaced three months apart. Josiane's daughter by her stepfather was three months younger than her half sister by him. When Josiane's mother discovered the second pregnancy, she beat Josiane and locked her out of the rooms they shared. The judge had the daunting task of finding a placement for the young mother and the two children and in subsequent hearings of convincing Josiane that she could not "make a family" with her stepfather. Judge de Maximy's colleague, Judge Courtier, who was appointed to the Twentieth South district courtroom in 2001, a notoriously difficult court with multiethnic, disadvantaged populations, admitted that she had similarly heavy cases that haunted her. By 2003 she had already decided to leave the juvenile court, confessing, "I cannot continue to do this. I take it home with me every night."

A CRITIQUE OF THE JUVENILE JUDGE AND HER COURT

The original 1945 ordinance gave juvenile judges unusual and anomalous powers in the adjudication of cases. These powers have been the subject of recurrent debate and periodic reform but little oversight. Judges combine functions that are normally separate in the French system: They examine charges and undertake investigations as well as conduct trials and render judgments. This has been controversial, given the inquisitorial legacy that mandated that the process of a judge investigating a case must remain secret. Judges preside alone over hearings in chambers that are closed to the public. Jurists have worried about the arbitrary exercise of power, the rightness of judgments, and the independence of judges who ruled alone. They have also worried about abuse of power because court personnel were not required to reveal the content of court files to families under supervision.[31] In 2002 families finally received the right to have access to their court files. Juvenile judges may initiate proceedings on their own authority and modify or reverse their own decisions, and their rulings remain in effect even during an appeal process. Except for the precise point in dispute, the same judge follows the case during the appeal process and may continue to make new decisions affecting the child. In a majority of appeal cases, the appellate court confirms the initial decision except when it is compromised by legal errors or obviously badly adapted to the individual case.

The 1945 law made little accommodation for an adversarial debate beyond notification of the charges in penal cases, particularly within chambers. It deemed that the juvenile judge was the best authority to advise the minor and, if his or her best interest demanded it, to recommend that the minor get an attorney. Despite the potential for the abuse of power and of arbitrary judgments, the obligation to provide minor defendants with legal representation became law in France only in 1989 under international pressure following ratification of the CRC, and then it applied exclusively to penal cases. Although social assistance (civil) hearings can result in the loss of parental custody or the temporary placement of children, the presence of a defense attorney in such proceedings is still the exception. Despite deep distrust of familiarity between judges and plaintiffs in adult jurisdictions because of compromised impartiality, legislators preserved the special mandate of the juvenile judge enshrined in the 1945 ordinance, believing that the efficacy of the judge results from just such familiarity and personalized relations.

In the 1990s as the punitive trend gained momentum, these powers formed the basis of a critique of the juvenile court from within the legal establishment and by court personnel, both practicing and former judges, psychologists, and éducateurs. This juridical critique built on long-standing sociological challenges on the left to coercive paternalism disguised as therapeutic intervention. It coalesced with criticism on the right from politicians, police, social scientists, and magistrates that demanded more individual accountability and less impunity for juvenile offenders. It coincided with the arrival of a new generation of judges in the late 1980s and early 1990s who defined themselves as magistrats first and juvenile judges second. They refused the label "social worker." They were, in the words of Thierry Baranger, "afraid of losing their identity by being too committed to one specialty and suspicious of certain forms of professional activism." This was a cohort of young professionals "who saw themselves as jurists as much as juvenile judges."

In a harbinger of the critique to come, Philippe Chaillou argued in his 1989 memoir for renewed judicial authority through a necessary "return to the law." Citing Foucault, he warned judges not to rely too heavily on the normative power of social professionals such as psychiatrists, social workers, and criminologists. This presupposed a narrow causal relationship between social context and troubled children. He was circumspect about the therapeutic paternalism long associated with the juvenile court and wary of the potential for abuse of power. In his view, the only way to avoid the moralizing admonishments often heard in juvenile court was for the judge to say: "You did this. It is forbidden. Here is the act that I as the judge posit as a response to your action."[32]

The most comprehensive reflection on the juvenile justice system from both theorists and practitioners came in the form of a 1993 conference, organized by Denis Salas and Antoine Garapon, eminent jurists, former juvenile judges, and senior fellows at the Institut des Hautes Etudes sur la Justice (in conjunction with the Protection Judiciaire de la Jeunesse), to mark the fiftieth anniversary of the 1945 legislation of French juvenile law. Published in 1995 under the title "A Changing Model of Juvenile Justice," the conference report showed that the organizers remained committed to juvenile jurisdictions separate from adult courts. However, they described the crisis of state institutions, the absence of social integration through permanent employment, and the appearance of "new" delinquents whose marginality, violence, and alterity posed challenges to the very foundations of the system. The authors centered on three crucial points: (1) they redefined delinquency as a problem of territorial exclusion and ethnocultural affiliations; (2) they conceptualized the problem as one centering on bad parenting and insufficient values; (3) they critiqued the juvenile court itself, suggesting that its informal justice and individual-centered rehabilitative model were no longer suited to newly emergent forms of collective deviance.

A Delinquency of Exclusion: A Coded Reference to "Immigrant" Offenders

In his essay, Salas argued that the CRC unsettled the reigning paradigm of the "psychologically weak, legally incapable, and socially maladapted" child. The post-1989 child had agency and choice even though the law maintained his or her legal dependency as a minor. This gave the child "room for manoeuver, choice, initiative, autonomy but also, potentially put him at risk," even as a victim. According to Salas, the paradox confronting delinquent youth was the blurring of the distinction between victims and perpetrators and the new standards of accountability to which the minor was held despite his or her vulnerability. On the one hand, Salas argued against the punitive trend and the risk posed for the rehabilitative state by more repression. He castigated the tendency to pathologize and distance young people. He and others worried about increased prosecutorial power and less receptivity to rehabilitation that was presented as enhanced respect for individual rights. Salas distrusted legal reforms that streamline proceedings and bypass juvenile judges in the interest of expediency and accountability such as mediation and reparation before prosecution as well as treatment in real time. On the other hand, Salas identified the "new challenge" for French juvenile law as a "delinquency of exclusion." This, he argued, is "a social phenomenon which has nothing in common" with earlier forms of deviance. Then, delinquents were immature youth experimenting with risky behaviors. Rehabilitation was necessary because those "delinquents" had families, grew up, straightened out, got jobs, and became part of mainstream French society. Then, it was justifiable to reduce sentences, erase police records, and prioritize prevention.

How, he asked, can we intervene with youth who now settle into a chronic marginality where they are "neither in danger nor delinquent?" He suggested that these youth were perpetually liminal and their delinquency was normalized to the point of becoming a lifestyle in which "every deviant act is stripped of culpability."[33] Who were these new delinquents? "Youth from an urban proletariat, born of school failure, lost in school tracks without potential, enmeshed with their families in a net of social assistance." Salas recategorized the perpetrators as child adults and concluded that the individual model of treatment based on "the error of youth" was no longer viable. Why? Drawing on sociologists of urban violence, he described "the young of the second generation of unemployment, have no plan to integrate to anything but their [own] values, codes, territories and not to a world of common references with adults and [French] youth."[34] While he ended his article by emphasizing the imperative to "reintegrate within a common space youth who are captives of rampant ghettoization and so many daily exclusions," his labeling work was complete. He demarcated the immature [French] youth of earlier periods whose illicit behavior could be seen as "normal" rite-of-passage risk-taking during adolescence. They stood in contrast to the current marginals whose violence is adultlike and linked to the cultural pathologies of their families and territories. The new delinquent could "no longer be the object of purely social [or rehabilitative] interventions since his actions do not result from individual emotional development but from collective processes."[35]

No Shared Values and Absentee Parents

In the introduction to the conference proceedings, Antoine Garapon and Denis Salas depicted French society as rooted in a "crisis of state legitimacy" in which core institutions such as the family, particularly parents, have failed. They described "the cutting of the social bond" as evidenced by "rising individualism in life styles" that paradoxically meant the "loss of shared values" on the one hand, and, on the other, the difficulty for "populations subjected to foreign customs to adapt [to French society]."[36] "Money" and "economic success" had become the universal references. They drew on the work of child psychologist Philippe Jeammet, whose testimony figured prominently in the 2002 Carle and Schosteck Commission Report on juvenile delinquency. The emergence of a normal childhood personality takes time (like the slow time of the juvenile court) and requires good parenting, proper structures, and shared [cultural] references. They wondered how to raise well-adjusted children if common values no longer existed.[37] This was a veiled reference to the Arab and African families overrepresented at court. As we shall see, some jurists expressed the view that prevention and rehabilitation—humanistic justice administered in chambers by one all-powerful juvenile judge—were no longer suited to a "new" delinquency of exclusion.

In that same year, 1995, Philippe Chaillou published a book in which he links delinquency directly to parents—the "weak father and the mother's suffocating love"—who lack the authority to impose limits on children and give them proper grounding. In the book, Chaillou insists that youth violence reveals a disorder that results from an absence of values and solid bearings. The etymology of the word *delinquent* means to dislodge things from their normal place. Thus, according to Chaillou, a delinquent's parents never taught the child his or her rightful place.[38]

Both Chaillou's book and the 1995 conference proceedings reflected a consensus among jurists and practitioners about the cultural deficiencies of the new delinquents. The tropes of absent bearings, no sense of limits, and lacking values figure prominently in court case files. Minors of immigrant and foreign ancestry were identified and tracked as problems by teachers and counselors in public schools and referred to the courts as social assistance cases. It was an implicit indictment of the children's parents, home life, and cultural origin.

Individual Rights, Judicial Subjectivity, and Sovereign Judges

The 1995 conference proceedings included an examination of the individual rights of minors in the juvenile court. Magistrats wrote about the limited protection of these rights for minor defendants, and Salas remarked critically on characteristics of the French system that were at odds with demands for international children's rights, namely "the lack of the presumption of innocence, the power of the prosecutor, the primacy accorded to the confession of culpability, and the total absence of the defense."[39] These critiques focused on the extraordinary powers of judges. Was the specialization of a judge who treated the case from beginning to end compatible with procedural guarantees, notably the principle of impartiality?[40] Contributors cited respected jurist Marie-Laure Rassat, who deemed the judge's investigatory powers to be "dangerous and totalitarian . . . incoherent and arbitrary." They quoted lawyer Daniel Soulez-Larivière, who compared the institution of the juvenile judge to "a true sovereign who rules over families with a total imperium."[41] Whereas many contributors recognized the need for a judge "who was capable of penetrating the changing personality of the minor" and for a jurisdiction that could attract and keep experienced judges, they noted that "out of 280 juvenile judges [in France in 1992], 89 have less than one year in their current posting, 59 have worked less than one year as juvenile judges, and on average juvenile judges stay less than three years in the same position."[42]

Garapon, Bruel, and others demanded more judicial rigor, particularly in the hearings heard in chambers. Bruel suggests that the distrust of the juvenile judge originated from the misperception that his judgments were based on subjective opinion. Bruel argues for a "total reform of existing practices." This meant caseworker reports that were factual and narrative rather than diagnostic and interpretive; judgments that did not predetermine outcomes; and proceedings that were based on the law rather than psychology. He urges "intentional judicial forgetting" to prevent the misuse of certain elements in the file and to enable youth to be agents of change through a re-appropriation of their own history. Finally, he argues that the contents of the file should allow open critique and an adversarial debate among all the parties.[43]

Antoine Garapon was in the vanguard of judges who initiated a critique of the informal justice in chambers, particularly in social assistance hearings.[44] Judges did not wear judicial robes in chambers, they sat behind their desks to receive families, and they developed personal relationships with the children. Divested of the judicial ritual and procedural formalities in the juvenile correctional courtroom, hearings in chambers were intended to be less intimidating and more conducive to communication between judges and families. In contrast, Garapon and others viewed the apparent informality, open dialogue, and legal requirement that juvenile judges seek the approval of the families before rendering decisions in chambers as an illusion that merely masked the unequal power relations between judges and lower-class families. It gave the dangerous impression that all of the parties were equal and that the decision was not coerced. These writers pointed out that families frequently faced judges without legal representation, were unaware of their rights, particularly with regard to the possibility for appeal of judgments, and, until 2002, had no access to their case files.[45]

In his concluding chapter, Garapon advocates a new model premised on a shift from judicial paternalism, indeterminate facts, and subjective judgments in favor of formal, legal, and adversarial approaches. He recommends that the judge as "arbiter and coach" be replaced by the judge as jurist and technician. His chapter is an apology for many extrajudicial measures, such as reparation; mediation; and expedited proceedings, such as treatment in real time, about which his colleagues like Thierry Baranger continued to express reservations in 2001. It is significant that he distances himself from Foucauld's critique of the modern juvenile court as a new means of social control and adopts the neoliberal discourse that migrated across the political spectrum. He admonishes adolescents to take responsibility and be accountable for their actions:

> It took us time to get ourselves out of the Foucauldian ideology of social control and to appraise the suffering hidden behind the marginality. We believed for too long that deviance was only [adolescent] rebellion and cultural difference a misunderstanding likely to disappear without approaching the delicate question of political identity. We are paying for decades of state welfare in which the law was limited to a blank check ("the rights to") that had the effect of depriving individuals of their personal responsibility.[46]

Garapon raises doubt about the prevailing juvenile justice model grounded in a generous welfare state, treatment, the confession, consciousness of illegality and the internalization of legal norms. He espouses an actuarial model predicated on efficacy, management by objective, and more latitude and legitimacy for prosecutors whose new role in favor of victims made them the public face of justice. He argues for sentences that would be more "systematic, global, varied, positive, and socialized." "In the final analysis isn't it a good thing to limit a kind of power [of the juvenile judge] that risked in the long term becoming intoxicating?"[47]

PUBLIC DEBATES: RESPONSIBILITY,
ACCOUNTABILITY, AND A REPUBLICAN ETHIC

As we have seen, 1999 was a pivotal year in the changed political debates over delinquency among magistrates and members of the Socialist government in power. The year began with the ceremonial exchange of New Year greetings between the French president and members of the government. President Jacques Chirac used that symbolic forum to register his concern over the worsening climate of insécurité and to renew his call for the Socialist government headed by Prime Minister Lionel Jospin "to mobilize against a plague that threatens national cohesion."[48] Jospin had preempted the president's position on delinquency in his own New Year interview with the press when he urged both a "return to a republican ethic" (a reference to secular, national values) and more repressive measures for "recidivist juvenile delinquents." Although he acknowledged poverty, unemployment, and the "social handicaps" of different linguistic and normative codes exemplified by young offenders, Jospin was unequivocal: "As long as we accept sociological explanations and don't question individual responsibility, we will not solve these problems."[49]

As we saw in Chapter 3, Jospin's own Interior minister, Jean-Pierre Chevènement, appeared on national television to declare "the fight against insécurité" to be his number one priority. He denounced "the soft line on delinquents" taken by Minister of Justice Elisabeth Guigou as "wrong-headed," even "anachronistic," when confronting what he termed "those little savages." Claiming that juvenile delinquency rates had doubled since 1992, Chevènement advocated the major overhaul of the 1945 ordinance he had outlined in a confidential memo written to the prime minister in May 1998. The memo provoked a heated debate within the Jospin government between defenders of the 1945 ordinance in the ministries of Justice, Labor, Health, and Environment and proponents of reform within the Interior and Education ministries. Justice Minister Guigou opposed Chevènement's radical suggestions but echoed the discourse on the individual responsibility of teenage offenders and reaffirmed the recent reforms of juvenile law outlining new offenses and creating harsher penalties and accelerated proceedings:

> The Left certainly recognizes the social causes of delinquency due to unemployment and marginality. But families and young delinquents with these handicaps have taken to living on welfare assistance. We are not denying this but must

now insist on individual responsibility. We must say to these young people, 'It's your life, your future, your responsibility.'[50]

The struggle between the powerful ministries of Justice and Interior and their respective allies launched a vigorous public debate among juvenile and family court judges. The previous June, in response to Chevènement's memo, Thierry Baranger and then-president of the Paris juvenile court Alain Bruel published an impassioned defense of French juvenile law. They saw existing statutes as the best means to mitigate the discriminatory effects of state institutions such as public schools, where a "pernicious" policy is "to exclude those who cannot or do not want to assimilate." They decried Chevènement's repressive project "as a perversion" whose goal was "to make the application of criminal law the only instrument of social cohesion and zero tolerance the alpha and omega of proper legal procedure, a move that dehumanizes juvenile justice and strips judges of their independence."[51]

It was in this political atmosphere that Philippe Chaillou delivered a ceremonial address to a gathering of magistrates in early 1999. In "The Delinquency of Minors," Chaillou, a member of the Paris Court of Appeal, declared that worsening youth crime, although a reality, should not be exaggerated. He debunked received wisdom on the juvenile court as too indulgent and rejected the notion of prosecuting cases involving incivilities. He reminded his listeners that juvenile justice was "more and more severe and had recourse more often to a standard penal arsenal: prison, probation, and conditional suspended prison sentences." He alluded to one court, without naming it, where 90 percent of the judgments in 1998 were penal. He noted the increasing frequency of firm prison sentences. Rapid penalization had increased by 46 percent the number of minors referred to juvenile judges between 1997 and 1999. He concluded that "the image of the juvenile judge as more social worker than magistrate must be definitively put aside."[52]

Evidence of the emergence of a new penal model was apparent at the Bobigny juvenile court headed by Jean-Pierre Rosenczveig. He was a regular guest on radio and television talk shows, ran an NGO devoted to children's rights, and, by 1999, was widely known for the new penal "revolution" he championed in Bobigny. He was the subject of a *Le Monde* series on prominent public figures in January 1999. Rosenczveig had institutionalized a zero-tolerance approach and immediate response to all offenses, particularly those of first-time offenders, by establishing immediate information sharing among public schools, police, prosecutors, and the courts to curb youth crime.

In the 1990s, Justice Ministry circulars (with the force of law) and new legislation heightened the visibility, legitimacy, and policies of the juvenile prosecutor's office in the treatment of delinquency and the protection of minor victims. Beginning in 1991, some courts introduced the "third way," allowing mediation and reparation measures supervised by prosecutorial representatives and diversionary measures for first-time offenses.[53] At the Bobigny court, Rosenczveig seized on these reforms to reinforce the prosecutor's role, reduce the delay of court summonses for all offenses, emphasize reparation measures for victims, and increase the pace and timing of prosecutions for minors who failed to "participate in rehabilitative projects."[54]

In his 1999 Le Monde interview, Rosenczveig noted that prison produced criminals and should be reserved for serious cases. Nonetheless, his insistence on individual accountability, parental responsibility, new forms of offending, and the need to end criminal impunity played to a political climate receptive both to punishment and quick fixes. His depiction of youth violence distorted the larger reality because it largely described only his suburban district. He emphasized the increasing banality of violence through dramatic and unrepresentative examples. In a pattern repeated in subsequent interviews, he noted the basic shift away from violence against property to violence against people, a shift not supported by national statistics or the reality in Paris.[55] Rosenczveig implicitly linked this shift to a crisis of socialization and delinquents' adherence to a culture outside of French society. He argued that deferred hearings and delayed sentences were a luxury France could no longer afford: "Today we cannot allow ourselves to wait for two to three murders, two–three rapes. It is urgency that is required. There is the imperative of an immediate response to a problem that in the past demanded patience, rehabilitation, and maturity."[56]

The very next day, Thierry Baranger and jurist Thierry Pech published a piece in the leftist daily Libération in which they reflected on Chevènement's use of the term petits sauvageons (little savages). For them the term evoked the anxiety surrounding adolescence and wrongly separated minors into two categories of incommensurate difference. There is the indulgence when confronted with "the pure and vulnerable innocent, the good savage, not yet corrupted by society," and the panic when faced "with the poorly domesticated foreigner-stranger, even the barbarian." This, they argue, gives rise to the ominous specter of new Apaches linked to a culture of poverty "without faith or law, [operating] with criminal networks, secret solidarities, music, and linguistic codes."[57]

Later that year Alain Bauer and Xavier Raufer, two of the new security experts with ties to the private security sector, French police and prosecutor associations, and conservative think tanks, published a book on urban violence in one of the most prestigious French university presses, Presses Universitaires de France, that became a best seller. It was an apocalyptic vision of a nation in deep denial with regard to its deviant youth, a disproportionate percentage of whom were of immigrant ancestry and had no moral or social bearings. In the same year, 1999, Jean-Pierre Rosenczveig also published a book on troubled youth. It too tells a compelling story of a justice system overburdened by dysfunctional families, both economically marginal and emotionally bereft; headstrong, angry, and unstable teenagers; street savvy vagrants; unprofessional social workers; bureaucratic indifference; and outraged victims. He recounts a day in the life of the Bobigny court to document what really happens there. The book explicitly addresses the "mistrust concerning juvenile judges" who are accused of being unable to respond effectively to all kinds of juvenile delinquency.[58] While he mentions the need for prevention and protection, he clearly argues in favor of a new model: "In the past the juvenile judge was the only true judicial actor, now we must include the prosecutor."[59]

One case described at length in his book gives pause, particularly in light of Rosenczveig's incessant public criticism of prison. It involves the case of Mohamed, a fourteen-year-old Malian boy whose eighth offense for driving a stolen car without a license occurred just three days after he was placed on probation (*contrôle judiciaire*). He was one of eleven children raised in a polygamous household. Fed up with his son's delinquency, the father planned to send his son back to his family in Mali—relatives the boy did not know in a country he had never visited. Given the boy's refusal to accept his father's authority and the deputy prosecutor's request to revoke probation and send him to prison, Rosenzcveig weighs the options. He shares his doubts regarding the incarceration order.[60] Was it the most appropriate response? Didn't the negative effects of prison risk being worse than those sought, namely protection for society? He reminds readers that although the 1987 law changed the rules for pretrial detention for thirteen- to sixteen-year-olds,[61] French law still permits prison for those accused of crimes and serious misdemeanors. The problem is the lack of secure residential facilities to provide alternatives to prison.

Although Rosenzcveig admits that very young detainees such as Mohamed typically view pretrial detention as a "judgment and punishment before trial," he insists that "generally the youth I send to prison accept my decision" and even say 'thank you, judge.' " Nonetheless, he confesses that the decision to commit Mohamed is difficult because of well-documented violence at the Youth Detention Center at Fleury-Mérogis, the facility where he would be detained (see Chapter 5). He notes that between 1997 and 1999 there had been a 20 percent increase in the rate of incarceration of minors. What about Mohamed? Rosenzcveig is very torn. He mentions the juridical arguments: Mohamed could not be detained for a simple misdemeanor, but since he had violated his probation it could be revoked. The penalty for violation is incarceration. Rosenzcveig wonders if the measure itself was legal. Had he been trapped by issuing such an order the preceding Saturday night? Too late; he has to be consistent. Mohamed would go to prison despite being only fourteen. Rosenzcveig claims that everyone supported the decision, even the defense attorney and the youth's éducateur.[62]

JUVENILE CRIME AND THE 2002 PRESIDENTIAL ELECTION

Fear of public safety dominated presidential campaign rhetoric and public policy debates in 2002. Presidential candidate Lionel Jospin, the Socialist prime minister; center-right incumbent president Jacques Chirac; and the far-right leader of the National Front, Jean-Marie Le Pen, attempted to outdo one another in their support for more repressive approaches to youth crime. Jospin outraged many on the Left, particularly members of the leftist Union of the Magistracy and the far-left professional association of the majority of public caseworkers (éducateurs: SNPES) when he famously reversed his position on two controversial proposals for juvenile law reform. He called for the reopening of "closed detention structures" that had been shut down by a rightist Justice Minister in 1970 as well as the institution of immediate judgments for recidivist offenders. Chirac likewise called for closed facilities for recidivists. As the rhetoric heated up, there were proposals to lower the penal majority from eighteen to sixteen, to reimpose pretrial detention for minors between thirteen and sixteen for all misdemeanors, to permit the prosecutor (versus the judge) to detain the minor, and to punish the parents of delinquent children. The tenor of the campaign was changed by strategic leaks to the media. First, there was the highly unusual first-trimester publication of police statistics from the Interior Ministry showing sharply higher rates of delinquency (arrest). These reflected poorly on the Socialist government's

ability to contain the problem of youth crime. Secondly, just two months before the election, the conservative newspaper, *Le Figaro*, obtained and published parts of the confidential pre-report evaluating the performance of
Protection Judiciaire de la Jeunesse. Completed by state auditors at the Cour
des Comptes, it was a devastating account of bureaucratic inefficiency, poor
oversight of personnel, and misallocation of resources. It depicted éducateurs
who refused to consider any repression as hopelessly anachronistic and an
agency "lacking specific policy objectives" that, along with the entire juvenile
justice system, gave "the impression of having been abandoned [by the State]
to their own devices."[63]

In the midst of the shrill campaign rhetoric, leftist judges and public caseworkers at the Paris court wrote a forceful statement on delinquency that was
also published in the media. They denounced the security discourse, the sensationalist media coverage, and the frequent conflation of mere incivilities, serious criminality, and life in public projects as both misleading and "socially
explosive." They worried that moral panics were not limited to talk and noted
the institution of curfews for minors under thirteen years of age, plans to prosecute the parents of delinquents in certain cities, and the "latest avatar of the
tense climate: the proposed law on internal security calling for the penalization
of gatherings in common areas of public housing and prison terms for repeatedly defrauding public transportation." They directly addressed the question of
statistics, insisting that those produced by the section Cities and Suburbs of the
Domestic Surveillance Service were unreliable. According to the judges, these
statistics reflected the difficulties associated with policing "sensitive" areas
rather than reality on the ground as well as "the overuse of infractions of insulting and assaults on police, riots, and public order infractions." Judges reminded readers of the forces driving juvenile delinquency, which included
increased economic polarization, new family models, weak bearings and frag-
menting social bonds in the form of single parent families, rampant individualism, a crisis of traditional authority structures, and conflicting social norms.
They denounced an "ethnicization of social ties" that creates "minority identities and a ghettoization of territories."[64] They clearly refuted popular images of
delinquent predators by noting that young people were the main perpetrators
and victims in a hierarchy of want:

> It is a delinquency of theft and burglary. The social pattern underlying this real-
> ity is classic: the poor youth steal from those who have more than they do, those

who aren't quite as poor, and from middle classes, the upper classes being protected by the distance and means [they have] to protect their property . . . paradoxically those who are overlooked by politicians and the state are asylum
seekers, unaccompanied minors, and delinquents who endure labor or sexual
exploitation by criminal networks.[65]

JUVENILE JUDGES AT COURT: REFLECTIONS
ON A PENAL MODEL

The juvenile judges at the Paris court and elsewhere who wrote the position
statement took a strongly anti-penal position on what they viewed as a worrisome trend: the steady penalization of juvenile justice by legislators on the Left
and Right, the growing power of the juvenile prosecutor's office to influence judicial practices, and the growing proportion of penal to civil cases within their
courtrooms. In my semi-directed interviews, informal conversations, social
gatherings with judges, and observations of them in court and in conversation
with one another, I came to see this as only one of two views represented at the
Paris court. These opposing views reflected a larger split within the legal community and among juvenile and family court judges. Despite a wide variety in
judging styles, those in what I call the anti-penal camp saw penalization as the
problem and those in the pro-penal camp viewed it as the solution. Both positions were linked to conceptions of childhood and adolescence and causes of
delinquency, its changing manifestations, and the judgments the judges favored to deal with it. Despite basic disagreements, both groups shared a consensus on popular folk ideologies regarding culture and, particularly, the
weight of tradition among children and families of immigrant and foreign
ancestry who constituted the majority of cases at court. For both groups, culture was a problem. Depending on the judge, cultural difference was either
pathologized and controlled or medicalized and treated. The handling of
cases in which culture was a factor echoed public discourses that ethnicized
delinquency.

Anti-penal Judges

The anti-penal judges included those at mid-career as well as senior judges
with more than twenty years' experience. They viewed childhood and adolescence as strongly influenced by social origin and milieu but not exclusively determined by it. They were guardedly optimistic that with the proper adult
interventions, the offending youth can be brought onto the right path, find his

bearings, accept limits, and make his way toward a productive adulthood. Judge Suchard expressed it this way: "Every minor is in the process of becoming. He is at the crossroads of life, he needs to be trained psychologically, scholastically, mentally. You cannot give up on him. You can accomplish many things. Nothing is set in stone." Rather than blame the minor, these judges viewed delinquency as having many causes, including structural conditions such as poverty, economic polarization, and institutional dysfunction; larger social transformations within French society, such as consumerism, individualism, and conflicting norms that resulted from ethnic [cultural] differences; bad home situations; and individual psychological problems. Judges—just as most of the French do—tend to believe that the essential work of socialization is completed by puberty. They deemed it critical to identify troubled children early, preferably in preschool or elementary school, as they associated the onset of adolescence with identity conflicts and rebellion against authority. Some judges clearly saw chronic delinquency as symptoms of parental deficiency and intergenerational disorders, whether psychiatric or cultural in nature, and demanded interventions, not only for the minor but for the whole family. Yet most of these judges adamantly resisted larger political pressures to punish the parents of severely troubled youth. In contrast to public rhetoric concerning negligent parents, a common refrain was this: "parents have not given up [démissionaires] on their children" but are resigned (démissionés) and deprived (démunis) and need help, not further obstacles to surmount.

In response to questions about what changes had occurred in the practice of juvenile law, these judges described an encroaching punitive model. They blamed this on a number of factors, including the changing professional culture among younger juvenile judges, the political context, and enhanced prosecutorial power. They described new zero-tolerance policies within the prosecutor's office, as well as deputy prosecutors, JIs, and juvenile judges who had become more repressive and, in the words of Judge Boyer, "tended to interpret a certain number of texts in a way that sometimes renders the law more severe for minors than for adults. The general principle is to prioritize rehabilitation. Even when the facts of the case are more serious and the personality of the minor no longer justifies only a lenient approach, we must still apply texts that are partly protective." Mixing rehabilitative and repressive reasoning to produce more severe judgments was to go beyond the law. Those with long years of experience noted the impact this had on judicial practice in the form of heavy caseloads at the monthly sessions of the juvenile court and the increased emphasis on penalty. Judge Bondy, who spent fourteen years at the Paris court between 1984 and 1998, noted that the proportion of civil to penal cases in her courtroom had changed from two-thirds and one-third to one-half and one-half, respectively.

Anti-penal judges, such as Judge Chaland, worried that prosecutors had forgotten the protective aspect of juvenile law. For the juvenile judge an offense means that a delinquent child is also an endangered child. Thierry Baranger feared that "a rehabilitative culture is disappearing in the name of an ethic of accountability and the dictates of immediacy." These judges had examples to offer of the increasing legalization of incidents and were particularly critical of public school principals who systematically referred "any and all problems" to juvenile prosecutors. These problems were defined ambiguously as "school violence." Judge Rabinovitch described a school fight with a ruler that ended up in her courtroom and wondered if delinquency had increased or tolerance had diminished. Judge Boyer related a much more disturbing incident that occurred in 2001. It concerned a twelve-year-old girl who shoved a teacher in the hallway of her middle school. Although it was a first-time offense and no one was hurt, the girl was expelled from school and a penal case was opened at court. In a context dominated by public order concerns and deepening professional outrage at school violence, teachers at the school went on strike to protest the lack of respect for their authority and to call attention to poor working conditions. Judge Boyer was deeply concerned

> because there were clear warning signs of trouble, the girl had been absent from school, and was demonstrating aggressive behavior. Four years ago they [prosecutors] would have opened a social assistance case, a protective measure, but here they opened a penal case. The problem in Paris is that we don't have the means to intervene in problem situations, not because we don't want to but because the necessary services are less numerous.

Anti-penal judges readily acknowledged that punishment was a necessary part of rehabilitation but feared that if they exercised retribution initially or exclusively they would lose the uniqueness of their function. In the context of repeated legislative reforms to the 1945 ordinance, Judge de Maximy proclaimed, "They want us to specialize in punishment and leave social assistance to the local-level departments." Judge Rabinovitch explained: "We must not become correctional [court] type penalists." She referred to judges who preside over trials [in adult court] immediately following arrest and issue sentences without any knowledge of personal background and mitigating circumstances. These judges saw evidence of coercive penality in new powers assigned to juvenile judges in 2003—they could, on their own authority and in chambers, revoke a probation—and in the use of prosecutorial delegates, many of whom were retired police officers or JIs, to hear first-time offenses in extrajudicial proceedings. They tended to oppose legislative amendments that limited their independent control over when and under what conditions to schedule trials. A number criticized the reforms of juvenile law permitting accelerated summonses and trials (*délais rapprochés*) that were legislated in the mid-1990s but only implemented in the Paris court in 2003. Under the logic of this law, children were tried by judges who were available to hear a case in the shortened timeframe mandated by the summonses, not by the judge who normally supervised them and knew their personal and family backgrounds. This struck at the very heart of the 1945 ordinance. These judges also found provisions of legislation passed under the center-right government in 2002 and 2003 to be excessively punitive, in particular the closed centers that had provoked such debate during the 2002 campaign and the creation of new public order violations punishable by prison terms. They were particularly critical of legislation punishing gatherings in stairwells and outside apartment buildings because it targeted youth in public housing projects.[66]

These judges were particularly reticent about the rehabilitative possibilities of incarceration, seeing it as appropriate only for those accused of crimes or as a last resort for youth whose recidivism or physical violence suggested incorrigibility. Some judges were concerned by the frequency of incarceration orders requested by the prosecutor's office and by the population disproportionately targeted by these orders, namely unaccompanied minors and irregular foreigners. My arrival at the Paris court in January 2001 coincided with the implementation of the law on the presumption of innocence and protection of victims that was intended to enhance due process protections for the accused and victims by limiting the extensive policing and detention powers of JIs and, by extension, those of the juvenile judge in his or her role as investigating magistrate in a penal case. This law created a new, nonspecialized magistrate, the *juge des libertés et de la détention* (JLD), to preside over all detention and release decisions.[67] Juvenile judges were opposed to a magistrate with no special expertise in juvenile law who was invested with the power to incarcerate youth. All of the anti-penal judges joined a 2001 demonstration against the creation of this new magistrate. In the months that followed January 2001, when the 15 June 2000 law was implemented, this judge was seen as an extension of the prosecutor's policies, since he approved all but 10 percent of the incarceration orders requested by the prosecutor's office. Judge Bondy described two cases in which a JLD had approved what she viewed as totally unwarranted incarceration orders. The first involved a pregnant sixteen-year-old Romanian teenager living in a squat outside Paris who had been arrested for theft, and the second involved an unaccompanied, irregular minor from Morocco who was accused of attempted theft with violence (he had shoved his male victim) and was in prison awaiting trial because the prosecutor argued that he was a flight risk.

Many of the anti-penal judges were outraged by the sensationalist media coverage of youth crime and insisted that only a small percentage of the minors they supervised were repeat offenders. Most were involved in group theft, mostly of cell phones, and even among this group the majority needed support, not punishment. These judges were strongly committed to an individual-centered model, emphasizing in interviews and in court, that a minor's route to successful integration within adult society was through individual effort based on school performance and an educational credential. They stressed the importance of good grades, the value of hard work, and the necessity to make an effort and to take initiative. This was striking, since the overwhelming majority of the teenagers in the courtrooms I observed were from disadvantaged or working-class backgrounds and all but a handful had been tracked early into the less-prestigious vocational track of the public educational system, often against their wishes.[68] Many were struggling to complete dead-end secondary diplomas that had no value in the job market. Nonetheless, all judges emphasized individual trajectories premised on an educational meritocracy. They insisted that youth stay in school and take exams even in programs for which they had no aptitude or interest. When I raised the obvious contradiction of urging youth to get vocational degrees such as the Certificat d'Aptitude Professionnelle (Professional Aptitude Certificate) in accounting, for which there were no jobs, anti-penal judges echoed larger neoliberal discourses on accountability and responsibility. It was clear that they, like their pro-penal colleagues and many others in the public arena, no longer saw these youth as a permanent labor reserve but maintained the fiction of possibility. As Judge Suchard said:

> Of course, it is true, [there is a real] economic problem. And all these kids who leave school at thirteen don't know how to read or write well, that is [also] the

problem. What they need to do is get mobilized, start learning to read and write. They can't avoid it. When they grow up, they want to make money.[69]

I asked her how they would do that if they were no longer in school. I mentioned the very high rate of unemployment for all but the most well credentialed young people. What sorts of jobs would they get? She admitted that the minimum credential demanded by French employers was now a long-cycle secondary degree: "These young kids already with their problems given their family history, on the job market, it's true, with the problem of unemployment, already young people who are qualified can't find jobs."

When asked to describe how the nature of delinquency had changed, most of the experienced judges mentioned "gangs," "collective phenomenon," and the "territorial nature of offending." Hervé Hamon, the court president, was particularly eloquent on this theme. Was an individual-centered model based on a one-on-one intervention in an open setting still viable if the main problems were now understood as the neighborhood and bad influences from street culture? Judges protested that French penal law only recognizes and punishes individuals, not groups. They must consider the collective offense, find the individual responsibility, isolate the act, and work on that. Echoing some sociological writing that puts gangs in historical perspective and downplays their importance, Judge Suchard insisted that they had always existed and that the black jackets of the 1950s and 1960s were every bit as violent as the contemporary groups depicted in the media. Yet, in an interesting rhetorical slippage, she described how she dealt with gang members, depicting them as outsiders and foreigners rather than insiders and citizens:

> Of course, the gang is a way to protect yourself from police, the justice system, from the adult world whose ideals one rejects by adopting shared codes, a language, and customs. I say if you are an interesting individual, you can bring something to this country, to France, to your neighborhood, we can work with you. The biggest part of our work is to extract them from the group and to take them individually because the law requires it.

Pro-penal judges

Pro-penal judges tended to view cultural and family origin as largely determining influences in the lives of the troubled children they supervised. Although they did not completely discount the possibilities for positive outcomes, they viewed the combination of dysfunctional families, cultural difference, the turmoil of adolescence, and at-risk behavior—from truancy to theft—as having a cumulative effect that offered little optimism. Like their anti-penal counterparts, these judges identified increased penal cases opened by the prosecutor's office as the most significant shift in French juvenile justice, although they linked this trend to the emergence of a new delinquency of young predators, "many only 10 years old." Rather than see the higher proportion of penal cases as an abusive state policy driven by public order concerns, they viewed it as a necessary response to a new category of offenders who were younger and more violent.

According to these judges, youth committed more serious infractions and had delinquent profiles that began in early childhood. Troubled children exhibited aberrant behaviors that originated largely with parental deficiencies in the home.[70] Like French child psychologists who tended to downplay the physiological effects of raging hormones and willful impulses in adolescence in favor of Freudian analyses centering in intergenerational struggles over authority and autonomy, judges focused on family pathologies as well as the typical profiles of at-risk teenagers. They blamed offending on family milieu, bad parenting, and individual psychology rather than on socioeconomic factors such as poverty or class and racism in public institutions. The pro-penal judges echoed public rhetoric that focused on social origin as a major causal factor in a downward spiral, ending in territorial violence and ethnic gangs. Judge Binet explained:

> The real problem is the young teenager, the thirteen- to sixteen-year-old. At that age they have only one desire and that is to do the least possible. They have no interest in exerting effort, they prefer easy money and leisure activities. You ask them to get up early and to study! They internalize a culture of idleness. There is a lot of unemployment among young people and their parents. Why should they get up when their parents stay in bed?

In contrast to anti-penal judges who criticized the mounting penalization within the court, these judges decried the feeling of impunity created by case backlogs and delayed hearings. They criticized their colleagues at the Paris court who were too lenient and too reluctant to impose sentences that demanded accountability by repairing the wrong and punishing the guilty. Despite the rapid amendments to juvenile law since 1995 and the recent creation of new infractions as well as stiffer penalties for existing offenses targeting youth, these judges were dissatisfied with existing law. Judge Bella believed that "We have reached the limit of the effectiveness of the 1945 ordinance." These judges wanted either more punitive legislation and/or texts that were specifically adapted to deal with the worsening problem of youth crime. Judge Binet, for example, complained that the 2002 law voted by the center-right government made it impossible for judges to impose probation on that most problematic group of teenagers, the thirteen- to sixteen-year-olds.[71] In contrast to many of their anti-penal colleagues, they viewed expedited hearings positively as long as the minor's background was known. This lessened the feeling of impunity by rightly raising the penalty for failure to appear. Judgments in absentia were followed by an incarceration order.

These judges specifically addressed the problem of prison but supported incarceration in some cases, both pretrial and postsentence, explaining that constraint and punishment were a part of any comprehensive rehabilitative system. In their view, it was not possible to implement penal law without establishing authority. The integrity of the system demanded that youth sometimes receive the ultimate constraint—doing time. Judge Binet explained that this did not imply interminable prison terms like "you have in the U.S.," but "there were times when it was essential to remove them from bad neighborhoods. For example when éducateurs are not making the necessary effort or it is impossible to find an appropriate placement outside the home."

Like some of their anti-penal colleagues, pro-penal judges favored sentences that reinforced individual responsibility, such as reparation measures in community organizations and accountability for all criminal defendants. Only two judges, Dinard and Franconi, were willing to demand accountability publicly of unaccompanied, irregular minors. Those who, according to Judge Dinard, "only live from theft, don't work, and accumulate long police records" deserve punishment and even prison. These judges tended to favor measures like pretrial probation because they had "meaning for young people" and carried consequences in the event of violation. Judges used measures such as conditional suspended sentences (*sursis avec mise à l'épreuve*) to impose multiple conditions on young defendants so that they "registered mentally the severity of the situation and had something concrete to work on," such as staying in school, maintaining grades, continuing to work, and avoiding certain neighborhoods. If a youth failed to comply and/or continued to offend, the judge could revoke the measure and incarcerate the youth. A number of judges avoided suspended prison sentences, saying that the sentence was meaningless to young defendants and provided only a potential trap for the

public space" of the court. As she explained, "In the veil there is a connotation of the submission of women, of the manipulation [of young girls], and of proselytizing that is absolutely shocking."[72]

CONCLUSION

This chapter focused on juvenile judges as the lynchpin of a system under siege. Currently judges experience the constraining neoliberal pressures of limited state welfare. The new penology links them more closely to policing and prosecutorial functions defined in terms of control, repair, and retributive solutions. At the same time this penology is premised on enhanced protections of individual rights and open debate associated with adversarial legal systems. The punitive trend and an increase in the number of penal cases have only exacerbated the tensions and contradictions inherent in their function. Judges find it difficult to treat more and more cases in shorter periods of time with the same methods and scarce resources.

Although defenders of the court see the unique contribution of juvenile judges to be their in-depth relationships with individual children and families, the reality is often quite different. The turnover is high and the work is time-intensive, emotionally draining, and stressful. Legal scholars and public opinion criticize juvenile judges precisely because their personalized judgments depart from and compromise the norm of impartiality. In contrast to U.S. judges whose appointment or election to their courts tend to reinforce their links to local communities, French juvenile judges are appointed by the Justice Ministry and, at the Paris court, rarely live in the districts they serve. Their physical separation from the children and families is mirrored in their social distance.

This chapter considered the impact of gender and class on professional identity and practice, concluding that the naturalized link between female magistrates and juvenile justice and the progressive overrepresentation of women in this function cannot be separated from the stigma attached to the juvenile court as a site more associated with personalized social work than with impartial judicial work. In Paris, the largest and most influential juvenile court, women judges dominate. It is no accident that a vigorous critique of the ideology and practice within the juvenile court was undertaken by predominantly male jurists, judges, psychologists, and éducateurs at a time when the punitive trend was not only attracting wide support but was being applied in jurisdictions with large multiethnic populations, such as the Bobigny juvenile court.

Assuming the mantle of a first-rate magistrate has been premised on accepting the penalizing function implicit in French penal code.

The enhanced media exposure and greater visibility of judges as public intellectuals potentially provided a forum for reframing critical social issues and shaping public policy. This forum was limited to debates among prominent jurists or male presidents of courts in or outside large metropolitan areas, particularly Paris. Despite the internal disagreement I document among Parisian judges, public opinion and legislative reform are moving steadily away from the model enshrined in the ordinance of 1945. This model was never based on the blameless child and has existed for a relatively short period of time. As we saw in Chapter 3, in spite of the nostalgia surrounding this model and the celebrations concerning its uniqueness, there is ample evidence to suggest that the actual practices in many juvenile courts remained both severe and punitive after 1945. Recall that the legislation instituting social assistance within juvenile courts was not enacted until 1958, prison-like detention centers were not closed until 1970, and pretrial detention for thirteen- to sixteen-year-olds accused of common misdemeanors was legal in France until 1987. As a result of legislation in 2002, youngsters in that same age group who are accused of misdemeanors and violate probation can once again be imprisoned before their cases come to trial.

In the 1990s the caseload and demand for service providers nearly doubled, but the Protection Judiciaire de la Jeunesse budget did not increase.[73] Dominique Dray, an anthropologist employed there, described it as the most marginalized agency within the Justice Ministry in terms of staff and funding.[74] The agency's budget represented only 10.5 percent of the total Justice Ministry budget and a mere 0.14 percent of the overall state budget.[75] Despite annual increases beginning in 1999, its share of the Justice Ministry budget actually fell over the four-year period culminating in 2002.[76]

The degree of anxiety French commentators have registered with respect to the "new" delinquents conveys a pervasive pessimism concerning the viability of French republican institutions, rehabilitative justice, and social values. Ever watchful of international trends, French politicians were attracted to the zero-tolerance model applied in U.S. cities to reduce urban crime. At the same time they and others worried about the encroachment of yet another unwanted U.S. import—the punitive model. Denis Salas, for example, denigrated American juvenile justice as "totally absent." Salas pointed to the tough penology, ethnic ghettos, and racialized prisons in the United States as a cautionary tale for those who would reject the rehabilitative legacy of the French welfare state for the American penal state. Nonetheless, Salas's writings send contradictory messages. Working closely with French sociologists, Salas provided one of the most vivid images of "immigrant" delinquents for politicians bent on retribution as well as eloquent testimony to the unprecedented nature of their deviance. He proclaimed that "this delinquency is neither initiatory nor individually pathological but applicable to a whole age cohort and [is] territorialized." On the one hand, Salas has repeatedly argued that the current rehabilitative model had broken down because of the challenge of "temporary or lack of employment, tired fathers, over-protective mothers, the violence of sons in closed projects" and "a counter-culture generating its own norms and turning its back on common law."[77] On the other hand, he urged that the state maintain its commitment to preventive justice over time. In a recent book, he warned against the dangers of an actuarial model gaining ground in France where the penal is reduced to its purely punitive function.[78]

These contradictory arguments are typical of the uncertainty surrounding theories of juvenile justice. They strongly suggest that a new kind of adolescent has emerged, one for whom the normal dispensations accorded the developmentally immature are no longer viable. This conception of adolescence radically adjusts the boundary of childhood downward for those in enclaved, ethnic projects and "adultifies" even young teenagers ascribing conscious and malevolent intent to them. When judges handle the relatively rare penal cases of adolescents from middle-class and mainstream backgrounds, they may still understand childhood as a malleable and perfectible stage extending to the late teens, but they increasingly challenge these assumptions for disadvantaged youth of immigrant and foreign ancestry.

This reconceptualization rests on the problematic notion—a legacy of Durkheimian sociology—that different [ethnic] values threaten the putative cultural homogeneity upon which social solidarity and legal norms rest in a "stable" entity described as French society. Given the socioeconomic upheavals and compressed change that have marked postwar French society, it is untenable to suggest that there has ever been a uniformly "shared idea of the right and the just" that had to be reconstructed in the face of challenges from "new" delinquents. Rather, the assertion of a "loss of a community of values" and the need "to recreate common rules" have more to do with the perceived effect of cultural outsiders on the inside and the problem of how to control adolescents whose deviance was viewed as fundamentally different in nature and scope. By linking personality development and shared references, they identified bad parenting as the problem even as they absolved overburdened public institutions such as the schools and the justice system from a responsibility or ability to fill the void and to create the social bond. Judges and jurists displaced the causes for delinquency from socioeconomic circumstances or individual psychology onto a failure of parental authority and deficient values in the home.

In the next chapter we move into the court system and experience it from the bottom up, beginning with the proceedings set in motion by an arrest, police custody, intake interviews, and the hearings before a judge that can lead to release, probation, or prison.

5 GETTING ARRESTED AND GOING TO COURT

THIS CHAPTER TELLS THE STORY of the first encounters between court personnel and youths after arrest and detention by the police. It centers on the procedures that take those youths through the court system, including a first meeting with an éducateur during an intake interview in jail, the initial court hearing, prison counseling, and the judgment after pretrial incarceration. This chapter confronts French normative constructions of family structure and childhood development with the behaviors and backgrounds of minors of immigrant and foreign ancestry. In addition, it explores how the notion of social personhood is embedded in the French model of rehabilitation. How do state institutions such as the juvenile court single out individuals, label them as problems, and sort them into a category of educability?

A JOURNEY THROUGH THE COURT SYSTEM: AN OVERVIEW

On a national holiday in late May 2003, I got a call from Caroline, the éducatrice on duty. As a result of arrests the night before, seven minors were in a holding cell and all had been referred for prosecution. The prosecutor's office had recommended that Abdellah, a youth from Senegal, be sent immediately to the Fleury-Mérogis prison. Although he had no police record, he and an accomplice had commandeered a taxi at knifepoint, an unusually serious offense in Paris where most aggravated thefts consisted of boys snatching cell phones or purses. In addition, a seventeen-year-old from Gabon was in custody for physical assault, along with five Romanians accused of theft, one boy and four girls (see Chapter 8). If I could get there in twenty minutes, she promised to postpone the required intake interviews until my arrival. I grabbed my things

and ran for the subway, relieved that there would no lines at the Palace of Justice. Caroline would be anxious to get started because more teenagers would
probably be transferred to the Palace from precincts across the city, and the
judge would want to finish early.

During my time there, detention in the "juvenile quarter" of the Paris jail, a
bleak, enclosed wooden cubicle surrounded by adult cells, began with arrest,
custody in one of the precincts, and telephone contact between the precinct
commander and the deputy prosecutor on duty in the centrally located Palace
of Justice. Before the 1990s and the politicization of juvenile justice, police in-
vestigators mailed notices of arrests to the prosecutor's office for all but the
most serious cases.[1] In the wake of public demands for an immediate response
to delinquency, prosecutors and police began to treat cases of suspects in "real
time."[2] Now, juvenile prosecutors are on duty seven days a week to take incom-
ing calls for all cases. They work in tandem with rotating teams of state caseworkers (éducateurs) who interview suspects and brief the juvenile judges who
conduct hearings following arrest.[3] Based on those preliminary telephone interviews with the police, deputy prosecutors have the discretionary power to
decide on whether and how to prosecute minors. They may refer petty offenses
for hearings in chambers or send serious misdemeanors before the juvenile
correctional court.[4] Conversely, all crimes are referred to a JI rather than a juvenile judge for the investigation. In my experience, this was increasingly the
case for repeat offenders accused of committing serious misdemeanors. When
the suspect is known to the court, the prosecutor issues a summons to appear
before a member of the judicial police,[5] one of the procedures newly legislated
in 1995 and 1996. This is a way to expedite the adjudication process and, not co-
incidentally, to sidestep juvenile judges in the initial phase. Alternatively, for a
first offense, prosecutors may order a formal reprimand (rappel à la loi) and
a reparation measure if the accused admits guilt, the victim agrees, and the
charges are not serious. Finally, they may decide not to prosecute and instruct
the police to release suspects.

THE PARIS SOCIAL SERVICE AND PROBATION
OFFICE (SEAT)

On that day in 2003, I crossed the city in record time, arriving at the Service
Educatif Auprès du Tribunal, or SEAT (the Social Service and Probation Office) out of breath but with five minutes to spare. The SEAT is part of the Protection Judiciaire de la Jeunesse, one of the three largest operational units

within the Ministry of Justice, whose mission is to implement court decisions for three populations: delinquent and at-risk minors under eighteen as well as young adults aged eighteen to twenty-one. The Paris SEAT is one of the largest in France, and in 2003, Caroline was one of thirteen éducateurs posted there.[6] The SEAT office, located within the court, was then and still is a place of high drama and raw emotion. On any given day the hallway outside the SEAT office or éducateurs' individual offices (where they schedule regular appointments) is a chaotic space. Here family members await appointments in varying emotional states of resignation, disbelief, pain, or hostility. Here they must confront, many for the first time, unwelcome truths and manage feelings of powerlessness and anger. It is, in the words of the SEAT director, "a beehive," where things happen all at once.

The hallway is a liminal space where waiting foregrounds an oppressive reality, multiple dramas are staged, and a host of people who are at their most vulnerable behave badly. The French middle-class norms that demand self-control and restraint under pressure are rarely in evidence. One afternoon in 2003 I spent at the court was not unusual. A middle-class white teenage girl ran away from home, her mother contacted the court, and the Brigade de la Protection des Mineurs (Child Protection Brigade), a special unit of the national police, brought her against her will to the SEAT. She shrieked at her mother "get out of my face" and told her to "drop dead." Her mother fainted dead away from the shock and struck her head on the floor; medical personnel had to be called. They arrived on the scene and moved quickly past an African mother who came to collect her son from jail. She had no child care and had three young children in tow, including a crying infant. Inside the SEAT office the éducatrice on duty faced an angry French teenager of Algerian ancestry who had missed a filing deadline for a state-funded trip. He staged a tantrum, cursed, and with the sweep of his arm sent a stapler and pencil holder flying. The caseworker lost her temper and screamed at him in turn, saying that "you must put at end to this violent behavior," prompting the director to rush in. Just as quickly, the commotion ended and a social worker from one of the affiliated private agencies arrived to announce that her service could admit a Tunisian teenager who had been sniffing glue and been arrested in an aborted attempt to steal a taxi. Three police officers had subdued the boy using force, including spraying him with tear gas at close range, and he had suffered second-degree burns on his face. After she left, the translator for the Romanian teenagers in jail arrived to assist with the intake interviews.

The SEAT is home to the state-recruited and credentialed caseworkers known in French as éducateurs, whose job is to monitor children with penal and social assistance cases that are open at court. Like public prosecutors and judges, éducateurs do monthly rotations on duty.

THE EDUCATEUR: SOCIAL WORKER
OR PROBATION OFFICER?

The profession of éducateur has had a vexed past and has an equally uneasy present. In 1912 legislators created an embryonic version of juvenile courts and borrowed the concept of probation from Chicago reformers as an enlightened alternative to confinement for troubled youth. This required a corps of "probation delegates" (délégués à la liberté surveillée), then consisting of largely middle-class volunteers from private agencies, to undertake investigations of the suitability of minors to be returned to their parents rather than committed to state institutions. The court's decision to keep minors within "open settings" (at home) was contingent upon regular supervision by probation delegates. They made regular home visits and provided normative evaluations of children's behavior. If children "behaved badly," judges could revoke probation and send them to state reformatories or agricultural colonies.

The 1945 legislation created a separate administrative unit, Education Surveillée, and institutionalized the recruitment of permanent, state-certified caseworkers. In an important symbolic and institutional shift, this office was removed from the jurisdiction of the departments of prisons, and éducateurs ceased being the direct subordinates of judges. Instead they reported directly to the head of the Education Surveillée, which in 1990 became the Protection Judiciaire de la Jeunesse, or PJJ. In 1956 caseworkers adopted the name éducateurs and forged a professional identity around youth advocacy, social justice, and a militant rejection of penal repression. They were recruited by state examination and became public employees but were drawn to the work, according to one senior éducateur, "because as leftist militants they believed in it."[7] The first professional éducateurs were predominantly young men who came from modest social backgrounds. Many had not completed the full cycle of secondary education or held the baccalauréat degree then synonymous with bourgeois status and, as a result, identified with the largely male working-class adolescents whose cases they handled. The same éducateur explained that an overwhelming majority joined the leftist trade union representing them because of its commitment to the integration of the underprivileged and to the fight against marginality, "a project union leaders espoused long before it came into vogue."[8] Educateurs lived in the local communities where they worked, forging personalized relationships with youth and insisting on their professional independence to ensure the integrity of the rehabilitative project.[9]

Today the profile of the profession, the requirements to enter it, and the nature of the work have changed considerably and stirred public debate. Critical attention has centered on administrators in the PJJ and éducateurs in SEAT offices throughout France in a context of heightened fears regarding a delinquency of exclusion and an actuarial penal model that is focused on results. Officials at the Cour des Comptes (equivalent to the Office of Budget and Management) and inspectors within the French Chancellery have sharply criticized administrative redundancy, bureaucratic inefficiency, lack of accountability to children and families, and workplace practices that subverted the professional ethos of prevention and education. They have noted that despite unprecedented budgetary increases for the PJJ and the addition of almost 1,300 new positions between 1998 and 2002, individual courts still experience considerable anomalies in resource allocation and work organization. Officials have posed hard questions. For example, why does the SEAT of Grenoble warrant six caseworkers, while Bobigny, which treats ten times the number of cases, only have eleven? Given the amount of time allotted for desk work, personnel meetings, and fifty-three annual vacation days, state officials have calculated that carrying a caseload of twenty-five children permits éducateurs to spend only four hours per month per case.[10] Despite the addition of new positions, inspectors described the growing backlog in the implementation of court-ordered measures. Nationally, in 2000 the average delay between the court-ordered decision and the caseworker response was forty-three days. In that same year at the Paris SEAT, which had one of the highest number of caseworkers on staff (thirteen), 18 percent of the measures ordered were delayed at least two weeks.[11]

Attention within the Chancellery and among state inspectors has also centered on the enormous social distance separating éducateurs, who are now largely middle-class and female, from the children they monitor. The minimum education requirement for éducateurs is currently two years of university study. In contrast, minors with open cases are predominately male, economically underprivileged, and scholastically challenged and come from large families headed by single parents who are of foreign or immigrant ancestry. Judges I interviewed deemed the increasing feminization and professionalization of the work problematic as legislators resurrected and sought to staff closed residential facilities for "violent recidivists" after 2002. Moreover, some judges in Paris viewed éducateurs less as social workers than as office workers who rarely left the confines of the Palace of Justice to follow children into their home settings, instead requiring that counseling take place at the SEAT office. Referring to a professional embrace that was close but conflicted, Judge Boyer described court caseworkers as our "brother-enemies" (*frères-ennemis*).

Although the SEAT éducateurs like Caroline are required to interview juveniles after arrest, monitor teenagers who are in prison, and speak for them at trial, many viewed the essence of their work as the supervision of children in an open setting, that is with parents, a court-appointed guardian, in a foster family, or in a special school. Because I initially saw them more as social workers (*assistant social*) than probation officers, I distinctly remember inadvertently using the term "social worker" to refer to a "court caseworker" (éducateur) and being immediately corrected by an attorney specializing in juvenile law. Although the term *éducateur* is widely translated as "educator" in English, this is a misnomer. The duties of éducateurs have always been ambiguously and unevenly positioned astride two roles—the one associated with the punishment and containment and the other linked to rehabilitation and integration. These roles are viewed as increasingly incommensurate. The reason has to do with the professionalization of casework and the penalization of juvenile justice. The new penology has required that éducateurs focus more on surveillance and control than on prevention and assistance.

My arrival at the Paris court coincided with a disturbing national trend. Between 1995 and 1999 penal measures increased 67 percent and represented two-thirds of all the interventions judges ordered in open-setting cases.[12] The most frequently pronounced penal measures were probation (*contrôle judiciaire*; 38 percent) and a conditional suspended sentence (*sursis avec mise à l'épreuve*; 22 percent), both of which impose conditions that juveniles must respect on pain of prison. The rapid penalization of juvenile justice after 1995 and necessity for éducateurs to assume the function of probation officers rather than social workers raised doubts and provoked resistance.[13]

In June 2003, éducateurs within the largest professional union, Syndicat des Personnels de l'Education Surveillée de la Protection Judiciaire de la Jeunesse, were on strike to protest working conditions, specifically retirement benefits.

They were dismayed at judges' increasing recourse to sentences imposing conditional suspended sentences on underprivileged youths. For those with little schooling, few skills, family problems, and long police records, this ruling imposed such unrealistic obligations after judgment that it virtually guaranteed failure. One éducatrice gave the example of Antoine, a young, mentally challenged man from the mainstream population who had served a prison sentence for theft and possession of a stolen car. His parole was conditioned on regular sessions with a psychologist, obtaining work or training, and repaying 18,000 euros to the owners of the car he had stolen and wrecked. His mother and stepfather wanted to help by hiring him but insisted that he accept responsibility by paying for his training. The teenager refused the offer, telling his éducatrice that he could make many times what his stepfather paid by selling stolen cars abroad. The éducatrice admitted to me that it would take him years to repay such a huge debt if he worked for minimum wage. She explained that he was personally responsible for the debt because his paternity had never been officially recognized by his biological father, a man who had spent most of his adult life in prison.

Although many éducateurs were vociferous critics of the penal trend, they were also ambivalent about the challenges of the "new" delinquency of exclusion and voiced contradictory opinions. As one senior éducateur put it, "How are we to manage probation, a containment measure that can lead to prison, if the young person doesn't comply? How can we treat it in a rehabilitative way? It is not in our work culture." He continued, "We've left behind the individual dimension of behavior, it's very clear with these youth in the projects, it is a collective phenomenon, tied to the neighborhood. It is very difficult to separate the youth from his territory, his milieu, he feels uprooted. The recognition of street values is very powerful."[14]

In 2000, when I first arrived in Paris, a new, "new" delinquency of exclusion perpetrated by undocumented, unaccompanied minors, the majority of whom were Romanian, had not yet burst into public view to destabilize the dominant national narrative equating lawlessness exclusively with non-European, Muslim delinquents segregated in bad neighborhoods. Nonetheless, judges and éducateurs considered it a significant problem, and, in an angry 2001 communiqué addressed to the Justice minister, they denounced "the repression" aimed at vulnerable youth from eastern Europe "without families, papers or protection" as well as the "steadily deteriorating situation within the PJJ." Despite the official pronouncements of outrage by the éducateurs' union leaders, Ministry of Justice officials were, in turn, indignant at the way éducateurs treated those same unaccompanied minors following arrest. In a 2002 evaluation of the Paris SEAT office, state inspectors issued a scathing indictment of the SEAT director (who left her post later that year) and the excessively punitive policies she and her colleagues used to deal with this vulnerable population.[15]

THE INTAKE INTERVIEW: TELL ME WHERE YOU
COME FROM AND I'LL TELL YOU WHO YOU ARE

When I arrived that May morning, Caroline was hanging up the phone. Two more minors had been brought in. We immediately left the building and headed for the dank medieval fortress housing the jail. Caroline knocked on an imposing twelve-foot-high iron door. A policeman answered, took our IDs, and disappeared to retrieve Abdellah. We settled into the glass cubicles where all the interviews are conducted. Caroline mused out loud about the gravity of the offense. It was rare for a first-time offender to use a weapon in a theft.

Immediately upon minors' arrival in the jail, éducateurs are required to conduct intake interviews. These interviews provide the preliminary social, psychological, family, and scholastic background information they need to brief the judges who must evaluate minors' state of mind as well as extenuating circumstances. In contrast to the U.S. juvenile court's concern with the moral character of offending youth, the French court is preoccupied with the causes of delinquency, how they connect to his or her social milieu of origin, and what this suggests about his or her prospects for integration. The court's initial determination that the youth is merely lost and redeemable or unformed and incorrigible relies heavily on the written and oral reports presented to judges by the éducateurs. Their reports focus on family structures within and between generations, housing, income, lifestyle, and educational level and draw heavily on a medical-psychological discourse to evaluate the child's personality and capacity for normal social interactions. Intake interviews are an important first phase in the constitution of a court archive on the minor. In the press of preparing for the mandatory hearing after arrest, éducateurs collect only basic autobiographical information and superficial social and psychological facts. Nonetheless, these data condition the substance of the case as well as normative evaluations regarding the child's psychological well-being and social behavior, which are central to later proceedings. The reports form a constituent element of a disciplinary system in which children are marked, evaluated, and categorized. There is a broad consensus among éducateurs about dominant mainstream values, codes, and practices. They are particularly attentive to matters of self-presentation, including dress, hair, bodily comportment, and oral expression. The necessary conformity to these codes and values is treated as a universal truth.

Both the oral interviews in jail and the written reports in the file open a window onto contemporary middle-class representations of childhood and adolescence. Socialization is understood as a process of continuous molding and ordering that transforms a raw, unformed being into a finished, social person. It presupposes a strongly adult-centric model that demands close supervision by appropriate authority figures and holds parents responsible for the actions of their children. This is true in a social and legal sense as parents are held liable for their children's delinquent actions and the damages that may result until they turn eighteen, the age of legal majority. Beginning with reports on the development of infants and toddlers under state supervision, éducateurs are particularly attentive to the emergence of what they view as proper personality structure and appropriate emotional expression. Here they use metaphors of containment and restriction to describe a solid structural frame that bears the imprint of its adult architects and is designed to last a lifetime. Proper childhood development has been linked to a child's inculcation of a sense of limits and clear boundaries in space and time. Although there are obvious parallels with child psychological theory elsewhere, the court personnel place particular emphasis on the connection between individual limits, spatial grounding, and personal, and, therefore, social identity. Without the appropriate structure, a child can have no clear sense of his or her bearings (*repères*) or place within family and society as a whole since bearings signify a firmly grounded sense of personhood and identity. The critical questions for the court turn on these understandings of a properly structured personality. Has he or she accepted and internalized the rules of social life and controls on individual behavior that are a prerequisite to integration within a larger social and moral order?

Given the importance of the social codes that govern food, oral expression, and self-presentation in France, éducateurs' evaluations assess the child's ability to conform to these codes beginning at a very early age. Although a report alerting the court to "a lack of bearings" and "a testing of limits" can and does describe children in general, when these terms appear in case after case of North or West African children, they become shorthand labels for "unruly," "loud," and "disruptive" boys of immigrant and foreign ancestry. They carry powerful received messages about who the at-risk child is and how he or she differs from normal [French] children who exercise self-discipline, respect authority, and act appropriately. An éducatrice who writes that little Mustapha displays "no structure" and regularly disrupts class is repositioning his behavior in a framework that will be viewed as an ominous portent of his future prospects. Little Mustapha will be put into a category of educability and acquire a reputation that will have profound consequences for his education and career.[16] The report recorded permanently in the court archive is a singular instance of the institutional power to single out, to name, and to stigmatize in the name of the social good, and, ultimately, public order.

The standardized interview protocol that is conducted in jail reveals much about French notions of group affiliation and group integrity. One of the central goals is to collect "facts" that can be linked to immediate risk factors. Children are asked questions about their parents and grandparents, with equal emphasis given to the ascendants of the child's mother and father. Educateurs record the birthplace, birthdate, and native languages of the child and parents and, in theory, carefully differentiate all relationships by blood and marriage. The resulting construct reflects a number of normative assumptions about the integrity of groups through time and the primordial ties that are said to stem from commonalities of place, blood, language, and custom. By emphasizing a child's roots and genealogical continuity, the interview questions take group affiliation as a given rather than as a situational and perpetually emergent phenomenon. These questions deny the fluid nature of group formation and the fact that individuals not only identify simultaneously with many groups but in a given context specify one affiliation rather than another, for strategic or pragmatic reasons. These notions are not surprising in a nation of people who have emigrated relatively rarely and have historically seen immigration as a problem of integration within a culturally homogenous body politic. The problem is that they serve as the basis for rigid conceptions of Otherness and reinforce the categorical assumptions that support the creation and preservation of what Brad Shore has called "our natives."[17] Recall the peculiar half-life of the label *petits sauvageons* (little savages), used by former Interior Minister Chevènement to describe "immigrant" delinquents without explicitly naming them. The term *sauvageons* is also an organic metaphor that can be translated as wild branches imperfectly grafted onto the French family tree. As such, they attract attention and spell trouble.[18]

In a situation in which the vast majority of the suspects in jail are minors of immigrant or foreign ancestry, this interview process is particularly problematic. Countries and nationalities serve as the standard measure of diversity, whereas, for example, the first-generation migrants from former colonies in Sub-Saharan regions differentiated themselves according to ethnicity. Moreover, the interview does not account for systems of affiliation and descent that depart from the cognatic model observable in "modern" French families where equal importance is given to the mother and father's line. It does not recognize ongoing transnational migratory flows rather than stable residential patterns or culturally divergent child-rearing arrangements that involve regular movement between places and produce "irregular" family genealogies. Children who revealed knowledge gaps or abnormal structures were judged negatively. Consider the French éducatrice whose misunderstanding of the common practice of child fostering in Cameroon led her to conclude that the African girls she interviewed "didn't know if the relative they lived with was their aunt or their sister."

A Question of Culture?

Despite their leftist politics and declared tolerance for difference, éducateurs generally have no training in culture or specialized knowledge of the ethnic groups they see in court. As a result, the briefings that éducateurs provide judges and the reports of social workers from outside the court often reveal the misfit between Western diagnostic and treatment models and the problems of children from radically different kinship and belief systems in Africa and Asia. Their attempts to interpret cultural differences too often result in ethnocentric stereotyping or in the reification of culture as a powerful and immutable force that blocks adaptation among immigrants of all types from less "evolved" groups or "advanced" societies, putting their children at risk for delinquency.

A particularly interesting example of this surfaced in an appeal of the juvenile judge's decision heard by the Paris Appellate Court in June 2005. The crux of this case centered on a Congolese family's beliefs in witchcraft and sorcery, which were described in the report. The appeal was brought by the mother of thirteen-year-old Kevin. This mother had initially accepted the judge's decision to temporarily award custody of her son to her husband's relatives, specifically her sister-in-law. After consulting an indigenous spiritualist (*marabout*) she changed her mind. Both she and her sister-in-law appeared in court to plead their respective cases. The president of the three-member appeal panel reminded her colleagues that the family had been under court supervision since 1998 because of continuous marital conflict and their son's "disruptive and provocative" behavior. According to the file, "the parents were powerless to control" behavior that began in preschool and "put others in danger."

Reading from the éducateurs' report, the president described the "mother's violent reaction" when they informed her of her sister-in-law's arrival from Kinshasa and plan to take Kevin to a special school recommended by the judge: "She attacked an éducatrice, striking her." When the magistrate asked the boy's mother why she changed her mind about the custody arrangement, she responded: "I was bewitched [that is, I couldn't be held responsible for my initial agreement]. I [later] saw a marabout who said, 'be careful with your son, she [the father's sister] is going to kill him.' Kevin had many accidents. She [pointing to her sister-in-law] gave my daughter underwear and since then she has had periods that don't stop. She called me a dumb beast." When another magistrate asked why Kevin's aunt would want to hurt him, the judge again read from the file indicating that a cultural mediation undertaken by cultural psychiatrists had been ordered by the juvenile judge. It revealed that the father was descended from a long line of powerful sorcerers and was adamant that his powers be transmitted within the family. Kevin's mother insisted that her husband threatened her and claimed that her refusal to surrender her son to his paternal relatives had caused a series of supernatural afflictions to befall her, her other children, and Kevin. When questioned about a possible alternative to the special schools, she insisted, "Send him to a school of the [French] Republic."

When the judge allowed the sister-in-law to speak, the contrast between the two women was striking. Kevin's mother was heavy-set, dressed in a traditional African *boubou* and headscarf, spoke heavily accented French, and not only gave voice to her "superstitious" beliefs but repeatedly broke into tears. Her sister-in-law was svelte, beautifully coiffed, and dressed in a chic, neutral-colored Western suit. She radiated poise and confidence without arrogance and spoke perfect French, taking care to address everyone in the courtroom. She cast the problem as a marital conflict and implied that the appeal had more to do with the suspension of monthly child payments for Kevin than a belief in witchcraft. She blamed her sister-in-law, "who does not work and stays out late" and insisted that she had come to France all the way from the Congo because of her concern for her nephew, "not because I need the [state] money." She emphasized her own success as a parent, explaining that she had a son who was a university-educated airline pilot and a daughter who held a ministerial position in the government. "My children have not become delinquents. I am not going to abandon my nephew." When specifically questioned about the witchcraft, she cleverly sidestepped the issue. "How can we evaluate it? This is not a problem of sorcery. She [Kevin's mother] must be able to separate family problems from marital problems." When invited to speak, the éducatrice summarized the case: "Madame has refused to see the éducatrice, they could not implement the court-ordered measure, there are serious problems in the marriage. Ethnopsychiatry can produce results but it is difficult where witchcraft belief is concerned."

When it came time for Kevin to be questioned, he produced a letter, which he prepared to read. I overheard the president, who whispered to her colleagues, "the letter was written [by someone else]." His delivery convinced the judges that he had been coerced:

KEVIN: [*reading the letter*] There are too many problems now. They want to force me to leave home for this school. I don't want to go. They accuse me of having stolen things. It is not true. I work at home. I do my school work at home by myself.

The president advised him gently: "Regular school is a bit hard for you. We'll have to see about something else." His aunt's facade cracked and she interjected sharply: "His mother made him write that letter."

As is customary in appeal cases after hearing from both parties, the éducatrices, and the child (in custody hearings), the prosecutor stood to represent the state. A former juvenile judge, she was unequivocal in her rejection of the mother's appeal:

PROSECUTOR: The public ministry looks after the interest of children. If families function well, so does society. The cost to society is very high when people behave badly. Madame, you find that your family is in danger. It is not true. Rather, Kevin's problem is the problem that his mother and father have between them and it affects him directly. You need to look at your own life rather than consult a mere fortuneteller. The problem is not outside the family, it is in the family and in you. Look at what is happening in your own house. Start by working on yourself and changing your attitudes.

Kevin's aunt staked her claim to custody in part on her embodiment of normative white, upper-middle-class Frenchness. By ridiculing her sister-in-law's accusations of witchcraft (that were attested to by her brother and substantiated by professional French-trained cultural psychiatrists) and by reframing the custody appeal as a money issue, she adroitly appropriated dominant discourses that stigmatized African immigrant parents as culturally backward and negligent. She offered herself as a parental model whose African children were exemplars of bourgeois success, not at risk for delinquency, as Kevin was. As Fanon has argued, in doing so she not only "whitened her race" and enhanced her credibility with the court but demonstrated the "double consciousness" among postcolonial peoples whose identities and practices are refracted through the internalization of hegemonic French linguistic and cultural norms.[19] Kevin's mother also demonstrated this double consciousness when she played on the powerful trope of the French republican school as the solution to Kevin's problems, although her ability to use it effectively was muted by her emotional distress, failure to embody dominant class norms, and reliance on a belief system based on witches. The ugly dispute and the name calling with roots in colonial racism speaks to the uneasy but powerful embrace of white Frenchness as well as its by-product of self-hatred. It was clear to me from the moment both women set foot in court that Kevin's mother never stood a chance. The Appellate Court upheld the juvenile judge's ruling, as it does in more than 80 percent of the cases brought before it. It transferred custody from Kevin's mother to his aunt and approved his enrollment in a special Belgian school.

In many cases that I observed, éducateurs and social workers, not to mention judges and prosecutors, who were called upon to analyze conflicts or problems linked to cultural difference, simply ignored or dismissed culture as a salient factor and interpreted the problem as individual abnormality or family conflict, imposing Western psychological models and psychoanalytic discourses with which they were familiar. One éducatrice, who was a fierce proponent of rehabilitation and who went on strike in 2003 to protest working conditions and the turn to repression, interpreted a violent attack initiated by a teenage African girl. I choose this example because the physical fight that landed the teenager in court involved the violence of a visual gaze. Hostile stares figured prominently as motives in infractions in cases heard both in chambers and the formal court. According to the éducatrice, a "brilliant eleven-year-old" who got excellent grades and was a class delegate (equivalent to a student council member) got into trouble for attacking a neighborhood classmate "who looked at her badly." The victim landed in the hospital with a broken tooth and other bruises. The éducatrice explained:

Her [the accused] grades had fallen, her attitude had changed completely. Her mother refused to admit that her daughter was at fault. What was the problem? She had the responsibility of watching her two younger brothers and a little cousin. One day her brother fell into a well and nearly died because she was not looking. So when she was assigned to our service we started to work on this hostile stare and how it was linked to her responsibilities to others. It was too much responsibility (to watch three young children) for an eleven-year-old. To repair her fault, we put her in a social service provider during her school vacation, in the reception area, where she had to meet people, to look at them, and to meet their gaze. Her case came before the court and she was judged. She is not a delinquent and was returned home but given probation until her eighteenth birthday.[20]

Here the court's mission was to contain and control the hostile stare by renormalizing it as social contact even as the larger circumstances informing the teenager's social relations with her neighborhood peers and her parents as well as their cultural background were ignored and set aside.

One Educatrice's Approach

Caroline was the only éducatrice at the Paris SEAT with extensive, specialized training in ethnopsychiatry from the Paris VIII–Georges Devereux Center. Although she opposed the punitive trend and favored rehabilitative approaches, her ethnopsychiatric training taught her to view culture as a fixed constellation of traits that persisted through time and were inextricably linked to specific ancestors, homelands, and histories. Even though Caroline, who was of Jewish ancestry, was herself a transplant from Morocco, her training and experience at court made her view the immigration and permanent settlement of disadvantaged North and West Africans in a new homeland as disruptions that put them at risk for cultural disorders and aberrant behaviors, in contrast to her own experience. Caroline expressed this view when she described the case of a teenager of Algerian descent whose disruptive behavior in English class eventually got him suspended. When I asked why he was acting out, she explained: "He was frustrated and will never be able to learn English or any other foreign language, for that matter. He does not know his native language." I wondered if I had misunderstood, because we had been discussing a young man who was the third generation to be born in France. Weren't we discussing Malek? "Yes," she explained, "but the problem is that he is searching for his [cultural] identity and his roots in Algeria. Things won't be right until he learns his first language: Arabic."

That day in 2003 brought another example of Caroline's approach to a situation in which culture was a factor. When police brought the first suspect, Abdellah, to our cubicle, Caroline used the familiar *tu* form of address with him even though he was close to eighteen years old. Other éducateurs and some defense attorneys systematically used this form of address as a way to break down barriers, to dispel anxiety, and to create a space for dialogue. This was a technique Caroline did with exceptional skill. However, adult authority figures' use of *tu* with younger people is always complicated since it contravenes the standard linguistic conventions of symmetrical forms of address and is embedded in complex power dynamics that send strong messages.[21] When adults choose to address young people familiarly instead of using the conventional *vous* form, it can convey empathy, solidarity, and benevolent paternalism. Conversely, as both TV police dramas and neighborhood confrontations document, it can be a naked assertion of superior power that relies on condescension and racist rejection. Based on my observations, the use of *tu* even among the best intentioned court personnel was never intended to equalize power differences. The young people who ran afoul of the law were not invited to enter the circle of social proximity implied by a reciprocal use of this form of address. Rather, the exchange between the youth at court continued to mark an asymmetrical power relation that separated those who represented the legal norm and those who stood outside it.

Caroline quickly established that Abdellah was from Senegal, had no police record and, significantly, had no papers. He insisted that he was underage and had entered France legally. He implored Caroline not to contact his father, declaring, "I prefer to assume responsibility on my own." When he claimed to have forgotten his father's phone number, she reminded him that if he wanted to avoid prison, as "the judge recommended," he should cooperate. Caroline was most interested in knowing more about where he had come from and about his family situation. Abdellah revealed that his father had remarried twice since divorcing his mother and had four children from his first marriage with Abdellah's mother, three of whom were successfully settled in France, and three children under the age of six with his third wife. Abdellah's mother had also remade her life, remarrying in Senegal and beginning a second family. His father had held an important position in the Senegalese government before coming to France three years earlier to begin a doctoral thesis. Because of the importance of education as an indicator of class and the rarity of middle-class defendants, Caroline returned repeatedly to the question of social status and its effect on the father-son relationship. Did they have good relations?

> ABDELLAH: [*with bitterness*] No, I feared him. I never saw him. It was all about politics. He has plenty of diplomas but never took care of us. Can you imagine a father who never took his son to the beach? A son who was never alone with his father? He was minister of culture and leisure and counselor to the president and is now a legislator. He has French nationality. He likes France too much. He worships French culture.

Caroline probed Abdellah's movement from Senegal to France, asking, "Are you no longer anchored in Senegalese culture?" "How did you do in school?" He responded, "I was a pretty good student but I didn't like it. I got stuck." He attempted to separate himself from the offense and acknowledged his shame at being fingerprinted: "I have brothers. I am telling you that I am not a bad person. I never did anything like this before." He revealed that he had not attended school for three years, had spent a year in Spain with a maternal uncle, and he had returned to France working illegally, first as an unskilled laborer and then as a pizza delivery man. Why had he migrated to France?:

> ABDELLAH: I was in the third year of the academic section in middle school but I stopped. I wanted to work in France. Everybody has dreams about coming here to get money. I wasn't fooled [about finding easy work] but I wanted to see my brothers. I regret it. I need to get training. I'm sick of doing nothing. I eat at my brother's house but don't sleep there. I need to be independent.
>
> CAROLINE: Well, today you will be lucky to avoid prison. You need a rehabilitative measure to guide you and to straighten things out with your father.

When she asked him a second time why he was not in school, he retorted defensively: "My father didn't enroll me. He kept my papers. My little (half) brothers are in school."

Caroline briefed the judge on duty, Judge Bella, in detail and located Abdellah's father, who came to court in a rush and was visibly shaken. The judge initially doubted that Abdellah was underage but ultimately accepted the identity papers provided by his father. She imposed probation (*contrôle judiciaire*) as a condition of his release and transferred the case to the suburban jurisdiction where his father lived. Her ruling placed him with a parent who had withheld

his identity papers and kept him out of school effectively eliminating the possibility for legal work, housing or education. Judge Bella warned that if Abdellah
did not register with his éducateur every two weeks and avoid further infractions the probation would be revoked and he would go to prison. Outside his
father insisted defensively to Caroline, "I didn't put him in school because he
didn't want to study. This case must not sully my reputation. What if the victim
(taxi driver) presses charges and wants damages? This must not affect me. My
other children don't have any problems. This one is no good."

THE INITIAL COURT HEARING

After the intake interview, suspects are taken back to their cells to await a pretrial hearing. At this hearing a youth's fate depends on the judge, who considers
arguments from the prosecutor and the éducateur's notes from the intake interview, as well as comments from a defense attorney. For example, Abdellah,
the Senegalese youth, narrowly avoided prison, in large part because the taxi
driver was unhurt, but in addition he had no police record and he had a respectable father, however reluctant, to vouch for his legal identity. In the cases
of repeat offenders, prosecutors can demand pretrial detention and, as a result
of legislative reform in 2000, argue their cases directly before the newly created
magistrate, the juge des libertés et de la détention (JLD), who makes the ultimate decision.

In mid-June 2003, I spent the day with the juvenile prosecutor on duty. The
offices of the head juvenile prosecutor and his deputies are separated from the
juvenile court in a space heavily guarded by police.[22] Only those in handcuffs
escorted by police or armed with the requisite identification can penetrate the
protective cordon at the entrance. Like most French judges, the deputy prosecutor was a graduate of the elite Ecole Nationale de la Magistrature. She had
spent two years as a juvenile judge, a fact she admitted sheepishly just before we
went into court later that afternoon. She had moved from the "bench" to the
"floor" to begin representing the state in 1992 and had been promoted to a senior rank in 2002.

This case involved a sixteen-year-old Romanian youth who was accused of
aggravated theft involving an elderly Cambodian woman. The youth had been
caught in the act and had admitted his guilt. The case had been investigated
and an indictment made by a JI, who recommended immediate detention. The
teenager had tried to snatch the victim's purse, but she had held on, had fallen,
and was dragged along the sidewalk, suffering a broken shoulder. The accused

was on probation, had two cases waiting to be judged at the juvenile court, and had received a suspended prison sentence of six months a year before. The theft was aggravated by three circumstances, which are outlined in article 311-6 of the French penal code: (1) serious physical violence, which is (2) perpetrated by more than one person, (3) on a vulnerable victim by virtue of age. The seriousness of the adult prison sentence of ten years and the fact that the accused was older than sixteen determined the pretrial detention period of four months, with the possibility of a one-time renewal. The prosecutor, who "did not believe for one minute" the youth's motive for the theft, reported by the éducatrice—that he owed money to a local thug and was under pressure to pay—and she argued strongly for detention.

In the early afternoon the supervising magistrate, Judge Rabinovitch, came to the prosecutor's office, where she was briefed on the case. I noted her initial incredulous reaction when she was informed about the demand for incarceration: "I really don't understand. He was placed [in a state facility] and is under probation. Yes, he has six or seven cases (for theft in a group), but only two are serious and he has never been violent. This is a kid who seems really sweet." When the prosecutor described the victim's injuries, Judge Rabinovitch was aghast: "The little jerk. Well, put him in prison then. Perhaps it is the best solution."

At 7:15 P.M. his hearing began in the chambers of the specialized magistrate, the JLD. French law requires an "adversarial debate" between the prosecutor and the accused's defense attorney. The prosecutor emphasized the seriousness of the offense, the extent of the physical injuries, the threat of recidivism, and the need to guarantee public order as well as the protection of victims. She argued that probation "had not born fruit. He has been offered assistance and had an éducatrice, but to no effect. I ask you to put him in prison tonight." His attorney was unusually strident in arguing for clemency based on his lack of maturity, economic marginality, and position outside mainstream French society. As an outsider to French society without the right bearings or personality development and subject to the pressure of true criminal elements, he could not be held responsible for his actions:

> ATTORNEY: It is obvious that he didn't want this to happen. When you are an adult, integrated in society, have bearings, and are well established, you stop and think. He sees the purse before seeing the lady. He had debts, he was under threat. It is mentioned several times in the report.

He panicked. It's not an excuse but an explanation. He was doing well on probation, his éducatrice says good things, and he has an internship proposal. It takes time to straighten out. Going to prison is certainly not going to do that.

When asked if he had anything to say, the youth shook his head. The JLD was unmoved by the attorney's plea. He claimed that the risk for the victim and to public order were "too great. . . . Besides, he has parents [who should, therefore, have exerted more positive influence]. The choice is his, to sink further into delinquency or to stop. He will have plenty of time to think." It is telling that despite the adversarial debate held in the JLD's chambers, everyone, including Judge Rabinovitch, assumed he would go to prison once they knew that a JI had requested immediate incarceration. In 2000 legislators who created the JLD sought to enhance the due process protections and the presumption of innocence of the accused and to lessen the powers of the JI by mandating that pretrial detention orders be reviewed by two different magistrates. The JI requests incarceration and the new JLD, after an adversarial debate in court, rules on the request. Nonetheless, these judges grant 90 percent of pretrial detention requests.

DOING TIME: THE YOUTH DETENTION CENTER
AT THE FLEURY-MÉROGIS PRISON

The Fleury-Mérogis prison is the detention facility for minors awaiting trial, as well as those who had been sentenced to prison. The Youth Detention Center at the prison underwent a thorough reorganization between 1999 and 2000 and prison wardens showcased it as a model of penal correction. The new experiment was well received, even in the leftist press.[23] In fact, the center was not only a model but an exception in the landscape of extreme overcrowding and deplorable conditions in French prisons, where the inmate population had increased steadily since the 1970s and exploded after the election of 2002 brought the Right to power. The prison population of minors temporarily decreased after legislative reform in 1987 banned pretrial detention for misdemeanors but rose steadily beginning in 1993.[24] The annual total of minors in prison went from 1,905 in 1994 to 4,542 in 2001. Over the same period pretrial detentions nearly doubled, rising from 961 to 1,665.[25]

The Youth Detention Center at Fleury made headlines in 1999 when psychologists, doctors, counselors, and teachers issued a manifesto to the Justice minister and the press in which they denounced the climate of violence.[26] Although the press and academics concentrated on gang violence and extreme anomie, the authors emphasized the institutional violence visited upon inmates as a prime cause of the brutality. They recorded the "routine" bruises, scratches, and open wounds inflicted by razors or bites, bone fractures, and missing teeth they observed on inmates. Brutal assaults occurred in spaces that escaped the guards' supervisory gaze, such as showers or the exercise yard, which guards watched via surveillance cameras but refused to patrol or to enter, claiming it was too "dangerous." In a "lawless, two-meter zone" of the yard, youths divided themselves into gangs and "marked out their territory with spit." If the point of prisons is to produce the docile bodies and disciplinary individuals whose internalization of regulatory regimes end in supervision of themselves, a disturbing pattern had developed at the Youth Detention Center. Inmates subverted the methods and rules designed to transform and improve them. Many youths were so terrorized that they refused to leave their cells for class, training, work, or the exercise yard. Did this represent a new heightened level of panopticism or the total abdication of panopticism?

Authors of the manifesto decried penalties imposed by the prison's Disciplinary Council as arbitrary. They noted that penalties focused largely on the protection of penitentiary personnel rather than on safeguarding the young prisoners. This was all the more troublesome as sixteen-year-olds were housed with twenty-one-year-olds and 60 percent of the detainees were held pending trial and had not been convicted of any offense. Although minor detainees represented less than one-tenth of the prison population, they made up a disproportionate 40 percent of those subject to disciplinary action by the prison's Disciplinary Council. The reasons for disciplinary action involved almost exclusively verbal violence, insults, and threats to guards and, to a lesser extent, extortion and violence to other inmates.

That manifesto precipitated a 1999 visit to the Center by the Socialist Justice Minister Elisabeth Guigou, who ordered immediate changes and released substantial resources to effect them. This occurred in the context of fierce and intensifying public debate about the purpose of incarceration. Debate was fueled by a best-selling exposé of the horrific conditions in one emblematic prison, la Santé. Three widely publicized state commission reports that appeared in 2000 vehemently criticized a penitentiary system deemed unworthy of a modern Republic, much less the vaunted country of the Rights of Man.[27] As a result, the Youth Detention Center was substantially reorganized. The detainees were grouped into small living units, where twenty-two supervisors (*surveillants*) were recruited to continuously monitor approximately sixty detainees, who were given access to recreational facilities and enhanced school and training programs by teachers accredited by the National Education Ministry.

Visiting the Prison

I visited the prison several times. A senior probation and integration counselor, Viviane Marshal, who headed the monthly meetings of the Paris Incarceration Commission in 2001, accompanied me to Fleury-Mérogis in April 2001, my first tour. Her superior, Maude Dayet, section head of the Juvenile Quarter, met me and explained that prison reforms had allowed them to individualize sentences, reduce violence, and reconceptualize the profession of "guard." Did I notice the terminology? She contrasted the outmoded term "guards [*gardiens*] who watch cows" with the "supervisors" (surveillants) of minors age thirteen to eighteen who received special training, wore civilian clothing, and volunteered to work in the small units. She described herself as the architect of the reorganization and explained that it was informed by her background. With an advanced degree in criminology and a master's thesis in juvenile justice, she was deeply implicated in the debates on the French prison as a "Republican institution." She also raised the issue of professional integrity:

> Our profession is not valued. On the outside we are not considered supervisors, we're guards, the public completely rejects us. Inside a lot has changed. Compared to the police, just look at the violence of an arrest, ours is a very humane profession. It is in our interest to have things go well. We manage human misery and must show humanity. The reality is we see the same faces because there is a high rate of recidivism. We want them to get training and education.[28]

After lunch, I had the opportunity to meet the probation and integration counselors who work with minors serving sentences after conviction. It is telling that the counselors with whom I spoke were adamant about distinguishing their work from that of the supervisors. One counselor emphasized that "we are not supervisors." He contrasted the regenerative, therapy-driven work the counselors did with minors to the authority-based, containment measures implemented by supervisors. He insisted that the counselors' task was to facilitate a consciousness of the futility of physical violence, the need for punishment in certain circumstances, and the reason for detention. In fact, counselors worked only with those who were serving postjudgment sentences. Apart from close observation by the prison supervisors, the 60 percent of inmates doing time pending trial received no psychological counseling because they had not yet been tried. Prison supervisors provided the close evaluations of their behavior that were the subject of the debriefing session.

Maude Dayet permitted me to attend the debriefing session on the detainees' behavior. That day, fifty-seven minors were in prison, 80 percent of whom were held pending trial.[29] The weekly debriefing reports were critical because they determined the boys' movement among the living units, which were differentiated by four regulatory regimes extending from the strictest to the most liberal. The evaluation of behavior relied on supervisors' continuous observation and evaluation of the small groups of boys assigned to them. Rewards included free TV at specified hours and degrees of access to activity rooms and sports areas. Punishments involved the withdrawal of privileges, such as taking meals with others, participating in activities, and using spaces other than the exercise yard. Penal offenses were meticulously catalogued and minutely subdivided into three degrees: 1) assaults and prison breaks, 2) insults and threats, and 3) refusal to follow orders, followed by a correspondingly detailed set of punishments, such as solitary confinement (for those older than sixteen) or loss of visitation rights.

What were the criteria for judging good versus bad behavior and according coveted privileges such as free TV? When she was interviewed by Cécile Prieur, a *Le Monde* journalist, Maude Dayet responded that "hygiene, politeness, assiduity in school . . . these were the behavioral goals."[30] When we spoke, she was less guarded saying, "Oh we don't claim to be able to succeed but we try to teach them the basics that they don't have. For instance, like learning to say hello and good-bye, getting up at the same time of the day, keeping their cell in good order. The problem is that we are at the end of a long chain of failures . . . parents, National Education, éducateurs, so we have to start again at zero."[31]

The prison day began early and was tightly scheduled around daily rituals of meals, classes or work, exercise, and activities permitted as rewards. Prison officials and some social workers I interviewed outside the SEAT presented this routine as an important structuring regimen for adolescents from poor families. One social worker recommended prison for a sixteen-year-old youth from Cameroon: "I visited the family's apartment. It stank to high heaven, there were bugs crawling all over, and eight people were crammed into two rooms. At least in prison it will be clean and he will have regular meals."

As Drew Leder has eloquently argued, the disordering of temporality that weighs heavily on adult inmates in the United States is also at work here, particularly for those minors who were foreign, spoke little French, and were detained pending trial for immigration violations or misdemeanor offenses.[32] They may be particularly susceptible to the shift from the infinitely elastic notion of time they have lived in the outside world to the rigid, static clock time of prison. The collapse of a "textured temporal field" bound up with individual histories, future projects, and social networks must surely pose a greater risk to those in France without family, who came seeking economic opportunity through school or work and ended up in prison after breaking the law on Parisian streets. Even life on the street is "nonetheless a life, with its own goals, rhythms, activities, and interactions."[33]

Time in the service of a future goal and enhanced potential becomes an instrument of disempowerment when controlled by the state. Trapped in a painful present, many of the adult inmates interviewed by Leder found ways to reclaim time by escaping productively into the past or constructing a future through study and work.[34] In the Youth Detention Center, 80 percent awaited trial and were unsure whether their detention would be extended and for how long. The indeterminacy of detention before sentencing made it difficult for these teenagers to escape a painful present. Given the lack of opportunity for legal work or access to school and training programs for undocumented migrants and the 2002 bilateral agreement between Romania and France to send unaccompanied minors home, release offered little hope.

What it was impossible to know except by visiting the Youth Center is that all of the boys in detention on that day were from working-class or underprivileged families of immigrant or foreign ancestry, a fact not mentioned in the press. This sheds new light on the normative imperative to socialize and civilize teenage boys. If one is to believe Youth Center authorities, the disciplinary regimen relied on rules as a moral imperative to instill values and prevent violence as well as a pragmatic means to impose order and affirm authority. But these rules have specific racial and ethnic overtones. To redeem delinquents, it is necessary "to start from zero" and to resocialize them. The focus is on individual maladaptive behavior and immigrant parenting practices—by implication absent fathers and protective mothers—as the problem, rather than the socioeconomic structures in which the teenagers are submerged. The debriefing sessions permitted supervisors to continually sort and re-sort inmates into categories of educability based on their weekly evaluations. The constant threat of movement from the most liberal units to the most restricted reinforced the behavioral norms considered ideal. Supervisors noted approvingly those boys who were "calm" and "quiet." Excessive "impulsiveness," "rapid mood shifts," and "willful isolation" were viewed negatively and recorded as suspect behaviors. One supervisor suggested moving a Chinese teenager out of the basic unit and into the more structured unit with fewer privileges because he kept a "dirty cell and didn't participate in activities or exercise in the yard." When Maude Dayet pointed out that he spoke no French, her colleague retorted, "Yes, he is in a bad way, but how will he evolve?" The fact that the prison provided no classes in French as a foreign language was beside the point. Given the importance of language mastery as a constituent element of culture, non-French-speaking foreigners were much more easily positioned outside of the social order and risked having their behaviors read as incorrigible.

The logics that fueled the massive expansion of the U.S. prison complex in the 1980s were at work here, including a punitive individualism that frames offending primarily or exclusively in terms of individual choice. The newly redesigned units in the juvenile detention center represent a distilling of this logic within the larger prison system as offering a set of rational and humane alternatives framed in turn by an ideology of choice. This logic rests on a larger neoliberal or neo-Darwinian conception of public order in which the young men who make the wrong choices are deemed unfit for civic life. The detention facility is part of the technology of responsibilization applied to all young people, including those who land in prison for immigration violations after fleeing political persecution, those who commit minor public order offenses or petty misdemeanors, and those who are wrongly accused. Responsibilization is a process whereby all are obliged to be free and to enact their lives as if they truly had a range of choices.[35]

Based on what I observed in the debriefing session, prison surveillants viewed any display of masculine mettle, through body language or verbal rejoinders such as the ritual insults or scatological references that are common currency in street culture as a sign of insubordination, as subject to punishment. The boys were expected to learn to exorcize defiance, suppress bad attitudes, accept the strict limits, and project at least an outward respect for authority. The enactment of docility was a prerequisite for privileges and survival rituals in the total institution of the prison. It nonetheless belied a more complex reality. Violence and extortion remained problems at the Center despite the 1999 reforms. Two surveillants, even in the presence of a foreign observer, mentioned incidents involving extortion and fights that had occurred the preceding week outside their purview, suggesting that the supervisory gaze remained selective at best. One noted the psychological fragility of an inmate who was both immature and physically small for his age. He had refused to leave his cell until two older inmates had offered him their protection. This implies that, in some instances, the same dynamics of group violence, the withdrawal of the state, and vigilante self-protection associated with the so-called "lawless neighborhoods" were reengaged in prison. The Youth Detention Center is the destination for detainees from the juvenile courts in Paris and the surrounding departments.

The very problems that contributed to detainees' incarceration were also mimetically reproduced in prison and fueled both frustration and despair. Their low academic levels hampered their performance in the Center's classes and exams. Even those who did well must have interpreted the prominently displayed posters in the prison stairwells advertising "careers" for unskilled, manual labor (*manutentionnaires*) as a cruel taunt. Social alienation, economic marginality, and psychological instability made extortion and violence unavoidable, if less frequent. The return to and reintegration within neighborhoods and schools after detention tended to extend the exclusionary tactics of the prison. Social workers and counselors found it extremely difficult to persuade public school principals to readmit teenagers who had served time even for short sentences lasting several weeks, despite the fact that school attendance is mandatory until age sixteen. Although school officials rarely refused directly, they resorted to other tactics, which had the same effect. School files were lost, paperwork was delayed, or decisions were deferred until important deadlines were missed and enrollment was impossible.[36] The undocumented foreigners with no legal papers or adult guardians and little knowledge of French or legal norms constituted a vulnerable and high-risk population at the Center, both as minors and young adults. They were doubly isolated, and those over eighteen were twice punished, subject to the double sentence of imprisonment for penal offenses and, upon release, deportation from France.

In the late 1990s, psychiatrists in the Center expressed grave concern about a special segment of the Center population from eastern Europe, West Africa, and China. These teenagers had entered France illegally, broken the law, were wrongly identified as adults by means of a highly controversial test of skeletal development, sent to immediate trial (*comparution immédiate*), given prison sentences, and incarcerated with eighteen- to twenty-one-year-olds in the Youth Center.[37] This was, in fact, the case of the homeless Gabonese minor who was in jail with Abdellah in May 2003. Without papers or family, he had been identified as a legal adult, sent to immediate trial, and served a year in adult prison at the age of sixteen. After a second arrest, he was granted minority status and sentenced to three weeks in the Youth Detention Center.

One psychiatrist noted that the loss of identity was particularly traumatic since identity constituted the only reference point (repère) remaining after the loss of home and family. Once again, it is instructive to note the French preoccupation with a loss of "social, cultural, and geographical bearings [repères]," particularly in the liminal period of adolescence. "Lacking a solid grounding and a favorable environment, the mourning for traumatic events such as war and massacres cannot begin and their ability to adapt is stifled."[38] Counselors and psychiatrists noted depression, insomnia, loss of appetite, despair, and self-mutilation as common reactions to trauma among inmates. They warned that suicides would likely result. This was not an idle threat. French rates of suicide among detainees have skyrocketed, and those in French prisons are seven times higher than the population as a whole.[39]

A Second Visit to Prison in 2003

In June 2003 I made my second trip to the prison. The day before this trip, I had spent time with the Paris juvenile court president, Hervé Hamon, who noted that the repressive political climate following the 2002 elections had led to the first-time use of fast-track judgment hearings (*comparution à délais rapprochés*) by the juvenile prosecutor's office in Paris. Consulting his figures for 2002 and the first trimester of 2003, he remarked that there had been fifteen such hearings per trimester, the average of one per courtroom. Although this was not excessive, the problem was that most of the expedited trials had been accompanied by detention orders and all involved foreign minors, the vast majority from North and West Africa. He worried that if prison became the unique warehouse for underprivileged immigrants and unaccompanied foreigners, the court would become a mere punitive apparatus bereft of any rehabilitative promise.

With this in mind, I traveled to the prison, accompanied by Caroline, who, like all SEAT caseworkers, was required to visit and evaluate incarcerated minors during her supervision. During our visit to the Youth Detention Center, Caroline was scheduled to meet with three minors, two of whom were awaiting trial while the third was nearing the end of a three-year sentence. All three were undocumented minors—one from China, one from Mali, and one from the "former Yugoslavia"—and only two spoke passable French. These meetings would form the substance of Caroline's report to the court. The pretrial counseling she provided was revealing. In spite of the 2000 legislation to enhance the presumption of innocence, no such presumption existed for the adolescents sitting in prison. After reminding them of the "facts" with which they were charged, Caroline's first questions to these boys concerned the reasons for their detention. This was the moment for them to explain what detention had meant to them and to show that they had put distance between themselves and the offense.

We visited the Malian youth, Amadou, whose case was complicated because he had been implicated in a violent altercation between the police and a group of youths that had resulted in injury to a gendarme. He had been identified as the main perpetrator and incarcerated pending trial. He had never been identified as at-risk or benefited from a social assistance case, in spite of the fact that French authorities had deported both of his parents to Mali because they had no legal papers. They were forced to leave behind four of their youngest children in the care of a family member who had a residence card. Amadou had spent almost five months in detention and had a court date scheduled for early July. Caroline warned him that the judge could give him a sentence greater than time already served, and it would be in his best interest to show that he had a plan in place. How did he see his future? What did he want to do? He replied that he wanted to spend summer vacation in Mali, return to France, and didn't know after that. Caroline insisted that this would not be well received by the court; he had to show that he had support. She began to read the preliminary version of the report she had already written and planned to present to the judge. Despite Amadou's low scholastic level and expulsion from school, Caroline had found an apprenticeship center willing to accept him in a remedial section and a state facility to house him. Amadou stopped her repeatedly to ask the meaning of both legal terms and French vocabulary. When Caroline described his behavior before prison as "immature," he asked her to define the word. Although he knew the term *probation*, he did not understand the word *majority* as a reference to legal adulthood. Caroline described the layout of the court and the key personnel. She admonished him to speak out loud and look the judge straight in the eyes, and she warned him again that he should tell the court everything he knew. His naive retort was, "They already know everything." When she asked if he had any questions, he wondered if she could arrange for his eldest sister to visit him. Five months was a long time to be without a visit from family.

GOING TO TRIAL, GETTING JUDGED

In contrast to Amadou, who was scheduled for trial in the juvenile court, the best outcome a youth in pretrial detention could hope for was a quick release and a judgment hearing in chambers, because in that venue judges are constrained as to what punitive sentences they can impose. In February 2001 I observed such an outcome in Judge Boyers's Eleventh District courtroom. It involved Abdel, a young man of Algerian ancestry, who was arrested as a runaway in a stolen car with Partha, a young woman from a South Asian family. The teenagers admitted to stealing a car while on the run, driving without a license, and snatching a credit card from an elderly woman after shoving her to the ground. The charge of theft was aggravated by three circumstances: with violence, in a group, and on a vulnerable person by virtue of age. Although neither had a police record, Abdel had spent two weeks at the juvenile facility in the Fleury-Mérogis prison in the summer of 2000, and Partha was given probation pending the court hearing. I was struck by this proceeding in part because of the reactions of Judge Boyer and the defense attorney. Both agreed that the case was custom-made for the 1945 ordinance. What did they mean? Was this a judgment on the redemptive potential of the young people in this case? Was it a statement on the 1945 legislative text itself as a still viable exemplar of the rehabilitative ideal and the individual-centered penology that its creators intended? Or conversely, did it speak to more exceptional situations in which the law's promise of assistance and prevention could be realized?

Before pronouncing judgment, the judge asked for the court-appointed attorney's observations. That day the attorney was the dynamic founder and director of the Juvenile Defense Bureau, Marie-France Ponelle. She informed the judge that both teenagers were enrolled in school and had admitted their guilt. She urged that the cases be tried together, and she argued for clemency given the mitigating circumstances. Looking at Abdel and using the familiar form of address, she said, "You had trouble adjusting to France. You were evolving and had possibilities. What happened? There were family problems. You ran away. It was dangerous. Crazy even." She characterized the delinquency of both teenagers as a "lapse," a temporary loss of family "structure," and of the bearings (repères) vital to normal childhood development:

ATTORNEY: Abdel is more mature now. There was an emotional slip and no structure. I ask you to give them both a solemn warning. They have taken hold. They were not equipped by life but now they can face challenges. He is enrolled in an apprenticeship program and she is pursuing secretarial studies. They got a good shock and are on the right road.

On the charge of possession of stolen property and underage driving, Judge Boyer pronounced them guilty, issued a warning, and returned them to their parents, a lenient, rehabilitative judgment. In judging the second case of aggravated theft, she was clearly concerned given the serious charges. She reminded them:

JUDGE: We do incarcerate minors when cases are serious because it is appropriate when there is physical violence. The victim will always be marked by this. She will always be afraid when she sees young people. She will think they are all bad.

Judge Boyer drew on the éducatrice's report to highlight the risks Abdel and Partha faced, to reframe the period of deviancy as exceptional, and to justify a judgment based on rehabilitation. Abdel's distress was caused by ongoing problems with a difficult stepfather and the sudden death of his grandmother. Partha's suffering resulted from the loss of her mother and a culturally repressive household. Before rendering judgment in the second case, she once again asked for the attorney's observations:

ATTORNEY: It's a pleasure to defend young people with a high intellectual level. They got in with the wrong people. They were both without protection, in a very vulnerable state, they put themselves at risk. That period is over. They need help. We will not solve anything by more punishment. I ask for a warning so that it will not affect his future.

The judge accepted her recommendation but warned Abdel.

JUDGE: It is important that you are able to speak honestly, you have accepted the wrong, and that you have put distance between your past and the present. If not, you would have been tried by the juvenile correctional court. You have had no new cases and you are capable of saying this is serious, I am afraid, I accept responsibility, I want to improve. We are testing your ability to respect the limits of the law. I have here a copy of your apprenticeship contract. You are leading a normal life. You could have ended up in prison, but I am pleased with this result.

This case was "custom-made" for the ordinance of 1945 because the delinquency of the young people could be interpreted as a temporary lapse on the metaphoric road to a normal adulthood. The defendants admitted their guilt, recognized the "facts of the case," and accepted responsibility for their actions. They also reinforced the authority of the court and the rightness of its decisions. In so doing, they claimed the rights and obligations that are the legal entitlements of French political subjects. They had "evolved" and changed, demonstrating the perfectibility of the adolescent maturation process. Their respectful demeanor and meek acquiescence allowed Abdel and Partha to isolate serious offenses from their sociocultural background without challenging the social and moral order the court must defend. The nature of the problem was construed as the result of broken families and deficient parenting that were serious enough to constitute sufficient extenuating circumstances. In contrast, "bad" youth were those who repeatedly tested limits, challenged authority, and broke rules and in so doing revealed their character flaws, lack of personal bearings, and overall incorrigibility. They refused to acknowledge the "facts" or to take responsibility, and they resisted attempts on the part of various social professionals to put them back on the right road. "Bad" youth were at risk to offend again and, as the judge put it, to end up in prison.

The legal mandate for the protection of at-risk children also implied protection from the "backward" beliefs and practices in Muslim families like that of Abdel, whose stepfather, we learned in the hearing, used to whip him as a discipline measure, and of Partha, whose father earned the disapproval of the judge and the attorney by positioning himself as the obsessive guardian of her sexual purity. The court framed and ultimately excused their deviance as individual responses to a set of abnormal pressures and losses originating within the home. The psychologization of delinquency treated the problem as an individual disorder associated at best with aberrant one-time behaviors or at worst with pathological defects that are traced to cultural differences. In this view, pathologies were spatialized and associated with a culture of poverty rooted in the segregated ethnic enclaves of bad neighborhoods and public housing projects. The court did not view the problem as a social and systemic product with deep roots in French colonial and postcolonial histories or discrimination within state institutions.

CONCLUSION

What do the cases of Abdellah, Antoine, Abdel, and Partha teach us about French notions of social personhood and the individual-centered model of rehabilitation still in play at court? French court personnel are recruited largely from the mainstream middle classes and draw on dominant, class-based understandings of childhood development and maturation. Origin and place in a social, cultural, and spatial sense are integral to this understanding. Children begin as clean slates. They are capable of developing normal personalities and internalizing correct norms when and if they come from the right families and locations.

The cases of Abdel and Partha were viewed as "custom-made for the ordinance of 1945" because they presented an exceptional set of conditions in which the rehabilitative and individual-centered mission of the law could be applied. Their offenses were framed as aberrant, one-time behaviors, caused by catastrophic loss and abnormal family pressures. They involved correctable mistakes. The case also turned on issues of individual choice and responsibility in the face of cultural pathologies. Before the hearing, the éducatrice had informed Judge Boyer of the strong objection of Partha's father to her intimate relationship with Abdel. In his court testimony, the father decried his daughter's disobedience and moral laxity. Although parental authority is clearly central to most hearings, the judge dismissed his objections, "which have no place here." She and the defense attorney made no effort to hide their support for the individual rights of young immigrant women to defy the backward social conservatism of their fathers (or mothers), to get an education, and to control their own sexuality. They rewarded the free choice of immigrant youth to be accountable and to separate their behavior from the negative cultural traits the court associated with their families. Despite their attorney's glowing assessment of their "high scholastic levels," Abdel and Partha were both placed in low-level vocational tracks with few outlets on the job market—he in an apprenticeship program and she in a secretarial track.

The case of Abdellah also turned on individual choice in the face of cultural disorientation. The éducatrice focused less on the teenagers' economic marginality than on the damage to the primordial ties of place, blood, and culture. For her, Abdellah's problems resulted from his estrangement from his Senegalese culture of origin. At the same time, both she and the judge deemed it important to return him "home" to a father who had neglected him and kept him out of school. The court put the onus of choice and responsibility on the teenager himself, despite difficult odds, to respect the terms of his probation and to stay out of prison.

The position of éducateurs relative to judges and families is also significant. As a profession they have achieved a measure of autonomy from magistrates and other social professionals by fervently defending the rehabilitative ideal. In the immediate postwar period, young male éducateurs from modest social backgrounds boosted their claim to expertise through intensive engagement with families and the appropriation of psychoanalytical models of diagnosis deemed appropriate to treat troubled individuals. Over a forty-year period culminating in the 1990s, the credentials and training changed along with the working conditions and the clientele. The profession attracted more women and solidified its middle-class image through the requirement of two years of university study. At the same time, the young women who began work in the 1990s faced a very different political context and judicial understandings surrounding delinquency. The specter of a "new" delinquency of exclusion, associated with children from marginalized Muslim families of North and West African origin, has come to be understood as both an enduring phenomenon and a more threatening social category. The overrepresentation of "immigrant" children in penal cases and prison is based on a conception of the minor as determined by his or her sociocultural milieu, a notion entirely consistent with French understandings of childhood and family. Even court personnel opposed to the new penality tend to contrast the problem child of the past, whose psychological or social vulnerability make him a subject for assistance and rehabilitation to the delinquent youth of the present whose cultural difference and marginality make him or her an object suitable for control and accountability.

In the next chapter we examine the civil and penal hearings held within chambers. These are central to judicial and public debates on the quality of judgments, the impartiality of judges, and the due process protections extended to the minors and their families, who are subject to the supervisory gaze of the juvenile court.

6 RENDERING JUSTICE IN CHAMBERS

NEXT, WE ENTER THE JUDGE'S CHAMBERS, the controversial venue where the impartiality of juvenile judges and the judicial rigor of proceedings have come under scrutiny. Critics of the procedures in chambers focus on judges' absolute powers, the lack of a true adversarial debate, the arbitrary nature of judgments, and the personalized relations between judges and minors that compromise the legal norm of neutrality.

When courts open files on minors, there is an immediate and ongoing categorization of a case as penal or civil. This occurs even when a judge orders both penal sanctions and social assistance measures for the same child. Here, I group penal cases by the themes that emerged based on the most common charges filed against juvenile offenders. These include (1) public order violations, such as rioting and loitering, as well as threats, insults, and assaults on public authorities, such as Paris police; (2) aggravated theft; (3) and cases in which non-Western cultural differences were believed to play a contributing role in the misbehavior of the minors. Some of the cases I discuss are representative of broader trends in juvenile justice and others are atypical but instructive in other ways.

In the civil cases, I focus on the factors used to determine what constitutes child endangerment as well as who is deemed responsible for putting a child at risk. I ask what circumstances entitle children to protection and what consequences abusive or neglectful parents suffer as a result of their maltreatment of minors. Class and cultural origin figure implicitly in psychiatric evaluations, social worker reports, school records, and judicial decisions. Both class and culture affect the outcome of hearings but in ways that were largely unacknowledged by court personnel.

CONSIDERING CASE STUDIES

I adopt a case study approach because this is the way court personnel organize and manage their work, as well as categorize and track troubled youth. Although few judges or éducateurs at the Paris court referred to specific cases by name, most remembered the details of many cases, endlessly comparing and contrasting them as a way to take the pulse of the court and, in the words of Judge Boyer, "of the wider society." State officials also viewed cases in a similar fashion. The number and type of cases juvenile courts handle are central to the periodic evaluations court presidents and Ministry of Justice inspectors make of individual judges and juvenile courts. The proportion of penal to civil cases, the caseload per judge, the number of new cases opened versus old cases pending, the type of penal sanctions imposed and rehabilitative measures ordered—all of these case-related data are carefully logged and repeatedly scrutinized. I begin with an emblematic case involving the Temba family. This case illustrates how social class, family structures, and ethnoracial categories intersect with psychology, economics, culture, and the law to shape court proceedings.

"YOU NEED TO MAKE YOUR CHILDREN TAKE RESPONSIBILITY"

In mid-December 2003, I observed penal hearings in the Eleventh District chambers of Judge Bondy, where I met, for the second time, members of the Temba family from the Central African Republic who fled political upheaval to settle in France. The juvenile correctional court had tried and acquitted the eldest son, Jacques, of aggravated rape two years earlier but imposed psychiatric treatment as a condition of his release (see Chapter 7). Madame Temba was already well known to court personnel, who thought she was "unbalanced" because of her outlandish histrionics in court. She was under psychiatric care and the entire family had earned a reputation as "difficult," a moniker that implied continuous court supervision. This time Jacques and his youngest brother, eleven-year-old Michel, were accused of assaulting an elderly deaf woman at a Paris municipal pool who, according to the police report, had objected to their rough play and looked disapprovingly at their big sister. The prosecutor's office had taken a hard line in light of the victim's age and disability. The deputy prosecutor issued an arrest warrant for Jacques and, under new rules, requested that Michel's hearing come before the formal correctional court rather than in the judge's chambers despite his young age. Judge Bondy took the position that such an approach was too harsh. Citing the added complication of dealing with "a hysterical mother," she scheduled the hearing in chambers. Only Michel, his mother, and father appeared, explaining that Jacques, now almost eighteen and a legal adult, had returned to Africa "to help his aunt."

The judge drew on police reports to establish the facts of the case, juxtaposing statements from the elderly woman with those from Michel, who was fiercely supported by his mother. Michel insisted that the elderly woman had glared at their older sister, demanded that the boys stop their water fight, insulted them, and argued with and then struck Jacques. In contrast, the woman told the police that she had asked the boys to stop splashing. They called her a "bitch" and attacked her, hitting her in the face and pulling her hair. A doctor documented bruises serious enough to warrant an incapacitation order of two days, the primary means by which the court assessed the severity of an assault and determined the penalty. She refused to testify at the hearing out of fear. Michel and his mother insisted that Jacques, not Michel, hit the woman, but only in self-defense.

The judge situated the case within an overall family history characterized by social dysfunction and deficient parenting. She recalled Jacques's psychological instability as well as the problems of the boys' first cousin, Robert, who also had a court hearing later that afternoon. His mother, Madame's younger sister, had gone to the United States, proof, according to the judge, that she "thought only about herself, not about her children." Finally, Judge Bondy confronted Michel's parents and quoted from district social worker reports who described "Michel's gang," a group of "incorrigible boys" reputed "to terrorize the neighborhood." She related an incident described to the social worker by neighborhood youth in which Michel attempted to steal a purse but failed and narrowly escaped arrest by hiding in a local bakery. Looking pointedly at Michel, she asked, "You don't remember that?" Unfazed, Michel glared at her and defiantly retorted "liars," provoking the hearty laughter of his parents.

When the judge responded stonily that "Michel will not be amused by the judgment at his trial," his mother angrily blamed her sons' problems on the overcrowded conditions in the "squalid hotel" where she lived with her four children (since Jacques's departure), a makeshift public housing facility similar to those in which nearly fifty residents, mostly women and children also from Sub-Saharan Africa, perished in suspicious fires in the summer of 2005. Madame Temba recounted the discrimination she faced from Paris municipal authorities who, she claimed, had called her "a dirty black" and repeatedly refused to provide decent subsidized housing despite "her heritage" as the grand-daughter of a French citizen. She grew more and more upset: "I was repatriated from Africa for nothing, to live in a filthy hotel. I wanted a good education. Look at my younger sister taking university courses in the United States and my other sister married and well established in Africa. We have been abandoned. I don't have a life here." The judge retorted: "Madame, you need to make your children take responsibility for their mistakes and to give them the proper bearings (repères) in life. They don't respect the rules. You are going to make them lifelong victims if you don't."

The Tembas were assigned a court attorney they had not encountered until their appearance that day. I met their attorney outside chambers as she was reviewing the file for the first time just before proceeding. When Judge Bondy asked for her input, the attorney had none. The judge indicted Michel for assault but suspended judgment pending rehabilitation. The use of the familiar *tu* form of address, normally appropriate for a youngster, in the formal indictment of an eleven-year-old defendant, gave the proceedings an unreal effect. The judge ordered a cultural mediation consultation with an African ethnopsychiatrist, justifying this approach on the basis of Jacques's mental instability and Michel's growing incorrigibility. Studying the court file, she asked, "Why is Madame so upset? It does not make sense." Madame Temba reacted strongly, saying, "I get mistreated [by the housing authorities]. They say 'if you're not happy, go back to where you came from.' They tear up my papers . . . Jacques isn't crazy. We aren't [mentally] ill. The problem is that he has a mother who lives in a hotel not fit for dogs." Looking at me, the judge conceded that the hotel in question was so bad it had made the newspapers, but she then turned back to Madame Temba, reassuring her that an ethnopsychiatrist would have particular expertise in African culture and language, which would help with all their cultural difficulties: "He is familiar with your country. Your son is not acknowledging his role in these incidents and his place in his own history." The mother acquiesced but added, "There is no one to help us, Jacques is going to turn eighteen and we will still be in that hotel. I am French by blood like you."

THE COURT FILE

This case illustrates what Bourdieu calls "the force of the law."[1] This force is evident in the power of the written case file to inform and condition court proceedings. As part of the judicial archive, it constitutes the official institutional memory of a particular childhood and its encounters with the law. Just as the colonial context worked to delegitimize certain kinds of precolonial voices and texts in imperial archives, the court archive is a depository of history that evolves over time and favors certain voices over others in the construction of individual cases.[2] The individual files archived at court thus constitute a determinate discursive formation in that they reflect the categories of key state actors. Through them the state literally produces the legal and the normal at particular historical moments.

The nature of the archive makes the issue of access to the written file all the more critical. The ability to read what is in the file bears directly on the ability of children and families to contest expert opinion, to refute charges, and to defend their rights. Until 2002, families under court supervision did not have the legal right to examine their own files, in particular the psychiatric evaluations and social worker reports which judges and defense attorneys used extensively to prepare for hearings. Even after 2002, many families were not aware that they could review their court file and even when they do problems remain. Parents with a weak grasp of French, little education, and no background in psychology or law are at pains to decipher the specialized terminology or to evaluate the importance of legal statutes. In the Temba case, the judge relied heavily on the file since she had been assigned to the Eleventh District in 2002. The family history constructed there emphasized Madame Temba's five children by two fathers and her single parenthood during the periods when her Senegalese husband returned to Africa to work. One might ask to what extent the family's "irregular" history, foreign origin, and transnational migratory patterns already in the file conditioned the judge's view of the case and of Michel's personality before the hearing began.

PENAL HEARINGS IN CHAMBERS

Police and Youth: Challenges to Public Authority

Strained relations between police and young men "hanging out" in the street or in apartment stairwells resulted from the frequent ID checks that rapidly degenerated into verbal and/or physical confrontations and often ended in their jailing on charges of rioting, and resisting police orders (*rébellion*), as well as insulting, threatening, and/or assaulting public authorities. The number of these cases tried in adult and juvenile courts increased substantially beginning in the mid-1990s, and their numbers continued to rise after 2000. Judges pronounced more severe sentences for these offenses in the 1990s than in the past. For example, between 1994 and 2006 the percentage of prison sentences doubled, the length of prison terms increased, and heavier fines were imposed. Physical assaults against the police actually decreased from a quarter of the total offenses between 1965 and 1984 to a sixth of the total today. Nonetheless, jail sentences for those convicted of assaulting the police soared and now represent more than one-third of all sentences.[3] Of the three most common public order offenses—resisting orders, insulting, and assaulting authorities—the one that increased the most was resisting the police, the least objectively verifiable offense. A new phenomenon emerged, namely civil damage awards made to police who joined the prosecution's case as civil plaintiffs. Claiming the status of victims, the police have constituted themselves as civil plaintiffs in two-thirds of the cases tried. This practice was virtually nonexistent fifteen years ago.[4]

The explanation for the rapid increase in offenses against the police vary. Some blame disaffected and more violent delinquents whereas others point to police tactics in neighborhoods and prosecutorial strategies in the courts rather than criminal behavior.[5] French police behavior was the object of international censure for more than a decade before a center-left legislature voted a law in 2000 to reinforce the presumption of innocence for suspects in criminal cases and the protection of victims seeking restitution. The European Court of Human Rights condemned France for police brutality against suspects during detention in 1992, 1999, and 2004. In the 1999 Selmouni case, the European Court ruled unanimously that France violated article 3 of the European Convention on Human Rights, not only "for inhuman and degrading treatment" of detainees but also for torture.[6] This made France only the second country after Turkey to receive such a finding.[7] Despite the 2000 legislation reforming police custody rules,[8] the 2004 case against France involved a juvenile suspect who, after being brutalized by a policeman, required surgery on his genitals.[9]

Despite the controversy created by the 2000 law, some jurists deemed it critical to modernize the French penal system and to align it with the "principles guaranteed by the European Convention on the Rights of Man."[10] The law stimulated considerable debate among police, magistrates, and attorneys. One the one hand, it had the enthusiastic support of The National Council of French Bars and the Paris Bar. Two of the three unions representing magistrates also supported it. On the other hand, its passage unleashed vehement opposition among police unions who objected strenuously to the new rights of suspects and the time constraints imposed on the police.[11] Police also resented the disruptions caused by defense attorneys who "demanded that interrogations end so they could meet with their client the minute they arrived."[12]

In December 2001, a French judge, Claude Schouler, wrote a book that was published by the leftist Syndicat de la Magistrature (Union of the Magistracy).[13] It denounced abusive police practices as well as the impunity enjoyed by police who broke the law. The book's cover featured a pig in a police uniform and provoked both the fury of police unions and the outrage of the Interior minister, Daniel Vaillant, who filed a defamation suit against the author, the publisher, and the artist of the offending cartoon. The same month that Schouler's book appeared, the Syndicat de la Magistrature, in conjunction with the League of the Rights of Man and the Union of French Attorneys, formed a commission to investigate allegations of police brutality in two suburban departments of Paris and in the twentieth arrondissement within the city. In their widely publicized report[14] the commissioners noted "numerous violations of the law by the police," including recurrent and abusive identity checks, excessive force, racist slurs, and unwarranted arrest and detention in police custody as tactics that provoked youth resistance to public authorities and produced urban conflict. They blamed the prosecutor's office for inadequately controlling the police and criticized judges "who when there is a dispute over the facts, tend to support the police over the accused."[15]

The defendants in the Schouler defamation case were not acquitted until 2006, prompting Aïda Chouk, a member of the commission and then president of the Syndicat de la Magistrature, and Alain Vogelweith, a juvenile judge in suburban Paris, to publish an editorial indicting the justice system's treatment of minority youth during the 2005 youth riots:

> The vast majority of those prosecuted for last fall's events were not delinquents. Rather, they were teenagers struggling to be seen as subjects of the law, who no longer expect much from French institutions, and whose feeling of being humiliated was greatly exacerbated in the dramatic context of the death of two of their own.[16]

In the descriptions of hearings that follow, there is a similar dynamic at work. Arrests for public order violations, such as loitering, rioting, resisting police orders, insults, threats, and assaults on public authorities resulted from confrontations between police and youth in the street. Young men of immigrant and foreign ancestry were rapidly targeted as matter out of place, particularly within the city limits of Paris.

I begin with a February 2001 case in the Eleventh District courtroom. This district, in the central eastern quadrant of the city, is experiencing a rapid influx of new migrants and uneven gentrification. The hearings on that day were representative of those I observed in the four district courtrooms to which I had regular access. All but one of the fifteen defendants were teenaged males, thirteen of whom were of North or West African ancestry whether or not they held French citizenship. The two others were unaccompanied Romanian children (see Chapter 8). The charges included simple and aggravated theft, attempted theft, physical assault, property destruction, possession of stolen property and/or public order violations following confrontations with the police.

I center on a case in which Ahmed, a minor of Algerian ancestry, was accused of rioting and inciting violence during a Bastille Day street party run amok. This case was unusual because Ahmed was not represented by a court-appointed attorney, but by a French attorney of Moroccan ancestry retained and paid for by his father—the only attorney from North Africa hired by the accused's family that I saw in court between January and April 2001. Ahmed's mother and father, his uncle, and his éducatrice all attended the hearing. The presence of the entire family was important given the public perception of the link between juvenile delinquency and cultural handicaps, such as unstable families and absent fathers. The case was also unusual because, in contrast to many of the underprivileged families in court, Ahmed's father, a successful accountant, was educated and middle class.

The case documented a very public accusation of racism leveled at the Paris police after they arrested Ahmed on 14 July 2000. On that evening, he attended a commemoration of the storming of the hated royal prison that had taken place in 1789. A typically rowdy gathering of young men with firecrackers formed in the street to celebrate the holiday. The police report, police court testimony, the accused, his father and uncle all agreed that trouble started when young men from a state residential facility for troubled teenagers, located on the same street, began to hurl firecrackers at passing cars. Neighbors called the police, who confronted Ahmed's two older brothers and cousin—all over eighteen and, therefore, legal adults. When they resisted, a fight ensued in which a policeman was kicked and Ahmed's older brothers and cousin were forcibly restrained. They were arrested, charged, and later convicted of resisting arrest and assaulting police officers. Upon observing the commotion, Ahmed had rushed into the street from the family's apartment with his dog, a pit bull, a fact emphasized in the police report. The police charged him with "riot" and "incitement to riot" and two officers, who had joined the prosecution as civil plaintiffs, were demanding the equivalent of $1,000 in compensatory damages for "moral harm."[17]

Despite his twenty-four-hour detention in police custody, Ahmed refuted the statement of facts presented by the police and insisted on his innocence. Although claims of innocence and disavowals of responsibility tend to be viewed very negatively, in this case the judge took them seriously given the facts presented by the police.

Judge Boyer began the hearing, as is customary, by reading from statements taken by the policemen who claimed that Ahmed "went into the street to insult the police." After reassuring the family that Ahmed was not charged with insult, she questioned Ahmed, whose court testimony echoed his police deposition. He insisted that he had immediately taken the dog back inside the family apartment when instructed to do so by the police, and then he had returned to the street: "I never insulted anyone. I just told them [his brothers and cousins] to calm down." After determining that the teenager's pit bull was castrated and registered by law, the judge read from the police report describing a confrontation between the police and the young men that expanded rapidly to include a crowd of neighborhood families. They angrily challenged and surrounded the police, who felt threatened and called for backup.

Judge Boyer asked the officer present to describe what Ahmed had done. He replied: "He was yelling insults, inciting the crowd and his brothers to rise up against us." Here the policeman's reference to Ahmed's "brothers" [in the 'hood] is strategic as the term is loaded. On the one hand, it indexes the important role of older brothers in North African families in public housing projects, where a strong divide between female indoor space and male public space assigns them the primary responsibility for younger siblings when outside.[18] The term *brother* signifies a kinship idiom where age mates are reclassified as brothers and sisters and incorporated within a fictive unit understood as the neighborhood family. This term was also used to promote the potentially beneficial impact big brothers could have in local anticrime initiatives by watching out for younger children, insisting that they attend school and avoid bad associations. On the other hand, the term *brothers* is also linked to the gang leader (*caïd*), a symbol of an illicit parallel economy based on drugs and stolen goods. It evokes the disaffected second generation of "immigrant" youth stuck in the projects, who initiate rather then discourage the young in deviant behavior. They are the oppressive guardians of their sisters' sexual purity. They disturb the moral and social order by initiating violent antipolice riots and destroying resonant symbols of public property. The 2002 state report on delinquency came to the extraordinary conclusion that even big brothers who succeeded in school were problematic role models. Why? According to the commissioners, "Because the big brother is condemned to low-paid, temporary jobs and, for that reason, is unable to leave home, he exemplifies an image of rejection for the young generation."[19] Here the apartment building was not subsidized housing but was located in a multiethnic district of the city in which underprivileged and upwardly mobile families of non-European ancestry, from North and West Africa and China, live alongside their middle-class French counterparts. The term *brothers* was intended to connote the loyalties that bind "immigrants" to kin and clan over the nation and the Republic. The crux of the case was that at a strategic moment, the arrival of police reinforcements, Ahmed had screamed, "Don't let yourselves get taken!"

In both the police record and his court testimony, one of the police officers expressed fury at the allegations of racism leveled at him and the law enforcement community. He made emphatic reference to a cultural expression of frustration and anger that, judging by his tone and affect, he clearly found both backward and repugnant. He described an elderly Algerian woman in the crowd "who completely undressed a little girl, yelling, 'this is what the French did to her daughter in Algeria,'" a reference to the use of torture by French paratroopers against Algerian resistance fighters, both men and women, during their war for independence from French colonial control. It is possible that this woman expressed personal grievances or referred to wrongs inflicted on Algerians and their French supporters. The Algerian war had resurfaced powerfully just a few weeks before when, in a June 2000 interview with *Le Monde* journalist Florence Beauge, Louisette Ighilahriz described her brutal torture and repeated rape by members of General Jacques Massu's 10th Paratrooper Division. The French generals Massu, Bigeard, and Aussaresses, who directed the war, all publicly responded afterward, reigniting debates about the lessons of the French-Algerian war.[20] Although the policeman did not mention it in court, the police report described another woman who was "overcome with an attack of hysteria" and threw herself "on the sidewalk flailing and shrieking." The policeman's attorney, provided by the state, insisted that Ahmed's words alone were "a serious incitement to violence" and added that, like his brothers and cousin, he was guilty and should be made to pay damages to the police.

Judge Boyer next invited Ahmed's father to describe his role in the confrontation because he had not been formally questioned by the police. Looking directly at the officer present, he explained calmly that the police had punched him and thrown him violently to the ground when he attempted to break their "stranglehold" on his eldest son who "suffered from physical problems," a condition the judge later explained to me was a congenital heart murmur. He also referred to the incident with the little girl, insisting that she was not undressed but in her pajamas because it was bedtime. When the judge asked the father if Ahmed was a behavior problem, he demurred, saying, "Like all kids these days, not without problems but nothing serious."

The judge next asked Ahmed's attorney for his observations. He used the stylistic elegance, rhetorical flourish, and subtle innuendo characteristic of French trial lawyers to excellent effect, impressing the judge, her clerk, and the social worker with both his manner and strategy. He emphasized that the original incident was not provoked by his client but by the "problem youth" in the state facility. He effectively contrasted the delinquents under mandatory state supervision with his innocent client, who lived at home with a two-parent family which, although of immigrant ancestry, was resolutely middle class. He adroitly raised the issue of police discrimination and brutality by insinuating, without explicitly mentioning racial or ethnic origin, that they chose to let the real perpetrators go and to target his Maghrebi clients for arrest. He stressed that "despite the perhaps overzealous police response" his client had "acted responsibly" (locking up the dog) and "with restraint" (going peaceably with the police):

> Let's remember the circumstances. Ahmed is not accused of striking the police. Furthermore where is the incitement to riot? The police first pursued the youth from the state facility and then they saw these young people [that is, of immigrant ancestry]. They felt violently and unjustly challenged. The police started to yell, allowed no exchange, things heated up.

Despite the fact that Ahmed was not enrolled in school or working and had a first-time shoplifting offense, two circumstances usually considered risk factors for delinquency, Judge Boyer acquitted him. She cited a doubt concerning his guilt and explained that his words were "perhaps inappropriate but they do not constitute a penal infraction." She also denied the request for damages for the police officers. Nonetheless, she worried out loud about the impact of her ruling. How would the police in the Eleventh Precinct headquarters view an acquittal and a rejection of a monetary award for their colleagues? In the informal commentary that followed, she and her clerk were effusive about the legal skills and social presentation of Ahmed's attorney. What went unsaid is what is often the most significant, namely that Ahmed's family had the economic means and middle-class demeanor to mount a convincing defense and to deflect the charges in a confrontation with angry and determined police officers. That this case came to trial, given the lack of evidence and discriminatory behavior of the Paris police, suggests that the process of adjudication itself, in the time and expenses required of the accused, constitutes the real punishment.

Issues of authority and respect due police were often at issue in confrontations that ostensibly began with violations of the traffic code such as driving without a helmet or loitering in the street. Police complained about insolent youths and parents who did not control their children. They readily became civil plaintiffs (partie civile) and requested compensatory damages in cases for being verbally insulted or having their physical integrity breached in any way. Juvenile defendants defended their behavior by accusing the police of harassment and/or excessive force. They complained about repeated identity checks (as many as five or six a day); unwarranted arrests and detention in police custody; racist insults against them and their families; systematic use of the familiar *tu* form of address (instead of the polite *vous* form) as a tactic to humiliate and disrespect them; beatings administered on the street or away from public view, in police vans, subway restrooms, or at precinct headquarters; teargassing at close range; harsh treatment in custody including tight handcuffing, slaps, illegal withholding of food and water; and the "accidental" loss of their clothes and shoes, a tactic that was particularly harsh for poor teenagers.

In the cases I observed, judges usually upheld the authority of the police and admonished teenagers to fall in line. One 2001 case in the Eighteenth South District courtroom resulted from an ID check after the police spotted a "known" Algerian youth riding a motor scooter without a helmet. They accused him of refusing to stop and, then, insulting them. He insisted that they never ordered him to stop but had positioned their vehicle to deliberately obstruct his passage, causing the bike to fall.[21] When two officers lunged at him, he admitted defending himself and calling them "dirty pigs." Although the judge noted significant discrepancies in the depositions of the two police officers, she supported them, indicted him, and sent the case for trial to the formal juvenile court. She admonished the defendant: "You cannot refuse an order to stop. The police must be respected. They have a job to do."

The most vulnerable youth were underprivileged foreigners who entered the country illegally and had run afoul of the law. In the Prologue to this book,

I described my first day at court and my observation of an Eighteenth District South case involving an Ethiopian girl of fifteen arrested with a false passport on a train bound for London. The girl I will call Salem had left Greece with the blessing and financial assistance of her mother, a legal migrant and live-in domestic who was working in an upper-class household. I served as the girl's interpreter that first day since no speakers of Amharic or Greek could be found. She had learned English from watching American crime shows and had an impressive legal vocabulary and a sense of righteous indignation to match. She was furious at the police who, she claimed, "had treated her like a common criminal," a phrase she uttered in English. Although the judge did not ask her for details of her forty-eight-hour detention and immediately censored my attempt to elicit this information, she issued a protective order, ensuring that Salem would be placed with social services and entitled to the same rights and privileges as French minors in state care. That teenager was one of the lucky ones.

Three years later in March 2004, the same judge was on duty. The judicial atmosphere had changed and the reception for irregular, unaccompanied minors seemed less hospitable. On that day, a homeless seventeen-year-old Algerian male was in jail on charges of insulting, resisting, and assaulting a police officer. The young man had no legal papers and a long record for theft, possession of stolen property, and illegal loitering. He had been incarcerated four times. The judge grew exasperated with his poor mastery of French but questioned his defense attorney on his allegation of police brutality. She asked his attorney if he had sustained any bruises after being hit with the handle of a gun, as he alleged, and not a nightstick, as the police maintained. She read from the police officer's statement: "He [the accused] spit in my face and when I recuffed him, he kicked me." Looking at the defendant, the judge shook her head, saying: "it serves no purpose to get upset. This is another case to be tried. You're illegal. You will never get a residence permit. You need to go back to Algeria. You are constantly in and out of prison here. We have tried to help you but nothing works." The JI requested a two-month detention order. Looking at the defense attorney, the judge proclaimed, "He's going to prison for two months. There is no point in having an adversarial debate."

Aggravated Theft: A Correctional Offense
In the 1990s French politicians demonstrated an increasing reliance on the law and the courts to settle social problems. Some examples include legislative and penal code reform to permit preventive identity checks in "sensitive" (that is, multiethnic) areas (1993), to create penal reparation measures for first-time

offenders (1993), and to introduce new accelerated adjudication procedures (1995 and 1996). The redefinition of juvenile law clearly reflected this shift. The majority of infractions committed by minors were property offenses and, within that category, the most common infraction was simple theft. However, the 1994 penal code reform transformed the definition of this offense through the addition of new aggravating circumstances, which substantially increased an offender's sentence, if convicted.[22] Theft aggravated by two circumstances—committed by more than one person and accompanied by physical violence—was a common charge in Paris and typically involved two or more male teenagers snatching a cell phone without the use of a weapon and inflicting no serious physical injury to the victim. Such an offense carries a maximum prison sentence of seven years and a 100,000-euro fine. Those convicted of this charge benefit from the excuse of minority that automatically reduces adult sentences by half. In the cases I observed, judges never imposed the maximum penalty. Their decision to hold hearings in chambers where the law restricted the severity of the sentences was itself an indication of leniency.

However, judges did damage to youths in more subtle ways through intrusive supervision without the necessary resources for rehabilitation and insertion within society. Even judges ostensibly opposed to the punitive model seemed less concerned with individual outcomes and more preoccupied with imposing a longer continuum of judicial control over youths. The perception of repeat offenders was particularly revealing. The urgency with recidivism had less to do with the success or failure of treatment programs or court interventions than with eliminating new public risks by identifying the perpetrators, detecting probation violations, and tracking new offenses. The retreat from a concern with outcomes has tended to reinforce the new meaning of penal hearings as a means of control through surveillance rather than as a possibility of transformation through rehabilitation. Perversely, the preoccupation with surveillance, containment, and prosecution has produced heavier caseloads, greater hearing delays and backlogs, making the decision to punish or rehabilitate seem like the luck of the draw depending on any number of factors extraneous to the case—from available state facilities and sufficient staff to implement court orders to the goodwill of school principals.

The new penology exacerbated existing tensions between social class and culture of origin as critical factors in deciding what constitutes at-risk and delinquent behavior and who is held accountable. Both factors affected the outcome of hearings, but in different ways. Of the hundreds of cases I saw from

2000 to 2005, there were only a handful of middle-class children. Their families could and did mobilize substantial resources, both material and symbolic, to protect their children from legal sanctions. The social proximity of middle-class parents to judges could give those parents an advantage in pressing their claims in court. As we shall see, this advantage did not always produce a long-term benefit for their children, particularly when children's rights collided with those of the parents.

In the case that follows, we meet Mustapha, a seventeen-year-old French teenager of Malian ancestry from a poor, single-parent family who had already been labeled a recidivist delinquent by virtue of his police record. He received a summons to appear in chambers of the Nineteenth East District Court of Judge Chaland, a strong opponent of the penal trend. In the hearing, Mustapha would confront François, a teenager from a white bourgeois family who claimed to have been the victim of extortion, harassment, and the theft of a motorcycle helmet. The case was unusual because the boy and his parents had waited more than a year to register a complaint with the police. The prosecutor's office had reviewed the charges and referred the case for investigation to the judge in December 2000. Since Mustapha vociferously refuted the charge of aggravated theft, the hearing was intended to allow both parties to press their respective cases with counsel present.

Judge Chaland briefed me on Mustapha, who had been under her supervision since he was twelve. His mother's health was precarious and he had three cases waiting trial at the juvenile correctional court, two for aggravated theft and a third for extortion and vandalism. Given this record, it was not difficult for her to believe that he had been implicated in the theft. She was both incredulous and scornful that Mustapha's mother had refused a more modern and larger apartment in subsidized housing outside Paris, given the decrepit state of the building in which they lived in the nineteenth arrondissement. The judge explained, "The mother was not cooperating with French social services and adamantly opposed the placement of Mustapha in a state residential facility." Judge Chaland described the "French" family as "bourgeois leftists, the mentality of '68. . . . they chose to live in the nineteenth. The father is a musician and the mother a secretary."

Mustapha, a handsome but sullen young man over six feet tall, arrived with his mother, a haggard, painfully thin woman. Behind them, François, slight and short, was accompanied by both parents. The judge began by establishing the teenagers' legal names and birthdates before asking François for his version of the facts. I was intrigued when François began to speak because he had adopted the intonation and accent of underprivileged youth from the projects (cité). His speech took me back to a birthday party organized for my best friend's daughter, before the second Palestinian Intifada in 2000 soured relations between many French Jews and Muslims. My friend was born in colonial Morocco, grew up in a Jewish family there, spoke Arabic as a first language, and attended French public schools. She left Morocco to settle permanently in France in the 1960s and, when I met her in the late 1980s, was raising her only daughter in the upscale sixteenth arrondissement. She maintained ties to Moroccan families, both Arab and Jewish, who stayed in North Africa or migrated to Great Britain, Canada, and the United States. At the party, her daughter's teenage friends, most of whom were middle-class French Muslims and Jews, regaled us with stories from school. One of the Muslim girls brought down the house when she imitated perfectly the suburban street style. François had adopted a toned-down version of cité style in court in stark contrast to the standard, educated speech of his father, who spoke for the family.

In response to the judge's questions, François admitted that Mustapha had not directly participated in the theft. Rather, he accused him of helping to plan the attack and of threatening François. He and his father competed for control of a narrative portraying Mustapha as a serious threat:

> FRANÇOIS: He didn't participate in the theft, there were two others, but in the planning, yes. He told his buddy I was an easy mark.
>
> FATHER: He [Mustapha] had weapons, two tear gas canisters concealed in his coat. He threatened François.
>
> JUDGE: Did you have trouble with him before this incident?
>
> FRANÇOIS: He threatened me before. He already said he wanted my helmet and would get it.
>
> FATHER: Well before we went to the police, we had problems with him.

The judge asked about Mustapha's role given the lack of a well-established chronology of events.

> FRANÇOIS: The problem is we don't know the others. We only know him.
>
> FATHER: [*interjects*] They hang out at all hours . . . until one or two A.M. Where are the parents? They are always together. They stare you down when you walk by. If we identify the attacker, the result is retribution. We need a guarantee of safety in our own neighborhood.

JUDGE: [*suddenly more attentive*] Are you afraid of him?

FRANÇOIS: [*indirectly makes a serious allegation*] I have seen an attack—a guy covered with blood.

JUDGE: Where did it [the incident in question] happen?

FRANÇOIS: It happened in front of my building. The other guy took off. My father approached him [Mustapha] after it happened. He lied and told him [my father] he was alone.

JUDGE: Does he attend the same school?

FRANÇOIS: No, he got expelled.

At this point, the judge reread Mustapha's declaration to the police in which he insisted on his innocence and that he was alone with François. It was greeted with sneers of disbelief from François's family. The judge was convinced that Mustapha was withholding knowledge of the real perpetrators and clearly supported François's version of facts. She grew increasingly impatient:

JUDGE: There are two completely different versions here. How can you continue to maintain this nonsense about being alone. The helmet didn't take off by itself. What was this [extortion] business about the fifty francs? Didn't you and your buddies surround François and threaten to beat him up if he didn't bring the money? Why don't you admit that there was another person present? You are going to catch it for everyone. Why would François make this up? The truth is you have bad associations and a buddy who gets you into trouble.

At this point, Mustapha's defense attorney interrupted to say that Mustapha was accused of the theft, not attempted extortion. Her direct challenge put Judge Chaland on the defensive and forced her to review the December 2000 proceedings and the police statements.

ATTORNEY FOR MUSTAPHA: Why did the father—because that is who we are really talking about—wait for a year before going to the police? Why do they focus only on Mustapha? They live in the neighborhood, why didn't they question other youth?

ATTORNEY FOR FRANÇOIS: We expect him to give the name of his buddy.

MUSTAPHA'S MOTHER: Because there are things he [François's father] refuses to see.

JUDGE: People have the right to live in peace. We must have your commitment to leave François in peace. He feels persecuted by you and your gang.

MUSTAPHA'S MOTHER: I object to this word. You all know one another well. You've been together in school.

FRANÇOIS: [defiantly] He saw everything. He was there. He knows who it is.

MUSTAPHA'S MOTHER: It's up to you to find out. You live in the same neighborhood. My son is always the target. He is tall and outside. They always blame him.

JUDGE: It is always the same, guys who are implicated in crimes and are protected by their friends, who disturb others and create a climate of fear. Your son does not do well in school. No, he didn't take the helmet but he was an accomplice. It is the climate he chose. They are all victims of this climate. He hangs out a lot. [to Mustapha] You need to choose a different best friend.

MUSTAPHA: He is not my best friend.

The judge decided to render her decision in chambers and, before asking for the defense attorney's observations, asked François and his parents if they were seeking compensatory damages. The son responded with an emphatic, "Yes." His father shook his head saying "No, we don't want to add to the family's problems because Mustapha is not a criminal. We just want a guarantee that there will be no more trouble." At the judge's insistence Mustapha assured them, "I will not bother them in the future."

ATTORNEY FOR MUSTAPHA: I have grave legal concerns about this case. There are no dates, no specifics, no one was arrested, this case barely meets the legal standard for prosecution. The accused totally contests the facts. Everyone agrees that the theft cannot be attributed to him. He was not indicted for extortion. Why was it mentioned? He did not threaten the victim, he did not participate in the infraction. We can only condemn the reticence of parents who wait a year before coming forward. He refuses to denounce witnesses. It is the neighborhood climate that demands that one keep silent in court.

The judge acquitted Mustapha in part because of his attorney's unusually aggressive defense, a ruling greeted with hostility by François, and incredulity by the judge's substitute clerk. After they left, she muttered, "I wouldn't want to meet him and his gang after dark. I can understand the father because that won't be the end of it. He is a bad one."

Two-and-a-half years later, in June 2003, it was François who was back in Judge Chaland's court, this time following a conviction in the full juvenile court for a hate crime he and another youth committed in the same neighborhood. In the intervening period legislative reform added racism as an aggravating circumstance to existing sentences for a crime or misdemeanor, substantially increasing the penalties for a conviction.[23] Considerable public attention centered on the rise in anti-Semitic incidents targeting the French Jewish community, the largest in Europe, since the beginning of the second Palestinian Intifada in September 2000. This rise was widely attributed to North African Arab youth, despite the fact that police and Interior Ministry statistics for 2003 and 2004 showed that they were responsible for one-third of the reported incidents.[24] François was arrested with a red marker and stains on his hands in front of a store owned by a Jewish family. The words "Dirty Jew" and "Son of a Whore" had been scrawled on the window. Following his arrest, he had adamantly denied the charges but ultimately admitted his guilt. During his trial, his parents had their turn to be put on the defensive. They declared that "they were mystified" by their son's behavior and insisted that "we have not raised a racist teenager. He has always had contact with all different cultures and has friends from many different nationalities."

The éducatrice's report noted that he had been under court supervision since early 2002 and had scholastic problems that dated back to elementary school. She attributed his difficulties to his parents' long-term separation and noted that he had dropped out of school despite "a good intellectual level, excellent ability to express himself, and a passion for music." The judge had postponed sentencing and imposed a reparation measure for him and his accomplice (who did not appear), which involved volunteer work with an antiracist NGO. François had designed a community project to spread a message of tolerance. During the June 2003 hearing, he appeared contrite and, surrounded by both parents, said all the right things in language devoid of its cité style. He admitted his fault and presented photos of the mural he said he had spent fifty hours painting on the wall of the lycée.[25] He insisted that it had inspired him to be a graphic designer and to eschew all bad associations. The prosecutor, the judge, and the assessors were duly impressed. He earned a dismissal of the sentence (dispense de peine).

One might argue that justice was done in both cases. Mustapha was given the benefit of the doubt and acquitted, whereas François repaired his debt and escaped a punitive sentence. Nonetheless, court personnel understood and handled their misbehavior differently despite striking similarities in their family situations and alarming differences in the charges against them. Mustapha was raised by a single mother struggling with health problems and François grew up in a broken home marked by conflict, a fact that did not surface until his own arrest. François's parents were middle-class leftists whose ideological choice was to live in an ethically mixed neighborhood. Their problems were depicted as personal not cultural. In contrast, Mustapha's difficulties were viewed as a product of the culture of poverty in which he (and his mother) preferred to remain despite other alternatives, and they generated little sympathy from the judge. His mother had, after all, refused a better apartment for the family and a placement for him in a state facility. His putative misbehavior was viewed as part of territorialized violence that created a climate of fear in the neighborhood. His voice figured little in this hearing except through his police statement read by the judge. In contrast, François's sense of entitlement as a victim empowered him to claim retribution and damages against Mustapha. Even in his role as a defendant in a hate crime, Francois was assertive. He adroitly framed his successful request for leniency in terms of hard work and individual accountability.

Here we see, as Appadurai has argued, the unequal possibilities for imagining social lives that are engaged by global flows of people, language, and cultural forms. Because of his parents' class position and the larger diacritics of power, François was relatively free to imagine a different identity by appropriating aspects of street culture such as dress and youth vernacular. When he got into serious trouble, he was also able to shed cité speech and to reassume an identity more acceptable to the court and his family. Mustapha, on the other hand, had no such alternatives. Given his long police record, upcoming hearings at court, and a poor school record, he no doubt saw his life as more of a compromise between what he could imagine and what he could realistically expect.[26]

Mustapha's mother raised police profiling by implying that her son was always targeted because of his "height." Suggesting that he was identified because of his race would have been impossible to prove and probably would not have been well received by the judge, since the court is officially color-blind. Mustapha was investigated for the theft of a motorcycle helmet by association, whereas

François was caught literally red-handed at the scene of a hate crime. This was an incident that, from the viewpoint of the Jewish grocer at least, surely added to a climate of fear. François's éducatrice told me that she had contacted the local rabbi, who had refused to meet with him, believing his apology to be insincere. She was outraged, citing the intolerance of the orthodox Jewish community. She framed François's problems against a backdrop of unanticipated personal misfortune and his parents' protracted divorce. These elements figured prominently as mitigating circumstances in her report. Despite the fact that he was a school dropout—in contrast to Mustapha, who was enrolled in school—the emphasis on François's intellectual potential and career aspirations was strategic. These represented symbolic capital associated with the middle classes, social goods she naturally ascribed to François. No one made such a case for Mustapha who was already known as a recidivist from a "bad" home.

Culture at Court

The preponderance of children of immigrant and foreign ancestry at court brought intense scrutiny of cultural traditions deemed at odds with mainstream French norms. "Traditions" such as arranged marriages, control over female sexuality, excision of female genitals, patriarchal domination, corporal punishment of children, belief in sorcery and witchcraft, and polygamy were identified as significant risk factors for minor children. In cases involving excision, the French courts have actively prosecuted both the practitioners and the offending families. Court personnel tended to be highly suspect of upbringing in homes where cultural norms differed radically from mainstream French society and deemed placing children in state institutions or in French foster families preferable to keeping them in such settings. Judges were particularly vigilant when they were alerted to the dangers posed for Muslim women by tyrannical fathers, backward mothers, and oppressive older brothers who monitored them, abused them, or threatened them with return to their parents' country and/or with forced marriages. Those who ran away, committed offenses while away from home, or sought shelter from the court stood a good chance of being categorized as victims and protected. Although female delinquents constituted only a small percentage of penal cases, less than 10 percent nationally, and only 5 percent of the cases I observed, I discuss the cases of several teenage girls of immigrant ancestry because of the dilemmas they posed for court personnel. Judges clearly viewed young women of immigrant ancestry as having greater potential to integrate within French society than their male counterparts even when they had few economic resources or educational credentials.

In the penal cases that follow, judges attended to the role played by culture in penal cases in one of two ways. Either it was stigmatized or criminalized and neutralized through the standard interventions at judges' disposal or it was medicalized and treated through the specialized services of ethnopsychiatrists. In all cases, culture was an obstacle to be overcome or treated.

Wayward Girls?

Unni Wikan has argued that for young daughters raised in the West, the costs of choosing to defy or to flee from observant Muslim families can be devastatingly high.[27] Faced with families' impossible demands or enforced estrangement from them, these young women experienced deep psychological distress and severe emotional deprivation. There were a number of cases in which adolescent daughters in conflict with their parents requested help and were placed with their full consent in state residential facilities despite their parents' vociferous protests. These cases involved Algerian parents, veiled mothers, abusive fathers, and the threat of kidnap and forced marriages. In the penal case below, the judge directly attributed the young woman's delinquency to her family milieu and sharply rebuffed her parents' requests to end her placement. Nonetheless, the court intervention that sheltered her from family abuse did not provide the guidance she needed to negotiate French social services or the educational system and did little to improve her life chances and career prospects.

When sixteen-year-old Fatima's 2001 hearing was scheduled in the Nineteenth East District Court of Judge Chaland, she had already been placed with French social welfare services for a year and her schooling was interrupted due to clinical depression. She had been sent back to Algeria, physically abused, and returned to France only after she attempted suicide. When she sought the court's protection, she was placed in a state home and treated with psychotherapy and medication. Because of her frequent absences and unfinished program the year before, Fatima was not enrolled in school. She had also been expelled from a state residence facility after an altercation with another teenager, her first and only violation of the rules. As a result she was temporarily moved to a makeshift facility, one of the hotels run by the city of Paris, where she was completely unsupervised. She was arrested for attempting to purchase clothes with a stolen check and identity card. As this was a first offense and she readily admitted her guilt, Judge Chaland indicted her but heard the case in chambers rather than the juvenile court.

When the judge asked about her parents, Fatima explained that after her arrest, she returned home, where "things went badly, they wanted to take me back [to Algeria], it was the same thing again." She requested placement at another state home. At this point, her éducatrice raised the issue of school and what she implied were Fatima's overly ambitious career goals. Ignoring her documented clinical depression, the éducatrice advised the judge that Fatima had "manipulated her problem to stay out of school longer than needed."

> EDUCATRICE: She can only be placed in a state facility if she is enrolled in 3e [the final year of *collège* or middle school]. She didn't do anything last year. She says she is interested in the medical-psychological field but she does not know what she wants to do. I mean . . . we need something more realistic for her. So much is unresolved.
>
> JUDGE: I agree that she needs to buckle down, but there is no reason that she cannot succeed. [*to Fatima*] You need to get to work. Are you feeling less depressed?
>
> FATIMA: Yes.
>
> JUDGE: Do you see your éducatrice on a regular basis?
>
> FATIMA: Yes.

The judge allowed Fatima to leave before seeing her parents, both of whom were French nationals and had lived in France for twenty-two years. Fatima's mother, a middle-aged woman who wore the headscarf, interjected:

> MOTHER: We were at the police station. We saw everything. I want my daughter back home, not in a hotel where she goes and comes when she pleases.
>
> JUDGE: Why? Things went badly at home.
>
> MOTHER: No, they went well, we allowed phone cards.
>
> JUDGE: It is not clear what is going on. Would you accept a family [cultural] consultation with a neutral person? (Although this judge was skeptical about the benefits of ethnopsychiatry, the consultation was suggested by the éducatrice and strongly supported by Fatima.) It will help to find out what is causing the conflict. To get all points of view, positive and negative.
>
> MOTHER: She does not need to be institutionalized. She is not lacking for anything at home. She is fine at home.

JUDGE: At one time she was not fine.

MOTHER: She is fine.

EDUCATRICE: She must take medicine prescribed by the psychiatrist. When she went home, her parents confiscated it.

FATHER: I take responsibility in my own house.

JUDGE: But it has to be without violence.

MOTHER: I never hit my daughter.

JUDGE: We'll order a consultation to gain a better understanding.

FATHER: Absolutely not, no one monitors my daughter but me. We want her at home.

EDUCATRICE: It's an untenable situation. Need I remind Monsieur that she made an attempt on her life while she was at home?

The judge refused to return Fatima to her parents' custody and judged her in chambers, issuing a simple warning. Given her expulsion from the Paris facility and the shortage of service providers in the city, the judge was forced to place her in a facility for high-risk teenagers outside of Paris, where she was surrounded by repeat offenders. In the months following the hearing, Fatima was still not readmitted to school and her chances for placement in an academic track to study psychology were slim to none. Her parents remained opposed to a cultural consultation and the family situation seemed hopelessly deadlocked.

Deviant Boys?

The question of the overrepresentation of young men from immigrant—particularly polygamous—backgrounds in urban violence was a subject of legislative debate following the 2005 riots. As the link between immigration and youth crime was naturalized, cultural origin and cultural traditions attracted the attention of the general public, school authorities, and court personnel. Sometimes a warning from a teacher, a school nurse, or a guidance counselor, or an anonymous call to the national abuse hotline, are the first steps in establishing social welfare intervention. In addition to questions of hygiene and school attendance, the pressing issues were the upbringing and disciplining of children within the family.

In late May 2003, I attended a penal hearing in the chambers of the Eighteenth District South court of Judge de Maximy. The eldest son of a respected leader in the Soninké community, Amadou, had been arrested and indicted for aggravated theft along with an adult felon and was violating the conditions of his probation: to stay off the streets late at night, to attend school, and to keep up his grades. The district social workers reported that the father had worked for twenty-five years in the same cleaning business, advancing to the position as foreman but, "despite having a regular income had continued to live in the same filthy, two-room apartment."

The hearing began late and on a tense note. The judge was furious because everyone in the family appeared—his father, his father's second wife, and their three young children—except Amadou. She was concerned that Amadou was not only doing drugs but also selling them. She chose to begin with the issue of corporal punishment because she had learned that the father was beating his son to enforce his authority. Initially the father adopted an authoritative tone and addressed the judge in broken French with the highly inappropriate familiar *tu* form of address:

FATHER: He don't listen. He went too far. I hit him. I don't want any problems. If I hurt Amadou, it's the fault of the French state.

This strategy backfired spectacularly and the judge immediately lost her temper, her voice rising:

JUDGE: If you are not happy in France, Monsieur, you can go straight back to your country. Here we don't have the right to hit children. We make them listen without beating them. French law does not give you the right to punish them like that. You are clearly backward in your view of child rearing. You only know how to impose your authority with your fists. Even in France a century ago, we locked children up and whipped them, but that is over. Little by little we have replaced corporal punishment with other means.

Challenged in this way, the father's bravado evaporated:

FATHER: Never I commit a crime in France. I have been here forty-six years. I respected the law. I done nothing. That shames me, shame in my family. I wanted that Amadou do like me. [*a long silence; his voice broke and he began to weep*] I go to the Mosque. Where is Amadou? I talk to everyone. I say you need to pay attention to the law, it's the law, morning, noon, and night, all the children but Amadou, no. [*weeping*] I am ashamed.

One of the neighborhood social workers tried to reassure him:

SOCIAL WORKER: You don't hit the other children. The French state is not accusing you of anything.

JUDGE: [*clearly affected*] Did you say it like that to Amadou? The problem is that he has difficulty imagining that punishment is anything but a beating. You were punished that way by your father. We give spankings to young children but not to teenagers. Parents must make children obey in French families as in other families. They don't have the right to go out after a certain time, they can't cut school. We have never tried to remove your parental authority. But here is the problem. [*to the caseworkers and the mother*] As long as his father hits him, he will continue [with his delinquency]. You must quit this feeling of shame. Amadou needs to make an attempt to structure his life and make the right choices. You all need a cultural consultation at the Devereux Center. I'll issue an assistance order.

SOCIAL WORKER: There are things that were never said. Things that he misses. The family history. His African culture and roots. It's too much for him.

The judge declined to revoke probation and instead issued an assistance order, adding it to Amadou's penal file. After the hearing, we went to lunch with another juvenile judge and Judge de Maximy described her outburst: "I sounded like Jean-Marie Le Pen [extreme right-wing politician noted for anti-immigrant rhetoric], telling them to go back where they came from." Her colleague dismissed this as nonsense. When I remained silent, she turned to me somewhat defensively and said, "That is the way you have to deal with Africans, you have to hit them head on."

The judge linked Amadou's delinquency to both bad parenting and an identity disorder resulting from suspension between two cultural systems. The more pressing issues of viable educational opportunities, bad neighborhood influences, and poor housing never surfaced. The judge gave a highly idealized view of the evolution of juvenile law and of parental practice in France to highlight what she perceived to be the backwardness of Africans. Her statements suggested that the problem of child abuse was limited to immigrant families and that France had evolved beyond this social ill. Such pious condemnations obscure the kinds of "not-so-benign social and psychological neglect that underlie so-called progressive practices of child rearing in the West."[28] They also ignore the complicated history of child abuse in France, where Napoleonic law gave fathers absolute authority in the family until legislation in 1889 limited paternal power in the name of child protection. Nonetheless, child abuse was not acknowledged as a social problem until the 1980s when public awareness campaigns exposed it as both serious and widespread.

Coutant studied the diversion program instituted at the Paris Palace of Justice in the late 1990s, interviewing a number of Maghrebi and African fathers whose sons had first-time offenses. All expressed their bitterness at what they viewed as the contradictory admonishments from court personnel with regard to child discipline. On the one hand, they were castigated as negligent parents who imposed no limits on their children, and, on the other, when they attempted to correct children "in their own way," they ran afoul of the law. The fathers, who were largely poorly educated or even illiterate labor migrants, distrusted the police and the legal system and were afraid of what their children would tell French authorities.[29] The exaggerated way in which Amadou's father related his own respect for the law was perhaps born of a fear that he himself might be subject to legal sanction. His initial bravado may also have been an attempt to counter a call made to the abuse hotline denouncing "the lack of hygiene, deficient child supervision, and frequent school truancy" in his home.

CIVIL HEARINGS IN CHAMBERS

Many judges saw their work in social assistance cases governed by the French civil code as less subject to "the dictates of immediacy" and the critique of penal hearings. Judge Boyer described social assistance cases as the best safeguard against judicial excess. "For one thing it is professionally salutary to be humbled by constantly confronting one's failures. There is the child who repeatedly runs away and the parents who refuse to accept their responsibilities. It puts the judge back in his place. This is work that requires time. Prevention and assistance don't happen over night."

The question of time is central to understanding the French conception of juvenile law and the process of assessing child endangerment. Jurists and sociologists of law distinguish two notions of time at work in the legal system. The first, *kairos*, refers to justice in the long term, requiring deliberation and reflection. This long-term perspective is contrasted to a much shorter, linear time span, *chronos*, linked to expediency and the demands of change. Chronos is the time frame dictated by social reality and its contingencies. As Bessin has argued, it is characterized by personal exposure as judges come under pressure from a variety of sources: the prosecution, public opinion, the defense, the media, and families. Confronted with time constraints, judges often referred to the notion of a reasonable length of time to show their reluctance to intervene right away and their unease at the delays inflicted on families. The word *kairos* refers to a more qualitative dimension of time since it implies that the timely moment has been chosen, the right distinctions have been made, and the best priorities have been set. Until recently there was a consensus that kairos is deemed the time scale theoretically best suited to the juvenile court, since the decisions are adapted to the personality and circumstances of the child.[30]

The crisis of the rehabilitative model has affected the management of time in civil cases just as it has in penal law. In recent years, there has been a substantial increase in the number of child endangerment reports (*signalements*) sent to the prosecutor's office, which has prompted emergency hearings in chambers and the immediate removal of children from their families, sometimes without the adequate preparation or consent of their parents. The prosecutor's office plays an increasingly important role in responding to emergency cases of child endangerment. In these cases deputy prosecutors act like judges and make decisions which quickly set in motion the machinery of justice, but in ways that can sidestep juvenile judges and adopt the short-term view.

Assessing Risk

The attention to child endangerment is a radical change from the past, when a "rule of silence" reigned among social workers and prevented many such cases from being handled in the courts. Pediatricians, psychologists, and psychiatrists in the late 1970s successfully focused on abuse as a physical condition that could be diagnosed and prevented through early detection and public awareness. National sensitivity programs in the media in 1985 and 1997, state circulars, and legislative reform in conjunction with 1990 French ratification of the CRC portrayed abuse as a dangerous social phenomenon that demanded public attention. As Serre has argued, the public recognition that transformed abuse into a commonsense category had contradictory effects. On the one hand, it made the question of state responsibility and the labeling of abuse a focal point of treatment and response, but on the other, the extension of the notion of abuse made it more difficult to define precisely.[31] Child endangerment reports were and continue to be based on article 375—and following—of the Code civil, all of which involve broad and ill-defined criteria such as the "health, security, morality and upbringing of the minor." Nonetheless, in adapting these criteria to individual cases, caseworkers, who alerted the court, drew on internalized professional practices as much as a normative view of the social order. In the 1990s, children at risk for abuse were considered victims of socioeconomic marginality and of a loss of bearings. These were often the same predictors for a delinquency of exclusion associated with immigrants and foreigners.

Social workers, who as a profession had resisted reporting abuse to the courts to protect the confidentiality of children and families, began to be subject to prosecution for their failure to do so in the early 1990s.[32] Despite legal pressure to report endangered children and new managerial rationales in state bureaucracies that used the child endangerment report (signalement) as a critical index of the quality and productivity of work, there was no uniform response by social workers. To the consternation of judges, some caseworkers covered themselves to avoid responsibility by systematically reporting minors "in danger" or projected the risk of abuse by making unverifiable allegations. Others resisted alerting social services or the courts, citing the ambiguity of the law, and reported only in good conscience based on their individual assessment of the degree of danger.[33]

Nonetheless, in the mid-1990s reports of endangered children increased along with the emergency placements of children in state institutions or foster families. This development increased the already crushing workload for caseworkers and posed dilemmas for juvenile judges and welfare services alike. Although judges were legally responsible for overseeing caseworkers, in a trend that has continued to this day, many found it difficult to find the time to go into the field. Caseworkers criticized judges' decisions as too rigid and hearings as too widely spaced to adapt to rapidly changing family situations. Anticipating the placement of a child demands thorough planning, specifically timing and careful choice of an alternative living arrangement. Although institutionalization is more costly than monitoring in families, placement can become a default solution when a family situation deteriorates rapidly. Research on emergency placements indicates that they occurred most often following situations of sexual molestation or the birth of a child. Typical placements affected large, broken families who were poor as well as single-parent households headed by women.[34] In other words, juvenile court personnel were predisposed to assess risk and remove children from underprivileged immigrant and foreign families with open social assistance cases. By 2000, a state-commissioned report recommended reducing the large number of child placements in order to assuage the concerns of parents who felt victimized by the practice.[35] What goes unacknowledged is the way class, culture, and gender combine to affect the assessment of risk posed by particular home environments and parenting practices. At what point do state agents deem that risk to be unacceptable by revoking parental custody?

Consider the case of Roger Leparquet followed by Judge Lebrun in the Eighteenth District court until 2000, when she left to assume duties in another Paris courtroom whose jurisdiction includes the First, Third, and Seventh districts. This was a case involving the sustained abuse of a boy by his father, a leftist intellectual, the respected director of a suburban theater, and an active participant in the parents' association of a prestigious Parisian lycée. Beginning in preschool in 1989 and again in 1992, 1994, and 1995, school authorities warned Roger's parents about his slow development and behavior problems— "anxiety, depression, tendency to self-mutilation, aggressiveness, refusal of social contact with peers, absences from school, and unkempt appearance"—but a formal endangered child report was not issued until 1994 when he was ten years old. The social worker explained that this lapse was due "to the refusal of Roger's parents to cooperate with French social services." A year later when Judge Lebrun was away on vacation, Judge Bella substituted in an emergency hearing and immediately ordered a formal social investigation.

The investigating social worker reported that the parents refused to allow her to interview Roger alone and his father demanded to know what legal statute he was accused of violating. She concluded that there was obvious abuse by the father that the mother tolerated. Despite hearings in chambers, summons before the Brigade de la Protection des Mineurs (Child Protection Brigade), a deposition from family friends who witnessed Roger's father burn him with a cigarette, and a notification from school that his hair had been torn out by the roots, the judge still took no action to remove Roger Leparquet from his home, citing lack of cooperation from the family. Finally in late 1998, his sister sent a wrenching letter to the court corroborating her brother's abuse as well as her own need for protection from the "serious and unrelenting violence" she suffered at her father's hand. She attempted suicide and mutilated herself. Only then, in 1999, when Roger was fourteen years old, did the judge place Roger in a state residential facility for two years.

French civil law—article 375 and following—requires the cooperation of the parents in cases where the "health, security, morality, and upbringing of the minor" are at risk and deems it best to assist children and parents in their home setting when children under fifteen suffer physical and/or psychological abuse.

However, penal law trumps civil statute, and the protection of children takes precedence over the rights of parents. Indeed, some jurists have suggested that the legal statute (line 2 of article 375 of the Code civil) requiring parental cooperation is problematic, particularly if their opposition has the effect of undermining legal action destined to protect severely abused children. They urge that this statute be deleted if certain safeguards are respected, namely that judges hear all sides and carefully justify their decisions.[36]

Why did the parents' refusals to cooperate with court personnel carry any weight, given the severity of the charges? Why did their adamant denials of culpability between 1989 and 1995 delay judicial action despite the overwhelming evidence of abuse? Why were their overt challenges to the very authority of the system itself tolerated? When I asked Judge de Maximy, who inherited this case, to explain what happened, she said, "The father is a big pervert who made everyone stop doing their jobs." [*Il a fait dysfonctionner tout le monde.*] How could one father accomplish that? It seemed clear that her predecessor, Judge Lebrun, was partly receptive to Roger's class position and prominence within the Parisian arts scene. This social standing, combined with an unusually aggressive self-defense, were enough to fend off the court. It is telling that a comprehensive social investigation and the collection of a family history were completed only after the parents lost their employment and social capital. When caseworkers finally interviewed them, they discovered an intergenerational pattern of abuse within both the father and mother's family and the fact that Roger's father was estranged from a first wife and children for pain and suffering inflicted on them. Roger's ordeal continued after his rescue from home. Two weeks after placement in a state facility, he got into a fight with other teenagers, was beaten up, and landed in the hospital. When told, his mother cynically observed, "Well for once what social services are saying is true. Since he left [home] I no longer sleep with my checkbook under my pillow. We have no pity for him."

It is instructive to contrast this case to the child endangerment file of Ali Dalim, a nine-year-old of Algerian-Turkish ancestry whose case was heard in the Twentieth District North court in April 2001. Judge Dinard's predecessor, Judge Corsini, presided in that courtroom between 2000 and 2003. Ali's parents had lived together briefly and separated acrimoniously and were locked in a bitter struggle over his custody and visitation rights. Both had immigrated to France clandestinely, lived on the street, and finally legalized their status, obtaining "permanent work and decent housing," but remained economically vulnerable. In 1998 French social services issued a warning based on Ali's be-havior problems at school, including "psychological instability, anxiety, and aggression," strongly urging that he be removed from the custody of his Alger-ian mother, whom they described, "as depressed, with dark thoughts, exces-sively rigid, and with an emotionally unhealthy attachment to her son (*rapport fusionnel*)." They noted that although both parents had made "significant ef-forts at professional insertion, the mother was still terrified of losing her child," a fact they held against her. They reasoned that "Ali was caught in a maternal discourse of violence and victimization. He is poorly structured, immature, lacks temporal-spatial grounding and needs to be placed in a state facility." Both parents reluctantly agreed to the temporary placement of their son in 1998, which was extended to the fall of 2000.

In October 2000, Ali's mother hired an attorney, requested Ali's return home, and raised the specter of his abuse by the father during summer vacation when the boy returned with the mark of a slap on his face. Family court judges (*juges des affaires familiales*) normally decide on parental rights and child visi-tation arrangements in custody disputes. Since juvenile judges only intervene in custody decisions when children are in danger, court personnel believed that some parents alleged abuse to obtain custody. They thought this dynamic was at work in Ali's case. In response to the accusation, the judge ordered a report from social services and a psychiatrist's evaluation of Ali. The 26 October 2000 social service report was dismissive of the mother's request for custody, sug-gesting that despite "the considerable efforts she had made to integrate herself within French society, a return to her would seriously compromise Ali's up-bringing and stability." A 25 March 2001 report submitted by a child psychia-trist also strongly recommended that Ali remain with French social services. The tenor of that report revealed the continued dominance of Freudian theory in the interpretation of family relationships. The psychiatrist described the "cultural difficulties faced by the mother which reveal the pathological mother-son bond" coupled with the "common history of uprooting from their coun-tries of origin" shared by his parents. She administered TAT tests in which Ali displayed "debilitating anguish, depressive posture, an inability to represent himself and an unresolved Oedipal complex."[37] In short, Ali had been denied his rightful place as a child and had been prematurely cast in the role of a par-ent. She advised against a return home.

Before the hearing began, Judge Corsini indicated that she agreed with the psychiatric evaluations that Ali was at risk, and she had already decided to keep him in state custody. She attempted to explain to the nine-year-old why he could not live with his mother as he wished. She alternated between speaking to him, the social workers, and attorneys. She rephrased the psychiatrist's report because it was "too full of professional jargon":

> JUDGE: [*to Ali*] You need to separate from your mother in your head. [*to others*] We need a link on the psychological level here. If not, we will face a catastrophe when he is a teenager. He must have psychological help to construct himself. [*to Ali and the others*] You will be at risk if you go to live with your mother. You must work to separate yourself from her. It is not good for you to live with your mother in this unhealthy dependency. There are the psychological problems of his parents. It is not an emergency, but we need a boarding school. The only solution is to see your mother once every other weekend. And your father. It will be important to maintain relations with both parents. I have a strong feeling that this will work for you. You are a wonderful kid. I am speaking to you as a woman. Is this clear?

Ali's mother became extremely upset and insisted that "he's my son and I am the one to decide what is best for him." She insisted that his grades had improved and he was calmer. The time was right for a return home. One of the social workers retorted that his grades may have improved but they were still "very, very, very weak" and his school behavior was very aggressive. She mentioned "complaints from other parents, violence at recess, and insults directed at the teacher." When the judge reminded the mother that permanent adjustments to parental custody were made by the family court judge and would entail an additional hearing, the mother lost her temper:

> MOTHER: I can't believe this! Do you realize that I have lost three jobs because of these summons? It is killing me. I have had it! For three years I have had to deal with this. I want a normal life with my son like everyone else.
>
> SECOND SOCIAL WORKER: I see her point. The boy made a lot of progress. These hearings take a tremendous amount of time. This time gets deducted from her yearly vacation.
>
> MOTHER: [*starting to sob*] When I left today my boss said [*sarcastically*], "what a great beginning." I'm all alone. I have been on the street for him. I've sacrificed for my son and I can't even live with him.

JUDGE: I hear you, but we have to make sure things continue to progress. We'll choose an establishment close to Paris. [*to Ali, using the familiar form of address*] You will continue to work with the doctor [psychiatrist]. This is necessary if you are going to begin to be independent.

ALI: I don't understand. What does that mean? I want to stay with my mother. I feel good with my mother.

JUDGE: It is too soon. I did not say it will be for always. Does that help? You'll be like kids whose parents are rich but very busy with work. Their kids go to this school.

In this case, behavioral difficulties linked to cultural origin and economic marginality were framed within the discourse of psychiatric pathology and Ali's unresolved Oedipal conflict with his mother. The psychoanalytic diagnosis embraced by the judge invested her decision with the authority of clinical expertise. Court personnel viewed French educators, counselors, psychiatrists, and caseworkers as better able to assure Ali's proper upbringing and to structure his personality than a single mother or a newly remarried father. Social workers attempting to make such a claim in Roger's case were repeatedly rebuffed by his family and a judge who apparently refused to see beyond their class position and their normative two-parent family structure. It is telling that, in contrast to Roger's case, there were no allegations of serious physical or psychological abuse against Ali's parents but rather excessive emotional attachment born of economic vulnerability and cultural difference. Although some of the same symptoms were reported by school authorities, they provoked very different responses. Both suggest child endangerment but are hardly equivalent. Nonetheless, Ali was immediately removed from his family against the wishes of his parents, whereas Roger's parents were able to challenge and successfully subvert court scrutiny for ten years before their child was finally rescued. Both ended up in state institutions, but ironically Ali, the child of newly legal immigrants, was sent to a well-known boarding school, whereas Roger, the son of a Parisian theater personality, was placed in a state facility for delinquents, a place where he encountered and perpetuated further violence.

Weighing Culture

As some of the preceding cases make clear, many court personnel evaluated cultural tradition negatively—particularly among the underprivileged Maghrebi and Sub-Saharan families within their purview—as a force with the weight of biology that determined the practices of peoples born into it. They viewed peoples from non-Western cultures as less evolved and less able to adapt or change. A number of judges routinely referred families to the Georges Devereux Center at the University of Paris VIII, which specializes in clinical psychology and the use of scientific psychiatric nosologies to treat culturally specific disorders. Two Paris judges, Thierry Baranger and Martine de Maximy, had advanced training in ethnopsychiatry and published a well-received book advocating its incorporation into the juvenile courtroom. They see this as a more empathetic approach to the "lost and wounded families" whose blurred identities made the court's approach seem "empty, without promise, and sometimes violent."[38] They argue that judges need to end the legal silence on cultural difference by addressing it openly.

They advise transforming the courtroom into a judicial clinic where the power relations of the traditional courtroom would be altered. With the help of indigenous psychologists, patients become active participants, speaking in their native language and describing problems within the appropriate cultural frame. They argue that this is the best way to handle cultural disorders that stemmed from migration. Migratory flows fracture existing kinship systems and force the suppression of belief systems, such as sorcery and witchcraft, which serve as a crucial means of social regulation and conflict resolution in Central and East Africa. Children who are suspended between two cultural systems need first to reestablish their place within cultural genealogies before they can begin to construct whole individual identities. They see culturally based psychological disorders as grounds for reduced criminal responsibility and as treatable conditions through the interventions of French-trained native ethnopsychiatrists and traditional therapies.

Despite their stated tolerance for cultural difference, the authors reaffirm the supremacy of French values and the "republican process of integration at a time when it appears threatened." They readily assume that the "shared norms" in question are those of middle-class, mainstream French culture.[39] In the cases I observed, the attempt to recognize cultural difference and to give voice to families with radically different belief systems never resulted in elegantly simple solutions, as the judges themselves admit. In fact, the ethnopsychiatric view of cultural tradition does not differ substantially from that of culture of poverty theorists or pro-repression advocates. Families were rarely as cooperative or the children as compliant as expected. Rather, children who were born or raised in France adapted and integrated in ways that could and did accommodate multiple belief systems. Even those who were well assimilated often had problems within their families that could not be blamed on group culture but on a range of individual disorders or a combination of the two. The fact that their parents may have believed in spirit possession (like the father in the next case), carried amulets, or feared witches explained little about their parenting styles or their children's misbehavior.

A Cultural Mediation

I attended a court-ordered cultural mediation in late January 2001 with another Algerian family and their daughter, in which the salient factors included family honor, child abuse, mental illness, labor migration, and a decision by French immigration authorities in the 1980s that might have precluded the case from ever appearing in court. Judge de Maximy inherited the case of Nadine from Judge Lebrun in the Eighteenth District South court and suggested a consultation between the parents, the child, and an Arabic-speaking cultural mediator. Despite poverty and adversity, Nadine had excelled in school and been admitted to the long cycle of the academic track in one of the most prestigious lycées in the capital. She had been raised by her father, a labor migrant whose wife and six children had remained in Algeria. There were gaps in the file. No one knew why she alone had been chosen to stay.

Nadine first came to the court's attention as a twelve-year-old following allegations of neglect and had been temporarily placed with a foster family. After an attempted suicide in 1999, Nadine was again removed from her father's custody and placed in a state home, a situation her parents found intolerable. In March 2000, she finally disclosed the "substantial physical abuse, persecution, and voyeurism" her father had inflicted on her. She narrowly escaped being hanged with a telephone cord when a neighbor knocked at the door. She suffered from debilitating bouts of depression and was ravaged by guilt for her revelations to the court. She was petrified to visit her family in Algeria because she was afraid she would never return.

The éducatrice described her father's well-documented "mental illness" and his systematic violation of the court's 2000 order that barred any unsupervised contact with his daughter. Nadine had written to the previous judge on two separate occasions, in 1999 and again in 2000, to explain that her father had withheld her identity papers, refused to permit her to go on school trips, and repeatedly thrown away her schoolwork. She begged Judge Lebrun, then the presiding judge, to make the harassment stop, suggesting that "perhaps the best solution would be her death."

When Nadine, her parents, the mediator, and the two social workers convened for a late-afternoon session in 2001, the atmosphere was tense. Her mother had made a special trip from Algeria to attend the hearing. Her father had convinced a French psychiatrist to write an affidavit certifying that he was not crazy. Nadine's mother was a heavy-set, veiled woman who spoke little French. Her eyes darted back and forth trying to read the expressions of the court personnel. Her anxiety and heartache were palpable. The judge had told me that during the previous hearing presided over by Judge Lebrun, the mother had fainted dead away. Was it the revelation of the abuse her daughter endured? or guilt? The judge reassured the family that the meeting was an attempt to reestablish family bonds. Looking directly at Nadine's father, she added, "But not by force." With the mediator translating for Nadine's mother and adding his own cultural commentaries, Nadine's mother began:

> MOTHER: I don't dare say too much. I want my family together. You, as judge, are defending certain principles . . . for instance, that Nadine not come home. We don't want her at the state facility. I want her at home. She was seven when she came here. We don't lack for anything. We can provide. It is a question of honor.

When the judge asked why Nadine stayed in France with her father, her mother explained:

> MOTHER: I was here in 1984. I was pregnant with Nadine, she was born in France, the only one born in France.
>
> MEDIATOR: Was it destiny? Why was Nadine the one to stay?
>
> FATHER: She was born in France. There were no problems with papers.
>
> JUDGE: Why was there no family reunification? [to allow Nadine's mother and other siblings to join her father who had entered France legally in 1960 to work for a French construction company]
>
> SOCIAL WORKER: Because the twins [boys] were already in Algeria, they could not get visas. The father couldn't bring the children because he had no housing. He asked for an apartment or house for fifteen years and never got it [because he did not have a resident family in France to justify the request].
>
> MEDIATOR: The twins stayed in Algeria and the mother suffered.
>
> MOTHER: [shaking her head and beginning to cry] I was in tears.
>
> MEDIATOR: [to Nadine] How was your arrival in France? Didn't you ask yourself why you were all alone in France?

NADINE: I never asked.

MOTHER: She was born here. She came back [in 1991] to live.

MEDIATOR: It was so hard for her to be apart from her daughter. It is a struggle between reason and the heart. She has trouble. Nadine is the only French girl of the family.

NADINE: [*simultaneously with her parents*] I am also Algerian.

MOTHER AND FATHER: She is also Algerian.

At this point the judge and Nadine's mother exchanged views on migration and roots. If Nadine was born on French soil, spoke and acted French, and, most importantly, excelled in French schools, she was French. Nadine had the courage to denounce parental abuse and differentiate herself from a "backward" worldview that included her father's belief in spells and the opposition to her premarital independence. The judge saw Nadine as a case of successful integration within France. From the perspective of her parents, this was precisely the problem. Because Nadine had a foot in both French and Algerian worlds, she had choices with regard to social norms.

JUDGE: [*commenting subjectively*] I'll say personally that I would have trouble accepting that my children settled permanently in another country, say Canada. In that case, I would have Canadian [not French] grandchildren.

MOTHER: [*obliquely criticizing French policy that separated husband and wife as well as parents and children*] This is the same thing. It is not accepted that your children leave. We have trouble with the idea that they stay in another country.

The judge tried to reassure Nadine's mother but she directly contradicted received French views on immigration that are wary of American-style multiculturalism. The French do not generally accept the possibility of two equivalent or "hyphenated" national cultural identities in situations of migration.

JUDGE: It is not the same thing. Children leave the country of their ancestors but keep their roots and their language. [*turning to me*] Suzanne, tell them how it works in the United States with immigrants. How it was in your own family?

It was rare for me to be anything but a silent observer during court proceedings. This invitation to bear witness to the immigrant experience was a shock, and I was initially stymied. Clearly I was being asked to describe what the French perceived to be the classic American trajectory in which immigrants celebrated their origins, maintained ties to the homeland, cooked ethnic cuisines, and continued to speak their ancestral languages. This was not the vision they generally had for immigrants to France, where there are strong pressures for assimilation to dominant norms. Nor was it my family's experience of immigration. Their story would have delighted French nationalists and proponents of integration. My father's people were of German ancestry who settled in a small Pennsylvania town and assimilated quickly, turning their backs forever on the mother country. My mother lamented the loss of her "good English name" when she married my father. She came from a line of small industrialists, one of whom tried his fortune in the United States, settling there in the late nineteenth century. Although my great-grandfather returned to England six times, the last contact between the two branches of the family ended with World War II. The only trace of ethnic cuisine that I knew was an Americanized version of sauerkraut and the sole vestige of German was an impatient "*raus*" my father shouted at the family dog. I learned French in a pilot language program in a U.S. elementary school. This was not what the judge wanted to hear. But to oblige her I described an "American" family, a group that linked Germans, Welsh, and English by blood, and by marriage, included a beloved Irish Catholic uncle as well as French Huguenots, a Basque, and Parisian emigrants to Canada. She nodded appreciatively, but Nadine's mother stared at me blankly. My saga meant nothing to her. She returned to the topic of the state home:

> MEDIATOR: [*alternating his commentary with a translation of Nadine's mother's speech*] The state home is seen as a place of punishment, as a space of incarceration. It is for those without money or status. The state home has a bad reputation. The mother says that Nadine's older sister is on the same path, is also very intelligent, attends university, has an advanced degree, lives in university housing. She has spent four years at the university.
>
> JUDGE: The state home where Nadine was placed is one of the best in Paris. It is a respectable institution and it is well run. You must understand.

The judge queried Nadine, and the teenager insisted that she be allowed to remain at the state home. Her father's impatience turned to belligerence and he angrily challenged the judge:

FATHER: I don't believe you [that the state home is good].

JUDGE: [*now bristling at the father's attitude and impatient at their intransigence*] We will reestablish the family ties but slowly. I am the one who decides on the visits, not the man. I am a senior judge at the Paris juvenile court. This young woman has a mind and personality just like you. We try to persuade families to accept the court's decision but the law must prevail. Nadine cannot return home yet. *I'll* say when she is ready for a visit. I am issuing a temporary placement order for six months. We won't make a decision today about Nadine's departure for Algeria this summer.

FATHER: I swear that she will come back.

JUDGE: I have had fathers not only swear but sign written statements and their daughters never came back. We will decide later.

In contrast to Fatima's penal case above, Nadine's family got an empathetic hearing and an opportunity to voice their pain and frustration. Ultimately, the session ended in the same disappointment and stalemate, although the court personnel pronounced it a success. They were encouraged that Nadine's father promised to stay in touch with the court and her mother returned alone to say in halting French, "I want my daughter, I count on you." The mediation turned less on issues of family reconciliation than on issues of judicial authority and legal control. Nadine and her parents exchanged no words directly. All communicative exchanges were controlled by the judge, with the mediator serving more as a translator than as a facilitator. The court order remained in place and Nadine was protected but at the cost of a nearly total rupture with her parents and siblings. Like the conflict resolutions described by Devine in his analysis of violence prevention programs, this one substituted the hypothetical for the real and dealt with the past and the future at the expense of the present.[40] It tended to equalize all past traumas—the father's frustration, the mother's pain, the daughter's isolation—and made it easy to escape harsh realities such as parental abuse. It avoided confronting serious issues for Nadine, such as her career goals, as she attempted to maintain her scholastic success under severe emotional duress. It ignored the government policies that force families in migration to make horrific choices, separating parents and children in the search for citizenship, a living wage, and a retirement pension. Nadine's father had been unemployed since 1990 following a work injury but stayed in France, according to the court personnel, to collect disability income and then to qualify for a retirement pension. Despite the past abuse and differing values, Nadine loved both parents and desperately needed to renew contact with her mother. She also wanted to see her father.

The use of ethnopsychiatrists to treat the cultural disorders that lead to abuse or delinquency is an attempt to cure a phenomenon without adequately diagnosing it. Despite their apparent refusal to judge cultural traditions that differ from French norms, the proponents of ethnopsychiatry locate the problem primarily in the children and families of immigrant ancestry, not in the host society, its policies, or its institutions. In the search for origins, the problem is the Other, not the self.

Confronting Religion: A French Muslim?

Just a few weeks later, a child endangerment case file was reopened in the Eighteenth District South courtroom of Judge de Maximy in the midst of heightened anxiety regarding Islamist fundamentalism and only eighteen months before President Jacques Chirac created a state commission that proposed a law banning ostensible religious symbols in public schools.[41] The mother, an observant Muslim who wore the headscarf, had been accused of neglect and physical abuse of her only child, a daughter, born in June 1999. Anonymous calls from neighbors and appeals from the child's maternal grandparents, as well as a message left on the child abuse hotline in late December 1999, prompted French social services and the Brigade de la Protection des Mineurs to alert the juvenile prosecutor's office. Judge Lebrun had ordered a social investigation and summoned the family to a hearing in her chambers in February 2000. As a result, she imposed regular consultations for mother and child at a child wellness center and mandated that the child be cared for at home rather than in the back room of the family grocery store.

In a July 2000 review, the social worker was cautiously optimistic, noting that the parents were "responding minimally to the child's socio-educational needs" in contrast to her first visit, when she noted that their "religious observances had been prioritized over their parenting obligations." She strongly recommended regular social worker visits to the home—a measure actively resisted by the mother. Suddenly the case acquired urgency in late January 2001, when the judge received letters from a neighbor and the child's grandparents outlining severe abuse and spousal manipulation. The neighbor claimed to have witnessed physical beatings, death threats, and several attempts by the mother to smother her child. The neighbor blamed the mother's psychological fragility and manipulation by a husband she described as "an Islamist extremist." The child's grandparents pleaded with the judge to end what they termed "the martyrdom of this child." Judge de Maximy responded immediately, issuing a summons for a hearing. What made this case unusual was that the mother of the child was not a foreigner or a French citizen of immigrant ancestry. She was born Françoise Tournier from a mainstream, middle-class Catholic family who had, against her family's wishes, married an Egyptian of modest means, Monsieur Fandy, and converted to a rigid, rule-bound form of Islam.

This case file revealed three distinct but interrelated strands to the narrative of child abuse constructed by court personnel. The first revolved around the circumstances and root causes of the abuse itself, which the mother rationalized as due to a difficult birth, medical complications, and her disorientation upon learning that she had delivered a girl and not the expected baby boy. When queried by the judge, Madame Fandy admitted past mistakes, accepted responsibility, and professed love for her daughter. She rejected as "outrageous nonsense" the neighbor's allegations of abuse, describing her as "mentally disturbed." Madame Fandy insisted that the personnel at the child wellness center accepted her explanation. She wanted to be left alone to care for her daughter "without court supervision" according "to her religion precepts."

The second narrative thread centered on Islamic extremism. The neighbor and the child's maternal grandparents blamed the mother's behavior on her Egyptian husband, whom they regarded as a religious fanatic. In a February 2001 report, French social services described the grandparents' dismay at their daughter's aberrant behavior, including her refusal of gendered toys and pediatric treatment for their granddaughter. They were alarmed to find one of the child's stuffed animals missing a head. Their daughter explained that "her action" (removing the head) was "in conformity with Islamic belief." Madame Fandy's parents were also shocked to discover that their daughter did volunteer work dressing the bodies of the dead in a Muslim morgue and had begun to wear the Islamic headscarf.

The central contention here was that Madame Fandy's conversion to a strict variant of Islam affected her ability to exercise her free will and to make rational choices that were in the best interest of her daughter. This was certainly consistent with the representation of the "veil" by French feminists and intellectuals such as Alain Finkielkraut, who saw it as a veil of ignorance that was impervious to critical thought or rational faculties.[42] Juvenile judges in Paris unanimously denounced the Islamic headscarf. For them, it symbolized an extremist version of Islam that was incompatible with the French republican values of female equality, tolerance, and freedom. They saw it as synonymous with regressive cultural practices that not only put the mental, moral, and physical health and well-being of minor children at risk but frequently required court intervention—in cases as varied as family conflicts over school activities, abductions of female children over summer vacations to Algeria, or arranged marriages.[43] For this judge, the veil was not a gesture of individual autonomy, a form of self-protection in repressive families, an expression of cultural identity, or a defiant reply to continued discrimination after immigration. Instead, it signified a dangerous threat and was synonymous with religious extremism, intolerance, and the subjugation of women. I was in France in December 2003 when the Stasi commission held public hearings on whether to ban religious symbols, specifically the Muslim headscarf. The judge made it a point to hand me material supporting such a ban, adding that her Muslim son-in-law supported it. This case muddied the waters. If the rejection of the veil by women of North African ancestry meant the protection of the French Republic against the destabilizing influence of Islam, what would it mean when worn by a French convert? Would the threat be the same?

The third strand, which was connected to the second, involved the embittered daughter, whose conflicts with her natal family began in elementary school, continued through her parents' bitter divorce, and were exacerbated with her mother's opposition to her marriage to an observant Muslim of modest means. In the February 2001 report, social workers noted that Françoise Fandy had expressed the desire to break with her family because of the grandmother's effect on her granddaughter's religious education.

When the judge's clerk called the Fandy family into chambers, only Madame Fandy and her daughter appeared. The judge began by reading from the social worker reports describing the neighbor's suspicions, her mother's charges, and the court's formal warning to her for child endangerment. Madame Fandy admitted that there was "a problem with her daughter" that lasted six months, explaining that she had "initially experienced only indifference" when presented with a baby daughter. When pushed to explain why her mother was so worried, Madame Fandy reframed the problem as one of French prejudice and ignorance against Islam.

MADAME FANDY: It was due to our religion . . . when you see what is broadcast about Islam in this country, the lies the media spreads, it is no wonder that people believe such things. You only see Muslim fanatics . . . the popular notions are due to ignorance.

The judge deftly raised the issue of gender and alternately probed the sensitive topics of family conflicts within Madame Fandy's family of origin. Madame Fandy's answers confirmed the family's adherence to a strict ascetic interpretation of Islam that precluded outside influences such as attendance in public schools, association with French rather than Muslim children, and the choice of toys. When questioned about the headless stuffed animal, she demurred, saying, "We have to be careful, if it has a soul, it could come to life." The judge suggested that Madame Fandy did not have the necessary distance (*recul*) with regard to her religion and declared herself "to be very worried that the child would be properly socialized." The judge viewed the isolation from French society as the result of tension within her natal family rather than cultural pressures from the religious community in which she lived and worked. She asked nothing about the husband's role despite the fact that he had consistently ignored court summons to appear. The initial allegations of neglect were premised on what the court viewed as an aberrant pattern of primary infant care. The child had spent six months in the back of the family's newly opened grocery store in her father's care rather than at home with her mother.

The judge repeatedly probed Madame Fandy's family history for the explanation of her religious conversion. Madame Fandy indicated her deep resentment against a mother who "left my father and preferred to remarry rather than think about the stability of her own children." When told that her daughter was expecting a child by her Egyptian husband, Madame Tournier had apparently advised her daughter to abort it, saying, "Don't ruin your life because of a child." The judge continued to suggest that Madame Fandy needed psychological help in her role as both a mother and a daughter. Madame Fandy was well aware that she and her family had become a case file known in terms of symptoms and diagnosis.[44] She refused the framing of her personal difficulties as psychological and deflected the accusation that she was troubled, insisting that she was "mentally fine." She appropriated medical-psychological discursive references to attempt to reframe her role as self-directed and maternal. "I know how necessary appropriate social and psychological development is for well-balanced children. It's obvious," she said. "Of course, I will take her to the doctor." She attempted to align her child-rearing practices with mainstream norms, but the judge persisted:

JUDGE: It is this certainty that bothers me. At the beginning you had trouble. How did you solve it? [*rhetorical question indicating abuse*] This problem with your mother is eating away at you. If you had a social worker, you would have someone who would listen without judging, come to see you and help you improve.

MADAME FANDY: I don't like to tell my life story. I have friends for that. They listen. I want to be left alone. Will I have you on my back until she is eighteen?

JUDGE: No, but because of the problems with your mother, I cannot close the case file.

The hearing ended with a vague threat by the judge that her role was to protect children and to remove them from abusive families if necessary. She imposed no other conditions on the family or protective measures for the child, such as a follow-up hearing, explaining afterward that she needed their cooperation and did not have it.

CONCLUSION

A central theme in this chapter is the critical role played by class, culture, religion, and gender in the determination of who lands in court and how risk is defined. It begs larger questions about the tolerance for cultural difference, understandings of legal responsibility, and the legitimacy of culture as a defense in court. The normative assumptions surrounding the selection of marriage partners, the possibility of divorce, the definition of family, the disciplining of children, the passage into adulthood, and the behavioral requirements for women and children are all intimately linked to citizenship and belonging.[45] The cases examined in this chapter reveal the difficult negotiations and outright disputes among judges, éducateurs, law enforcement, and members of minority groups over what forms and degrees of cultural diversity are permissible. The limits of tolerance for certain types of cultural difference emerge in the encounters of minority groups with various agents of authority such as police, school officials, district social workers, and psychiatrists as well as neighbors and coworkers. On the local level, in the neighborhood, the apartment building, and the school, cultural differences read as dress, language, gestures, looks, family forms, and public behavior are the primary means for differentiating among the mainstream French and their Others—primarily disadvantaged children of immigrant and foreign ancestry. These are often understood, like race, as invariable and immutable clusters of traits that are passed from generation to generation.

Once in court, this population is treated by a paradigm based on social origin and cultural difference. However, class, culture, and gender combine to affect the outcome of hearings in paradoxical ways. Class can, and sometimes does, trump culture, as in the case of Ahmed, when parents claim membership through "appropriate" behavior in the French middle class. However, because of their immigrant ancestry, Ahmed's parents had to go to considerable expense to prove their son's innocence in court. On the other hand, full-time employment, legal status, access to court files, and paid legal representation did not guarantee a positive result in civil proceedings when the court framed risk as a matter of cultural difference based on foreign origin. Ali's mother, despite earning high marks for her integration, still could not regain custody of her only son. Conversely, allegations of severe abuse and neglect directed against parents from privileged class backgrounds did not necessarily provide legal protection for abused or neglected children. Their parents had the economic means, social status, and cultural capital to keep court personnel at bay, a situation that was catastrophic for some children.

A delinquency of exclusion, associated with the troubled children of disadvantaged immigrants like the Tembas, was seen as a pernicious amalgam of chronic poverty, an urban underclass, school failure, and welfare dependency. It was based on a conception of the minor as determined by his sociocultural milieu. Many court personnel agreed that the "new" offenders who were appearing in their courtrooms, such as Michel Temba and his "gang," were mired in their own cultural codes and territories and seemed resistant, if not impervious, to the redemptive power of both French norms and laws. The trope "gang" appeared frequently in the discourses of judges to impute criminal intent to groups of young men who spent too much time in the street. Michel had already been identified by school authorities and social workers as *"turbulent"* (unruly) and without bearings (repères). Given the family's housing in a converted hotel room for four children and two adults, it was likely that Michel would continue to hang out with his "gang," get into trouble, and get placed in a track for underachievers.

These cases return us to *The Just* by Paul Ricoeur. The legitimacy of democratic institutions like the courts relies on able subjects whose rights and obligations are grounded in mutual recognition and acceptance of shared rules. Can this be said of the angry youth, outraged victims, misunderstood parents, indignant public officials, and moralizing court personnel? A recurrent theme involves visual contact as a prelude to visibility and recognition. Its opposite is embodied in the hostile stare that emerged in many cases. It is a look that forecloses recognition, erects boundaries, projects negative emotions, and often precedes confrontation and sometimes violence. In the first penal case involving the attack there was no mutual tolerance or recognition between the elderly French woman and the Temba boys. This led to unconscionable violence and increased alienation when the victim refused to testify out of fear, and the judge had to serve as her proxy and to recount the suffering she endured. She declined to join the prosecution as a civil plaintiff, surrendering her rights to be recognized as a subject of rights. It must also be said that the Tembas' right to decent housing and public security were largely ignored, abrogating an obligation implied in Ricoeur's democratic contract.

In the case involving the charge of violence and incitement to violence heard in the Eleventh District court, one of the reasons Ahmed got into trouble was his sense of moral outrage. After witnessing the violent confrontation between the police and his family, he considered them to be victims of police brutality and racism. Moreover, his warning "to not allow themselves to be taken" is an echo, verbatim, of the testimonials collected from other French victims of crime who insisted on their need to act, to redress the wrong done to them, and to demand that justice be served.[46] The irony in Ahmed's case was that as a subject of the law who was attempting to exercise his rights to security and peace, he should have been charged with disorderly conduct and incitement to violence. The fact that justice was served and an acquittal obtained did not negate the reality of an unwarranted arrest and arbitrary detention. The police, on the other hand, used a frivolous and, ultimately, baseless charge of disturbing the peace, when the real issue was the assault on their moral and professional integrity through the public allegations of racism and brutality. There was no mutual recognition, respect, or esteem grounded in shared rights as political subjects. Rather, an embittered colonial past was recalled and repeated for the accused and his family. This same past was evoked and disputed by the police.

Many civil plaintiffs who claimed to be victims turned out to be police officers. The majority of those claims for compensation were for minor physical injuries or merely symbolic insults. Their demands for "justice" and damages in court rested on their very power as public authorities to accuse and arrest, begging the question, in the wake of violent unrest in 2005, of who would hold them accountable. The confrontations of police with juvenile defendants rested on a set of categorical oppositions that precluded mutual recognition. For the police and prosecutors, the young offender too often represented social chaos, gratuitous violence, and immigrants, in contrast to public order, legitimate defense, and *Français de souche* (the pedigreed or true French). Although some judges rejected police claims as spurious, the majority took the word of the police and of French civil plaintiffs over that of juvenile defendants. To insist that the courts are color-blind, when the majority in penal hearings are African and Arab, makes a mockery of the status of victim as well as of the accused and ignores the peculiar nature of "republican racism" in historical and contemporary France.[47]

In the cases of Nadine and Madame Fandy, the French convert to fundamentalist Islam, social origin was prominent in the determination of risk. Nadine's birth in France provided her with citizenship, but political enfranchisement and state assistance was predicated on her isolation from her Algerian family, public testimony to the abuse she endured by her father, and a lonely struggle to attain the independence social services deemed important for such children. In the case of Madame Fandy, the risk was abrogated rather than assigned based on her French origin. Despite clear evidence of past neglect, new accusations of severe abuse, and eyewitness accounts of child-rearing practices culturally marked as abnormal, the court declined to intervene. The case exemplified the principle of categorical mixture that produced cognitive anxiety and led to rejection. For her own mother and the neighbor from Brittany, Madame Fandy's origin in the French middle class, marriage to a working-class Egyptian, and conversion to a rigid, rule-bound version of Islam were disturbing. She became part of an anomalous social category that became all the more threatening after she was suspected of abusing an infant.

The judge viewed the Fandy case in individual psychological rather than collective cultural terms. She interpreted and attempted to address the situation on the basis of Madame Fandy's social origin in the French middle class rather than her ascribed identity. The judge recognized her as the psychologically troubled victim of a broken home and an unhappy family history with a right to individual therapy and the obligation to provide good parenting. However, there was less space for the child as victim than for the mother as victim. Despite the prior history of maltreatment and possible continued abuse of her child, Madame Fandy clearly saw herself as a good mother who rationalized her past behavior as unintentional. She explained it as a temporary lapse born of frustration, inexperience, and disappointment, not to be compared with the actions of a bad mother.[48] As an educated French person, Madame Fandy had the authority to refute the allegations, refuse regular social worker visits, and, at least temporarily, forestall court intervention. It is hard to know what the consequences will be for her daughter. To my knowledge, the case did not resurface in court. For many nights afterward I dreamed about that tiny, solemn-faced figure in the pink coat who reluctantly gave up the doll from the judge's toy box as she left chambers with her mother.

In the next chapter, we move inside the juvenile court, a judicial venue that has generated debate. Its defenders contend that formal proceedings are necessary to communicate the power of the law and the social order upon which it depends.

7 JUDGING DELINQUENTS IN THE JUVENILE COURT

IN THIS CHAPTER WE MOVE INSIDE the formal juvenile court, which is the venue for the trials of thirteen- to sixteen-year-olds who are accused of serious misdemeanors and crimes. This court is the scene of highly ritualized confrontations among court personnel as well as victims, the defendants, and their parents. The cases we examine in chambers and those heard by the formal juvenile court reveal different understandings of violence and the dilemmas of classification. If the legitimacy of liberal democratic systems is underwritten by able subjects whose responsibility to one another is enhanced by their mutual recognition of the rightness of shared rules and privileges, the adjudication of these cases begs the question of how court personnel, children, and families imagine themselves and one another as social persons and political subjects.

Because of the continuing and rapid amendments to juvenile law over the past fifteen years, more offenses have been recategorized as "correctional" infractions that must be tried in this court and carry stiffer sentences for convictions. The most common cases heard before the Paris juvenile court involved charges of theft aggravated by one or more circumstances involving (1) an infraction by a group versus an individual; (2) with physical constraint; and (3) on public transportation or in public areas. Despite the menacing tenor of the moniker "aggravated theft," the charges in the vast majority of the hearings I attended centered on the theft of cell phones, designer sunglasses, clothing, motorcycle helmets, wallets, and cash.[1] Both the accused and the victims tended to be minors or young adults. When one of the aggravating circumstances was physical constraint (*avec violence*), it rarely involved a weapon or serious physical injury. When it did, the weapons were sticks, bottles, razors, or knives, not guns.

In 2003, Justice Ministry officials conducted a comprehensive inspection of the Paris juvenile court. Comparing the types of judgments and sentences rendered in Paris to suburban jurisdictions, such as Bobigny, Créteil or Nanterre, inspectors concluded that Parisian judges handed out rehabilitative measures at the lowest rate (only 4.9 percent of the total) and dispensed some of the most severe punitive sanctions. The most frequent were firm prison terms, suspended sentences, and conditional suspended sentences. Inspectors identified the increasing proportion of minors tried in the formal court versus chambers coupled with the fact that on average, only 20 percent had the benefit of court assistance and/or supervision before trial and sentencing, a phenomenon that was all the more problematic due to the long delays between indictments and trial. Inspectors noted the lack of in-depth investigations into the personalities of troubled minors, particularly those investigations that were conducted by a team of social professionals over a six-month period (versus a one-time evaluation by a social worker or psychologist). These inspectors criticized the unacceptably high number of minors judged in absentia (65 percent in 2001 and 55 percent in 2002) and the insufficient oversight of postsentence measures imposed by the court.[2]

The juvenile court is a privileged arena in which to observe the new penology at work as it centers on group offending, pathologizes culture, demands individual accountability, silences excuses, redefines causes, and, through a consensus on judgment and sentence formed among judges, prosecutors, and defense attorneys, separates offenders into uneven categories: the minority associated with the lost and redeemable child for whom scarce resources may be recommended versus the majority identified as unformed, incorrigible minors for whom assistance measures are viewed as unrealistic. This pessimistic outlook is expressed in the prosecutorial pleas emphasizing the need for harsher punishment for the repeat offenders whose cases fill the dockets of the juvenile court.

The space of the juvenile correctional court can be read as a reflection of the broader context in which the legal system brings together, at least for a time, different publics. The forced geographical proximity of these groups in the juvenile court proceedings is a painful reminder of the social distance and the collective entitlements that divide them. For the minors (and their families) who are tried and sentenced before the court, it is impossible to ignore the imbalances of state power, the selective supervisory gaze of the court, and the polarizing nature of its judgments. The most obvious manifestation of difference is that of the magistrats, those who stand to represent the state (le parquet) and those who sit and preside over criminal proceedings (le siège). In 2004, all eight prosecutors in the juvenile court were from the mainstream, middle-class French population. Among sitting judges on the court, all but one were from the majority population.

The class and ethnocultural homogeneity of magistrats also characterized other key personnel at court, including the attorneys, police, bailiffs, clerks, and secretaries. There was no ethnic and little gender diversity among the éducateurs, who interacted most closely with the overwhelmingly male minors and their families, until 2002, when two male éducateurs—one of Maghrebi ancestry and the other of West African ancestry—were appointed. Of the thirteen éducateurs, eight were women, including the director, and four were men. Defendants at the Paris court saw no Arab or black faces when they stood trial and faced the court. Minority defendants had little opportunity for legal representation by attorneys from their own groups because these groups are underrepresented in the magistracy, the bar, and law enforcement. Throughout France the courts are run by mainstream French professionals who prosecute and try those of immigrant and foreign ancestry. The implicit message is that the juvenile courts are not "for" the French except in the relatively rare cases where those from the mainstream population end up at trial. Although foreigners and [French] youth of immigrant ancestry are the main objects of the court's jurisdiction, the courts are not "for" them either.[3] The juvenile correctional court functions less to protect and rehabilitate than to contain and control a population whose deviance is increasingly depicted as a threat to the basic social order.

GOING TO COURT

Hurrying to get to court on time for the start of hearings, I often saw disoriented families who mistakenly attempted to step through the majestic entrance of the Palace of Justice with its grand iron gates and imposing central staircase. Police on guard brusquely directed visitors to the public entrance equipped with a metal detector. Once through this hurdle, they had to find their way into the labyrinth of the Palace itself and locate the Twenty-fifth Chamber. If they were fortunate, someone would point them to the door marked Y, and from there they would see the entrance marked *Tribunal pour Enfants*. Once inside, they might well ask themselves if this was indeed the juvenile court, a barren hall with two rows of wire benches screwed to the wall and a tiny, spare wooden desk manned by a lone, and usually bored, policeman. At 9:00 A.M., the time when proceedings were scheduled to begin, the hall was already crowded with children and parents, all African and Arab and mostly poor and of the working class or lower middle class. There were typically no "French" middle-class teenagers. The parents anxiously scrutinized the faces of white people like me who walked by, wondering if I was a judge or someone "official."

The halls were generally full by that time because the court summons instructed all the defendants and their families to arrive by 9:00 A.M. However, no court personnel ever arrived then—not the bailiff who served as both gatekeeper and master of ceremonies, not the defense lawyers, not the presiding judge. Typically the first to arrive in the deliberation room behind the courtroom were the two lay assessors who attend the trial and assist the judge in the judgment and sentencing deliberations.[4] The judge usually arrived sometime after 9:00, and she and her assessors waited for the ritual greeting of the deputy prosecutor in the deliberation room before the court session began. The prosecutors always entered and left from the outside door of the deliberation room, never using the door leading directly into the heart of the court chamber. Once when I naively asked why, one of the male assessors explained condescendingly, "It's the prerogative of the bench. The prosecution and the bench are separate; They have entirely different functions." Later when I considered the spatial arrangements in and movements through court, my question did not seem so absurd. When the hearing officially begins, despite the different routes they take, the prosecutors, sitting judges, assessors, and clerks assumed their rightful places on a raised dais separate and opposite from attorneys, victims, defendants, their families, and court caseworkers. As we shall see, symbolic form corresponds to judicial function. Despite apparent differences, judges and prosecutors in the inquisitorial tradition of the French court are on the same side. They uphold and defend the integrity of the law and public order.

WAITING FOR COURT TO BEGIN

I had imagined that the time preceding a trial would involve substantive discussion of the cases and would preclude exchanges between the prosecution, the bench, and the assessors. In fact, assessors did discuss cases, but they and magistrats, both the judges and prosecutors, also raised broader issues that spoke directly to the population under scrutiny. The issues they discussed and the opinions they solicited often reflected a general consensus based on their class position and educational background. On one occasion in June 2003, in the midst of the debates on secularism and talk about possible legislation to ban religious symbols from French public schools, specifically the Islamic headscarf, one assessor, a middle-school principal with long experience at the court, recounted an experience that shocked his listeners. He described the end-of-year exam period during which "a Muslim student" in his school had demanded the right to pray in the exam room. He described his response: "I refused, offered a room separate from the exam site, he rejected it, got upset, insulted me, addressed me [inappropriately] using *tu*, and then a group of teachers went on strike to support him." The prosecutor and judge greeted this story with expressions of outraged disapproval and unanimous censure of the striking teachers as an overly politicized response. They all expressed sympathy for the principal's position. The prosecutor lamented, "What are we coming to in this country?" The judge exclaimed, "You were absolutely right to refuse. You upheld *laïcité*" [state policy regarding religion in public schools]. Later that summer, in the minutes before hearings began, the Islamic veil again surfaced as a topic of conversation among a different group of assessors. One of them, a businessman, vehemently decried the veil as a "kind of fascism." When I asked why he used that term, he explained that the veil represented the repressive subordination of young women in the service of rigid religious fundamentalism. This was a viewpoint that his middle-class female colleague unequivocally shared.[5] These exchanges were usually truncated by the clerk's appearance, who, after consultation with the bailiff, entered the deliberation room to ask if "the court" was ready to begin.

ENTERING THE COURTROOM

In a typical trial the clerk works from a court docket furnished by the prosecutor's office. The prosecutor assigned to a particular district establishes the cases to be tried after consultation with the presiding judge. There could be last-minute changes or modifications on the order or number of cases, based on a decision to postpone a particular hearing because an attorney was unavailable or a defendant was delayed. Only the court personnel were advised of these changes. None of the accused or their families know ahead of time in what order the cases would be called. Only those whose cases are heard could enter the courtroom. With the exception of family members, social workers, attorneys, police officers, and other persons authorized by the court such as judicial interns, the proceedings are closed to the public. In contrast, the pronouncement of the judgment is public and open. This means that if the court docket is heavy—a docket can include ten or more cases—and all the defendants appear for trial—indicating that they received the summons, their parents were able to leave work and to arrange for child care for young siblings—the session could well continue until early evening, requiring that families spend all day waiting for cases to be tried.[6]

As the cases are called by the bailiff, defendants enter a proceeding which, because of its elaborate ritual apparatus, has been compared to the temporal and spatial strictures of French classical theater organized by the three unities of action, place, and time. Like its adult counterpart, the juvenile trial occurs in one place, the hearing room, and unfolds at one time, beginning and continuing to its inexorable conclusion with a judgment. It involves one action, the infraction for which the accused is judged.[7] The trial is the scene of flamboyant spectacle and highly ritualized confrontations between the legal order and the youth whose offense violated that order. It is organized to accentuate the authority of its decisions through the intimidation and isolation of the accused. These confrontations depend on an elaborate symbolic apparatus and spatial arrangements modeled on the adult court, which dramatize the solemn nature of the proceedings. The symbols include ceremonial black robes for prosecutors, judges, clerks, bailiffs, lawyers, and uniformed police, archaic formulaic language, and legal protocols such as the opening bell.

Next, the judge, his or her assessors, and any judicial interns solemnly enter the courtroom to the sounding of the bell that opens the court proceedings.[8] They join the juvenile prosecutor and the court clerk, who are already in place. When the accused is escorted into the courtroom by the bailiff and police, he assumes a liminal status and enters a highly policed space. Although understated compared to the grandiose chambers elsewhere in the Palace of Justice, the Twenty-fifth Chamber is still imposing in contrast to the modest offices of juvenile judges. The move from the noise and commotion in the adjoining hall into the silence and solemnity of the chamber is unsettling. The accused confronts the symmetrical organization of judicial space as he moves up the center aisle of the courtroom. In this way he immediately faces the judge who, from a central position on an imposing elevated podium, presides over and controls all communicative exchanges in the trial. The judge is flanked by the two assessors and is equidistant from the prosecutor and the court clerk, who face one another from opposite sides of the room. Opposite the judge's podium is the bar, which stands alone in an empty but symbolically resonant space. It is here to which all persons—the accused, court professionals, and material witnesses—are summoned to stand and answer questions unassisted by counsel. On the right of the central aisle are benches reserved for the accused and his family. Their defense attorneys and social workers sit behind them. To the left are the benches for the victims, witnesses for the state, and their attorneys.

CALLED TO STAND BEFORE THE JUDGE

Movement through and in this space is governed by largely unwritten codes and rules. The intricacies of court ritual and the opacity of legal language are such that no one instinctively knows how to act, where to stand, or what is expected in terms of appropriate speech. During my time there, although it was the responsibility of defense attorneys (and, to a lesser extent, éducateurs) to prepare the accused for his or her court trial, the actual preparation minors received was very uneven. Court-appointed attorneys were assigned by the Antenne des Mineurs (Juvenile Defense Bureau) to cases on a rotating basis, depending on the hearing date and the availability of the attorney, not on the case. Thus, defense attorneys did not necessarily follow the same case from beginning to end, and underaged defendants were likely to have one attorney for the indictment hearing and another for the trial.

The accused's ignorance about court protocols is a problem, since he or she must be seen to participate fully in the judicial ritual that produces the judgment and the sentence. Prosecutors and judges pay close attention to the behavior of juvenile defendants and their families in court. They must display a consistently appropriate and properly deferential demeanor. Their ability to stand straight, speak clearly and correctly, look directly at the interlocutors, wait their turn, and register both respect and restraint all count. The transgression of judicial protocols—such as when to remain standing, when to sit, whom to address when questioned, how and when to approach the bar—frequently results in corrections. Any deliberate or oppositional affirmation of the gestures, affect, stance, and slang associated with street culture provokes immediate reprimands or sarcastic denunciations from prosecutors, such as "the accused mocks the court" or "he cannot stand and act like a human being." Reprimands are intended to reinforce feelings of moral culpability and to promote social conformity, although they sometimes had the opposite effect, prompting expressions of hostility and resistance. Only the display of a proper (middle-class) demeanor and the acceptance of responsibility allow defendants to isolate the offense from their sociocultural background without challenging the legal and social order the court must defend.[9]

The juvenile judge has an expansive role at the juvenile correctional trial. Although the composition of the docket is determined by the prosecutors, the questioning of the accused and witnesses as well as the order and timing of each individual trial are controlled by the judge. In contrast to the often theatrical posturing of the prosecutors, the sitting judges are understood to be "more deliberative and methodical."[10]

After the ringing of the bell, the first case is called. Proceedings begin with what is termed an adversarial debate during which the accused is called to the bar to hear the charges and is asked to confirm or deny the facts of the offense as they appear in the file. This is the only portion of the trial transcribed directly into the court record by the clerk. In this introductory phase, the judge confronts the facts of the case—with mitigating circumstances of the youth's personal and family background—presented by éducateurs and his parents or guardians. The judge first addresses the minor, his parents or guardians, and the éducateur who has been assigned to the family before allowing questions by the prosecutor, the attorneys, and the two assessors who participate in the judgment. Victims' testimony precedes the prosecutors' pleas, and the defense attorneys have the last word before the court adjourns to deliberate.

In contrast to the U.S. juvenile court, where the causes for offending are relatively less important than the moral character of the youth, the French court is very much concerned with root causes because of what these reveal about the nature of the offense, the guilt of youths, and their capacity for social integration.[11] In France, the basis of the charges draws directly on statements and confessions obtained by police. The court relies heavily on these statements, signed by the defendants, victims, and witnesses, and resists any attempts to reframe or retract the version of events presented there. It likewise resists attempts to undermine police credibility and integrity, as these constitute an attack on the moral authority of the justice system. In my observation, judges' rhetorical style during questioning thus was premised on the individual responsibility of the youth and his or her acknowledgment of the wrong done to the social order. Claims of innocence and belated alterations of the facts before the bar were viewed very negatively as acceptance of culpability was considered a precondition of rehabilitation. Judges' questions were conducted so that there could be no legitimate reason or justification for the act that could be maintained or defended. Despite a growing ambivalence about the capacity of the "new" delinquents to be rehabilitated, the judges I observed considered individual motive and its relation to the whole person because of the pedagogical role and structuring dimension of French law. On the one hand, their training conditioned them to see the law as a means to reintegrate the "bad" citizen through the internalization of legal norms and an appeal to shared social values. On the other, their practice and experience within the court increasingly called this possibility into question.

ANSWERING THE JUDGE'S QUESTIONS

The tenor of the judges' questioning was verbally aggressive in the trials I observed. It involved the skeptical query, the incredulous probe, and the vigorous evaluation of any inconsistencies. At the same time, judges always invited minors to reflect critically on their acts by eliciting personal statements that suggested they have been renormalized and integrated within the social order. The timing of this questioning at the very beginning of the trial reinforced the power of the court over minor defendants, particularly illegal foreigners and lower-class French citizens of non-European ancestry. The defendants I observed in court were, on the whole, largely passive, disengaged, and reluctant, answering with monosyllabic answers or phrases and in low voices to the torrent of questions directed at them. Sympathetic judges have argued that the ignorance of French legal protocol, judicial terminology, and penal statutes can render the accused "mute and stupid" and produce the erroneous impression that they are recalcitrant, belligerent, or duplicitous. French attorneys have described how difficult it is to defend minors because of their complete disinterest in and refusal to participate in their own defense.[12] Because the trial is premised on the admission of guilt as a precondition of rehabilitation, the court resisted judicial procedures, such as a true adversarial debate among all parties, that allowed an alternate version of the truth to surface. Minor defendants rightly saw themselves as objects of a legal process with a predetermined outcome rather than subjects empowered to act on their own behalf.

Nevertheless, some minors were assertive during questioning, giving as well as they got, or expressed resistance, refusing for prolonged periods to answer questions or employing other techniques to avoid sanctions. In contrast to their portrayal as passive, intimidated, or ignorant, some who were the most marginal and had the least to lose demonstrated considerable agency, mental agility, and creative thinking in their court performances. They revealed a certain understanding of French law and made an instrumental use of it. They attempted to resist accusations of culpability and to lessen the severity of punishment through a variety of strategies. They acknowledged responsibility for lesser charges carrying lighter penalties, they shifted responsibility from themselves to their parents or peers, exercised the right to have cases retried when sentences were excessively harsh, changed their stories, and constructed narratives that countered the facts recorded in police statements.

The 2003 case of a French seventeen-year-old of Antillean ancestry is an example of a teenager who was failing in school, had a long police record and few job prospects, was alienated from productive networks of exchange, and found himself literally, in Robert Castel's phrase, floating unmoored among the "disaffiliated."[13] He provoked the judge's ire by refusing to accept his part in an attack on an unarmed youth in the Paris metro; because of a "hostile stare." The judge established his identity and discovered to her dismay that his mother had not come to court. She elicited his version of the events. Narrating in passive voice, in a move likely intended to erase agency and responsibility, he declared that "a fight had broken out, insults and shoves were exchanged, and he was punched hard in the stomach" before he responded in kind by hitting "his assailant" over the head with a "whisky" bottle. The judge countered this version by reading from hospital records—which certified bruises on the victim's skull—and the victim's police statement:

> I was waiting for my girlfriend when I saw two individuals, of the African race, leave the train platform and approach me. They stood in front of me and tried to block my path. They started to insult me and tell me that I was looking at them in the wrong way. I told them I hadn't done anything wrong. One of them grabbed me by the neck. I pushed him away and the other took out a bottle and hit me over the head with it.

When the judge demanded that the accused justify the discrepancy between the two accounts, he refused to answer. She began to lose her patience. "What is your problem?" she asked. "You get angry over absolutely nothing. Why can't you keep the damned peace?" Confronted again with his silence, she looked at his file, saying, "This is your eighth offense since February 2002. You have to stop this violence. This is not the first time you've used a bottle as a weapon. What do you think about this?" At this point he attempted to deflect blame for the attack, saying, "it wouldn't have happened if I had not been having problems with my mother." After hearing from the éducatrice that his "problems in school had gotten worse," that he was "too subject to peer pressure," and was very "rowdy" (turbulent), she and the prosecutor were clearly both pleased and relieved to hear that the family intended to send him back to his father in Guadeloupe. The court's leniency was premised on this return to the Antilles and enrollment in a taxi driving training course. It was framed as an issue of individual accountability and personal responsibility. The judge admonished him to remember, "It is not inevitable [this behavior], things depend on you, on your choices."

In my experience, the attempt to resist accusations of wrongdoing and to deflect individual responsibility was viewed as deeply subversive because the juvenile court rituals were structured for the accused to acknowledge guilt, to convey the intention to avoid offending, and to underwrite both the ideological hegemony of the court and the moral authority of the legal order by accepting responsibility.[14] When juveniles insisted on their innocence or changed their stories and disavowed earlier statements to escape conviction out of fear of reprisals, outrage at police abuse, or shame in the presence of their parents, they incurred the strong displeasure of court personnel. This took the form of moralizing disapproval from éducateurs, sharp rebukes from judges, and, sometimes, demands for stiffer penalties from deputy prosecutors.

One of the most serious cases I heard involved the eldest son Jacques of the Temba family whom we met in Chapter 6. The case was exceptional because it involved the crime of aggravated rape.[15] It was also unusual because of the young ages of the accused (thirteen) and the victim (six) and because the accused and his mother insisted on his innocence and obtained a rare acquittal. Here the prosecution insisted on the guilt of the accused, blamed a culture of poverty, and painted a vivid picture of absent fathers, negligent mothers, and wild children left unsupervised. The crux of the case turned on the lack of physical evidence of sexual molestation but centered prominently on scars found on the victim's arms. Furthermore, Judge Boyer, who investigated the case, thought it significant that the young victim's mother did not join the prosecution as a civil plaintiff. Did a sexual attack occur? If so, did it also include a physical beating as the prosecution alleged? Or were the victim's own relatives guilty of disciplining her with a belt as Jacques's defense attorney successfully argued?

Both children lived in the same welfare hotel in the eleventh arrondissement, which the éducatrice depicted as "indescribable" in its state of disrepair and filth. She informed the court that she had monitored Jacques for two years, that he did not speak French well, that he had been out of school during that period (that is, had been expelled for truancy and was never readmitted), and "repeated attempts to integrate him had failed." After his arrest, Jacques had been removed from his family and placed in a residential facility for the most incorrigible offenders outside Paris. She continued, "Jacques reacted very badly to the separation. There were violent altercations among the youth there and Jacques got mixed up in it." She gave no details on what transpired or who was to blame and declined to describe Jacques's injuries beyond mention of a three-week hospital stay and his return to his mother.

> JUDGE: Did he receive psychiatric care?
>
> EDUCATRICE: Yes, he received care at the Adolescent Care Center in consultation with the Salpetrière Hospital. He followed the treatment as an outpatient.
>
> JUDGE: [*reading from the case file*] The little girl, six years old, denounced Jacques, saying he put his hand in her vagina and also hit her. The gynecological examination was normal but the marks on her arms were consistent with a beating with a belt. Jacques has always denied the facts but the young girl was questioned by the Brigade de la Protection des Mineurs and maintained her statement. Her mother insists that Jacques sexually molested her daughter but did not beat her. She asserts that the molestation took place in his room and he took photos.
>
> JUDGE: [*to Jacques*] What do you have to say about this?

Jacques adamantly denied the charges, provoking a spirited exchange with the judge. I noted that, despite the éducatrice's report, he spoke well in French and demonstrated considerable presence.

> JUDGE: With whom did you dance?
>
> JACQUES: Girls came to dance with me.
>
> JUDGE: Did you commit this act?
>
> JACQUES: Why would I have done such an act? Why would I touch a six-year-old girl like that?
>
> JUDGE: Why would she invent such things?
>
> JACQUES: I don't know. I have little sisters. I have trouble understanding. I have never hit children.
>
> JUDGE: She came up to dance with you?
>
> JACQUES: She came up two times but I told her to go back down. I said go down. Why would I touch a child like that?

JUDGE: You got angry with her.

JACQUES: No.

JUDGE: You were tired of having these children bother you all the time.

JACQUES. No.

When the judge asked if some parents in the hotel punish their children by beating them with a belt, Jacques responded yes, adding that the little girl's aunt beat her, and her mother, who worked late, neglected her. He indicated that on several occasions the police had to bring the child home because "she was allowed to wander alone in the street at night. Late at night." Unsolicited denunciations of this type were a risky tactic because they claimed entitlement based on the integrity of the youth even as they threatened adult rectitude and parental authority. They were also risky because they mirrored the very judgments leveled against African parents not only by officers of the court but by French public opinion. The court scrutiny was intensified by sharply contrasting normative conceptions of parental authority and modes of discipline within "modern" French families and their "traditional" African counterparts. These exaggerated contrasts tend to obscure the history of child discipline in France and the many shifts that coalesced to end the broad public tolerance for corporal punishment that predominated in the past. Over the last century, parental relations with dependent children were transformed by a decrease in infant mortality, control over fertility, the emergence of childhood as a distinct stage in the life cycle, the rise of child psychiatry establishing early childhood as the essential building block of the adult personality, and new labor market demands requiring prolonged schooling.[16] The child, whose links to parents were now more personalized, lasting, and affective, could no longer be physically punished. Newer models of parental, versus paternal, authority were based on the reasoned negotiation of rules and the necessary provisioning of conditions for realizing the child's full potential.[17]

The prosecutor's summary was a plea for guilt mitigated by a commitment to therapy for "an obviously troubled teenager." Nonetheless, she linked a poverty of culture to a culture of poverty and was clearly irritated by the persistent protests of innocence by the mother and son. Their claims confirmed for her both the teenager's mental illness and the backward culture of origin. She maintained that the "crux of the matter" was the "overcrowded conditions in the hotel," where "poverty of several different kinds is put on trial." She admonished the court not to forget Jacques's "cruel, brazen behavior" and his "brutal uprooting from Africa to France" and urged that he be removed from his home environment. Here the prosecutor was ascribing intentionality and bad character in an attempt to adultify Jacques in her plea for guilt. She admitted that there was "no formal proof," but she added that it was "completely unacceptable for him to treat the little girl like a sexual object." At the same time she was predicating therapeutic intervention on an absence of individual volition by blaming his African cultural roots. As a foreign transplant out of his element, his cruel behavior was predictable.

In recent years, strong tensions have arisen between court personnel and families, particularly Maghrebi and African fathers, whose use of sometimes harsh corporal punishment to discipline children and to maintain parental authority has drawn the censure of representatives of numerous French institutions, including teachers, school nurses, doctors, social workers, and the police. These disciplinary methods are legally categorized as abuse and parents themselves have been threatened with penal sanction, a charge some found incomprehensible.[18] This case illustrates the contradictory signals sent by the court, which suggests, on the one hand, that families do not sufficiently supervise their children and, on the other, are overtly harsh in their discipline. For the prosecutor, this case concerned not only a sexual assault aggravated by violence. It also pitted two qualitatively different cultural systems against one another. One is associated with Africans, whom she implied are less evolved, resistant to cultural adaptation, and difficult to integrate. The other is French society, in which civilizational standards are supposedly higher, children are not treated as sexual objects, and the law safeguards victims of sexual assault by punishing offenders. Given the fact that French social services could find only one room in a squalid converted hotel for a large family and that, after two years, a caseworker had still not managed to get a teenager reenrolled in public school, this case also begs the question of what kinds of violence against children the French state will tolerate.

THE PARENTS' TURN TO SPEAK

After questioning the accused, judges typically invited parents to comment on their relations with their children, along with the child's actions, development, scholastic achievement, and future plans. Parents' presence in court, deference to judicial authority, respect for the power of sanction, realization of the consequences, composure, ability to follow the proceeding without requesting clarification or repetition, and ability to express themselves in correct French all had an effect on the judge and the assessors, positive or negative. The parents I observed in court were deferential, passive, bewildered and, in some cases, shamed. For poor and working-class immigrant families in particular, an appearance in court was particularly traumatic, because the stigma of cultural difference they had hoped to keep at bay was both visible and intensified under court scrutiny. They felt targeted as bad parents and judged along with their children. For Algerian and African parents, and fathers in particular, children who caused trouble were doubly illegitimate. Fathers who spent their lives in hard, poorly paid jobs nourished the dream of social mobility for their children. In return they demanded that their children remain both loyal to their parents' culture and be successful in French schools. When the children failed in or were expelled from school, broke the law, and landed in court, it was both humiliating and unforgivable.[19] The fathers and mothers who had lived in fear of the police and bosses were suddenly forced to defend their parenting in court. This meant public scrutiny of methods of discipline, hygiene, nutrition, rules with regard to homework, curfews, and social boundary mechanisms related to friends. All these were subject to the normative judgment of and comparison with French middle-class values and practices.

A case tried in June 2003 in the Eighteenth District South court illustrates the way the court gaze settled on and stigmatized the families of deviant youth, particularly those who resisted the pedagogical and structuring function of the law by refusing to admit culpability. Here we meet Mustapha, a seventeen-year-old who was born in the Eighteenth South District of Paris to working-class Malian parents. Although living in a famously "bad" neighborhood, he was enrolled in the final year of a baccalauréat program in a professional lycée and had no police record until he was arrested in a drug bust involving several adults. He was accused of possession and sale of marijuana and crack cocaine. He had acknowledged his role as the "banker" in a well-known and dangerous drug ring run by adults, served four months in pretrial detention, and upon his release from prison in May 2003 was removed from his parents' home, put on conditional parole, and placed with his paternal uncle in a different area and a new school, a move that set him back emotionally and scholastically. I was present with Judge de Maximy the day before the trial when the deputy prosecutor arrived to discuss the case. They both agreed that, given Mustapha's admission of guilt and the positive social report, they should be lenient and sentence him to the time already served.

In court the judge turned to his parents and asked them to comment on their son's behavior since his return from prison:

FATHER: Since prison he has worked hard, no longer associates with the wrong people. He goes to school, has stopped his stupid behavior.

JUDGE: [*to Mustapha*] Was it so easy to stop that behavior? [*goes on without pause*] You were arrested by the police in the middle of a transaction involving crack cocaine with Abdel, a well-known drug dealer. You were arrested just when a female drug addict gave you money. [*looking again at the file and musing out loud*] It is true that they don't exactly say that it is you. They mention "two African individuals." When the police searched you [meaning his person and his room at home], you had 30 euros [on his person], they also found [in his room] 92 grams of marijuana, in bars for sale, a nightstick, 325 euros, money earned illegally, three hoods, a pistol, an automatic weapon! A small arsenal! Abdel is a criminal known to the court. These associations have to stop! What do you have to say?

MUSTAPHA: It is difficult to deny.

JUDGE: So you admit the facts?

MUSTAPHA: Yes, I was selling marijuana.

At this point the judge turned again to the police statements and pointed out that the police had placed a unit in the area conducting surveillance. It was apparent that the big dealers had escaped their dragnet. She looked at Mustapha and asked him to identify his cocaine suppliers for the record, saying, "I know it is difficult to say this in front of your parents, but you have to stop sheltering these people." He looked petrified, his body went rigid, his eyes stayed fixed straight ahead and he abruptly changed his story, insisting that he had never intended to sell drugs. This visibly frustrated the judge, exasperated his defense attorney who shook her head in disbelief, surprised his parents, and infuriated the prosecutor.

When the prosecutor made her plea, she put her outrage on display and drew me into her performance. This was the only occasion when I was invited to sit next to the prosecutor. As an observer associated with sitting judges, I usually sat on the opposite side of the courtroom next to the court clerk. I became the perfect pawn, invited to express horror as she brandished photographs seized by the police showing Mustapha and his school friends smoking cigar-sized joints and to register disapproval at obviously negligent parenting.

The case shifted from Mustapha's vulnerability at the hands of a local gang in a bad neighborhood to the negligence of his parents:

PROSECUTOR: He is the gang leader of the eighteenth [arrondissement], giving the impression of the big gangster selling crack cocaine. He is selling death in small doses. What kind of a state does it put them in? We cannot ignore the ravages wrought by this drug. I am quite willing to accept that he is changing, but he must adopt a different tone. [*sarcastic tone*] He did four months in preventive detention. The parents are here. How are things going at home? Don't they feel challenged when they find objects like these under their son's bed? Why didn't they know? I know what is under my children's bed. 92 grams is substantial. [*producing a photo*] These are not little joints. They are smoking *enormous* joints. What is their life going to be? They must be able to change their life and attitude. Look at this. Look at Madame's reaction [*referring to me; I reacted with surprise at her tactic, not at the photo.*]. They take pictures of themselves with these joints and bottles of Pepsi [a clear reference to the consumption of multiple drugs such as marijuana, sugar, and caffeine]. They are on a downward spiral. It is people like them who make the eighteenth an unlivable place.

Mustapha's refusal to divulge the identities of the adults in the drug ring provoked the prosecutor to change her plea:

PROSECUTOR: I was hoping for a different attitude. It is not very smart because it is going to worsen his case. It is critical to be able to admit his responsibility. It is important to be able to admit his role, only his role. [*adopting a sarcastic tone*] So I suppose the French police invent stories and teenagers exchange candy outside grocery stores. It is a bit much to accept . . . I revise my request. He is obstructing justice. Four months in prison was not enough. He is mired in delinquency and needs more punishment. I request a year of prison, with six months suspended. I demand two additional months. We released him from prison so he could take the [professional baccalauréat] exam. Well, he failed. He is not capable of passing it. He is obstinate, isolating himself, and continues down the wrong path.

The court found him guilty, giving him an eight-month suspended sentence with a conditional probation of eighteen months, in addition to the obligation to stay in school and avoid his old neighborhood, on pain of incarceration.

THE EDUCATEUR WEIGHS IN: IS A CHILD LOST, OR MERELY UNFORMED?

Before or after questioning a minor's parents, judges always turned to the éducateur following the case.[20] Judges' determination that a minor was receptive to rehabilitation and assistance depended on the facts of the case, his behavior, his background reported in the written reports archived in the file and the oral testimonies provided by éducateurs. Written reports included psychological, social, physical, and scholastic evaluations of the children. They also focused on family structures within and between generations, housing, income, lifestyle, and drew heavily on a medical-psychological discourse to determine the accused's capacity for normalcy or to register patterns that signaled trouble. Educateurs prepared for court by condensing complicated family histories and selectively presenting elements to present in court. After hearing many such summaries and reading scores of written reports in court files, I came to see that the form taken by their reports was a distinct genre. It was a family narrative, recounting the history of the family and interweaving it with the minor's personality. The goal was to synthesize a child's formative experiences and to predict his future prospects. They situated observable behavior amply documented by state authorities in key venues, such as the public school or the home, within a matrix of explanatory factors to construct a coherent narrative. This allowed them to distinguish the lost child or potential citizen whose misdeeds were a temporary and reversible digression from his movement along the right path from the unformed child or future delinquent whose early deficiencies set him irredeemably on the wrong path. In both cases, family origins, parent-child relations, intergenerational bonds, and social *habitus*, understood as internalized predispositions and immediate influences, were central elements of the plot. Whereas an integrated welfare system theoretically makes no distinction between endangered and delinquent children and favors prevention and protection, in reality, given the scarce resources and limited access to therapy, training programs, paid internships, and entry-level jobs, strategic decisions are constantly made as to who is deemed worthy.

One of the most significant factors for consideration in penal cases was the section in these reports devoted to the personality of the youth. Here the court was particularly attentive to the proper structure of the personality. Did the youth have a clear sense of his bearings (repères) or place within his family and social structure, which both signify a firmly grounded sense of personhood and identity? Had the youth accepted and internalized the limits (les limites) or the controls on his behavior as an individual that are a prerequisite to integration with a larger social and moral order? Or as one judge put it, had the accused "become a delinquent with problems of individuation and the manifest inability to detach from a family with pathological relations."[21] Whereas psychology was and remains a major factor in explaining childhood abnormalities, the new explanations for the causes and persistence of a delinquency of exclusion, offered by sociologists, politicians, jurists, and ethnopsychiatrists, centered on culture. The individual child was seen less as an autonomous individual and more the product of a group culture. Cultural difference and origin have been added to and conflated with psychology, class, and economics as the most significant risk factors at a time when a majority of the penal defendants were minors of immigrant ancestry, resident foreigners, or illegal migrants. These factors were indexed indirectly in social services reports in lifestyle sections and descriptions of the parent-child relations. Despite the weight of cultural disorders and deficiencies, the minor who broke the law was admonished to demonstrate his capacity to integrate within French society and to internalize legal and mainstream social norms by demonstrating his capacity as an individual with the free will and agency to take initiative and be responsible.

Educateurs sometimes unequivocally positioned children as either lost minors or unformed children, but more often their reports were necessarily ambiguous and open-ended. Such ambiguous summaries combining characteristics of both lost and unformed children provided the basis for leniency and rehabilitation as well as for punitive sanction. This gave judges, prosecutors, and attorneys the material and the power to selectively appropriate salient aspects of the report and to present the story of a temporarily lost but ultimately redeemable "good" child versus an unformed and menacing "bad" child. Opposing narratives ostensibly divided the judge from the prosecutor or the prosecutor from the defense attorney. In fact, careful attention to the pleas, verdicts, and sentences revealed that a consensus formed around one narrative, usually provided by the judge. This narrative was often endorsed by all the parties, including the defense attorneys, giving that narrative authority and allowing it to form the basis of the judgment. Although prosecutors' pleas seemed to depart from this narrative, despite the hyperbole that accompanied their sanction demands, these did not differ substantially from the actual sentences imposed by the judges.

Consider the narratives that surfaced in three cases tried together involving two young men and one young woman accused of theft and property destruction directed against the young woman's parents. All three of the accused shared troubled backgrounds and were known to the court. Two were foreigners, a Haitian male and a young woman of Japanese ancestry. I knew from the court file that sixteen-year-old Aimé, the Haitian minor, had eleven infractions and had already served eight months in prison for aggravated theft, vandalism, and extortion. Neither he nor his single mother appeared for the trial. Mathieu, the second male, the French son of middle-class parents—an Algerian father and a French mother—had an even longer record consisting of twenty-three infractions. He had been expelled from school at fifteen and had served a one-month prison term. Yukiko, the only female, had never been in trouble until after her parents' divorce. She had suffered sustained abuse from her mother, who was a violent alcoholic. She was removed from her mother's home at age thirteen and custody was awarded to her father and stepmother. She had conflicts with her stepmother, ran away, and, at the age of fifteen, lived on the street for six months, sleeping in an abandoned car, where she was raped. Although she came to the attention of social services during this period, no alert was sounded. It was only after the offense brought her to the prosecutor's attention that a juvenile judge intervened and placed her in a residential center, where she adapted well, got back in school, and excelled.[22]

Because Yukiko had not been assigned an éducatrice, the judge had only a written report filed by a social worker from a different service provider. Judge de Maximy was disgusted with its poor quality, exclaiming in a brief exchange with the prosecutor, that "it said nothing." The report included a highly truncated family history that erased Yukiko's troubled childhood and portrayed her deviance as intentional, conscious, and immoral. It provided no specifics concerning her mother's alcoholism, the rape, or her life on the street. The report began after the divorce of her parents and the remarriage of Yukiko's father to a younger Japanese woman. It described their jobs, monthly income, two children, and his inability to pay fines incurred from Yukiko's misbehavior. It indirectly assigned her the blame for conflicts with her new stepmother. It had virtually no information on her schooling, beyond listing the "many" establishments she attended, implying recurrent expulsions, and it highlighted her truancy from school.

Eliding the abuse she had endured, the report interpretively framed her behavioral problems through the strong tropes of race and sexuality. The "problems" Yukiko created with the son of a Chinese foster family and her association with her "co-detainees" who were "boys living at a hotel" hinted at sexual promiscuity. Summing up her personality as an unformed child, the social worker concluded: "Behind the fragile exterior, there is a determined character, obstinate, and rebellious. Seductive, she can play on her undeniable little Asiatic charm with her svelte silhouette. The fact remains she is a teenager without any grounding or references." Yukiko's "anguished memory of terrible arguments," the "emotional deficit of her home because she has not known any tenderness," and abuse by her mother and neglect by her father put her, "in perpetual danger" and boded ill for the future. The normal dispensations that should be granted to an abused adolescent, who must be assertive when faced with the total abdication of adult responsibility and who must protect herself when alone at fifteen and sleeping in an abandoned car, were withdrawn from her by this social worker. Through the use of Orientalist images of potent sexuality and skillful deception, the social worker made Yukiko an adult figure whose deviance took on a conscious and sinister tone.

In contrast, Judge de Maximy cited the conclusions of the medical-psychiatric evaluation she had ordered. In that report, Yukiko was depicted as a lost child who had been "affected by the emotional deficiencies in her family and had made bad choices." In this way, the judge substituted a new narrative for Yukiko:

JUDGE: Yukiko is intelligent, affectionate, athletic and immature, but not violent. She is in moral danger and needs a firm hand.

Yukiko's defense attorney informed the court that Yukiko had been readmitted to the academic track of a French lycée, had a fiancé with whom she was expecting a baby, and had applied for the special social assistance available for young adults aged eighteen to twenty-one. She added a mitigating circumstance not mentioned by the social worker report by describing Yukiko's rape and her attacker as a serial rapist currently serving a prison term. Despite this, the prosecutor argued that because the offenses were premeditated and motivated by revenge, and none of the three had shown remorse or apologized, she insisted on accountability and asked for a three-month suspended prison sentence for Yukiko and Aimé and a 300-euro fine for Mathieu. Nonetheless, the narrative constructed and imposed by the judge was affirmed by her assessors, and the court was lenient with regard to Yukiko and Mathieu. Aimé's case was rescheduled.[23]

It was rare for éducateurs to construct and defend unequivocal narratives of either lost or unformed children. It was also unusual for them to use their reports as a vehicle to register protests against police brutality or other institutional injustices. One example was an unusually detailed written report in the file of a seventeen-year-old Malian national, Amadou, whose case was scheduled for trial during the same court session as Mustapha's. Amadou failed to appear, and the report was never made in court, but I rescued it from the obscurity of the court archive as a means to publicize what the éducatrice denounced as systematic police harassment. Amadou had no legal status and was accused of threatening and insulting the police and violently resisting arrest during an ID check. He had already served six months in prison for selling drugs, and his parole from prison had been conditional upon regular school attendance and satisfactory grades. The éducatrice described his attempt to stay in school and to keep up his grades as "an effort demanding extraordinary will power given the systematic harassment to which he is subjected in the neighborhood by the CRS [riot police] in the eighteenth." She noted a specific incident in which the police stopped a car in which Amadou was riding. They questioned him about the new Nike shoes he was wearing, assuming that he had stolen them, detained him at the local police headquarters, and confiscated the shoes. He was held without charge or access to an attorney and released four hours later, barefoot, onto the street, on the pretext that his shoes could not be found. To justify her defense of Amadou's character, the éducatrice described him as a lost minor who was well brought up "according to the criteria of French culture" and added that he was "not devious [as one may suspect?] but rather direct, simple, and generous." This narrative prompted no direct comment from the judge, but the prosecutor acknowledged in open court "the widespread problem of harassment by riot police in the eighteenth." His case was judged in absentia and he received a one-month prison sentence.

THE PROSECUTOR'S *RÉQUISITOIRE*

Although judges play an important role through their control of courtroom proceedings, juvenile prosecutors also exercise considerable power. Prosecutors decide who to prosecute after arrest, control the court docket, determine which judges' decisions to appeal, and have access to case files at any time before trial. Nonetheless, there is a functionally complementary relationship between judges and prosecutors. In spite of the vivid spectacle on display in the juvenile court and the apparently opposing roles of judges and prosecutors, in reality judges and prosecutors enact similar functions and work together closely as professional collaborators on the cases that come before the juvenile court. They discuss cases in detail and, as we saw in the case of Mustapha, often come to a consensus on judgments and sentences before the trial begins. Despite the flamboyant histrionics and incendiary rhetoric used by prosecutors, the outcomes of verdicts and sentences are often predetermined and the deliberations presided over by judges and assessors rarely produce surprises. Recent reforms of juvenile law, inaugurated with the Justice Ministry circular of 15 October 1991, have heightened and revalued the specialized role of the juvenile prosecutor's office in the containment of juvenile delinquency and the protection of victims. Similarly, legislative reforms in 2002 and 2004 have added to the already extensive powers of the juvenile judge by making the judge the sole sentencing authority. In this new capacity, the judge enjoys the weighty prerogative of revoking all or part of a conditional suspended sentence and incarcerating a minor.[24]

Prosecutors' sanction requests (*réquisitoires*) come after the adversarial debate between the judge and the accused. The réquisitoire is considered an integral part of the juvenile court ritual because it symbolizes the power of the state to accuse and to identify the threat posed by a delinquent youth. When prosecutors stand to deliver their pleas, they embody that power. They defend the authority of the law by building cases through a selective emphasis on elements taken from police reports, signed confessions, witness and victim depositions, medical examinations, psychiatric evaluations, and physical evidence. They mine details from these sources and reorder them into legal facts that could have only one conclusion—the criminal intention and bad character of the accused. They create a selective but logically coherent biography of the stages of a delinquent career in order to recast offenders' behavior in opposition to the normal social order. In the trials I observed, this biography often included highly subjective commentaries that reflected their own class position and reproduced a stigmatizing discourse on the lack of integration among the defendants facing trial.

Although French law recognizes only individual culpability, prosecutorial summaries centered explicitly on culture. They tended to criminalize the cultural difference of minority groups through a focus on their families, communities, and cultures. They manipulated and reinforced public perceptions concerning juvenile offenders as dangerous predators (even in cases in which physical injuries are minor) and their families as both socially dysfunctional and culturally alien (even when they were born in or lived in France for many years and were citizens). I attended nine sessions of the full juvenile court between 2001 and 2003 in which six prosecutors presided. All but one tied sanction requests—particularly for offenses involving physical attacks—to behaviors they attributed to origin and upbringing. One prosecutor noted "the accused's obvious inability to integrate within French society" and "the swagger of the accused when he enters the courtroom." Another stressed the incivility of the defendant: "He approaches the bar at the wrong time, insists on HIS right to talk, interrupts the court, and will not be quiet." In a case involving a knife attack, another prosecutor informed the judge, "I'm told that in North African culture, it is customary to hide a weapon in one's sleeve. That may be custom in those countries but even in the twentieth arrondissement in Paris, we don't see attacks like this." In a mugging case, one of her colleagues could not contain his fury: "Their [a sixteen- and seventeen-year-old's] violence is completely unacceptable. It is not the act of someone with a normal personality. The parents defend their sons as good people. I say, 'not at all.' " That same prosecutor was even more hyperbolic in a case in which a brawl broke out among opposing groups of soccer fans after a match: "These youth carry out a lynching with crow bars, bottles, and knives. They need to understand that we are civilized in this country. It is not the survival of the fittest."

The prosecutor's réquisitoire is a bounded and stylized linguistic event that involves expressive body gesture, theatrical language, hyperbolic images, and the dissection of the minor and his family. The impact is all the more effective because in this phase of the trial the prosecutor completely ignores the minor and his family, never making eye contact or even glancing in his direction. She addresses only the judge and makes the minor invisible by describing him in the third person and denying him the right to speak. For those who have never been tried in the juvenile correctional court, the role of the prosecutor is both mystifying and alienating. It is left to the minor's attorney to address and contest the facts as presented by the prosecution.

THE DEFENSE ATTORNEY'S *PLAIDOIRIE*

Defense attorneys speak last and have the last word before the court recesses to decide the verdict and sentence. The *plaidoirie*, or plea, of the defense attorney in a criminal trial has been described as symmetrical in form but different in style from the prosecutor's réquisitoire. It has been compared to an incantation, the stylistic elegance, rhythm, and poetry of which appeal more to the senses than to reason.[25] This description does not apply to the juvenile justice system in which defense attorneys played a limited role until legal reform required their presence throughout the penal process from arrest and detention in police custody to trial and sentencing. In the context of enhanced children's rights and better protections for abused minors, experimental juvenile defense bureaus were created in juvenile courts around the nation with the approval of the French Chancellery.[26] These initiatives had the support of the leftist Syndicat de la Magistrature and were undertaken by well-established attorneys, the vast majority of whom were women. Their goal was to improve the quality and availability of defense counsel. These efforts coincided with and were facilitated by a number of factors, including available public funds remunerating court-appointed attorneys for indigent clients and wider access to the justice system for both victims and minors. Following France's 1990 ratification of the CRC, attorneys functioned within a shifting penal model premised on newer understandings of children as rational, responsible agents who were accorded rights and deemed accountable, responsible subjects.

In Paris, court-appointed defense attorneys rather than attorneys hired by the accused predominate at the juvenile court trials. They are recruited from the Juvenile Defense Bureau created in 1994 and operated under the aegis of the Paris Bar Association. Attorneys in Paris complained about the constraints they faced in fulfilling their functions. Many insisted that the requirement that minors have court-appointed attorneys was a major impediment in establishing the trust necessary to build a viable defense and to convince minors that they needed defense counsel. They bemoaned the indifference of their clients "who didn't give a damn about having an attorney," explaining that this was why they often met their clients and families for the first time in the hallway before trial. This was also why they found it so difficult to prepare their clients for trial and to educate them on their rights and duties as well as the likely outcomes in terms of verdicts and sentencing. Attorneys also complained about the problems of gaining access to the file and, in the case of repeat offenders, of having the time to read it in its entirety. I counted five occasions when court-appointed attorneys actually admitted during their pleas that they had not read their client's case file. One can only wonder how many more were unprepared but attempted to hide it.

In contrast to the much more detailed, lengthy, and colorful réquisitoire of the prosecutor, the attorneys' pleas suffered by comparison in the trials I observed. They lasted on average no more than several minutes and were usually much less detailed. In this short time, they had to address the facts as they were recorded in the file. The attorney drew the basis of his or her plea from the file but proposed an alternate reading of it by confronting it with the life and background of the minor. In most cases, attorneys did not contest the guilt of their clients or advise them to plead innocent but rather urged them to confess, to accept responsibility for their actions, and to collaborate with the judge when the judge asked defendants to explain their version of the facts. In this way attorneys participated in and reinforced the culture of confession that characterizes the juvenile justice system. They articulated their defense within the procedural orientation already defined and recorded in the file by the more powerful actors such as the judge and the prosecutor. This aligned the defense with the important elements already contained in the file, such as the type of infraction, the substance and length of the police record, the age and personality of youths, and their attitude with regard to the court and their own defense.[27]

On the one hand, defense attorneys were at a structural disadvantage with regard to juvenile judges because of the judge's power and often superior knowledge of the case. They had to narrowly model the substance of their pleas on the prosecutor's réquisitoire and recognize the prosecutor's position as defender of the social order and beleaguered victims. On the other hand, attorneys could attempt to take advantage of the presence of changing actors in the courtroom, such as the éducateurs and expert witnesses who were perceived as legitimate social professionals and legal informants. It was imperative that they respond to the plea for justice by the victim's attorney—an actor who, since the 2000 legislation enhancing victims' rights, now enjoys more public visibility and moral suasion in the French legal system.

Defense attorneys had the opportunity for strategic maneuvers and employed their own theatrics to limit the credibility of witness depositions and victims' accounts as well as to create empathy for the accused. They disrupted the solemnity of the court by initiating loud side conversations and attracted attention through their appropriation of courtroom space and use of both expressive body language and facial movements to maximum effect. I distinctly remember my surprise the first time I observed a French defense attorney openly mimicking a witness for the prosecution whose testimony she was attempting to convey as ludicrous. At first I assumed her to be unprofessional until I subsequently observed other incidents of attorneys performing, in open court, exaggerated reactions of irony, scorn, horrified disbelief, or celebratory triumph like Daumier caricatures of nineteenth-century professionals, particularly figures from the courts. Until I sat in on a French criminal trial and observed robed attorneys, I never really understood the expression "*effet de manches*," or pronounced theatrics.[28]

Coming at the end of the trial, immediately after the prosecutor's réquisitoire, the lawyer's plea was a response to the accusations and demands of the prosecutor. Depending on the plea he chose, the defense attorney had to take the facts, reorder them, and interpret them. It was both an objective demonstration based on the facts and a plea that sought to seduce and convince by eliciting the subjectivity of the court and by appealing to leniency. The attorney's plea included eight more or less distinct parts. Attorneys began with the ritual greeting addressed to the court and went on to recognize the facts and the points of law that are necessarily linked to the offense, such as the elements that constitute the infraction, the proof, and the degrees of motivation, of participation, and of responsibility. They discussed extenuating circumstances and provided an overview of the scholastic background, upbringing, and personality of the youth, as well as a summary of his or her delinquent career and prior offenses. They gave their version of equitable penal responses, pled for clemency, and finally addressed questions raised by victims' attorneys and requests for compensatory damages.

The majority of pleas conditioned the rehabilitation of minors on their acceptance of guilt and their conscious recognition of legal norms and social taboos. Because they implied complicity between magistrats and attorneys in the advancement of the mission of the court, a mission still ostensibly committed to the rehabilitative ideal, these pleas were centered less on the facts or proof from a juridical point of view than on the imperative for youth to accept responsibility for past mistakes as a precondition for future progress. Most attorneys readily sacrificed the presumption of innocence before judgment because they viewed acquittals as antithetical to the rehabilitative goals of the court. Conversely, some attorneys opposed this approach and concentrated their strategies on avoiding penal sanction for their clients. They used juridical arguments as much as or more than those linked to the background and personality of their clients, defending them as they would adults by using all the tools at their disposal.

All attorneys walked a fine line between, on the one hand, appearing to excuse transgressive behavior through their appeal to the extenuating circumstances of poverty and neglect that inhibited the development of a normal, structured personality and, on the other, building a case for the individual progress that was demanded as a prerequisite for rehabilitation and a justification for clemency. They suggested, as do other court personnel, that the legal mandate for the protection of at-risk youth also implied protection from the dysfunctional aspects of their cultural backgrounds. Thus, defense attorneys emphasized where possible the efforts of young people to establish physical, psychological, and social distance from bad influences and neighborhoods. Recall the case of Mustapha, who was accused of possessing and selling drugs and who angered the court by changing his story. His defense attorney began her plea by admitting that she had not read his case file but aligned herself with the judge and prosecutor by admonishing him to admit that he sold drugs to provide for his own needs. She addressed his refusal to accept culpability for the cocaine sale by emphasizing his fear of reprisal from drug dealers and reminded the court that, given the aberrant cultural codes prevalent in bad neighborhoods, "We should not deceive ourselves . . . we cannot hold him to too high a standard." She evoked "the code of honor in the projects," and suggested that even if he was guilty of selling crack, "he was not the intended beneficiary." Besides, she added, "it was to his credit, even reassuring, that he was in school, in the professional baccalauréat program." In another 2003 case involving a neighborhood fight, one defense attorney focused on his client's "potential." "When he [the accused] first arrived, he gestured like an animal in the circus. I really have to fight for him, because he really wants to learn and to get on with his life."

Only one judge allowed me to observe the deliberations between her and her assessors that determined the verdict and sentence for trials.[29] I noted that not once did the judge or any of the assessors mention the plea of the defense attorney as having any effect, positive or negative, on the determination of the culpability of the minor. This may be one measure of how little impact defense attorneys' pleas are perceived to have on the outcome, their relatively recent specialization in juvenile justice, and/or a recognition of their complicity with the view of the case favored by the judge.

A NEW PENAL MODEL: GHETTO YOUTH ON TRIAL

I end this chapter with a case from the Twentieth South District which pitted the hyperbolic *réquisitoire* of the prosecutor, known for his explosive outbursts in court, against the pleas of the defense attorneys, who advanced juridical arguments based on the law and witness depositions in support of an acquittal. Despite the prosecutor's incendiary rhetoric, Judge Courtier and her assessors shared his position. This case was representative of the majority of those I heard in other sessions of this and other juvenile district courts where the defendants were teenage males of Antillean, African, or Maghrebi ancestry who were charged with aggravated theft. Police reports and witness depositions gave contradictory accounts of an encounter between two groups of teenage boys, one group of white French teenagers from a vocational high school (*lycée professionel*) and the other a group of twenty teenagers of Antillean, Arab, and African ancestry from a housing project in the Twentieth South District well known to the court.[30] Among nine witness depositions, there was no clear consensus on either the number of youth involved or the exact identities of the perpetrators. Nonetheless, Kévin and Antoine, both from the projects, were arrested and prosecuted for theft aggravated by two circumstances of violence perpetrated in a group. They were accused of stealing a cell phone and a phone card from one of the vocational students.[31] The latter followed their attackers into the projects where insults and blows were exchanged. Three of the vocational students were injured and one student landed in the hospital with moderate injuries.

This case was interpreted by court personnel as ghetto youths defending their territory, and although Judge Courtier said little she largely concurred with the narrative constructed and imposed by the prosecutor. This case did and still does speak to increasing conflicts in public schools in which the possibilities for social mobility have been reduced and mapped onto definitions of cultural proximity that have shifted and become progressively more Europeanized. In addition, it speaks to the frustrations and anger of underprivileged youth of non-European ancestry, who are more likely to be labeled as problems, drop out, be expelled, or be tracked early into devalued, dead-end vocational programs in public secondary schools for which there are no jobs or other outlets. In contrast to earlier groups of unskilled youth whose violent rebellion against authority figures and subversive cultural forms could be channeled into ideologically safe locales such as the factory floor or the labor union, these youths face a labor market in which manufacturing jobs have been replaced by low-wage service sector positions based on new workplace norms. They spend longer periods in school and strive for diplomas that will allow them to escape the manual labor and harsh working conditions of their fathers, but they suffer academic failure and have little chance of economic opportunity. In a context of stiff competition for unskilled jobs, young men whose street cultures, affects, and argots are stigmatized are particularly disadvantaged. Some French employers have instructed employment agencies not to hire people of color in service jobs because of the perceived negative impact on their businesses from disgruntled customers.[32] These youth are reduced to alternating periods of legal employment on temporary or part-time contracts or participation in *le business,* the informal economy of bartering, petty dealing, and reselling stolen property. Relegated to degraded urban spaces, they develop identities and solidarities tied to both neighborhoods and, increasingly, ethnic and racial affiliation. This has produced tension that explodes in violent confrontations in the subway and on the street.[33]

Kévin accepted responsibility for the theft but vehemently denied committing the physical attack, an aggravating circumstance that could substantially increase the penalty if he were convicted. He was accompanied by his parents, both French citizens of Antillean ancestry, who were well dressed and well spoken. They advised the court that he would return to Martinique to finish a two-year vocational course in plumbing. In contrast, Antoine, angry, sullen, and uncooperative despite obvious coaching from his attorney, categorically refused to accept guilt for the theft and the attack. He was in court with his single mother, a social worker. In response to the judge's questions, he indicated that he had left school, was unemployed, and had no career plans. The judge next turned to Antoine's éducatrice, who provided an ambiguous report:

> EDUCATRICE: He comes regularly to appointments. He wants to make something materialize, but it is very difficult for him to follow through. It's hard to have confidence in him. His family group is good. They try to support him in his determination to find training but he never finds it. He has completely given up since eighth grade [a critical orientation year]. In this situation there are things he can do, but he was so disappointed by his father's lack of commitment. He does not want to talk about it. His father hardly sees him during his visits to Guadeloupe. He was so hurt that his father didn't come. I monitor him because he has a penal case open with the juvenile judge. He has not respected the obligations of a conditional suspended sentence imposed by the court. He does not take the necessary steps."

The judge invited Antoine's mother to describe her relations with her son. Since court personnel view children from single-parent homes headed by women as particularly vulnerable, Antoine's mother attempted to deflect blame from any suggestion of bad parenting by presenting his problems as personal and psychological, not familial, and by emphasizing that he had a sister who was academically successful. She also hinted that he was at least partly to blame for his own plight and should take initiative in the way his sibling did:

MOTHER: I divorced his father eight years ago. It is so difficult to control him. I do not know what is going on in his head. At twelve, he tried two or three times to commit suicide. [*Antoine angrily elbowed her and earned a strong rebuke from the judge.*] I must say that his sister has succeeded well. It is painful because he never looks for work.

When the judge questioned one of the victims on the impact the attack had on him personally, he indicated that it had affected him deeply. He had changed his plan to study law and he had moved out of the twentieth arrondissement. Given the floor, the victim's attorney adroitly appropriated media images of the projects and insisted that Antoine in particular, because he refused to accept his guilt, deserved to be punished. Despite the resort to physical violence on the part of both groups, the court prosecuted only the "ghetto youth." The defense attorney racialized delinquency and made a point of announcing her physical discomfort when close to the violent and unrepentant Antoine:

VICTIM'S ATTORNEY: Antoine does not admit his guilt. He lacks maturity. He makes me uncomfortable. The facts of the case are obvious. You must punish teenagers who injure others. I am sorry that Antoine does not admit his fault. He is recognized numerous times by witnesses. Kévin, on the other hand, admits the theft. They are young, a cell phone has value. Remember, the injuries are described by the doctor, they didn't happen out of the blue. Here we have yet another example of kids who defend their territory in the projects. We need to remember that in the French Republic there are no lawless zones!

In his plea, the prosecutor echoed the attorney's emphasis on territorialized violence, suggesting that he was more inclined to be indulgent with Kévin, whose middle-class demeanor, two-parent family, and plans to leave Paris for Martinique favorably impressed the prosecutor. It is telling that although Kévin, like Antoine, was born and raised in metropolitan France and held French citizenship, his departure for Martinique, an overseas department of France since 1946, is depicted as a "return home" (*retour au pays*). In the

Antilles, Martinicans and Guadeloupans are distinguished in numerous ways, but in France, politicians, landlords, employers, police, and court personnel tend to categorize them with other Africans and immigrants. Despite their long-standing ties to metropolitan France, Antilleans' association with immigrants makes it impossible for them to claim that they are simply French. Despite the inclusion of Martinique and Guadeloupe as departments within France, French people do not consider the islands a part of France.[34] When questions of public order and national security become prominent policy issues, those with roots in the islands versus metropolitan France, particularly young teenagers, are subjected to intensive scrutiny on the basis of their perceived alterity. The prosecutor blamed France's urban problems and youth crime on "outsiders" and suggested that integration outside of France is promising although still not certain. The rigid and distorted distinction between victims from a local lycée and perpetrators from the projects was also revealing:

PROSECUTOR: I want to congratulate the two young victims for being here personally. Nothing replaces the physical presence of witnesses. In spite of their presence, Antoine denies the facts. Just imagine if you [to the victims] were not here. The task would be even more difficult for the Public Ministry. The victims tell us they no longer venture into those neighborhoods. They should not be the ones deprived of choices. Siding with people like Antoine who make their own law in the projects is the world turned upside down. We hear about lawless zones. But I say it is the territory of the Republic and it is not hoodlums who make the law. Both of them are drowning in this notion of the group, a group of violent youth who hit and then claim they couldn't be identified by witnesses. We have a thief and a liar. But we also have witnesses who without exaggeration or fear offer corroborating stories. Let's talk about the personalities. It is a different situation in each case. Kévin will leave for overseas. This confirms for us that it is kids coming from outside of France who create a mess. A return home will do him good. It will cut him off from bad associations in the projects. So there is some hope for his integration. Alas, Antoine is hardly in the same situation. He is not working. Here we are in the month of June. We ask him if he is looking for work and what does he say?!? "I'm waiting until September." [his voice rising, his tone angry] So when is it time to work? I look around me, ten minutes from the Palace, you can find work. I have seen job notices with my own eyes. [*shouting*] It is too much to hear this. They turn up their noses at temporary work! I remember the hearing last week of a victim, a young pastry maker who got attacked, who goes to work at four o'clock in the morning. I hear young people say it's too hard to find work. I say go to McDonald's or to Quick [French fast-food hamburger restaurant]. Of course, that won't appeal because you have to work at night and on the weekend. I say, they are adults now and repression is warranted. I ask the court for a six-month suspended prison sentence and a fine to serve as a pedagogical tool. They should pay the fines themselves instead of using their parents' insurance. Let them work like dogs in the summer, twelve hours a day if necessary. Thank you.

Antoine's defense posed a particular challenge. Here his attorney painstakingly led the court through the conflicting statements of nine witnesses, some of whom insisted that there were seven individuals present, others swearing they saw only five. He insisted that his client had come home and returned to the scene only after the events and, therefore, deserved an acquittal. He was nonetheless constrained to recycle the same trope of territorialized violence used so adroitly by the prosecution:

DEFENSE ATTORNEY: I understand the suffering of the victims but Antoine told you, he was not there. True, it is the same group phenomenon in the twentieth arrondissement at one o'clock in the morning. There were fifteen individuals. Today you have only two brought before the court. The victims indicate that the attackers divided into small groups and when the police arrived they ran away. One witness declared, "There were two individuals, a European and an African. I can tell you that they were there but I cannot tell you if they played an active role." Another witness declares: "I did not see them hit any one." A third: "I recognize these two, one of them arrived just before the gang of attackers got there. I am not sure if he hit anyone." Antoine was there but after the theft and the physical attack. Examination of the facts does not permit us to conclude that he did the hitting. He has personal problems. He is registered with the national unemployment agency. He has a social worker and a mother who takes care of him. It's a typical family scenario. He is affected by the absence of a father who couldn't bother to come here today. He is waiting for an internship. He does not have what it takes. I ask you to acquit.

Kévin's defense attorney relied on a similar tactic but explicitly targeted the prosecutor's strategy of stigmatizing groups by insisting that "in France collective responsibility does not exist." She too argued for acquittal on the charge of physical violence. She urged the court to consider the contrast with the unformed child, the violent delinquent, described in the file as "destructured, unstable, subject to bad influences, and involved in gangs" with the young man whose life was being rebuilt in Martinique," and whose "progress" held out hope for his integration as a productive citizen.

The court adjourned to deliberate and I followed the defendants and their parents into the hall to await the verdict and sentence. Judge Courtier did not allow me to attend the deliberations so I planned to take a few minutes to check my notes and eat a yogurt, when I saw Judge Rabinovitch and greeted her. When the bailiff saw us chatting, she joined the conversation. We were standing within earshot of the waiting families when the bailiff announced that she had an "amusing story to share" from the court that heard medical malpractice suits. She reported that one of the plaintiffs, "an Arab," brought a case after being rendered impotent by treatment for erectile dysfunction. The court rejected his demand for compensation and damages. I remember feeling quite uneasy, wondering what could possibly be amusing when the bailiff delivered the punch line: "When the public prosecutor came out of the court, he whispered to me, 'That Arab got just what he deserved [*il en a pris pour sa gueule*].' " With that she threw back her head and laughed heartily. Judge Rabinovitch and I looked at one another in utter disbelief. The judge turned on her heel and walked away. Mercifully the policeman on duty motioned to the bailiff that the court had reached a verdict.

The court returned a guilty verdict for both defendants but moderated the prosecutor's plea by sentencing them to a four-month suspended prison sentence, a 150-euro fine, and payment of the victims' medical bills, attorneys' fees, and damages. When I returned to France later that year and interviewed Antoine's defense attorney, I discovered that Antoine had been convicted of selling drugs and was in prison, serving a four-month sentence. For his part, Kévin had left his home in France and settled in Martinique. No one could tell me if he was enrolled in school.

PUBLIC POLICY AND THE FAILURE OF INTEGRATION

I began this chapter by discussing the conclusions of an internal Justice Ministry Inspection of the court, which documented a growing punitive trend. It manifested itself in the rapid rise of the proportion of penal to civil cases, which rose from 50 percent of the total to 75 percent from 1998 and 2001; in higher rates of prosecution of penal cases, an increase of 43 percent from 1998 to 2003 particularly for public order violations; and in more punitive sentences, including firm and suspended prison terms with intensive or conditional probation.[35] Since I spent so much time with sitting judges, I periodically interviewed Yvon Tallec, the head of the juvenile prosecutor section, about the general direction of the juvenile court. In extended interviews just before the inspection in 2003 and then again in 2005, he spoke at length about the substantial increase in prosecutions "not only in the number of cases but also in their complexity" and noted the "poverty of resources," complaining that the number of deputy prosecutors in his office had not increased since 1992.[36] He added:

> Although we have virtually all the legislative tools [meaning, the recent amendments to juvenile penal law] we need to prosecute, we don't have facilities to place delinquents. The recent legislation [2002 and 2003] called for more reinforced closed centers and for certain minors it is the best solution. The problem is that in Paris there still aren't any. There are only three in the whole country so when we have an emergency situation we have to request a detention order and send them to prison.

I knew Yvon Tallec was approaching the end of his tenure as the head juvenile prosecutor in 2005, so I asked about unfinished business at the court. He indicated his dissatisfaction with the formal juvenile court trials that he found "too long, dense, insufficient in number, and scheduled much too long after the offense." I raised the issue of how young people get identified as delinquents and end up at court and asked for his reaction to a then-recent study documenting police harassment in the form of abusive identity checks, racist slurs, and unwarranted, targeted arrests of minority populations in "bad" neighborhoods on charges of insulting, threatening or attacking the police.[37] He responded not only as a prosecutor but provided a thoughtful and critical commentary based on France's fraught postcolonial history:

> We must recognize that we deal with populations who are not easy to manage . . . who manifest an extreme violence and respect nothing and who hardly show a peaceful attitude with the police. Of course, as you know, in France we have a very ambivalent attitude toward the police. We only call them

when we have a serious problem. If not, we prefer not to have to deal with them. But the police do need training in order to deal with these types of people. I will admit there is the risk of mistakes on their part [police] and we must not cover that up, but the police also have the right to be afraid in certain situations when they are outnumbered. The reality is that our delinquents are from immigrant backgrounds. It is irrefutable. Eighty-five percent or more are children of immigrants. Now why is that? We are paying the price of our colonial past. The migratory flows [after decolonization] continued and, unfortunately, with enormous disparities between the former colonial powers and the colonized. Those north–south power inequalities have been reinforced with the fall of the Iron Curtain, the opening of China, and all the rest. To bring it back to the discussion at hand, confrontations with the police are more and more violent because, in part, the police have not been helped by the policies on integration. In France we have a policy of ghettoization. The problem we are now facing is linked to the history of integration. Earlier waves of immigrants—the Italians, Portuguese, and the Poles—wanted their children to be completely French and there was a pressure for integration through language and all the rest. Now I am not convinced that the Muslim immigrants want to integrate because of the ambiguities related to our colonial past. We are both former colonizers and the land of Eldorado. So what happens? We have an egalitarian discourse with regard to educational opportunity but in reality there are enormous gaps and few possibilities for social mobility. That generates violence. For twenty years public discourse has been egalitarian but the reality contradicts it.

CONCLUSION

There has been a decisive shift away from the older penal framework in which the goal was to reduce delinquency and to provide assistance in the hope of reintegrating young people through labor markets and educational institutions. In the new penal model the retreat from a concern with outcomes tends to reinforce the new meaning of imprisonment and probation as a means of control rather than as a possibility for transformation. Its concerns with recidivists have less to do with the success or failure of treatment programs than with eliminating new risks by detecting violations of parole or probation and tracking new offenses of criminals. The repeat offender who is given a suspended prison sentence with conditional probation and a fine or community service as an alternative to prison must take responsibility for a long list of obligations that can include avoiding certain neighborhoods, finding work, and staying in school. Failure to meet obligations and accept responsibility can land him or her in prison and does so more often.

Although this model still accords an important role to expert opinion from psychiatrists, sociologists, and criminologists, professional expertise is used less to diagnose or treat individual children than to identify at-risk groups and situations in order to better contain and control them. Court personnel tend to ignore social science research, which explains juvenile delinquency as a temporary deviation from normal behavior or theorizes it as the result of individual pathology and flawed parenting. While older explanations have not disappeared or been discredited, they are much less relevant to policy makers and court personnel who see the "immigrant" delinquent as the problem, not the wayward (French) child. At a time when juvenile delinquency is a highly politicized issue, a model that emphasizes individual accountability, blames the offender, silences excuses, redefines causes, and views restitution and punishment as proper responses had broad appeal among the public and politicians. The new at-risk groups are defined on the basis of criteria linked to cultural or ethnic origin.

The shift away from classic penal welfarism can be heard in the discourses of judges, prosecutors, and éducateurs who focus on civility, respect for mainstream values, and individual responsibility. Like the "white trash" studied by Hartigan, the stigma attached to the "immigrant" delinquents reflects a tendency to imagine them as a threat in bodily and behavioral terms.[38] Their speech, stares, gestures, postures, gaits, dress and family backgrounds all breach mainstream middle-class codes. "Immigrant" delinquents present an unacceptable image of Otherness that conflates class, race, and ethnicity. They fuel anxiety about the basis for belonging within mainstream French society. Those who come from "a culture of poverty," lack initiative, and fail to surmount challenges can be discursively constructed as unformed and poorly integrated children who did not warrant scarce institutional resources because "they do not have what it takes."

This penal model accords a more important place for restitution to victims of crime and institutes various forms of mediation and reparation. The goal is to oblige perpetrators to confront victims and to allow victims to voice their pain. It is presumed that such encounters will foster mutual recognition as a prelude to repair, restitution, and enhanced tolerance. A recurrent theme in the cases in both chambers and the court is the lack of mutual human recognition.

As we saw in Chapter 6, the challenge to mutual recognition is precisely the inability to situate people apart from their social origin and the cultures associated with their upbringing. Misrecognition marks many encounters between angry youth, overwrought judges, ambivalent éducateurs, outraged prosecutors, and exasperated attorneys.

In the cases of Jacques, Kévin, and Antoine, there was a prominent place for the testimony of victims and the suffering they endured but little room for the doubts raised as to their responsibility for serious offenses involving aggravated rape and aggravated theft. Although Jacques was acquitted, Kévin and Antoine were convicted of the charges. In their cases both the victims' attorney and the public prosecutor relied on a series of categorical oppositions between the delinquent predators from lawless, liminal spaces, on the one hand, and the French students from lawful, good neighborhoods, on the other. The violent nature of the conflict implicating both groups was lost in the trial.

The label of the delinquent depends necessarily on generalization, simplification, and exaggeration. As a category it relies on morally charged characteristics that fit neatly with Mary Douglas's description of matter out of place. As one who is dangerous and violent, the delinquent is conceived of as contaminating and can be situated outside the domain of the social. Although French law recognizes only individual culpability, prosecutors in this and other cases criminalized the cultural difference of minority defendants through a focus on their families, communities, and cultures. They reflected and reinforced public discourses concerning juvenile offenders as violent predators and their families as socially dysfunctional and culturally alien. In the case of Kévin and Antoine, the prosecutor's demand that work be imposed as a punishment for the young defendants mirrored not only older penal understandings of crime but also the talk of victims who wanted their abusers "to suffer, to be locked up, and to work at hard labor."[39]

The issue of who qualified as a victim and who as perpetrator figures prominently in the cases discussed in the next chapter. Yvon Tallec had strong views about the criminality of the young Romanians but, like many others, was ambivalent about the creation of a special court and the capacity of one judge to deal fairly with a growing caseload. The issue of how to categorize a rapidly increasing population of minors involved in illicit activity became a divisive issue within the Paris court, the departmental social welfare services, the legal establishment, Paris-based NGOs, the French Chancellery, and at the highest levels of the government. Tallec's view became institutionalized as this population was systematically penalized despite the opposition of the president of the juvenile court, the Syndicat de la Magistrature, the union of éducateurs, and many juvenile judges. The head prosecutor believed the court was well within its purview to punish minors, unaccompanied or not, who broke the law. Although "it is noble to want to provide humanitarian assistance to this population," he firmly insisted, "we do not have the means to do so." The heated debates, media representations, and judicial practices surrounding these minors are the subject of the next chapter.

8 NEW BARBARIANS AT THE GATES OF PARIS?
THE PROBLEM OF UNDOCUMENTED MINORS

ON THE FRENCH ASCENSION holiday in late May 2003, I accompanied the case-worker on duty to the Paris jail, where she conducted intake interviews with the minors who had been arrested and held in police custody. Of the seven children in lockup, five were Romanians (four girls and one boy) accused of theft. The Romanian boy, whom we will call Marius, was sixteen years old and well known to the police and the court. He had arrived in France at thirteen without a passport, visa (required before 2002), or knowledge of French. Immediately abandoned by an adult smuggler, he had joined other Romanian children who were living on the street, stealing and prostituting themselves for food, cloth-ing, and money. By his own account, after rescue in 2001 by the Brigade de la Protection des Mineurs, he had "been in and out of every state home in Brit-tany" but had returned intermittently to the street, using three different identi-ties and accumulating a long police record. He had been arrested with a French adult for attempted theft of a motorcycle. Like Marius, the four Romanian girls were economic migrants and not asylum seekers, but in contrast to him, these girls were (with one exception) first-time offenders. They had been arrested for shoplifting and had no identity papers, addresses, or parental guardians. De-spite this, the juvenile judge and prosecutor on duty accepted both their claim to minority status and their right to a hearing at the juvenile rather than the adult court.

Three years later, in November 2006, a Romanian girl without identity pa-pers was arrested for theft and sent to prison on the strength of a controversial X-ray test of skeletal development determining her age as sixteen and making her eligible for pretrial detention. She was examined by a doctor and questioned by a prosecutor and juvenile judge at the Paris court, who, when the case made national news, declared that "nothing [was] out of the ordinary."[1] In contrast, the prison doctor insisted that the girl could not possibly be old enough to be incarcerated for a misdemeanor. A relative ultimately produced a birth certificate showing her legal age as eleven and prompting her immediate release. What is striking about this case is that the controversy centered on the age of the defendant, not her incarceration for theft. Based on her past record as a "recidivist thief," all assumed that she was an accountable delinquent rather than an endangered teenager. The assumption that she was an un-moored vagrant without intergenerational ties was also wrong.

Beginning in 1997, growing numbers of unaccompanied, undocumented minors from eastern Europe, primarily Romanians, appeared in the Paris juvenile court. Although they were officially categorized as at-risk minors under French and international law and entitled to social assistance and rehabilitative interventions, juvenile prosecutors at the Paris court prosecuted this population in disproportionate numbers compared to suspects of other populations. Like Marius, the street children were caught without legal papers or visas; claimed to be squatters living in abandoned buildings, trailers, or camps on the city periphery; used false names; and refused to give reliable information about their families or lives in Romania.[2] Between 1997 and 2001, they were systematically prosecuted for destruction of city property and the theft of the hefty cash proceeds from Paris parking meters, a loss then estimated at 60 million francs annually.[3] In 2000 when Paris municipal authorities switched meters from coin to card payment, street children abandoned this activity for more precarious sources of revenue. They turned to begging, shoplifting, purse snatching, prostitution, pimping, and, burglary. The arrest of Romanian minor girls signaled a relatively new trend. Increasing numbers of these girls entered France with legal papers and tourist visas. Many stayed beyond the three-month limit, and some were drawn into organized theft and prostitution rings. The head of the Brigade de la Protection des Mineurs told me that by 2003 the occasional prostitution of Romanian boys had largely given way to the organized prostitution of eastern European females. These were Bulgarian, Moldavian, Latvian, and Romanian women over the age of eighteen, and of Romanian minor girls between the ages of sixteen and eighteen. During the last six months of 2003, there had been a spike in the number of underage Romanian girls apprehended for prostitution.[4] Although undocumented migrants comprised only one-fifth of the 5,200 minors arrested by Paris police in 2001, they represented fully one-half of the cases referred for prosecution to the juvenile court.[5] This trend continued in 2002 and 2003 with these minors representing 45 percent and 47 percent, respectively, of the total cases prosecuted at court.[6]

Until 2001 a virtual justice approach was developed to handle what had become known as "the Romanian problem." Unaccompanied minors arrested for petty crime, such as Marius, were detained, indicted, released pending trial, judged, and sentenced in absentia, disappearing and reappearing multiple times with different identities. Hervé Hamon, the then-president of the Paris juvenile court, was deeply concerned by the penalization of what he viewed as a vulnerable population, and in 2001 he created a special court, Court L, to deal more humanely with this population's special needs. He wanted unaccompanied minors to voluntarily seek assistance at the court. The creation of Court L was controversial from the beginning. Just two years later most judges at the Paris juvenile court opposed it, and French Justice Ministry inspectors declared it a "failure."[7] The inspectors criticized the high proportion of in absentia judgments made at trial (84 percent) and the punitive nature of pre- and posttrial rulings, notably probation (contrôle judiciaire; 34 percent);[8] pretrial detentions (39 percent), and prison sentences (34 percent), despite the fact that 89 percent of the infractions heard there involved nonviolent property offenses.[9] In contrast to the stated humanitarian goals, the vast majority of children (80 percent) came to penal hearings at Court L under constraint following arrest.

This chapter examines the shortcomings of the French juvenile justice and child welfare systems in the treatment of unaccompanied, undocumented minors who were prosecuted for illicit activity. It explores the inadequacies of these systems to properly identify the minority status of undocumented children and the gaps that exist in the services that are legally mandated for underage defendants in the French criminal justice system, regardless of nationality. It centers on the discourses of judging and the slippages between official rhetoric, legal norms, and judicial practice within Court L during the pivotal period of 2003 to 2004. It considers the binary of agents versus victims and the power structures within juvenile justice systems. Despite the mandate for social professionals to empower children, children's voices become subject to practices of translation, mediation, and interpretation that do not always serve their best interests.[10]

Social welfare systems are based on a universalist definition of childhood in international and human rights law. This definition assumes a universally applicable model of childhood development; presupposes a consensus on the public policies best suited to the categories of vulnerable children such as "child laborers," "child prostitutes," "child soldiers," and "child vagrants"; and views them all as objects of adult abuse. International law builds on humanitarian understandings of such children as exploited, powerless, in need, and without legal agency.[11] This view tends to violate evolving local and national understandings of blameworthiness and justice regarding children across the globe.[12] It also contradicts the real-world experiences of children in the historical and ethnographic record whose understandings of their own behavior in wars, at work, or on the street do not conform to the modernist, Western representation of the child built on arbitrary, chronological boundaries separating youth from adults.[13] These cases speak to the ambiguities surrounding legal definitions of the child victim versus the juvenile delinquent; the question of agency and empowerment versus accountability and punishment; and the shifting conceptions of childhood and adolescence in an era of globalization.[14]

CRIMINAL VAGRANTS AND PERVERSE CHILDREN

As noted in Chapter 1, in the 1990s the category of the child became an increasingly contested domain of public policy and cultural politics. In international legal instruments such as the CRC, children can claim new rights and entitlements but must accept enhanced moral and legal responsibility for their actions.[15] This redefinition of the child has coincided with harsher punishment for public order breeches as part of a move to governance regimes that shift responsibility and accountability to individuals, parents, and families.

In France, one of the central issues in nineteen-century debates on "perverse" children focused on vagrancy, which was viewed as a public threat and was criminalized as a misdemeanor until the mid-twentieth century.[16] As the century progressed, growing bourgeois fears of "homeless, roaming waifs, abandoned children, and young beggars" who "infested" the streets of Paris[17] explain in part why convictions for vagrancy multiplied sevenfold between 1830 and 1896.[18] In the early twentieth century, the 1912 law creating an embryonic juvenile court system was presented by a famous French jurist as a necessary legal protection against the "public danger represented by Bohemians, Romanichels and Gypsies."[19] In the twenty-first century changes to the penal code in 2003 that facilitated the removal of unwanted itinerant Roma and criminalized loitering and begging in public spaces suggest an enduring preoccupation with vagrancy. The specter of foreign street children involved in criminal activity is deeply threatening at a time when Fortress Europe is increasingly anxious about migratory flows and border crossings. The prosecution of undocumented, unaccompanied migrants who travel through a number of countries before and after arrest marks them as global subjects even as it challenges the regulatory and surveillance capacity of the nation state and the European Union.

The proliferation of "child criminals" also intensifies debates on normality, deviance, and agency. Dominant notions of the "good" childhood, the "right" family, and the "proper" upbringing are challenged by groups of children deemed "matter out of place," whether at work, in the press, on the street, or in prison.[20] The very mobility of street children, their use of false identities, and their (often) intentional erasure of their earliest formative experiences, or habitus, and family history subvert the court's supervisory gaze and threaten the processes of identification and control that only take into account blood relationships and birthplace. These children blur the accepted boundaries between the child and the adult. Their transgressive behaviors simultaneously highlight both their agency and marginality.

THE CHILD VICTIM: A CONTESTED CATEGORY

The alarming numbers of unaccompanied minors in the asylum and migration pipelines of Western nations is also disturbing because they are mostly categorized as victims of trafficking and viewed as vulnerable to sexual and labor exploitation. Yet many adolescents are knowingly complicit in irregular migration and participate in a range of illicit practices that unsettle conventional narratives of the child victim, complicating efforts to understand and treat them fairly. Street children like Marius defy easy categorization and challenge how we think about agency and childhood. Whether migration was a choice or obligation, it involved complex negotiations of their gendered identities and social personhood. It resulted in a search for and ambivalent embrace of alternative subjectivities that were largely unavailable to them in the places where they grew up.

Migrants from poor, rural backgrounds like Marius rejected the patriarchal norms and conservative morals of their home villages in favor of what they viewed as an individualized Western lifestyle predicated on money, education, and sex. European consumer culture provided the narrative and visual script through which alternative models of personhood and everyday practice were imagined. In this script they understood migration as a condition of deterritorialization, uprooting, and constant movement in search of other life worlds. At the same time, some unaccompanied migrants struggled to reconcile new aspirations for education and goods with their established roles as loyal sons and daughters who are expected to provide for the extended family but have no legal right to work. They squatted in countries where legal protection precluded their deportation and illegal activities were the only sources of revenue. They were easy prey for criminal networks and abusive families as well as police arrest and court sanction.

In contrast to the generally accepted human-rights depiction of undocumented migrants as vulnerable victims, the subjects—even relatively young minors—saw themselves as young adults with the heavy burden of choice, freedom to pursue their own agendas, or a weighty responsibility to provide remittances to their families. They felt infantilized and victimized by the very instruments of protection that prevented them from working legally and living in abandoned buildings or on the street.[21] It is no accident that punitive retribution became the default policy for unaccompanied children at court at a time when they seemed to straddle the categories of child and adult, appearing like helpless victims in one instance and willful criminals the next.

Paris court personnel began to construct new categories that informed judicial practice with respect to the Romanian street children. They distinguished the delinquent child whose agency and choice make him more accountable for his actions and more liable for control from the victimized child whose vulnerability and manipulation by others make him less responsible and more eligible for protection. A 2005 state study commissioned by the Labor minister and the Delegate minister for the Fight Against Poverty and Exclusion, Dominique Versini, discussed the newly emergent categories based on rootedness, contrasting the "good" migrant who "could be integrated" and had expressed a desire "to settle into a path of insertion," such as Chinese and South Asian youth, to the "bad" vagrant who merely passed through, was caught red-handed in "delinquent acts," and "could not be counted in official statistics" such as the "young Romanians."[22] Unaccompanied, irregular migrants from poorer regions in the east and south whose survival strategies in Paris included stealing, sex work, pimping, and burglary exemplified the principle of categorical mixture that produced cognitive anxiety and led to public rejection and legal sanction. They were increasingly situated outside of the legal order and placed within the anomalous and liminal category of the child-adult.

JUVENILE LAW AND JUVENILE JUSTICE FOR
UNACCOMPANIED, UNDOCUMENTED MINORS

In the debates surrounding unaccompanied children, we see conflicting and impassioned public statements and policies that are directed at one or both of two populations now entering France illegally: those involved in illicit activity, the majority of whom are economic migrants, and those fleeing turmoil and trauma, most of whom are asylum seekers. These statements range from outright hostility to irregular immigration, intolerance for asylum seekers, and fears of predatory vagrants to a humanitarian concern to protect parentless minors, stateless children, and neglected minorities seeking to settle within French society. The case of unwanted Others suggests that repression and compassion are not opposed but inextricably linked. As Didier Fassin has argued, the political encompasses the humanitarian, which in turn redefines it.[23]

French legal statutes view unaccompanied minors—both French and foreign—to be endangered by virtue of the lack of "parental supervision." In such situations French civil law requires social service agencies to alert public prosecutors and to seek protective measures through the juvenile court. In penal proceedings, French law mandates that unaccompanied minors appear before a juvenile judge and receive emergency social services, including shelter, food, medical care, and schooling. Until 2003, all foreign unaccompanied minors who received services from the Aide Sociale à l'Enfance or ASE (Child Welfare Agency) were eligible for French citizenship at the age of eighteen and were entitled to a child representative (*juge des tutelles*) to represent them in legal matters. French law forbids deportation and the imposition of the now-infamous double-sentence policy involving punitive legal sentences plus forcible deportation.[24] Yet there have been reports of deportations and the double sentence being applied to unaccompanied minors as young as fourteen.[25]

To manage vagrants on French territory involved in illicit activity and detainees in fenced holding centers requesting political asylum, successive governments adopted three strategies to disqualify them as endangered children and to categorize them with irregular immigrants. The first strategy was dissuasive and was based on the principle of deterrence through unlawful restrictions of welfare benefits. It consisted of the refusal to open social assistance cases on the rationale that the danger to the child was not established, continuous, or linked to parental neglect or abuse; the reluctance to provide temporary placement in state residential facilities or with foster families; the delay or refusal to appoint court guardians (juges des tutelles) to represent them in court; and the refusal to enroll them in school or training programs because of the presumption that migrant status and weak proficiency in French amounted to low scholastic ability. Admittance to France was made on a case-by-case basis and was based on a hierarchy of qualifying criteria, with minority status and verifiable identity as the most important. Exceptional humanitarian claims, such as serious illnesses or permanent loss of blood relatives, were also pertinent.[26]

The second strategy was repressive and consisted of detaining, prosecuting, and sentencing unaccompanied minors to punitive sentences for nonviolent property crimes. It also included the detention of unaccompanied minors with foreign adult asylum seekers in overcrowded, insalubrious conditions within what are euphemistically called fenced "waiting zones" (zones d'attente).[27] The goal to drive back increasing numbers entering France illegally was pursued by confining them in these detention centers while eligibility for admission to France was considered, denying high numbers of asylum requests once admitted to France (only 34 percent of the 949 requests were granted in 2003 by the Office français de protection des réfugiés et apatrides [French Office for the Protection of Refugees and Stateless People] [OFPRA]), and legislating restrictions on other forms of legalized status through residence permits and French citizenship.[28] Legislation voted on 26 November 2003 gave French authorities the right to deny French citizenship to unaccompanied migrants who had not registered with child welfare services for three consecutive years before their eighteenth birthday. Since 60 percent of Romanian migrants arrived after the age of sixteen, this effectively excluded the majority from acquiring French nationality.

The third strategy was categorical and redefined unaccompanied minors in two ways: first, as irregular immigrants or criminal vagrants, and second, as adults with no systematic right to protection. In Paris, prosecutors continued a long-standing practice of contesting minors' underage status and subjecting them to mandatory and controversial scientific assessments of bone development to determine age. The clinical examination included a wrist X-ray and a comparison with samples of a large study conducted in the 1930s among a white, upper-middle-class North American population.[29] Taking these tests to be definitive, discounting personal narratives of family origin or ignoring current living conditions, prosecutors declared these minors to be adults. They denied them not only the dispensations normally extended to immature teenagers but also the eligibility for welfare benefits. These declarations had potentially devastating effects, such as immediate trials in adult court, incarceration in overcrowded adult prisons, and denial of social services. All three strategies contributed to the confusion in public rhetoric between children as economic migrants and political refugees, a confusion that adversely affected both groups.

PUBLIC POLICY, POLITICIANS, POLICE, AND THE JUDICIARY

Tracking children who use false identities; have shifting territorial anchors; speak the local language imperfectly, if at all; and move constantly across borders poses significant methodological and epistemological challenges. They come into partial focus only when they break the law or when they are rescued by law enforcement, acquiring exaggerated and unreal forms refracted through the distorted lenses of the police report, the court file, the news item, and the politician's tirade. These elements form part of an ideoscape that is centered on youth violence and shaped by new retributive forms of penology and that circulates globally, creating moral panics and public outrage.[30] I concentrate on the attempts by the personnel within the Paris Palace of Justice to apprehend and manage a phenomenon that represented a growing percentage of the penal caseloads within individual courtrooms.[31]

The Romanian children described here posed not only a policing and public order problem for the city of Paris but were part of a highly charged political issue—irregular immigration—implicating the reputations of two nation-states in the global arena. As the preeminent champion of the Rights of Man, France had to be perceived to be upholding a humanitarian standard in the treatment of a vulnerable population and to fend off condemnations by the European Committee for the Prevention of Torture and Inhuman or Degrading Treatment or Punishment of the Council of Europe after periodic inspections of airport holding facilities, prisons, and jails.[32] At the same time, the legitimacy of successive governments depended in part on solving the problem of insécurité, given the importance of youth crime as a recurring public policy and campaign issue in the national elections since 1995. As a would-be candidate for membership in the European Union, Romania was particularly sensitive to news coverage using the term "new barbarians" at the gates of Paris in the guise of Romanian street urchins snatching purses and picking pockets in the city's upscale neighborhoods in broad daylight.[33]

The Romanian problem was closely linked to the criteria of admission to the European Union. The candidacy of nations such as Romania, which did not have a juvenile justice system or adequate child social services, posed a problem. The EU conditions for membership and complex negotiations with French partners on redressing this lack indirectly shaped the justice dispensed within Court L. Beginning in October 2002, the presiding juvenile judge of Court L was an active participant in working groups seeking solutions to the problem of unaccompanied minors on French territory. A series of bilateral Franco-Romanian accords signed between March and October 2002 produced an operational liaison group of French and Romanian magistrats and police to implement policy recommendations on an issue conceived largely in law enforcement terms.[34]

The following year, in 2003, the secretary of State for the Fight Against Poverty and Exclusion commissioned a study of unaccompanied minors in the greater Paris area from the prefect of the Ile de France region, Bertrand Landrieu, who concluded that "the best way to guarantee the child's protection and normal family life" was through "the return of foreign minors to their country of origin." Landrieu also recommended limiting the legal advantages said to be attracting foreigners; article 21-12 of the French civil code permitted any "child raised by a French national or registered with the ASE" and residing in France the right to declare French nationality at eighteen years of age.[35] This recommendation was incorporated into the new law on immigration and naturalization voted several months later along with legislation creating a commission to train future Romanian juvenile judges.

Recall that part of the anxiety created by vagrants resulted from the state's inability to count and track them accurately. Reliable, comprehensive statistics on the nature and scope of the problem were not available from the juvenile court, government ministries, or private NGOs. Moreover, the statistics disseminated in the media by government officials, activist judges, or concerned NGOs differed widely and reflected contrasting ideological agendas. Media coverage was nonetheless a critical primary source here for two reasons. First, given the rapid changes in irregular migration to France, investigative reports were an important source of factual information and a bellwether of public anxieties regarding a new menace. Media coverage also shed important light on the deep divisions within and among the French Chancellery, the national government, the Paris juvenile court, and human rights activists. Second, the content and tone of reports in national daily newspapers evidenced the national pulse across the political spectrum. These reports shaped public perceptions of crucial social issues such as delinquency and migration, influenced legislative agendas, and also indirectly and directly affected judicial practice within the courts.

NEW BARBARIANS IN PARIS? REPRESENTING A "ROMANIAN" PROBLEM[36]

In contrast to ubiquitous media coverage of youth violence in the famously stigmatized suburbs since 1980, there was comparatively little press coverage of rising delinquency rates within the city of Paris or of Romanian children involved in criminal activity until the late 1990s. This changed starting in 2001, with coverage centering on Romanian criminal rings forcing children into theft, begging, and prostitution.[37] Estimates on the numbers of street children varied widely. This was a result of difficulty identifying and tracking them as well as the motives and politics of the source. In early May 2001 an *Agence France Presse* report put the number of Romanian street children at approximately 3,000 to 5,000 and the number of squatter camps outside Paris at 100.[38] In an interview at the end of that summer, Parisian juvenile judge, Thierry Baranger, an outspoken children's advocate and critic of the penal trend, contrasted the 486 unaccompanied minors seen in the Paris juvenile court in 1999 with the 1,100 arrested the following year.[39] One year later, in 2002, in the context of negotiations concerning Romania's admission to the European Union, the Romanian deputy secretary of the Interior, Alexandre Fracas, insisted that only 100 Romanian street children were in Paris.[40] At the same time, Dominique Versini made a well-publicized visit— along with the also newly appointed prime minister, Jean-Pierre Raffarin— to Lazarus Center, a French NGO providing humanitarian assistance to Romanian street children. In a bid to highlight the problem, she estimated the total number of unaccompanied minors to be between 1,000 and 5,000. This number was immediately disputed by the office of the Socialist mayor of Paris, who opposed the law-and-order policies of the rightist Raffarin government.[41] The mayor demanded that the state commit to helping the city pay for mounting costs incurred by the "exponential increase of unaccompanied minors on Paris streets."[42]

By 2001 more public attention was given to the victimization of children as part of an increasingly complex "Romanian problem." Drawing on NGO and state ministry reports, French and Romanian journalists described Romanian children who were the unwitting victims of human traffickers operating criminal gangs for profit or smugglers who promised passage, job training, and work and/or housing for a large fee and then abandoned children once they were in France. There were also stories of impoverished parents in rural Romania who were selling or renting their children in exchange for monthly cash payments and of the rescue by police of minors who had been burned, cut, or beaten by their adult handlers. This coverage produced fear of a "new" urban menace linked to public order violations, such as shoplifting in upscale Parisian stores, prostitution in chic neighborhoods, purse snatching in broad daylight, and Roma children begging in the metro.[43] Some reports bore an uncanny resemblance to late nineteenth-century diatribes against marauding hoards of child criminals who were uprooted, unpredictable, and beyond both parental and state control.[44]

In a short time the category of unaccompanied children, which included Asian, South Asian, African, and eastern European migrants, became conflated in public discourse with marginalized Romanians, both Roma—long the object of discrimination in France and Romania[45]—and non-Roma. This occurred at a time when the "Roma problem" became explicitly linked to delinquent vagrants and the "difficulty of youth protection." It was one of the points said to be closely followed by public opinion in a speech by then–Prime Minister Lionel Jospin during a July 2001 visit to Romania.[46] There were a few high-profile cases of Romanian Roma adults coercing children and the handicapped to beg and steal, but only a small number were actually unaccompanied migrants. According to one estimate, in 2002 seventy-seven Roma children were "given, rented or sold" in Romania to adult smugglers who brought them to France and made them work.[47] Paris NGOs, court personnel, and Brigade de la Protection des Mineurs officials reported few Roma among the street children arrested for theft and prostitution in Paris.

The best way to assess critically media depictions and judges' claims is to observe the unfolding adjudication of individual cases. It is also to listen to the children themselves, who voted most eloquently with their feet by refusing to return in large numbers for trial to the Palace of Justice.

PROTECTION OR PROSECUTION AT THE PARIS PALACE OF JUSTICE?

The prosecution of street children prompted persistent outcries on their behalf by activist judges and child advocates. In 2000 there was a strong consensus among éducateurs and a majority of Paris juvenile judges that the street children were coerced into criminal activity and needed protection, not prosecution and punishment. On 16 January 2001 leaders of the leftist Magistrate's Union (Syndicat de la Magistrature), to which a number of activist Parisian juvenile judges belonged and the largest union of court caseworkers (*Syndicat des Personnels de l'Education Surveillée de la Protection Judiciaire de la Jeunesse*) sent a protest letter to then–Justice Minister Lebranchu. They lamented "the catastrophic conditions in which penal cases are handled at the Paris court," noting the flood of irregular minors "without families, papers or protection" arriving from eastern Europe, primarily Romania" and "the woefully inadequate means" to deal with the attendant explosion in penal cases. They were outraged that despite the Socialist government's rhetorical commitment to rehabilitation, "repression" had prevailed.

The judges' concerns were shared by the Children's Rights Commissioner, Claire Brisset, who demanded that the age of sexual majority be raised from fifteen to eighteen to allow sixteen- to eighteen-year-olds engaged in prostitution to be classified as victims of adult exploitation. She castigated French police and prosecutors "for denying and minimizing the severity of the problem."[48] Judge Boyer voiced a widely shared view when she asked, "How is it possible to talk about protection when they [juvenile prosecutors] prosecute a thirteen-year-old [Romanian] boy who stole the wallet of the [French] adult with whom he had oral sex [for money]?"

Nonetheless, this consensus was not absolute. In 2001, there were heated disagreements between prosecutors and judges on the treatment of unaccompanied migrants. In April 2001 a Romanian sociologist, Dana Diminescu, who studied undocumented migrants in the greater Paris region, came to court. She disputed the widely held view of Romanian street children as unprotected victims completely separated from their families by affirming that only 20 percent were unaccompanied and exploited in criminal rings. She reported that 80 percent of the Romanians she had interviewed lived with (at least periodically) or had contact with someone from their immediate or extended family or natal village. She outlined migratory flows organized for economic reasons and produced photos of the "dowry homes" or home "additions" constructed with the cash sent back by irregular minors.

By the time a special court for unaccompanied foreigners was created in the fall of 2001, sociologists, aid workers, and Brigade de la Protection des Mineurs officers had provided a more complete understanding of Romanian migratory flows and the motives driving them. Although some children were coerced into migration; endured emotional abuse, as well as horrific labor and sexual exploitation; and lived in appalling conditions, others arrived with their parents' knowledge and consent in search of education, training, and jobs. A common refrain among some children interviewed by NGOs was "we promised our parents to get trained, find a trade, and send them money. But upon arrival we found nothing." Many Romanian children came from Northeastern Romania, an area with a long history of outmigration where children were expected to work and contribute to family income.[49] While many children left behind family in Romania, some traveled to France with a family member who left them there and then returned to Romania. Others, such as Marius, joined or had regular contact with extended family already living and working in France, legally or illegally. Some children worked in the underground economy selling a variety of goods or begged and sent home remittances that their parents used to finance dowries, purchase land, and build or improve existing houses.

Romanian street children posed a dilemma for the caseworkers at the Paris SEAT. Between 1994 and 1997 the proportion of unaccompanied minors seen by them averaged 21 percent. In 2000 this figure more than doubled to 49 percent; a year later it dropped slightly to 46 percent, then 45 percent in 2002 and 40 percent in 2003. As minors without parental supervision or legal guardians, they were by law entitled to placement with the local ASE. Nonetheless, between 1999 and 2001 many caseworkers there refused to open cases for these minors, noting their reluctance to seek or accept help, their "difficulty assimilating" into French society as adults, and the scarcity of foster families, group homes, and emergency service providers.[50] They and many court guardians (juges des tutelles), appointed to serve as their legal representatives, claimed that these children fell outside their jurisdiction and expertise. ASE officials demanded that the national state, not the local département, assume financial responsibility for them. Local departmental councils refused to allocate the necessary funds to process their cases.[51]

The street children posed a thorny problem for Paris police and prosecutors because, despite their criminal activity, French and international law precluded their deportation. Prosecutions were straining limited resources and exacerbating staff shortages at the Paris court in a number of ways. They increased the pace and volume of intake interviews by court social workers following arrest; generated mounting penal cases and mandatory hearings before judges, requiring both state-funded and appointed interpreters and attorneys; and created overloaded dockets at the monthly trials held in the juvenile correctional court.

In the late 1990s and early 2000s efforts of court personnel to identify the leaders of the criminal networks and to rescue children by providing emergency shelter were unsuccessful. Following their release from jail and escort to group homes, most street children like Marius left immediately, returned to the street, and never honored court summons to appear for trial. As Diminescu writes, migrants such as Marius also saw migration as an opportunity to break with what they viewed as backward lifestyles, oppressive local cultures, and familial expectations.[52] Romanian judges, social workers, and interpreters described a culture of remittance based on "the cult of cash" channeled into consumer goods as tangible symbols of family honor and professional success.[53] The activist judges I observed or interviewed were reluctant to acknowledge that some Romanian children were complicit with rather than coerced into illegal activities. Their show of agency did not correspond to the image of victimhood that juvenile judges felt comfortable defending.

Failure to respond to a court summons was an established pattern in 2001. Following hearings and indictments, they were routinely released pending judgment and given trial dates. Precluded from pronouncing judgment in absentia in chambers, judges automatically referred cases to the juvenile correctional court hearing cases of serious misdemeanors and crimes (committed by minors who were thirteen to sixteen years old), where minors were found guilty, sentenced in their absence, and regularly received suspended or firm prison terms. Despite this impasse, arrests, indictments, and prosecutions continued. In contrast to French citizens of non-European ancestry who were widely associated by the public with serious violence and recidivism, irregular Romanian migrants were represented as victims but were largely treated as delinquents in the adjudication of cases by the very judges and court caseworkers who appeared to be their strongest advocates.

THE POLITICS OF "PREVENTION" VERSUS "PUNISHMENT" IN 2003

By the summer of 2003, most judges and éducateurs were opposed to Court L and the working atmosphere was extremely tense. Almost all of the judges, clerks, and attorneys with whom I interacted that summer mentioned this tense environment. Both the Paris juvenile court president and the judge of Court L were increasingly isolated in their support of Court L, viewing it as a means to prevent "a delinquency driven by poverty, not criminality." The goals were to collect accurate information on their identities, personalities, and families; to offer placement in open settings, either group residences or foster families; and to provide a variety of social services. These were conceived as first steps to return home or to integration in France through admission to public school and, ultimately, acquisition of French nationality. They hoped to encourage voluntary appearances to the court by holding daily hearings. Their efforts relied on cooperation with the ASE and with French and Romanian NGOs in Paris as well as their Romanian counterparts in an embryonic juvenile justice system, particularly prosecutors, judges, and social workers. The safe return of "trafficked and exploited children" was contingent upon investigation of the families to whom they would return. To make sure they stayed at home, training programs and jobs had to be created in Romania.

These ambitious goals were undermined by national and international circumstances, particularly the preoccupation with public security and irregular immigration. Following the 2002 return of the center-right to power, the new government continued efforts begun by Jospin's Socialist government to contain the problem of Romanian street children. After the highly publicized July 2002 dismantling of a Romanian Roma criminal ring exploiting the handicapped, the Interior minister, Nicolas Sarkozy, traveled to Romania to complete negotiations of a bilateral agreement to facilitate the "identification, protection, and definitive return" of Romanian street children.[54]

Although these accords were driven by both public order and political concerns, they were framed and presented to the French and international public as primarily humanitarian issues involving the protection of children "from pimps and pedophiles."[55] Nonetheless, human and children's rights organizations complained about an increase in police brutality, forced expulsions of Roma from camps,[56] public trials of Roma parents for inciting children to beg,[57] and the impunity enjoyed by adult clients of child prostitutes.[58] One prominent NGO associated with the highly visible president of the Bobigny juvenile court in the suburban Paris region, Jean-Pierre Rosenczveig, accused the French government of using "humanitarian window dressing" as a cover for repressive policies in the service of political motives.[59] How did police officials view government and judicial efforts to protect and return unaccompanied Romanian minors? When I interviewed the head of the Paris Division of the Brigade de la Protection des Mineurs, Madame Bertrand, on 12 March 2004, she described work as a member of the Franco-Romanian liaison group in the effort to break up criminal rings exploiting minors for labor and sex. She noted that by 2003 the occasional prostitution of

Romanian boys had given way to the organized prostitution of eastern European females.[60] She claimed that there had been a lull in sex work for the first six months of 2003 and then a spike beginning in July 2003. She described a raid on a camp outside Paris that yielded the arrest of thirty-three adults and the rescue of thirty-two exploited children:

> BERTRAND: They are very mature, hardened, not like our children. They are here to make money. [*to me*] You have seen them. I talked to two Romanian judges, who said, "Here in Romania the child has a commercial value." It's true. Romanian parents do not have the same view of their children as we do here in France. From the moment they are just a bit mature, they must make money. Of the thirty-two rescued, we placed fifteen by 10:00 P.M. of the same day. By the next day there was only one left. A young girl who was pregnant and had a sexually transmitted disease. She only stayed five days. Yes, I consider it a failure of policing, judicial, and rehabilitative institutions. My judgment is not shared by the Paris SEAT.

When I asked how she viewed minors who chose sex work versus those who were forced into it, Madame Bertrand insisted that "the minor who prostitutes herself is an endangered child. We are obligated to withdraw her from danger. We need to coordinate immediately with the SEAT so a placement can be arranged as quickly as possible and not in the Paris region." But in the same breath, she added:

> BERTRAND: We also realize that these girls come to France to make money. At 50 euros per client and four clients a night, that's not bad when the average [monthly] salary [in Romania] is 80 to 100 euros. The pimps are smart enough to give them a little of the salary. Some think that to come to France and sell sex is an opportunity given the huge problems they have at home. I had one girl last night who has been here since January and managed to send back 6,000 euros. That's easy money.

How did she view the response of the SEAT at the Paris juvenile court? She shook her head dismissively, "At the rehabilitative level they have nothing to offer these young people. They don't suggest anything innovative, not anything that responds to their needs. Frankly, they couldn't care less."

The judge of Court L was equally pessimistic about the success of social assistance in France or the prospects for voluntary return to Romania:

JUDGE: Take the case of a voluntary return involving a girl caught in a prostitution ring. I organized an international investigation which failed when the Romanian prosecutor warned one of the members of the ring. I sent her back and what happened? The family was threatened and harassed. The Romanian law protecting families is not enforced. There are other problems with Romanian judges and social workers. There is no work on prevention or assistance for children at risk in an open setting (at home). It is placement in an institution or nothing. In France, too, it's complicated because we are not committed to providing the necessary funds for training or education. Whether children come with their family's blessing or not, we have little to offer. In many cases I have no choice but to end a placement.

A Romanian caseworker, Manuela Neagu, who worked for the NGO Parada, corroborated this when we met in 2003. Families whose children migrated to France were pressured by Romanian authorities to depict their home situations in a favorable light and were "forced to agree" to the return of their children regardless of their socioeconomic circumstances.

COURT L IN 2003: A HUMANITARIAN SOLUTION?

The first opportunity I had to observe hearings in Court L came in the summer of 2003. The judge heard an average of three to four cases per afternoon.[61] Despite the intention to encourage voluntary appearances, 80 percent of the children came to court after arrest. Of that number 85 percent were Romanian and the remainder were North African. The 20 percent of social assistance cases involved unaccompanied minors from Africa, Asia, and eastern Europe seeking welfare benefits and legalized status as political refugees, legal residents, or naturalized citizens.

The judge's considerable outreach efforts and frequent trips to Romania had produced what she termed "the perverse effect" of stimulating rather than preventing further migration from Romania. News of the French judge had apparently reached even far-flung Romanian villages. The ambitious plans to return children according to the 2002 guidelines were compromised both in France and Romania by a number of factors. In Romania, these included underfinanced schools, outdated training programs, economic underdevelopment, and rural poverty driving out migration; shortages of trained social workers to provide reliable follow-up on families; and political corruption within the Romanian judiciary and among border police.[62] In France, inadequate funding and insufficient specialized and emergency service providers (only one specialized reception facility for unaccompanied minors was created in October 2003); no clear channels of communication between the court, police, and NGOs; a stagnant labor market even for well-credentialed French youth; conflicts between prosecutors and judges at the juvenile court; and political animosity between the leftist city government and the rightist national government made coordination between public and private service providers very difficult.

I turn first to the emergency hearings of the Romanian girls in lockup with Marius in late May 2003 and compare them to regularly scheduled civil hearings in June and December 2003.

EMERGENCY HEARINGS

The ages of the girls in a holding cell with Marius ranged from thirteen to sixteen. All came from disadvantaged backgrounds, and all left Romania with the knowledge of their families. They described having to quit school after the primary level for lack of funds to pay secondary school fees. The éducatrice asked if they wanted to learn a manual trade, apparently assuming this was their best hope. The girls instead described their desire to pursue careers in fashion design, modeling, computer science, and the law. When challenged about how they intended to support themselves, since theft was too risky and legal work was impossible under sixteen, they mentioned work as domestics cleaning houses. When offered help—meaning, placement in a state facility—the girls seemed genuinely perplexed, insisting that they already had good families. Three out of the four claimed that they intended to return to Romania. The oldest, a sixteen-year-old, had arrived from Romania with her maternal aunt to join her widowed mother, who was already living and working in France as an undocumented domestic. Her brother, also in France but "with legal papers," had supposedly found a baker who agreed to employ her legally. This, she insisted, would be a stepping stone to her ultimate goal of studying law.

Through their Romanian interpreter the teenagers described their police custody. They had not slept or washed, had eaten only one meal, and one of the fourteen-year-olds had received no sanitary protection despite having her period. When the éducatrice left the Romanian interpreter and me alone to take a phone call, the interpreter volunteered the following assessment: "They were recruited to steal. It's clear. Their handler knows the police, and when he saw them arrive [to make the arrest] he took off. They end up in jail and he goes free. The next stop for them [the girls] is the sidewalk [that is, prostitution]." Later that day the girls were indicted and released by Judge Bella.

PENAL CASES IN CHAMBERS

The first afternoon I spent in Court L in June 2003, the judge heard cases involving one voluntary presentation at court and two penal hearings following arrest. One of the latter involved a fourteen-year-old Romanian boy who was arrested and held in police custody for possession of stolen property, a wallet and a cell phone, a charge he denied. He had two prior convictions, one for theft in a group for which he had received a warning, and a second for the same charge for which he had been imprisoned in the Fleury-Mérogis prison for a month. Released to a temporary placement in Paris pending transfer to a residential facility in the southwest before repatriation to Romania, he had left immediately. His recent arrest prompted the prosecutor's office to recommend a commitment order. When the youth insisted that he had stopped stealing and had only left the Paris facility to visit his mother, the judge lost her temper and threatened to return him to prison:

> JUDGE: Liar! So you were just walking by, saw the wallet and picked it up. So the police are the ones who lie? How can we have any confidence in you when you refuse to respect the law?

She indicted him but instead of prison imposed probationary supervision with the requirement to meet with an éducatrice once a week, and she scheduled judgment for early September. Later on in the evening I literally ran into that young man on the street as I was coming out of a phone booth in front of the Palace of Justice. Our eyes met, there was a flash of recognition, and I stepped out of the way. He and his Romanian buddy were eager to make a call.

CIVIL CASES IN CHAMBERS

That same afternoon the judge heard a civil case involving a fifteen-year-old from northern Romania who had entered France three weeks before and sought help from a Romanian NGO in Paris, Parada, after adults in a squatter camp tried to force him to steal. Parada aid workers informed him that the prosecutor's office would only open a child endangerment inquiry (signalement) with a juvenile judge if he could provide them with valid identity papers.

He returned with his passport and with their help scheduled a hearing at Court L. The youngest of twelve children, he was forced to quit high school because his family could not afford the school fees. He had heard that in France "minors are protected," and with his mother's consent he paid a smuggler to take him to France. The judge questioned him closely, through an interpreter, on his family background. The Romanian NGO report described him as "shy and respectful but disoriented by his new-found independence."[63] The youth wondered if he could stay permanently in France. The judge issued a six-month placement order ordering the ASE to provide social services from shelter to schooling (although after the hearing she aired her doubts about the possibility of getting him into school). She was much more circumspect on his future.

> JUDGE: You came here illegally. You need to learn French first before you can even enroll in school. We need to see how you adapt and manage separation from your family. It's too soon to say if you can stay. Nationality decisions are not made until closer to eighteen.
>
> YOUTH: I want to teach history. What school would best prepare me for university?
>
> JUDGE: [*impatiently*] You will study where they put you. The educational systems in France and Romania are very different [meaning, those in France are more advanced]. We'll see how things go. We'll reevaluate in six months.

When I returned to France in early December 2003, the administration of Court L had changed in response to vociferous protests by sitting judges and the prosecutor's office. As of 1 October 2003, the judge of Court L heard only social assistance or civil cases and all the penal cases were assigned to courts with lighter caseloads. One of those judges whose court included the fifteenth arrondissement sarcastically described the new arrangement: "I don't agree with it at all. You know she no longer sees any penal cases in chambers? After arrest they [unaccompanied minors] see the judge on duty, but when they are referred for prosecution, they are given a summons to her court. The case is registered on paper in her court but if they come [to the Palace of Justice] they don't go there [but to one of the other designated courts]. That's quite a unique [*original*] system, don't you think? Of course they never come, they don't see caseworkers, nothing has changed."[64]

In December 2003, I attended civil hearings in Court L in the midst of a Justice Ministry inspection of the court and after new legislation on immigration had been put in place. The mood was somber and the tenor of the hearings more ominous. One case involved a young man, Sombo, who requested the status of political refugee. He had been imprisoned with his parents, who had opposed the political regime in the Democratic Republic of the Congo. His father had died in prison and Sombo had been separated from his mother upon his release. He spent five months with an aunt before fleeing to France without proof of identity. He had been admitted to French territory and placed in a boarding school, where his performance was deemed "satisfactory" and his attitude "serious." His teachers and caseworkers agreed that he could integrate well and should begin an internship as a commercial truck driver. Unfortunately, he needed legal papers to get a work permit and to drive. His request for a court guardian was "in progress" but the judge advised him that the main obstacle remained the establishment of his "civil identity." The open question was the effect of the new law on immigration on his asylum request and naturalization process: "We now need a three-year period of guardianship with the ASE." An éducateur reminded the judge that he had a serious medical condition, hepatitis B. The court personnel exchanged hopeful glances, implying that this could constitute the basis for a successful claim and agreed that he needed to see a specialist immediately.[65] Although only a tiny fraction of unaccompanied minors are admitted to French territory from detention zones on humanitarian grounds, the illness clause amended in 1998 to the ordinance of 1945 on the entry of irregular immigrants allows residence permits for applicants with serious illnesses if they are unable to obtain treatment in their home countries. The illness clause, instituted as a humanitarian provision, now plays a critical role in the politics of immigration for adult migrants. Although enacted through a moral imperative for compassion, it forms part of flawed and failed human rights discourses and practices by French state and nonstate actors whose effects can be violent and exclusionary.[66] As Miriam Ticktin has argued, according entry and rights to undocumented migrants on the basis of disease makes illness a social resource even as it strips suffering bodies of their full humanity and eviscerates asylum claims of their political content. The judge confirmed Sombo's placement for six months after suggesting two avenues for caseworkers to explore to establish his legal identity and facilitate naturalization.

This case was followed by one that involved unusual complications. The judge had first met Natalie, a tiny, emaciated seventeen-year-old, the preceding May when she was admitted to France under the exceptional circumstances provision by border police. She had described her parents' murder before her eyes in the Democratic Republic of the Congo and her flight with a smuggler who took her money, held her hostage, and raped her systematically for weeks before she escaped to France and discovered she was pregnant by him. She was placed in a home for single mothers and enrolled in a remedial correspondence course to prepare for a secondary-level diploma as a nurse's aid. She had given birth to a healthy baby boy in mid-November but the social worker report described numerous problems:

> Natalie does not communicate with the social work team or the other mothers. She keeps inside what she has experienced but constantly demands the attention of the social worker. She refuses to do the required tasks or to eat (at scheduled times), complains like a little child, has dramatically changing mood swings, shows frustration, has difficulty accepting authority, changes from joy to pouting, refuses to be patient. She is clearly in a state of distress but is also willful and determined. She cannot express her pain.

Natalie was in a state of legal limbo like Sombo. She was also waiting for her own minority status to be confirmed and for the results of the test determining her age to be communicated to the ASE so that a court guardian could be appointed. With no papers and legal identity, Natalie could not open an account at a French bank, and the post office could not deliver the child allowance payments for her baby to which she was entitled. The psychological trauma of accepting a child of rape was evident. The social workers insisted that establishing a proper "mother-child relation" demanded that she nurse the baby but then were surprised and judgmental when she rejected the baby, blaming her moods, distress, and "willful" refusal to accept authority for "not wanting to see him." They advised the judge that the "baby was not gaining weight." One of the two social workers present complained that "with eight young girls and four babies under two months at the home," she had too much work "to coddle one who stays in her room with the door closed." When asked if it was necessary to issue a judicial measure of protection, the other social worker insisted emphatically, "Yes, I can't get through to her, she shuts down, there are constant conflicts. She just does not have enough perspective to take responsibility." As an afterthought she added, "Of course, there is the fact that she was a victim of violence."

Turning to Natalie, the judge attempted to explain the rights and duties of French parents citing almost verbatim from article 375 of the French civil code which, she noted:

requires you, although you are still a minor, to protect the child, his health, conditions of upbringing, education, and morality. If you agree to do this alone, if you are strong enough, if you win the right to conclude contracts on your own, the ASE helps single parents raise children. Can you do it without close supervision from a judge? Do you understand what I am saying?

During this speech, I had watched Natalie closely. As the judge intoned authoritatively using abstract legalese, Natalie began to withdraw, stopped concentrating, and her gaze became fixed on a point in space, somewhere between the judge and me. It came as no surprise when she replied, "I don't understand at all." When the judge attempted to clarify by explaining the possible need for "arbitration" given the conflicts between her and the staff, Natalie asked tentatively if the judge was informing her that she had to surrender custody of the child? "No," was the emphatic rejoinder from the judge followed by several more attempts to explain that were no more successful. In the hierarchy of need with which the court must deal, the judge prioritized the attribution of parental authority and the obligations of the young mother of a child of rape over the supervision of a vulnerable minor who was the victim of rape. The judge confirmed Natalie's placement at the home until her eighteenth birthday but issued no additional protective orders.

LESSONS FROM COURT L

In 2003 the adjudication of cases involving street children revealed the blurred boundaries between agency and constraint, victim and perpetrator, insider and outsider. Romanian children learned quickly from their court appearances, access to court-appointed attorneys, conversations with interpreters, intake interviews with court caseworkers, and indictment hearings with judges. They learned that placement in foster homes or residential facilities meant social isolation, continued economic marginality, or a rigid integration process predicated on knowledge of mainstream linguistic and social norms. Most foreign minors were too young to work legally, had only grade-school educations, knew little or no French, and realized that there were limited opportunities for education or training programs. They were quick to grasp the limited legal opportunities in the formal job market for un- or semiskilled workers. Their complaints about or refusal of these constraints earned them reprimands from éducateurs, whose reports to judges carried considerable weight. Some accepted the bargain, attempted to conform, and sought legalization as political refugees, French citizens, or legal residents. For those who played the game, sought assistance at court, or turned to officials at the local prefecture, the stakes for losing were high. Rejection of residence permits as refugees or ineligibility for citizenship meant a return to the street and irregular status with the threat of punitive sanctions and forced deportation.

Despite these constraints and obstacles, undocumented minors who appeared in court in 2003, some of whom had been in France for two or more years, demonstrated an impressive understanding of French law and the due process protections reinforcing the presumption of innocence legislated in 2000. Some claimed they were innocent, while others acknowledged only the lesser charge of simple theft carrying reduced penalties. Some children dared to complain to social workers and judges of mistreatment or neglect by police during custody. This included rough handling, blows, tight handcuffing, and/or lack of food, sleep, and sanitary protection for young women. A few intended to appeal harsh sentences handed down by juvenile courts. One of the thirteen-year-old girls mentioned above intended to appeal a ruling from the St. Etienne juvenile court near Lyon. She and three other children had inadvertently damaged an expensive computer display case in a department store and been sentenced in absentia to a four-month prison sentence. These tactics were risky and rarely produced acquittals. Instead, youngsters collected long police records and encountered formidable obstacles to their "social integration."

Despite the arrival of a new director of the Paris SEAT in 2002 and goals to make more assistance available, the virtual justice continued. Social assistance was defined largely as placement in state institutions versus access to education and training. The judge of Court L rarely exercised the placement option. When I interviewed SEAT director Delphine Bergère on 10 March 2004, she produced the following statistic: Out of 634 unaccompanied minors prosecuted by the juvenile prosecutor's office in 2002, only 30 social assistance measures were opened by éducateurs. She also opposed Court L largely on procedural grounds—"it was an aberration for one judge to deal with half of the court's prosecutions"—but like her colleagues, she resisted unchecked irregular immigration: "Our organizations have been instrumentalized by foreign networks. They are perfectly conversant with French law. They know their rights, they can't be deported. . . . I recognize that with street kids it is different. But we can't adopt policies that encourage criminal gangs. We are torn between the need for protection of endangered minors and the protection of French territory and our institutions."

On 6 March 2004, I attended the meeting of the Incarceration Committee, which included representatives from the Youth Detention Center at Fleury-Mérogis, regional service providers, and Paris court personnel. We learned that out of 171 minors from Paris incarcerated in 2003, 79 were "unaccompanied," and of that number 41 were Romanian, 19 were from the former Yugoslavia, 15 were from Africa, and 4 from elsewhere. More disturbing was the revelation that 29 of the 171 were under the age of sixteen. All had had their minority determined by the X-ray test of skeletal development. The judges present were deeply concerned by the high number of unaccompanied minors in prison. When Delphine Bergère arrived, they pressed her to explain how so many under sixteen ended up in detention. The director repudiated the statistics just given by her colleague, saying "they had no utility" since the test consistently used by the court to determine age was not definitive. This, she explained, falsified the data! When the judges urged her to give the average length of incarceration as well as the type of offenses (property versus people), she simply pleaded ignorance and moved to the next agenda item.

CONCLUSION

Back in the Paris jail, the éducatrice began her intake interview with Marius. She remembered him well and greeted him warmly, remarking on how much he had grown since his first arrest. When she admonished him to provide his real identity, he agreed and described a chain migration to France including two other brothers and a married sister. He added hastily that "none of them stole for a living." He was obviously intelligent, highly perceptive, and had excellent representational skills, anticipating and answering the caseworker's questions with a sense of humor and a flair for irony. When asked the stock question about his "future plans," he insisted he would never become "a forest guard like his father." None of us could resist laughing when he added mischievously that he intended to be "either a French professor or a policeman." When challenged about his failure to answer a summons to appear in Court L, he demurred, adding that he was attending free language and computer classes offered for Romanians at several NGOs in Paris.

I accompanied the éducatrice to brief Judge Bella before the indictment hearing. She gave a glowing report on Marius, emphasizing his initiative and his fluency in French. The judge was unimpressed. When Marius arrived by police escort, the judge read from a long list of his convictions, including his own role as a pimp organizing the prostitution of newly arrived Romanian

children. She was annoyed when he changed his story, insisted on his innocence, and attempted to distinguish between himself and the French adult with
whom he was arrested, who, Marius proclaimed, "was an ex-con." The judge
indicted him and set a trial date in the formal court but admonished him to
seek financial help from France and return to Romania. She held up a letter
from his father forwarded to her from the Romanian consulate requesting that
he return home. This was something Marius had promised to do on a number
of previous occasions. There were dozens of boys like Marius who had spent
considerable time away from home, in France and abroad. While they remained attached to family, they no longer necessarily constructed place-
centered identities. The allure of fast money and the freedom of life on the
street in Paris was too great. Besides, these boys often had family close by.

I last spent time in Court L in March 2004. In between hearings, the judge
took a call from a juvenile prosecutor at a suburban court in Créteil, outside
Paris. He alerted her to a disturbing situation involving an unaccompanied
West African minor in a state residential facility there. The prosecutor took a
call from its distraught director earlier that morning after fifteen policemen
arrived unannounced with sirens blaring, burst in shoving the staff aside,
searched his room, and arrested and handcuffed him because of his "criminal
activity." When the director insisted that he was a minor but could provide no
identity papers, the police warned him that both he and his charge were "illegal." During police custody, the examining physician sent the youth to the psychiatric unit at the Kremlin-Bicêtre hospital in Paris as required by law. The
examination revealed serious psychological problems. The prosecutor resolved
the situation by allowing police custody to extend beyond its legal limit,
thereby ensuring that the charges would be dismissed on a technicality and he
would be released. According to the prosecutor, "it was nothing, he was riding
a bus without a ticket [and ID]." The judge was clearly upset when she hung up.
"It seems to be open season on [irregular] foreigners in France now."

Under existing court conditions of overloaded penal dockets, scarce service
providers, public pressure for greater accountability, anti-immigrant bias, and
a stigma surrounding criminal vagrants in France illegally, the judicial apparatus prioritizes prosecution and punishment over assistance and rehabilitation.
This is particularly true of unaccompanied, irregular children whose mobility,
vulnerability, legal minority, and lack of parental guidance all challenge the
court's supervisory powers—its ability to control, its capacity to protect, and
its will to integrate. Despite a rhetorical and institutional commitment to the

humanitarian goals of assistance, Romanian and other foreign migrants were repeatedly denied social services that were guaranteed by law and disproportionately subjected to prosecution. Moreover, the vast majority were issued summons for hearings that could not be delivered, tried, and sentenced without being present, and given relatively harsh penalties for nonviolent property offenses. Recall that all of the irregular minors I met in the juvenile quarter of the Fleury-Mérogis prison were awaiting trial. Some had been detained for theft or immigration violations. After the bilateral agreement between France and Romania, protection and assistance was predicated on the accused returning home. Restrictive legislation regarding the legalization and naturalization of irregular immigrants made integration and settlement in France increasingly difficult, if not impossible.

Groups of unskilled and unschooled young people could not be recognized en masse as economic migrants, because they were too young to work or had no skills except in the building or clothing sectors, where irregular workers were still a source of cheap labor. Their participation in both the informal economy and in criminal activity shaped public rhetoric and legal policy within the National Assembly and at court. In a context where there is no demand for an unskilled "immigrant" labor force and considerable suspicion about economic migrants from the east and south taking advantage of the generosity of western Europe, ambivalence about the proliferation of child criminals could be displaced onto the criminal organizations that helped them cross the border. When they continued to offend and to resist efforts to reform, they were denied the dispensations accorded minors, classified as adults, and subjected to more severe standards of accountability.

The creation of Court L did not accomplish its goal of dealing more humanely with unaccompanied minors apprehended for criminal activity. Court personnel, Justice Ministry inspectors, and outside observers agreed that it was having the effect of reinforcing and institutionalizing the very judicial practice it was created to prevent, namely the penalization of marginality. In fact, it may have actually exacerbated a punitive approach by encouraging more transnational migration in a judicial context marked by scarce resources, increased border controls, and bilateral agreements between France and Romania to eradicate a highly visible and politically embarrassing public order problem. Critiques of the treatment of unaccompanied minors by NGOs and child advocates highlighted the failure of a variety of French institutions—including border and municipal police, the juvenile court, and the ASE—to assure basic protections for some of the most vulnerable recent migrants. They fundamentally challenged the national and international representation of France as a preeminent champion of human rights and a preferred destination of asylum seekers. Moreover, French and Romanian attempts to return and keep Romanian children from migrating have been unsuccessful. When asked why the policy of voluntary repatriations financed by France had produced such meager results–only twenty-one returned to Romania as of September 2003—then-Interior Minister Nicolas Sarkozy replied testily, "The problem lies with conditions in Romania. I have no control over that. I'm not the Interior Minister of Romania."[67] Now that Sarkozy is president of France, the category of criminal vagrants that was so useful in prosecuting the *petits Roumains* may well be applied to groups of unwanted Others.

9 CONCLUSION

DURING HIS TENURE AS PRIME MINISTER from 1997 to 2002, Socialist Lionel Jospin was fond of repeating that "security is a right and the lack of security is a social injustice." He meant, of course, that the fear and effects of crime have the largest impact on those at the bottom of society.[1] The appeal to social justice as a rationale for the intensified containment of targeted groups in both suburban projects and city neighborhoods should give us pause. That rhetoric arbitrarily redefines security as linked to criminality. The exclusive focus on penality decouples it from the other critical spheres we associate with security, such as employment, income, housing, health care, and safe schools. It likewise separates it from the other inalienable human rights guaranteed in article 2 of the Rights of Man, such as the right to resist oppression or the right to legal rights extended to children in the CRC, to which France is a signatory.

The reality is that security is increasingly a privilege reserved for the well-heeled in highly policed city neighborhoods rather than a right for the poor in underserved public projects. This privilege is contingent on increasing restrictions on legal immigration as well as mounting intolerance for admittance of irregular immigrants in any form—either economic migrants or asylum seekers. Between 1980 and the late 1990s the attitude of state officials toward asylum requests completely reversed, shifting from one of relative tolerance to one of systematic refusal, except in the case of serious illnesses such as AIDS.[2]

The reliance of center-left and center-right governments on zero-tolerance policing means selective sweeps and arrests in targeted neighborhoods as well as more prosecution of public order violations, of infractions against public authorities, and of so-called violent offenses such as aggravated theft. This has resulted in a huge increase in both the overall adult and juvenile prison populations. Between 1994 and 2001, the number of firm prison sentences for minors went from 1,905 to 4,542 per year, and over the same period the numbers of pretrial detentions virtually doubled.[3] Between 2001 and 2003, 13,000 prisoners were added to the overall French prison population as a result of "bureaucratic and political pressure on judges" to accelerate adjudications, stiffen penalties, eliminate alternate sentences and early parole, and to hand down prison sentences.[4] In June 2003, after inspections of French prisons, the European Committee for the Prevention of Torture and Inhuman or Degrading Treatment or Punishment published a devastating report on the severe overcrowding and high rate of suicides in filthy, run-down prisons with occupancy rates of 239 percent (Loos prison) and 240 percent (Toulon). As Loïc Wacquant has so passionately argued, "where the so-called plural left [in power from 1997 to 2002] criminalized misery in a shameful and hidden way, the republican right openly acknowledged its choice of containing the disarray and social disorders . . . in neighborhoods ravaged by mass unemployment and flexible work by fully deploying a repressive apparatus."[5]

The policy of flexible incarceration produces not less but more insécurité in poor neighborhoods and public projects through the devastating social effects of doing time. Although there are no data on the race or ethnicity of inmates, statistics on income level, educational attainment, and class position reveal that French prisons are populated by the most marginalized members of French society. Foreigners are overrepresented in prison (24 percent), as are French citizens with fathers born abroad (25 percent). Serving time only exacerbates their social and economic marginality and places heavy emotional and financial burdens on the families they leave behind. It begs the question of why debate about crime centers "on loitering in project stairwells rather than on misdeeds in the offices of town halls, on the theft of book bags and cell phones rather than on stock market fraud, labor code violations, and tax evasion."[6]

Political rhetoric and criminological attention have centered on the rapid rise in the 1990s in public order violations, thefts aggravated by violence (*vols avec violence*), and drug-related offenses. Although the rise in aggravated theft began twenty years ago and has continued steadily but slowly since that time, the vast majority do not involve physical injury or use of a weapon of any kind. Drug offenses have also figured prominently in the media portrayals of the cités. Public fears focus on the new prominence of drugs in parallel economies within the suburban projects and the affirmation by police commissioners and new security experts that organized drug trafficking networks operate on a massive scale within "lawless zones." This rhetoric and the crime literature ignore the long history of drugs in French working-class neighborhoods, as well as the fact that drug consumption is not limited to suburban projects or bad neighborhoods.[7] Most consumption involves marijuana, spans all social classes, and, among certain age groups, is even more prevalent in middle-class milieus. Rather than violent drug kingpins driving luxury cars or mafia-style crime families earning vast wealth, a better label for those who sell drugs is "minimum wage dealers" (*smicards du bizness*). They preside over the majority of dealing in most poor and working-class neighborhoods, where the drug of choice is marijuana, which circulates in limited local networks among young men who are primarily users, not dealers.[8] In a context marked by high youth unemployment for all but the most credentialed, stark deindustrialization, limited blue-collar work, and a tight labor market favoring temporary, insecure employment contracts, it is little wonder that parallel economies have grown or that French and foreign employers in France readily hire undocumented immigrants precisely because they can be denied all rights. The reality for the majority of second- and third-generation children of Muslim immigrants and newer arrivals from eastern Europe and elsewhere who are poor and unskilled, is one of economic marginality and frustrated aspirations.

In the many proceedings described here the voices of court personnel dominate; those of children, parents, and even defense attorneys are muted or silent. No doubt, the silence had much to do with their sense that the hearings and trials were a formality and the outcomes were largely predetermined. It was a process in which they had much to lose and little to gain. The court determines how families should be organized, how control should be maintained, disputes resolved, wrongs redressed, and equitable punishments exacted.[9] Nonetheless, there were cases in which young people and their parents refuted the charges and spoke out. By challenging the facts, they challenged the court's attempt to manage doubt and to control the construction of authoritative narratives of reality. They critically commented on the cultural categories and, therefore, the social reality, on which the law is based. They attempted to alert the court to the contaminating effects of power on the law—racism, intolerance, different normative systems, and class differences. They demanded accountability, staked a claim, and sought different outcomes from the legal system by highlighting institutional injustices and emphasizing mitigating circumstances.

They warned of the hazards of bureaucratic indifference, the dangers of ethno-racial stereotyping, the hostilities born of social inequality, and the costs of economic polarization. The final examples that follow allow some of the most vulnerable minors and their families—homeless, impoverished, or undocumented foreigners—to speak their truth to power.

Tran, a sixteen-year-old Vietnamese teenager, was arrested in early February 2001 for violating the conditions of his probation. He was estranged from his mother who spoke no French, was illiterate, and homeless. He angrily challenged the judge:

> I don't understand why they arrested me. I am not the only Asian guy in the sixteenth [arrondissement], you know. I have witnesses who saw me in another part of the city. No, I told the police I don't live with my mother and she won't come to court. She never came before. I told them I want to get back in school. I want to live in a state residence facility or with a host family. I have asked several times and the court does nothing.

Around the same time, a seventeen-year-old Muslim of Malian ancestry was scheduled for a court hearing. He had been arrested and accused of insulting and assaulting a public transit worker. Homeless and mentally disturbed, he wrote a letter to the judge requesting leniency in an upcoming hearing. He asked to be placed. Could she get him placed with child welfare services? Could she put in a good word so he could get one of the entry-level state jobs reserved for young people? He failed to appear so his case was referred to the juvenile correctional court for sentencing.

A fifteen-year-old girl of Congolese ancestry who lived with her mother and stepfather ran away from home, began to smoke hashish, and got arrested for shoplifting. After the teenager complained about her parents' harsh rules and backward [cultural] attitudes, and her caseworker backed her up, warning the judge that the "stepfather was a whacko," the judge suggested a cultural mediation. Her parents vented their frustration and refused the offer. Her mother demanded, "Did she tell you why she ran away? Why she was digging in my purse? She was looking for money for hashish. Ask her if we didn't see her outside in broad daylight doing drugs. What will a mediation do about that?" Her husband was equally outraged. "You don't hesitate to lecture African parents on how to raise their children. Let me tell you that [in the Congo] the children of our spouse are considered like our children. For the French, I am considered the stepfather, not the biological father. For the French there is a distance. Well, for me, no. She is my daughter and I am her father even if her mother has children with different fathers. We accept them, not like you in France. You judge others who are not like you."

The rapid reform of juvenile law accelerated under center-right governments beginning in 2002. Nicolas Sarkozy, first as Interior minister and now as president, has favored more accountability and punishment for juvenile offenders. After his election as president, he named a forty-one-year-old woman of Maghrebi ancestry, Rachida Dati, to be his Justice Minister.[10] As part of Sarkozy's inner circle since the 2002 presidential elections, Dati oversaw the politically charged issues of juvenile delinquency and the banlieues. As the head of the Justice Ministry, her first priorities were to effect two revolutionary reforms of the French criminal justice system: the creation of automatic minimum sentences for recidivists and the lowering of the age of penal majority from eighteen to sixteen years of age, a return to the Napoleonic penal code statutes of 1810. A poll conducted during the 2007 elections by the Institut des Etudes Politiques indicated that these reforms would have broad appeal among French voters. Sixty-three percent of those questioned felt that juvenile delinquents should be treated just like adults in the French criminal justice system.[11] This confirmed an Ifop opinion poll published by the conservative daily newspaper *Le Figaro* in September 2006 in which 77 percent of the respondents declared that the judicial system was not harsh enough on young offenders.[12]

As the French continue to amend existing juvenile law, they would do well to consider the United States and the consequences of implementing a system in which minors are tried as adults and subject to mandatory sentencing mandates that exclude individual background and mitigating circumstances. Research here over the past ten years has reassessed the effects of legislation to punish juvenile offenders as adults in the interest of promoting public safety and crime prevention. Rather than reducing youth crime, trying youths in adult criminal court actually increased the chances that they would reoffend and commit more serious offenses.[13] Juvenile judges, child advocates, academic researchers, legal experts, correctional administrators,[14] and editors in newspapers of record are at long last beginning to speak out against "juvenile injustice" in the United States.[15]

It is estimated that as many as 200,000 youth are prosecuted as adults in the United States every year.[16] Despite the intention of state legislators to target serious juvenile offenders, most of those who enter the adult court are charged with nonviolent offenses. Once in adult court, however, they face the same punishment as adults, serve time in adult prisons, and may receive life sentences without parole. The only punishment they are spared is the death penalty.[17] Since 1990 the incarceration of youth in adult jails has increased 208 percent[18] despite the fact that the promised waves of young superpredators[19] never materialized and that juvenile crime fell over that same period and is now at a thirty-year low. When tried and incarcerated as adults, thousands of young people are put at risk of isolation, severe abuse, and psychological problems. They face harmful and irreversible consequences because of the stigma of a criminal conviction and many experience difficulty getting a driver's license, finding employment or affordable housing, getting federal financial aid for a college degree, and being able to vote. This is all the more disturbing, since we know the degree to which youth of color are disproportionately affected by statutes mandating transfer to the adult criminal justice system.[20]

We live in perilous times when more than 2,000 American youth are serving life sentences without any possibility for parole and the Bush administration's war on terror has created legal anomalies, such as the detention camp at Guantánamo Bay, Cuba, where minors as young as fifteen are held as enemy combatants and are subject to trial by Military Commissions which effectively give them no chance to defend themselves and allow evidence obtained through torture.[21]

I end this book where I began, with a discussion of the 2005 riots. Recall that members of the French government depicted those events as dangerous threats to the republic and vilified the perpetrators as confirmed delinquents operating in organized gangs. In fact, the vast majority (75 percent) of those tried were minors who were enrolled in public school and who had no police records; one-third of them were under sixteen years of age and two-thirds were aged sixteen to eighteen. All were born in France. The most common charges were for insulting or resisting public authorities and property damage, but the determination of individual responsibility for specific infractions was virtually impossible because of the mass arrests (4,500) and detention in police custody (*garde à vue*). A number of those in detention reported being arrested the day after the riots based on the word of informers or the police. There were no groups of "criminal, Islamist instigators" at work. Nonetheless, the courts were harsh and heeded then–Justice Minister Pascal Clément's instructions "not to hesitate in requesting firm prison sentences." The average penalty was five weeks in prison, and 800 young people served time. Since 2005 legislation has increased punitive surveillance and control of minors and their parents from the inclusion of youth offenders in a national DNA database to immediate trials in juvenile court.[22]

French reformers should reconsider their own difficult past in Africa, Algeria, and Indochina. They would do well to recall the wisdom contained in the preface of the 1945 ordinance justifying an individual-centered and rehabilitative approach to delinquency.[23] That sentiment is echoed in the words of a petition circulated by French judges in July 2007, which opposed legislation to try adolescents as adults and to increase prison sentences for repeat offenders. It was signed by over 8,000 people in France and abroad.

In the text [of the proposed law], the theft of a cell phone, committed after two prior infractions, mandates a two-year prison sentence. This will produce an increase in the number of teenagers in prison. 15,000 youth [out of 15 million], aged sixteen to seventeen, are arrested several times during the course of the year. Most [of them] have been out of school since the age of fourteen, have no skills and cannot get jobs. Perceiving themselves as useless, humiliated by repeated failures, they "hang out," get into trouble, and commit most of their offenses in groups. Are these the teenagers who will be singled out and treated as adults? Are these the teenagers for whom France will abandon every effort of rehabilitation?[24]

NOTES

Prologue

1. Catta 1988:59.
2. Once an investigation, or *instruction*, has been opened, the suspect, or *mis en cause*, in an inquiry becomes the accused, or *mis en examen*. This investigation "represents the paradigm model of investigation within French inquisitorial procedure" (Hodgson 2005:209). In less serious offenses involving minors, juvenile judges investigate the same cases they later try. See Chapter 2.
3. Augé 1986:26, 28.
4. *Le Monde*, 19 January 1999.
5. Coutant 2005.

Chapter 1

1. The town of Clichy-sous-Bois has no regular train service, social welfare offices, outdoor markets, or police headquarters.
2. The prosecutor's office did not open a criminal investigation into the incident until November 2006. Two policemen who were originally questioned as material witnesses were formally investigated (*mis en examen*) by the Bobigny court on 7 February 2007 for violation of the law requiring assistance to persons in danger (*Le Monde*, 8 February 2007).
3. This built on inflammatory remarks Sarkozy made in June 2005 on the need to clean out the nearby suburb of La Courneuve with an industrial power washer.
4. The measure originated from a 1955 law targeting the Algerian freedom fighters and was used twice in metropolitan France during the Algerian war for independence.

293

5. *Le Monde*, 8 November 2005. Close to 4,500 arrests were made in nearly 100 municipalities. On 15 November the National Assembly voted by an overwhelming majority—of three to one—to extend the state of emergency from an initial period of twelve days to three months.

6. *Le Monde*, 16 November 2005.

7. *Le Monde*, 27 June 2006.

8. Cole 2007.

9. Beaud 2002.

10. Salas 1995:41–62.

11. Compare the monstrous traits associated with "white trash" (Hartigan 2005).

12. See Copfermann 1962 on the "black jackets"; Fishman 2002 on delinquency between 1912 and 1945; Mucchielli 2002 on contemporary delinquency; and Nye 1984:171–226 and Savage 2007 on the urban Apaches of the early twentieth century.

13. Sarkozy 2007.

14. I borrow the term *adultify* from Ferguson 2001.

15. These sanctions are modeled on the adult penal code. They center on judicial control over young children's spatial movement, social contacts, and personal property. The 2002 law permitted ten- to thirteen-year-olds to be held for longer periods for questioning by the police. See law 2002-1138 of 9 September 2002 (www.legifrance.gouv.fr).

16. As a result of law 2002-1138, minors from thirteen to sixteen years of age who violate the terms of probation pending trial (*contrôle judiciaire*) may be sent to closed juvenile centers or prison. Many judges saw the law as a means to exercise broad discretion in imposing detention. I thank Andy Bickford for suggesting the term "flexible incarceration."

17. The excuse of minority automatically reduces the adult penalty by half. Judges may continue to use juvenile sentencing guidelines even for recidivists, but this has become the exception rather than the rule. They must impose minimum sentences on repeat offenders for physical assault, sexual offenses, and crimes carrying a ten-year prison term.

18. See 10 August 2007 Law no. 2007-1198 reinforcing the fight against the recidivism of adults and minors (Journal officiel 185:13466, 11 August 2007). There was considerable opposition to this law on the part of judges, caseworkers, and academics. On 17 July 2007 I was asked to sign a petition that was being circulated by French juvenile judges opposed to the law. It already had 8,000 signatures.

19. Compare Hajjar's 2005 treatment of the Israeli military court system in the West Bank and Gaza.

20. Durham 2004.

21. Stephens 1995.

22. Hodgson 2005:34–36.

23. See *Selmouni v. France*, 28 July 1999.

24. See Council of Europe, 1991, 1996, 2003, 2006; Herzog-Evans 2000:42. The Council of Europe's report based on the inspection conducted from 14 May 2000 to 26 May 2000 noted only marginal improvement (www.cpt.coe/int/documents/fra/ 2001-10-inf-fra.htm).

25. Ariès 1962; Scheper-Hughes and Sargent 1998:26.

26. This notion builds on hierarchies of class, race, and gender inherited from colonialism (Cole and Durham 2007:6–8).

27. See Bell 1993; Garland 1996, 2001; Muncie 2007:30; Rose 1996, 2000.

28. Muncie 2007:31.

29. See article 61 in the original version of law 2003-239, 18 March 2003, on internal security, which amended article 126-2 in the public housing code to punish deliberate obstruction of access or movement in stairwells and entrances as well as threats to the safety and security of public order within state housing units. It instituted a maximum penalty of two months in prison and/or a fine of 3,750 euros (www .legifrance.gouv.fr).

30. Compare Susan Coutin's work (2000) on Salvadoreans in the United States whose appropriation of the self-empowering term *refugee* versus *immigrant* collided head-on with vicious anti-immigrant politics in cities like Los Angeles.

31. There are two ways to report crime in France. The Interior Ministry records figures on suspects accused of infractions, whereas the Justice Ministry reports convictions after trial. Between 1990 and 1999, a period associated with a rapid rise in youth crime, the number of minors convicted of all types of offenses hardly changed: 38,507 in 1990 versus 38,580 in 1999 (Jérez 2001:283). In contrast, there was a dramatic increase in the proportion of minors to adults accused of illegal activity: In 1990 13 percent of suspects were minors versus 21.32 percent in 1999 (ibid.:288). According to police statistics, the number of minors accused of nonlethal assault increased fivefold between 1993 and 2001. However, these statistics are misleading. The 1994 penal code revisions reclassified assault without injury as a serious misdemeanor if accompanied by a series of aggravating circumstances, such as on a vulnerable person, in a group, or with the use or threat of a weapon (Robert quoted in Mucchielli 2004:112). Only half of the assaults were serious enough to warrant hospitalization or absence from work (Mucchielli 2002:67). Similarly there were fewer juvenile homicides in 2000 (26) than in 1984 (32) and in 1990 (33). The category of assault that received wide media coverage in 2001 was gang rape, particularly when the perpetrators were of Muslim ancestry

(Mucchielli 2005). The public perception that gang rapes increased dramatically is not supported by Justice Ministry figures. Moreover, in surveys for the Paris region, victims defined "assaults" as verbal insults, threats, and even hostile stares in half of the cases studied. Only 3 percent of those questioned reported being victims of actual physical attacks (Pottier, Robert, and Zauberman 2002, quoted in Mucchielli 2004:112). The short-term spike in minor arrests between 1990 and 2000 results partly from more aggressive policing and prosecution.

32. Alain Morice and Véronique de Rudder illustrate how the categories used in the annual survey of French attitudes on racism and xenophobia by the National Consultative Commission on the Rights of Man actually reinforce stereotypes and construct immigration as a problem comparable to terrorism, religious fundamentalism, loss of national identity, and environmental pollution (*Le Monde*, 22 March 2007).

33. Reporting in the national daily *Le Monde* during one week of May 1998 is emblematic in this regard. Three separate cases of juvenile homicide in different areas, two in different suburban areas of Paris and one in Marseille, received national coverage and were exploited by then–Interior Minister Jean-Pierre Chevènement as proof of a "culture of hate" and a "deep crisis" to justify a more repressive approach to youth crime (*Le Monde*, 11 May, 12 May, 14 May 1998).

34. See Mucchielli 2002:12–25; cf. the depiction of the murderous hoodlums in "Ados: La spirale de l'ultraviolence" in *L'Express*, 7 December 2000, with Laurent Mucchielli's account of having provided statistical documentation refuting the increase in juvenile homicide to *L'Express* journalists (Mucchielli 2005:15). Although he is a recognized expert on the subject, they completely disregarded his data.

35. See Nicolas Sarkozy's speeches on 13 October 2005 and 15 November 2005 (Sarkozy 2005b, 2005a). Sarkozy noted that "crime against persons represents only 10% of all delinquency" (Sarkozy 2005b).

36. Caldeira 2000:53–101.

37. Historian Sarah Fishman describes the repressive turn of contemporary juvenile courts and "the usual tendencies" for "white middle-class judges, social workers, and doctors, to intrude into, supervise, and attempt to control immigrant and working class families" (2002:233). However, she concludes that the French system remains "extremely, intrusively therapeutic" in part because "it is embedded in a society that places tremendous value on its children and young people" (ibid.). Had she actually observed the court from the inside and contrasted the written file with the oral proceedings, she would find it difficult to downplay institutional racism or to argue that intrusive therapy characterizes the current court system.

38. See Foucault 1977:293; cf. Rufin 1996:82

39. See Donzelot [1977] 1997; Meyer [1977] 1983; cf. Horn 1994.

40. Léger 1990; Rufin 1996:80–81.

41. Donzelot [1977] 1997:139–149. During this period, activist psychiatrists such as De Almeida (1975) denounced their predecessors' collusion with the colonial order and the system of domination that psychiatric institutions wielded over immigrants from French colonies in Africa. De Almeida founded centers that provided social services for patients and training for social workers.

42. Meyer [1977] 1983.

43. See Bauer and Raufer 1999, 2005; Grémy 1996.

44. See Bailleau and Gorgeon 2000; Bonnemain 2000; Collovald 2000; Mouhanna 2000; see also Bourdieu 1986.

45. During debate in September 2007, lawmakers adopted an amendment to the new, and particularly restrictive, immigration control bill. It proposed to legalize the collection of statistics on ethnic and racial origin "as a means to facilitate research on the diversity of origins, [forms of] discrimination, and integration" (*Le Monde*, 14 September 2007). One of the major French antiracist associations, SOS Racisme, circulated a petition demanding the withdrawal of the amendment and requesting the removal of questions on respondents' skin color that had been included in a public survey to be conducted in 2008 by two state agencies. In November 2007 the Constitutional Council struck down the legislative amendment on procedural grounds but suggested that it could have been struck down because of its alleged incompatibility with article 1 of the 1958 Constitution. See decision n° 2007-557 DC, 15 November 2007, http://www.conseil-constitutionnel.fr/decision/2007/2007557dc.htm.

46. See Hargreaves 2000:93; Noiriel 1992; Rudder, Poiret, and Vourc'h 2000:8.

47. Dubois 2000:5–6. There have been state attempts to combat discrimination. In 2005 a new agency, the Haute autorité de lutte contre les discriminations et pour légalité (High Authority for Antidiscrimination and Equality), was created to promote greater opportunities for minority populations. Despite increased debate on the use of ethnoracial statistics, most French policymakers and scholars strongly support continued color-blind approaches.

48. Crenshaw 1995:105.

49. Ibid.:106.

50. I take issue with Beriss's notion of culture-as-race because it downplays discrimination based on racial attributes such as skin color. This is all the more surprising given his own experience of profiling by French police based on his putative physical similarity to Arab men (2004).

51. I support Wacquant's critique of postmodern accounts that are limited to a study of discursive formations on race rather than pursuing a rigorous analytic of race

based on institutional practices (1997b). However, discourses are inevitably part of institutional practices even or particularly when these include silences and omissions on the unrecognized category of race in the French court.

52. Silverman 1995.

53. Silverstein 2006:2–3.

54. Consider CNN journalist's Christiane Amanpour's interview with Prime Minister Dominique de Villepin in late November 2005, when he rejected American affirmative action–type quotas as a means to address inequities that fueled the urban unrest, "because in France everyone is considered equal."

55. On racism in the workplace, see Bataille 1997. A case in point is the recent scandal at the Paris Montparnasse office of the Zurich-based Adecco temp agency. French recruiters rated candidates by race in order to comply with their clients' supposed refusal to employ people of color in visible service sector positions. A recruiter of Antillean ancestry quit his job and exposed the system in a letter written to SOS Racisme describing how his French colleagues did not think they were discriminating (*Washington Post*, 15 January 2006). The arsenal of antiracist laws offers no protection against those who deny their motives or against institutions whose practices disadvantage minorities. On racism by the police, see Jobard 2002; in housing, MacMaster 1991. On immigration policy, see Weil 2005.

56. For documentation of police abuse, see Chouk, Gillet, Spire, and Terray 2002.

57. Mucchielli 2002:8.

58. The labels assigned to problem youth depend on the jurisdictions that manage them. When youths enter the juvenile justice system, they are labeled "delinquents"; if transferred to the adult system, they become "criminals." In contrast, educators and mental health practitioners may describe the same individuals as "antisocial," "aggressive," or, in more severe cases, "conduct disordered." It is now commonly accepted that ADHD is a risk factor for serious antisocial behavior, and it is grouped, along with conduct disorder and oppositional defiant disorder, as disruptive behavioral disorders (Wasserman, Miller, and Cothern 2000). The psychologists consulted in my sibling's case concurred that his problems included aggression, resistance to authority, refusal to accept adult rules, and compulsive lying. In 1994 the American Psychiatric Association officially grouped these symptoms together, termed them pathological, and created oppositional defiant disorder (ODD), classifying it as a mental illness (American Psychiatric Association 1994).

59. They had to compile these data from individual state departments of corrections and other sources because there is no national database tracking child offenders sentenced to life without parole (hrw.org/reports/2005/us1005/5.htm). *Frontline's* 8 May 2007 broadcast, "When Kids Get Life," focused on Colorado and the stories of five individuals sentenced to life without parole for crimes committed when

they were under the age of eighteen (www.pbs.org/wgbh/pages/frontline/when kidsgetlife/etc/synopsis.html).

60. Here I have been inspired by Lisa Hajjar's differentiation between political and ideological hegemony in her superb analysis of the Israeli military court system (2005).

61. Ricoeur 1995.

62. See Cicourel [1967] 1995; Emerson 1969; Hirsch 1998, 2006; Philips 1998.

Chapter 2

1. "Paradoxically, the search for a more systematic means of gathering legal evidence led to the use of torture. Torture was used to supplement evidence considered inconclusive such as testimony provided by a woman or by one witness instead of two" (Herzog-Evans 2000:9).

2. Hodgson 2005:15.

3. Einaudi, Colinet, and Pouget 2002:1.

4. Nye 1984:24, 26–27.

5. They were more concerned with the offense than the offender in establishing the punishment (Ancel 1960:2–3). Legislation on recidivist offenders, both adults and juveniles, adopted on 10 August 2007 created minimum sentences for the first time. This law mandates graduated prison sentences for those convicted of a third offense (articles 1 and 2). Article 5 suspends the automatic reduction of penalties for those repeat offenders aged sixteen to eighteen whose offenses include physical or psychological injury, sexual aggression, or a misdemeanor aggravated by one circumstance of assault (Law no. 2007-1198, 10 August 2007).

6. In contrast, in counterrevolutionary periods, such as the first Napoleonic empire, during which internal disorder threatened in the form of increased crime, the rhetoric of the common good was eclipsed by that of public order and private property (Lagrange 2001:127).

7. There was a return, specifically, to the ordinance of 1670. See Herzog-Evans 2000:10. Napoleon Bonaparte's rise to power and his emphasis on political and legal centralization led to the adoption of the *Code civil* in 1804. The process of legal codification that began in 1791 with the *Code pénal* continued with the *Code de procédure civile* in 1807, the *Code de commerce* and *Code d'instruction criminelle* in 1808, and an amended *Code pénal* in 1810. The original 1810 penal code rejected the notion of the individualization of punishments by ruling out mitigating circumstances and dismissed the concept of rehabilitation of the offender by reintroducing horrific punishments from the pre-1789 Old Regime. It reinstated branding, mutilation, and death for some property crimes but inserted them into the new

logic of penalties ranked according to the severity of the offense. The penal code was reformed in 1832 to allow judges to consider extenuating circumstances and to impose a lesser sentence (Ancel 1960:8–9).

8. Herzog-Evans 2000:10.

9. Salas 1992:85–86.

10. Esmein [1913] 1968:437; Salas 1992:86.

11. Herzog-Evans 2000:8.

12. Hodgson 2005:17.

13. Ibid.:17–18.

14. See the interview with Renaud Van Ruymbeke in *Le Monde*, 19 January 2006.

15. Antoine Garapon and Denis Salas argue that the judiciary did not become truly independent until the Fifth Republic in 1958. They point to the 1958 creation of the ENM, which "marked the first break between the judicial and the political"; the 1968 founding of the Syndicat de la Magistrature, which "saw the beginnings of judicial syndicalism" and the emergence of the magistrat as a political actor; and the 1993 reform of the Conseil Supérieur de la Magistrature requiring that it comprise a majority of judges rather than state officials (Garapon and Salas 1999:35–36).

16. Bell 2006:55.

17. Hodgson 2005:19.

18. Herzog-Evans 2000:57.

19. In 1958 amendments to the *Code de procédure pénale* created a clear separation of the investigation from the prosecution and removed the JI from the jurisdiction of the prosecutor's office. Reforms in 1993 and 2000 enhanced the rights of suspects and material witnesses in police custody. Law no. 2000-516 of 15 June 2000 sought to improve due process protections by mandating that pretrial detention orders be reviewed by two distinct magistrats as opposed to a lone JI. This legislation created a new judge—the *juge des libertés et de la détention* (JLD)—and instituted different procedures. The JI now requests a detention order and the JLD rules on this request after an adversarial debate in court.

20. See the interview in *Le Monde*, 19 January 2006.

21. Garapon 1997:149.

22. Ibid.:169–170; Herzog-Evans 2000:20.

23. In cases in which no investigation or prosecution has been initiated, victims may activate proceedings directly. The 15 June 2000 law also strengthened victims' rights. Currently up to one-third of the cases handled by the JI have been opened by the parties civiles rather than the procureur (Grévy 2003, quoted in Hodgson 2005).

24. Hodgson 2005:21.

25. Herzog-Evans 2000:24.

26. Hodgson 2005: 21.

27. Soulez-Larivière 1995.

28. Garapon 1997:159.

29. Laws no. 93-2, 4 January 1993, and no. 93-1013, 24 August 1993, mandated that police notify suspects of the nature of the offense, of their right to see a doctor, and to inform someone of their detention. It also permitted suspects to see a lawyer after twenty hours in police custody.

30. Suspects in France are not compelled to answer or to provide self-incriminating evidence. However, prior to 2000 only those suspects appearing before a JI were informed of their right to silence. The 2000 law required the police, for the first time, to inform suspects of this right as well as the nature of the offense. This was fiercely opposed by police unions and was later repealed (Hodgson 2005:119).

31. See Law no. 2000-516, chapter 1, section 1 (Rules relating to police custody) and chapter 2, section 3 (Rules limiting the conditions or the length of pretrial detention).

32. De Beaumont and de Tocqueville 1833.

33. Law of 22 July 1912.

34. Ibid.:3.

35. See Fishman 2002:34–39; Lefaucheur 1993; Léger 1990; Rufin 1996:80.

36. Law of 22 July 1912:3.

37. The 1912 law continued to criminalize vagrancy and to make frequent use of pretrial detention, often in adult prisons (*maisons d'arrêt*). Vagrancy was not decriminalized in France until 1935.

38. See the excellent history of the 1945 ordinance by Fishman 2002.

39. Jérez 2001:336.

40. Catta 1988:173.

41. Jérez 2001:334–335.

42. As in the adult system there are three jurisdictional levels: minor offenses are tried in chambers by one juvenile judge as in the *tribunal de police*; the formal juvenile court, including a judge and two nonjudicial assessors, hears cases for juveniles thirteen to sixteen years of age accused of crimes and for all those under eighteen accused of serious misdemeanors like the *tribunal correctionnel*; and the *cour d'assises pour mineurs* tries sixteen- to eighteen-year-olds accused of crimes.

43. Touret-de-Coucy 2004.

44. Nicolau 1996:99.

45. Some critics focus on judges' sovereign powers, the lack of judicial rigor, and the arbitrary nature of judgments (Rassat 1990; Soulez-Larivière 1987). Others note

the paternalistic and personalized relations between judges and minors that compromise the legal norm of impartiality (Garapon 1997; Salas 1995). In contrast, defenders of the court, largely influential jurists who began their careers as juvenile
judges or the presidents of minor courts, cite the adversarial debate as the hall-
mark component of the juvenile court (Baudouin 1990). They argue that the adversarial debate permits a focus on the youth's personality and family situation,
thus safeguarding the universalist guarantee of individual rights derived from the
French Revolution (Bruel 1995a). They insist that it remains the best defense of the
accused's rights (Nicolau 1996), the surest guarantee of the recognition of the other
(Paperman 2001), and the best way to continue the pedagogical function of the
law, namely to integrate the wayward child through a forceful confrontation with
legal norms (Touret-de-Coucy 2004).

46. See article 769-7 of the *Code pénal* procedure amended by Law no. 2004-204 of
9 March 2004.

47. Touret-de-Coucy 2004.

48. Nicolau 1996:159–160.

49. *Le Monde*, 15 December 1999 and 23 May 2003.

Chapter 3

1. *Le Monde*, 29 May 1998.

2. Pretrial imprisonment for thirteen- to sixteen-year-olds accused of misdemeanors
was outlawed in 1987. Its reinstatement in 2002 signaled a return to more repressive approaches in dealing with juveniles awaiting trial.

3. *Le Monde*, 12 January 1999.

4. Tribalat 1998:290–291.

5. Debuyst 1995.

6. See Mack 1909; Scott and Steinberg 2003; Talbot 2000.

7. Both the conceptual underpinnings of the rehabilitative model and the image of
the adolescent offender as a wayward child came under attack beginning in the
late 1960s. Following the 1967 Supreme Court ruling on Gault that spelled out long
overdue constitutional safeguards for minors, the system was criticized for its procedural lacunae, therapeutic paternalism, and inattention to the legal rights of
children. These safeguards included the right to notification of charges, assistance
of counsel, adversarial debates, and the privilege against self-incrimination in *In re
Gault*, 387 U.S. 1 1967 (Allen 1964). Periods of increased violent juvenile crime generated intensified concern and demands for change from right-wing advocates of
reform who insisted that the rehabilitative model had failed to reduce crime and
to protect society.

8. See Scott and Steinberg 2003, notes 47 and 48; Bridges and Steen 1998:561–564.

9. There was no consensus on the need to import an American penal model. Many politicians were attracted to more punitive approaches but opposed borrowing extreme measures such as "three strikes and you're out" sentences.

10. Salas 1997.

11. Chazal 1946:35–36.

12. Ibid.:30

13. Ibid.:13.

14. Ibid.:13–14.

15. Heuyer 1914; Lefaucheur 1989; interview with Nadine Lefaucheur, 6 July 2000.

16. This theory was opposed to the Italian Lombrosian school of criminal anthropology based on the born criminal whose physical deformities reflected a primitive ancestral type. Rather, French psychiatry posited a different sort of biological determinism in which the criminal represented one end of an evolutionary continuum whereby the degenerate inherited a predisposition to develop physical or moral deficiencies (tare) rather than fixed criminal traits.

17. Chazal 1946:14.

18. Ibid.:15.

19. Lacassagne 1885, quoted in Lefaucheur 1989: 13 (synthèse)

20. Raux 1890b.

21. Heuyer and Dublineau 1932, 1934.

22. Chazal 1946:16–17.

23. The consensus on the link between family breakdown and juvenile delinquency borrowed from Heuyer, as well as the dominance of Freud, was challenged soon after the publication of Chazal's book. A study undertaken in 1948 in Heuyer's clinic tracking more than a thousand adults led its authors to question the dominant concepts informing child neuropsychiatry and to conclude that there was no direct correlation between the experience of family breakdown during childhood and their subsequent social adaptation (Lefaucheur 1993:138). Beginning in the 1960s, psychoanalysts René Spitz, John Bowlby, and Jenny Roudinesco-Aubry began to question family breakdown as the primary explanation for juvenile delinquency by examining the quality of maternal care and emotional identification in the earliest, pre-Oedipal stages of childhood (Mucchielli 1994:387). This group of psychoanalysts looked to deficiencies in the mother-child relationship as the cause of personality and emotional disorders that eventually led to antisocial behavior and crime. Their analysis shifted from the structural shape of the family and ties of blood to the relationship among its members and the function of parental figures. See also Mucchielli 1994:400.

24. Duché 1983, quoted in Lefaucheur 1993: 139–140.

25. Lebovici 1993:114–115.

26. Another research group affiliated with the University of Paris II, the Laboratoire de Sociologie Juridique, also conducts research on the cultural disorders of postcolonial peoples after migration to France.

27. Nathan 2001.

28. Fassin and Rechtman 2005:349.

29. For a history of how this occurred, see Fassin 1999 and Fassin and Rechtman 2005.

30. Ethnopsychiatrists contrasted the conception of African culture as a group superego that controls the actions of the group with Western notions of individual rights and responsibilities that inform the French penal code. In a 1993 trial of a Bambara mother, Bintou Fofana-Diarra, who allowed her daughter to be excised, Nathan used article 64 of the penal code, which states that "there is neither crime nor offense when the accused . . . has been compelled by a force that he has been unable to resist." He argued that she could not be held criminally responsible: "For the Bambaras, excision is a veritable ritual of initiation that is both systematic and governed by intangible cultural codes. . . . 'Traditional' logic categorically excludes the idea that a child can have a different 'nature' to that of her parents. If one wishes to remain within this logic, there is thus no possibility of individual choice in any area of acts of initiation. After having examined her, we can affirm that Ms. Fofana shows no sign of psychiatric or psychological disorder. The excision of her daughter must be considered an act beyond her own free will" (quoted in Winter 1994:949–950).

31. Nye 1984:98–99.

32. Vieillard-Boyer 1996.

33. MacMaster 1991.

34. Nye 1984:197.

35. Nye 1984:199–200; cf. Savage 2007:47–48.

36. *Petit Parisien*, 2 April 1901, quoted in Nye 1984:208.

37. Savage 2007:47–48.

38. Abu-Lughod 1980; Çelik 1997; Rabinow 1989; Wright 1991.

39. Collovald 2000:40–41.

40. Ibid.:43.

41. Ibid.:47–49. This pattern was evident in reporting on the 2005 riots. Kathy Schneider, professor of international relations at American University, interviewed banlieue residents and the Clichy-sous-Bois victims' families in 2006. These victims indicated that none of the French journalists covering the riots ever contacted them to get their version of the story. The Kojo Namdi Radio Show, National Public Radio, "The French Riots, One Year Later," 23 October 2006.

42. Bui Trong 1993:235–236.

43. "Banlieues: The Big Scare," France Channel 3, 9 November 2005.

44. *Boston Globe*, 5 November 2005.

45. Body-Gendrot 2000.

46. On spatialized poverty, see Beaud 2002; Bordet 1998; Duret and Augustini 1995; Lagrange 2001; Lepoutre 1997. On Wacquant's anti-ghetto position, see 1992, 1997a, 2005a, 2005b.

47. *Libération*, 3 March 1998.

48. *Le Monde*, 1 October 2001.

49. Bauer and Raufer 2005:19.

50. This was informed by a pseudoscientific racist theory, the threshold of tolerance, which became local housing policy and was widely used to impose strict limits on ethnic concentrations in excess of 15 percent in order to preclude the exodus of French families (MacMaster 1991; cf. Silverstein 2004:97).

51. Peyrefitte Commission Report 1977:25.

52. Ibid.:34.

53. Ibid.:103.

54. Ibid.:127.

55. Ibid.:363–364. They cited the testimony of a social worker who reported that one young person had been stopped thirty times in one month by the police.

56. This involved assigning a multidisciplinary team comprised of psychologists, youth counselors, and social workers to evaluate a minor and his family and to implement plans to eliminate risky or dysfunctional behaviors. Social assistance in an open setting means that the judge deems it important to keep the minors in their normal living arrangement whether it be at home, with a relative or foster family, in a boarding school, or an educational facility. When judges remove minors from their home environment and place them in closed residential facilities for a specified period, the minors are required to remain there.

57. See Fishman 2002, who argues that 1945 represents the triumph of a rehabilitative model. See Wyvekens 2004 on the limited role of prosecutors in juvenile justice until the 1990s. See Peyrefitte Commission Report 1977:399.

58. Bailleau 1996: 108.

59. Ibid.:113–114.

60. Meyer [1977] 1983:68.

61. Donzelot [1977] 1997:115.

62. Interview with Dominique Dray, anthropologist at the Protection Judiciaire de la Jeunesse, 26 January 2001.

63. Bonnemaison Commission Report 1982:31.

64. Ibid.:34.

65. Ibid.:48.

66. Body-Gendrot 2000:85–86; Monjardet 1996.

67. Aubusson de Cavarlay 1999; Wyvekens 2004.

68. Bailleau 1996:94–95.

69. Nonetheless, for all children under court supervision, the scholastic level was low and the professional training they did receive was liable to have little value as it prepared them for entry-level positions in retail sales, the building trades, or the service sector (Bailleau 1996:116–123).

70. Mary 2001; Nye 1984.

71. For example, aggravating circumstances included theft in a group as distinct from an organized gang, theft committed in public transportation, or theft accompanied by property destruction of any kind. See Code pénale, article 311-4, under the category of theft (www.legifrance.gouv.fr). Since 1 March 1994, article 311-4 has been amended twice, first by ordinance no. 2000-916 of 19 September 2000 and then by law no. 2004-204 of 9 March 2004.

72. Lazerges and Balduyck Commission Report 1998:194, 174.

73. Ibid.:174.

74. Pujadas and Salam 1995.

75. The law called for court hearings to be held no longer than three months after a misdemeanor offense if an investigation of the facts was not necessary and the court had complete background information on the personality and family of the minor. It permitted judges to issue sanctions immediately if guilt has been established. These sanctions include reminder of the law, warning, return to parents, mediation-reparation, or exemption from sanction.

76. Rufin 1996:38.

77. Ibid.:69.

78. Ibid.:65.

79. Interview with Dominique Dray, 26 January 2001.

80. Broken windows theory posits that the image and upkeep of neighborhoods are important factors in reducing crime and in maintaining community controls.

81. Roché 1996; 2000:390–391.

82. Bonnemain 2000.

83. Villepinte, les actes du colloque 1997:41. For the two variants of the culturalist argument, see Mucchielli 2002:8.

84. Villepinte, les actes du colloque 1997:65–67.

85. Ibid.:30–34.

86. Lazerges and Balduyck Commission Report 1998:9, 11.

87. *Le Monde*, 4 September 1998.

88. Lazerges and Balduyck Commission Report 1998:19.

89. Aubusson de Cavarlay 1998:274; cf. Wacquant 1999:58–59.

90. Lazerges and Balduyck Commission Report 1998:21.

91. Ticktin 2006.

92. On the changing French family, see Théry 1998; Lazerges and Balduyck Commission Report 1998:26–28.

93. There are distinct parallels here to Daniel Patrick Moynihan's denunciation of the "tangle of pathology" in the black family, particularly its matrifocal organization as the central cause for the persistence of poverty among urban African Americans in the United States (Rainwater and Yancey 1967).

94. Lazerges and Balduyck Commission Report 1998:193–194.

95. Fassin 2005; Ticktin 2006.

96. Jean-Marie Bockel, the Socialist mayor of the city of Mulhouse, gained notoriety when he publicly supported Tony Blair's policy of zero tolerance and youth curfews. He proposed that the juvenile court assume control of the child allowance payments (*allocations familiales*) made to the parents of repeat offenders. Under French law, juvenile judges usually control household expenses for families under court supervision for periods of two to three years.

97. On U.S. crime prevention, see Dray 1999:23–43; on the lack of common values, see ibid.:138–140, 210–211.

98. *Le Monde*, 7 January 1999.

99. Bachman 1992:128–152.

100. On the constitution of his sample, see Dubet 1987:44–46. On his rejection of the Chicago School of Sociology, see ibid.:124–142. On his definition of violence, see ibid.:14–15.

101. In contrast to Shaw and McKay's classic 1929 study on delinquency in Chicago in which the authors wrote that crime was a symptom of the disorganization of urban life and the degenerative forces that shattered the culture of immigrant newcomers, the French note that crime is a reflection of the growth of delinquent subcultures that draw on aberrant "immigrant" values, practices, and attitudes. On the polemics fueled by the culture of poverty debate, see Bourgois 2001; on the "underclass debate" sparked by W. J. Wilson's *The Truly Disadvantaged* (1987), see Katz 1989 and Wacquant 1997a.

102. David Lepoutre's well-received book, *Coeur de banlieue*, is emblematic in this regard. His citations include classics from the American sociological canon, such as

Cloward and Ohlin's *Delinquency and Opportunity: A Theory of Delinquent Gangs* (1961); Cohen's *Delinquent Boys* (1955); Gans's *Urban Villagers* (1962); Thrasher's *The Gang* (1937); and Whyte's *Street Corner Society* (1955).

103. Bordet 1999; Duret and Augustini 1995; Lepoutre 1997; see the review in *Le Monde*, 8 October 1998.

104. Duret and Augustini 1995.

105. "Because he is condemned to low paid, temporary jobs, and unable to leave home, the big brother exemplifies an image of rejection for young people" (Carle and Schosteck Commission Report 2002:55).

106. Although Lepoutre argued that middle schoolers abandoned violent street culture and conformed to mainstream social norms as they matured, this fact was lost on many reviewers of the book and on state authorities, given their uses of it.

107. Lepoutre 1997:278–280; cf. Mauger 1995, 1998.

108. Bauer and Raufer 1999; Body-Gendrot, Le Guennec, and Herrou 1998; Bousquet 1998; Bui Trong 1993; Lagrange 2001; Roché 1993, 1996, 2001.

109. The IHESI is the predecessor of the renamed Institut National des Hautes Etudes de Sécurité. The Institut's journal also changed from *Les Cahiers de la Sécurité Intérieure* to *Les Cahiers de la Sécurité* (www.inhes.interieur.gouv.fr/L-INHES-3.html).

110. Lagrange 2001:87.

111. Ibid.:272–274.

112. On distinctive cultural communities, see Roché 2001:204; on the necessity to consider ethnicity and race, see ibid.:205. To prove that disadvantaged teenagers preferred to stay in the projects and avoid contact with other groups, he took a quote out of context from a young informant of Lepoutre. The informant described bourgeois kids in Paris as "little rich assholes" (Lepoutre 1997:114).

113. Roché divided his sample into four distinct categories. Those most closely integrated within the nation by birthright and roots had two parents born in France and constituted the vast majority of interviewees. The next group included those with at least one parent born in France. The final two groups were constituted by teenagers whose parents were both born outside of France. Here the hierarchy of alien Others is significant. The third group consisted of any combination of foreigners, European and non-European alike. The largest number of Others were those whose parents were born in the Maghreb. Roché correlated frequency of criminal activity with what teenagers reported about the size of their families, parental supervision, school experience as measured by amount of time devoted to homework, absences, suspensions and perception of performance, and friends or siblings with police records (2001:199–229). This categorization by parentage and blood parallels the racial ideologies identified in the United States (Smedley 2006).

114. Carle and Schosteck Commission Report 2002:41.

115. Ibid.:46; *Le Monde*, 4 December 2001.

116. Carle and Schosteck Commission Report 2002: 35, 40, 39, 47.

117. Bailleau 1998:296.

Chapter 4

1. For purposes of confidentiality, I changed the names of all the judges at the Paris court, with the exception of those who hold leadership offices within the profession, such as Thierry Baranger; those who are known as public intellectuals and expert practitioners, such as Denis Salas, Hervé Hamon, and Alain Bruel; or those who have published memoirs based on their court experience, such as Elisabeth Catta.

2. See the memoirs by Baulon (2000), Chaillou (1987, 1989), and Rosenczveig (1999) for a few examples.

3. Catta 1988:88.

4. Chaillou 1989:15.

5. In 2001, there were fourteen judges, including the president of the Paris juvenile court. Of the twelve I was able to interview, seven intended to enter juvenile justice, whereas five entered it accidentally or reluctantly. Only one of the remaining five claimed to enjoy the work. As a result of one retirement, one death, and five promotions, six judges assumed positions at the Paris court in 2003 (leaving one courtroom vacant). I interviewed all six of those judges, for a total of eighteen interviews of Parisian Juvenile Judges.

6. Catta 1988:55.

7. A lawyer who was an active member of the Paris Legal Defense Bureau for Minors shared this story with me, and his legal assistant confirmed it.

8. Interview, 27 July 2000.

9. This court hears appeals on specific points of law and may function as a full appellate court if new factual evidence is produced to suggest judicial errors in the original trial. Since 2000 it is also the avenue for the reexamination of cases in which the European Court of Human Rights finds against France.

10. Cf. Chaillou 1989:197.

11. Baudouin 1990:168.

12. Baulon 2000:31.

13. Baudouin 1990:168.

14. Catta 1988:35.

15. In 2001, out of fourteen judges at the Paris court, nine were women, and in the summer of 2003, eleven of thirteen judges were women.

16. Conseil Supérieur de la Magistrature, *Rapport d'activité* 2003, quoted in Bell 2006:54.

17. Bell 2006:53.

18. Interview, Madeleine Sabatini, 15 February 2001.

19. Ecole Nationale de la Magistrature, www.enmjustice.fr.

20. Catta 1988:29.

21. Quoted in Scott 1996:173.

22. For comparative studies of professional women facing the challenges of work in patriarchal institutions, see Enloe 1988; Fisher 2004; Kwolek-Folland 1994.

23. Scott 1996:173.

24. On the differential treatment of working-class and/or minority defendants in the United States, see Cicourel [1967] 1995; on complainants in lower courts, see Merry 1990; Yngvesson 1993.

25. Catta 1988:59.

26. Chaillou 1989:27.

27. Inspection Générale des Services Judiciaires 2004, Fiche 9:4.

28. Rosenczveig 1999:46.

29. Other judges preside over cases involving child custody decisions following divorce, change of name, and legal guardianship.

30. Chaillou 1989:195.

31. Baudouin 1990:58–60.

32. Chaillou 1989:201.

33. Salas 1995:55.

34. Ibid.:56.

35. Ibid.:61.

36. Garapon and Salas 1995:1–11.

37. Ibid.:3.

38. Chaillou 1995:38–39.

39. Salas 1995:60.

40. Allaix 1995:77.

41. Quoted in Allaix 1995:77.

42. Ministere de la Justice, *Etude sur les juges des enfants*, Direction de la Protection Judiciaire de la Jeunesse, Bureau K2, quoted in Allaix 1995:77.

43. Bruel 1995a:70–71.

44. Garapon found the flamboyant ceremonial atmosphere of the formal juvenile court less detrimental to the accused and their families. He suggested that the sym-

bols, rituals, and spatial hierarchies of the formal court trial signify the force of the law and convey more to the accused than the "complicated technical vocabulary and paternalistic speech" of the juvenile judge in chambers.

45. See Chaillou 1987; Garapon 1985, 1997; cf. Donzelot 1977; Meyer [1977] 1983.

46. Garapon 1995:146.

47. Ibid.:152.

48. *Le Monde*, 11 January 1999.

49. *Le Monde*, 7 January 1999.

50. *Le Monde*, 24-25 January 1999.

51. *Le Monde*, 2 June 1998.

52. Chaillou, January 1999 address, "La Délinquance des Minors," page 3, author's files.

53. *L'Humanité*, 29 November 2001.

54. The first way to treat a case referred by the police is to close it, the *classement sans suite*, and the second way is to prosecute the case either by sending it to a juvenile judge or to a juge d'instruction in the juvenile court sector. The third way, instituted by a Ministry of Justice circular of 15 October 1991, highlights both the specialization of the juvenile prosecutor's office and new possibilities to curb delinquency and protect victims. It consists of a rapid response to a first offense that bypasses court hearings through measures such as mediation and reparation presided over by prosecutorial representatives, not judges.

55. Theft constituted the largest category of offenses at the Paris court, and in the hearings I attended the coveted object in eight cases out of ten was a cell phone.

56. *Le Monde*, 22 January 1999.

57. *Libération*, 23–24 January 1999.

58. Rosenczveig 1999:10–11.

59. Rosenczveig described the new role for the prosecutor's office: "We can say that the new prosecutor has arrived. He works in real time, that is to say that he is informed by the police and the gendarmerie, by telephone, as soon as minors are arrested. And the reaction is immediate. Registering of the case and first investigation. No more question of treating cases that have gone astray or gone cold. . . . He will be able to have him [the youth] referred for prosecution immediately after police custody, if he considers that the facts and the personality of the minor are already known and justify it. Conversely, if the facts are less serious, he will contact the [juvenile] judge in a more standard fashion. He will have the possibility of summoning first-time delinquents to the court with their parents. He will give them a summons to return in forty-five days. That is the case for a little more than 60% of the young people on this track" (1999:400–401).

60. *Contrôle judiciaire* before the legal reform of 2002 is the pretrial probationary supervision outlined in articles 137–143 of the *code de procédure pénale* and article 8 of the 1945 ordinance. During the investigation of an offense for which the sentence would be a prison term, this measure allows the judge to release the minor subject to a number of conditions. These include remaining within specified geographical boundaries; making periodic court appearances; obligatory attendance at school, training programs, work, or treatment regimens; interdiction to frequent certain persons or engage in certain activities; proof of discharging financial obligations. If the minor does not honor the conditions of his probation, it can be revoked and the minor can be incarcerated (Jérez 2001:475–479).

61. It only ended pretrial detention for those accused of petty offenses such as simple theft and possession of stolen property.

62. Rosenczveig 1999:128–129.

63. Cour des Comptes 2003:110.

64. Association Française des Magistrats de la Jeunesse et de la Famille 2002.

65. Ibid.:5.

66. As we saw in the preceding chapter, center-right legislators voted procedures for issuing expedited summonses and hearings in 1995 and 1996. Judge Bondy referred to those reforms as well as certain statutes of Law no. 2002-1138, 9 September 2002, that began to be applied by the Paris juvenile prosecutor's office on a limited scale in 2003. This reform of articles 5, 12, and 14 of the 1945 ordinance related to the cases to be tried on an accelerated schedule in the formal juvenile court rather than in chambers. It applied to offenses carrying a sentence of three years if caught in the act or equal to or greater than five years in other cases where investigations on the facts or on the personality of the accused were unnecessary. The time limits for the trial and judgment were extremely short given the constraints under which judges operated: not less than 10 days and not more than one month. The judge and many of her colleagues also mentioned the "closed educational centers" established under article 33 of this law where minors who had violated the conditions of probation or a conditional prison sentence were to be placed "for measures of surveillance and control to allow a reinforced educational and pedagogical follow-up adapted to their personality." Violating the terms of placement would lead to pretrial detention or incarceration in prison. The problem was that despite ambitious plans to build new centers or convert existing centers, few such centers existed and those that did were tainted by scandal. Judges also referred to new public order violations and stiffer penalties created in Law no. 2003-239, 18 March 2003, on internal security.

67. Commentators depicted the JLD created in Law no. 2000-516 of 15 June 2000 as a revolution in penal proceedings. It transferred to this new judge powers previously exer-

cised by JIs and juvenile judges. These included the prerogative to rule on pretrial detention, on release, on extending police custody, on visits during detention, and on procedures related to the stay of irregular foreigners in France (Jérez 2001:467–468).

68. In France as elsewhere in western Europe, the educational system is centralized and run by a national Educational Ministry. The secondary system consists of four years in the equivalent of middle school termed the first cycle and three years in high school, the long cycle, culminating in a competitive national exam required for university study. At the completion of the first cycle in middle school at the ages of fourteen or fifteen, students are ranked, sorted, and definitively tracked into vocational or academic tracks, a decision that largely determines their career choices. The most marginal of the vocational programs offer no competitive skills, lead to dead-end certificates, and provide little prospect for employment.

69. Although education is compulsory until age sixteen in France, many of the "problem" youth at court had been expelled repeatedly from one or more schools and stopped attending and/or could not find school principals willing to enroll them.

70. All judges were generally positive about the therapeutic resources available for young children under ten years of age but readily admitted the myriad problems posed by a scarcity of resources for older children as well as the developmental obstacles posed by young teenagers.

71. Judge Binet referred to the new rules governing probation under the Law no. 2002-1138 of 9 September 2002. In fact, article 8 of the 1945 ordinance was modified to include articles 10-2 and 11 explaining that thirteen- to sixteen-year-olds could be placed on probationary supervision but only if the prison sentence for the offense of which they were accused was equal to or more than five years and when the minor had already been the object of one or several rehabilitative measures or been convicted of a newly created "rehabilitative sentence" for ten- to thirteen-year-olds (article 17). Judge Binet may also have been referring to the fact that two other judges in addition to the juvenile judge were empowered to impose probationary supervision—the JI and the JLD—after an adversarial debate in chambers with a prosecutor, defense attorney, and the accused.

72. Compare the accounts in Bowen 2007.

73. The number of minors supervised by the PJJ went from 11,300 in 1993 to 19,160 in 1996 (Lazerges and Balduyck Commission Report 1998:179) and orders for outpatient and residential services increased by 83 percent and 94 percent, respectively, between 1994 and 1996 (ibid. 1998:180).

74. Interview, 26 January 2001.

75. Lazerges and Balduyck Commission Report 1998:183.

76. Carle and Schosteck Commission Report 2002:105.

77. Salas 1997: 64–66.

78. Salas 2005.

Chapter 5

1. Lazerges and Balduyck Commission Report 1998:145.

2. The policy of treatment in real time received the official imprimatur of the Socialist minister of Justice, Elisabeth Guigou, who recommended it in a 15 July 1998 circular to all juvenile courts.

3. Prosecutors also received alerts from municipal and school social workers regarding cases in which minors were endangered by maltreatment, abandonment, or homelessness. I focus here only on penal cases, but in later chapters I will examine civil cases as well as those of irregular, unaccompanied migrants.

4. The cases of minors sixteen to eighteen years old who commit crimes are prepared by a juge d'instruction and tried in the juvenile Assizes Court.

5. The *Officier de police judiciaire* is a police officer who conducts a criminal investigation.

6. In 2001, ten of the éducateurs at the SEAT attached to the court were women, including the director, and three were men. In 2003, of the thirteen éducateurs, eight were women and four were men. There were three new arrivals, including a female director and two men, one of Maghrebi ancestry and the other of West African ancestry.

7. See Ferguson 2001:77–96.

8. Shore 1996:55.

9. See Body-Gendrot 2000:96.

10. Fanon [1952] 1967:47.

11. Interview, Nicole Van Loyen, 6 June 2003.

12. See Morford 1997.

13. Interview, Dominique Cazier, 5 April 2001.

14. Ibid.

15. In addition to published scholarship on éducateurs, this section is based on interviews with Dominique Dray, Madeleine Chami, Marie-Colette Lalire, and Dominique Cazier at the Protection Judiciaire de la Jeunesse; Nicole Van Loyen, a caseworker at the public service provider Centre de l'Assistance Educative in eastern Paris; Delphine Bergère, head of the Paris SEAT in Paris and éducateurs on staff from 2000 to 2003; and primary sources such as the comprehensive report on the PJJ published in July 2003 by state inspectors at the Cour des Comptes.

16. Cour des Comptes 2003:39–40. In Paris, thirteen éducateurs carried an average of ten cases at any one time but this figure does not reflect the disturbing reality that fully half of the prosecutions of minors in 2003 involved unaccompanied minors.

Of the 634 minors prosecuted, only 30 had open files and social assistance measures ordered for them.

17. Ibid.:65–66.

18. Ibid.:65.

19. The creation of closed detention centers for repeat offenders in 2002 required staff who were not trained to deal with such demanding populations and who were unwilling to accept live-in positions in these residential facilities.

20. Interview, Dominique Cazier, 5 April 2001.

21. Inspection préliminaire. SEAT de Paris, 16 January 2003; Inspection, Rapport final. SEAT de Paris, 14 May 2003.

22. In 2003, the juvenile section of the public prosecutor's office was headed by Yvon Tallec, who had held that position since 1992. A team of seven prosecutors served under him.

23. See the accounts in *l'Humanité*, 27 May 2000, and *Le Monde*, 21 May 2001. Although prison officials had allowed journalists from French TV channel Canal+ and *Paris Match* magazine to take photographs and to film inside the center, I waited for months until my visit was approved in April 2001. Even then I was expressly forbidden from bringing a recording device into the facility.

24. Floch 2000.

25. Wacquant 2004:124. For powerful accounts of the global exportation of the U.S. prison complex to the developing world, backed by private security companies and supported by drug, anti-gang, and juvenile justice legislation, see Nagel and Asumah 2007 and Venkatesh and Kassimir 2007.

26. *L'Express*, 25 March 1999, posted on http://demlib.com/sec/edi/pris/art/CJD.htm, accessed 1 July 2001. Three physicians, two educators, and a sentencing magistrate (*juge d'application des peines*) prepared the report, titled "A Juvenile Quarter at the Youth Detention Center: An Appropriate Response to Violence at the Center?"

27. See Vasseur 2000 on conditions at the Santé Prison. See also Cabanel 2000; Canivet 2000; Floch 2000.

28. Interview, Maude Dayet, 18 April 2001.

29. Sixty percent of the cases involved misdemeanors and the remaining 40 percent were classified as crimes.

30. *Le Monde*, 21 May 2001.

31. Interview, Maude Dayet, 18 April 2001.

32. Leder 2007.

33. Ibid.:57.

34. Ibid.:58.

35. See Rhodes 2005:389 and Rose 1999.

36. These issues were discussed at the 25 January 2001 meeting of the PJJ's Incarceration Commission attended by prison administrators, the SEAT director, caseworkers, school guidance counselors, psychologists, and Judge de Maximy from the Paris court. The problem of reenrolling minors in school who have been suspended, expelled, or served time in prison was also dealt with in an interview with social worker Françoise Cattanéo, 12 April 2001.

37. *Comparution immédiate* is a procedure for immediate trials and judgments following arrest and police custody that is reserved for adults. It applies only if the penalty is a prison term of at least two years and not more than seven years. Defendants can ask for a delay to prepare their defense and have access to counsel but are detained pending trial. If convicted at the hearing, they go directly to prison.

38. *Libération*, 15 September 2000.

39. Terra 2003:9; Floch 2000:224.

Chapter 6

1. Bourdieu 1986.

2. See Dirks 2002:47–65.

3. See Jobard and Zimolag 2005 and the editorial published by Jobard in *Le Monde*, 31 October 2006.

4. Ibid.

5. On the prosecutors' strategies, see Jobard and Zimolag 2005, and on new policing tactics read Mucchielli 2004.

6. See Selmouni *v.* France, 28 July 1999, quoted in Herzog-Evans 2000:42; Tomasi *v.* France, 27 August 1992.

7. Hodgson 2005:37.

8. Law no. 2000-516 of 15 June 2000 mandated notification of the right to be informed of the nature of the offense with which one was charged, to remain silent, to have immediate access to legal counsel (not available until the twentieth hour of a twenty-four-hour detention period), to obtain a medical examination (if requested), to be allowed required periods of rest (if not sleep) during detention.

9. Hodgson 2005:37.

10. Lazerges 2001:3.

11. Failure to conform to the new procedures by notifying the prosecutor's office or by contacting defense attorneys at the outset of a new detention could result in dismissal of the case by the court. Police and gendarmes were sharply critical of their obligation to inform the accused of the right to remain silent, equating it with a loss of their authority and a disruption of the basic purpose of custody which, in their view, was to obtain a confession. One judicial police officer's commentary was

telling: "After reading [them] their rights, minors no longer feel like delinquents . . . they are in a position of power with regard to the police (quoted in Dray 2002:11).

12. Dray 2002:21. The major cause of hostility to the new legislation centered on the requirement to videotape and seal in the file all depositions given by minors during police custody. This obligation was viewed by police and gendarme unions as an indictment of their professionalism and a symbol of unwanted legislative distrust (ibid.:25).

13. The book's title was *Vos papiers! Que faire face à la police?* (*Your Papers: What Do You Do When Facing the Police?*) by Claude Schouler (2001).

14. *Le Monde*, 9 July 2002.

15. Chouk, Gillet, Spire, and Terray 2002:13. The commission included a judge, Aïda Chouk, then president of the Syndicat de la Magistrature; Antoine Spire, an attorney; Laurence Gillet, a journalist; and a university professor, Emmanuel Terray.

16. *Libération*, 21 June 2006.

17. If convicted of this charge, the maximum adult sentence is six months in prison and a 7,500-euro fine. Incitement to riot carries a 7,500-euro fine. The excuse of minority would cut the penalty in half.

18. Duret and Augustini 1995; Lepoutre 1997.

19. See Carle and Schosteck Commission Report 2002:55.

20. See Le Sueur 2006:xiii–xxv; French journalist and supporter of Algerian independence Henri Alleg's account of his arrest and torture by French paratroopers ([1958] 2006); and Louisette Ighilahriz's memoir (2001). See also Paul Aussaresses's unabashed defense of torture and the technique of "disappearing" prisoners that he and Bigeard perfected (Aussaresses 2001).

21. I observed this exact scenario repeated in three other cases. One of those cases produced an unusual acquittal, this time in the Nineteenth District East courtroom of Judge Chaland. A seventeen-year-old Malian youth with no police record had initially benefited from a diversion measure, and his case was referred to a prosecutorial delegate rather than a juvenile judge. The driver of a motor scooter had been charged with excessive speed and refusal to stop. The delegate was outraged that the young man "refused to accept the facts and insisted on his innocence." The delegate sent the young man back to court. The facts were eerily reminiscent of a 1990 incident involving a motorcycle that set off deadly riots in the Lyon suburbs. In the Lyon case, the police had deliberately positioned their unlit van in the middle of the road, obstructing the path of the scooter and making a collision inevitable. In Lyon, the passenger, Thomas Claudio, who fell from the bike, died from his injuries. In Paris, the passenger on the cycle had his leg broken in several places and a passerby was hurt. Although Judge Chaland admonished the defendant to respect and obey

the authorities, she acquitted the accused. Privately she wondered why the case ever ended up in court.

22. Mucchielli 2004:109.

23. This infraction is aggravated when it is committed against a person who belongs to or is believed to belong to an ethnic group, a nation, a race, or a specific religion. It is considered an aggravating circumstance when it is accompanied or followed by words, texts, images, objects, or actions of any nature that impugn the honor or the consideration of the victim or a group of people because of their membership in an ethnic group, nation, race, or religion.

24. From 2003 to 2004, hate crimes rose 88 percent and targeted both Jews and Muslims. A report released on 21 March 2005, by the National Consultative Commission for Human Rights revealed that these crimes were seen as less directly connected to events in the Middle East. Although anti-Semitism represented 62 percent of the incidents recorded, other forms of racism and xenophobia increased by two-and-one-half times, surpassing the highest levels measured in 1995, and were directed largely at the Maghrebi or Muslim population (*Le Monde*, 21 March 2005).

25. Lycée refers to the last three years of the secondary education cycle in France.

26. Appadurai 1996:58–59.

27. Unni Wikan, lecture delivered in the Department of Social Anthropology, Harvard University, October 2005.

28. Scheper-Hughes and Sargeant 1998:8.

29. Coutant 2005:98–128.

30. Bessin 2004.

31. Xuereb 1982, quoted in Serre 2001.

32. Serre 2001:72.

33. Under article 434-3 of the penal code, individuals must report child abuse. It is a misdemeanor not to report knowledge of abuse inflicted on a minor under fifteen or on a person vulnerable by virtue of age, illness, infirmity, physical or mental deficiency, or pregnancy and is punishable by three years in prison and a 300,000-euro fine. This excludes those covered by client privilege. Nonetheless, different statutes of the French penal code suggest contradictory mandates—on the one hand, that social workers may maintain professional silence or break the code of silence and speak to authorities when abuse is suspected (article 226-13).

34. Bessin 2004:382–383; Serre 2001:73.

35. Naves and Cathala 2000.

36. Huyette 1999:146–147.

37. The TAT, or Thematic Apperception Test, is a personality test consisting of standardized pictures that reflect everyday characters in a variety of moods and situa-

tions. For each picture the research subject is asked to make up a story with a definite plot and outcome and to explain the feelings of each character in the story.

38. Maximy, Baranger, Maximy 2000:38.

39. Ibid.:29.

40. Devine 1996.

41. See John Bowen's (2007) thorough and trenchant analysis of the period leading up to the legislation banning religious symbols in French public schools.

42. Bowen 2007; Scott 2007.

43. The judges' negative view of the Islamic headscarf is widely shared. For example, France's highest administrative court, the conseil d'état, upheld a decision to deny citizenship to a Moroccan mother of four French-born children. At issue was the woman's radical practice of Islam—wearing a facial veil—and the incompatibility of this practice "with basic values of the French community" (Decision du 27 June 2008, no. 286798, Mme M.).

44. See Rhodes 2004.

45. Shweder, Minow, and Markus 2002:2–3.

46. Dray 1998.

47. Dubois 2004a, 2004b.

48. There are strong parallels between this case and Korbin's study of abusive mothers and their treatment by social professionals in the United States. Korbin documented the willingness of caseworkers in social welfare agencies to retain children in or return them to homes where maternal abuse had occurred, as well as the collective denial and minimization of abuse by those in the wider family network. These actions had the effect of reinforcing the mother's sense that the harm was not serious, allowing her to maintain a self-concept as a basically good mother and/or to see herself as misjudged by the experts (1998:261–263).

Chapter 7

1. Prosecutors and judges tended to try multiple cases of the same offender during one court session. Although they explained this as a pragmatic, time-saving device, it had the effect of magnifying the impression of the offender's incorrigibility and distance from mainstream society.

2. Inspection Générale des Services Judiciaires 2004, fiche 5:10–15.

3. Hajjar 2005:81.

4. At the time of my research, there were fifty-nine assessors at the Paris court who were assigned in groups of four to the same judge, and they participated on average in one juvenile court session every two months. They received training that included a theoretical introduction to the law and judicial procedure, were interviewed by the

juvenile court president, and had to demonstrate an interest in the welfare of children. By virtue of their professions in education, civil service, or business, they were all members of the mainstream middle or upper-middle classes.

5. I note a similar discussion concerning veiled women during the June 2005 deliberations of the Twentieth Chamber of the Correctional Appeals Court in Paris, which Elisabeth Catta kindly arranged for me to attend and which the president of the court, Evelyne Verleene-Thomas, graciously permitted me to observe. The court president insisted that it was not the religious sign per se that made her uncomfortable: "Some French lawyers wear small crosses in court, but [it is] rather the fact that young girls who wear the veil in school don't participate in other school activities such as gym." Her male colleague insisted that he didn't like religious symbols of any kind in [institutional] public spaces and, when faced with an attorney wearing a kippa, refused to allow it. He felt "assaulted by such signs." Another female judge noted the discomforting reality in her neighborhood where "one saw more [Muslim] women dressed in black from head to toe, even wearing gloves." See Bowen's discussion of the Islamic veil as synonymous with extremism, sexism, and violence against women (2007:156–181).

6. The average length of trials in Paris was from three to eight hours, depending on the courtroom. The average number of cases scheduled was twelve to fifteen, whereas the average number of cases tried was ten to twelve per court session (Inspection Générale des Services Judiciaires 2004, fiche 3, p. 8). The courtrooms with the heaviest penal caseload were those representing the Twentieth North, the Nineteenth North and East, the Eleventh, and the Thirteenth districts (Inspection Générale des Services Judiciaires 2004, fiche 3:2).

7. Garapon 1985:16.

8. I use the ethnographic present in the description of the courtroom to highlight the power and immediacy of criminal proceedings for defendants.

9. Cf. Emerson 1969:194.

10. Garapon 1985:88.

11. Emerson 1969.

12. On judges, see Garapon 1997; Catta 1988. For French attorneys' perspective, see Benec'h-Le Roux 2004.

13. Castel 2003.

14. Garapon 1997:152–153; Emerson 1969:175–186.

15. In the Law of 23 December 1980 (and article 222-23 of the penal code), the definition of rape was broadened to include any act of sexual penetration committed using violence, constraint, threat, or surprise. Under article 222-24, the act can be aggravated by any combination of seven circumstances when, as in this case, the victim is under fifteen years of age. The maximum penalty for an offender, if con-

victed of aggravated rape in an adult court, is twenty years in prison with the possibility of additional sanctions, such as the interdiction to have regular contact with minors, to exercise a particular profession, to carry a weapon, to have one's civil rights suspended, or to be ineligible for public office.

16. Théry 1998:34–38.

17. In 1970 the Code civil was modified to replace the notion of paternal power with parental authority in the interests of the child; cf. Murard 2000.

18. Sayad 1991.

19. Ibid.; cf. Beaud 1994; Masclet 2002.

20. In some instances in which children have been placed in state facilities or placed with foster families outside of Paris and were monitored by different social workers, there were a number of reports in the file.

21. Catta 1988:281.

22. The cases involved two separate offenses: the theft of proceeds from the restaurant managed by Yukiko's father and the theft of personal items from her mother's apartment. Yukiko's mother filed a complaint requesting an award of compensatory damages from her daughter as a result of a fire that partially destroyed the apartment building the same evening of the burglary. She described herself as unemployed, homeless, alone, alcoholic, suicidal, and indigent. She claimed her only possession was a Hermès handbag.

23. The depictions of Mathieu and Aimé were also illustrative. Here the report submitted for Mathieu described him as "high strung, resentful, and easily influenced" on the one hand but "brave and respectful" on the other. There were no details about Mathieu's family history and, since his parents had not come to court, his defense attorney objected strongly, demanding a second evaluation of his personality. During her direct questioning of Mathieu, the prosecutor repeatedly called him "a delinquent" and contrasted his twenty-three offenses for theft, burglary, and extortion to his privileged social background. Mathieu was expelled from school at fifteen for fighting, arrested for aggravated theft, put on probation and sentenced to a one-month prison sentence for violating the terms of his probation. Just as she had done with Yukiko, the judge drew on the psychiatric evaluation to emphasize his immaturity, poor judgment, neglect at home, and to reposition him as a teenager who had temporarily lost his way:

JUDGE: [*reading from the report*] He has normal intelligence, was not mature, was destabilized by his home life, had insignificant psychological pathologies.

As in the cases above, the social worker report on Aimé was equivocal and superficial. Little information on Aimé's family history was given except to emphasize the vulnerability of his mother as a single working woman lacking the emotional resources to cope with her "problem" son, and the absence of a father as well as his "affection and authority." The report identified the lack of paternal authority as the source of Aimé's "rebellious behavior" and added, "He is cold, detached from reality, and has a hardened character." It advised sending him "back to [his father] in Haiti" despite the fact that he had never lived there or with his father. The judge quoted a more recent psychiatric evaluation of Aimé, which viewed him as on the wrong path but redeemable:

JUDGE: [*reading the psychiatric evaluation*] He is mired in delinquency, needs to be monitored by the court, has no relationship with his father, his mother wanted to send him back to Haiti, he is in school, in BEP electronics, is sad, depressed and needs help.

The depiction of Aimé as a delinquent provoked no challenges by the defense attorney but provided grist for the prosecutor's plea. The fact that he had run away and was absent at the trial confirmed his deviance. It is instructive to note that, in contrast to Mathieu, Aimé had a much shorter police record with half the number of offenses, despite his conviction for prison, and he was enrolled in school.

24. On the collaboration between judges and prosecutors in the juvenile court, see Baudouin 1990. Formally article 20-9 of the 2 February 1945 ordinance, it was introduced by the Law of 9 September 2002 and modified by the Law of 9 March 2004.

25. Garapon 1985:131.

26. Juvenile defense bureaus were created in Bordeaux, Clermont-Ferrand, Evry, Lille, Lyon, Marseille, Paris, Rochefort, Rouen, Strasbourg, and Versailles. See the reform of family law enacted on 8 January 1993.

27. See Benec'h-Le Roux 2004.

28. I also observed parts of the 2001 Paris criminal trial of the accused serial killer Guy Georges.

29. I attended court deliberations on two occasions, in 2001 and 2003, when that judge presided.

30. With a population of 182,000 inhabitants, the twentieth arrondissement is characterized by the large number of minors accused of physical assaults, aggravated thefts, and drug offenses. The southern quadrant of the district is quieter than the northern section. Between 2001 and 2003, there were 657 new penal cases versus 475 civil cases in the Twentieth; minor arrests have also increased since 2001.

31. Their infraction was considered a correctional offense because it involved theft aggravated by two circumstances: by violence and in a group of two or more persons. The maximum penalty for an adult convicted of the charges is five years in prison and a 75,000-euro fine, assuming the injuries did not incur a victim's physical incapacity of more than eight days.

32. See the account of the race-based categories established by job recruiters in the Paris office of the employment firm of Adecco (*Washington Post*, 15 January 2006).

33. See Tribalat (1998:282–285), who shows that teenage boys of non-European, particularly Maghrebi ancestry, face significant obstacles finding a first full-time job. This is particularly true for those without degrees but also applies to those who hold vocational diplomas below the level of the baccalaureat degree, such as the CAP or BEP. These young men spend more time looking for work and are unemployed for longer periods than their French and European immigrant (Spanish and Portuguese) counterparts. She argues that the stagnant labor market, stiff competition for scarce jobs, and anti-immigrant racism among French employers have combined to produce a "mimetic anti-French racism" that explodes in violent confrontations in the subway, at school, and on the street (ibid.:291). For the structural transformation of the banlieue and its effects on working class youth see Bonelli 2007; Ossman and Terrio 2006; Silverstein 2004).

34. Beriss 2004:20–21, 61.

35. Inspection Générale des Services Judiciaires 2004, fiche 25, p. 5.

36. I interviewed Yvon Tallec on 18 June 2003 and 15 June 2005.

37. The report by the Committee for Rights, Justice, and Freedom was commissioned to investigate policing in two Parisian suburbs and in the twentieth arrondissement in Paris by the Ligue des Droits de l'Homme (League of the Rights of Man), the Syndicat des Avocats (Union of French Lawyers) and Syndicat de la Magistrature (Union of Magistrates) and was made public in 2002 (Chouk, Gillet, Spire, and Terray 2002).

38. Hartigan 2005.

39. Dray 1998:105–106.

Chapter 8

1. *Le Monde*, 16 November 2006.

2. As a result of a bilateral agreement between France and Romania in 2002 and establishment of a working group that included police and magistrats from both countries, participants later discovered that many children had correctly identified their region of origin and villages in northeastern Romania.

3. *Agence France Presse*, 15 May 2001.

4. Interview, Madame Bertrand, Head of the Brigade de la Protection des Mineurs, 12 March 2004. By law, minors selling sex were considered endangered, entitled to social assistance, and referred to a unit of the Brigade de la Protection des Mineurs specializing in sexual violence or physical abuse outside the family.

5. Carle and Schosteck Commission Report 2002:40.

6. Inspection Générale des Services Judiciaires 2004, fiche 21:9.

7. Ibid., fiche 21:11.

8. As a result of the law of 9 September 2002, minors aged thirteen to sixteen who violate the terms of probation pending trial may be sent to prison.

9. Inspection Générale des Services Judiciaires 2004, fiche 21:8.

10. James 2007.

11. Panter-Brick 2002; Pupavac 2001.

12. Rosen 2007.

13. Ariès 1962; Bourgois 1995; Goldstein 1998; Mai 2007; Rosen 2005.

14. Cole and Durham 2007:14–15.

15. Cole and Durham 2007; Doek 2002; Scheper-Hughes and Sargent 1998; Stephens 1995.

16. Vagrancy was not decriminalized until passage of a 1935 law (Fishman 2002:38–39).

17. O'Brien 1982:114.

18. Meyer [1977] 1983:19.

19. Aubin 1996.

20. Stephens 1995:12–13.

21. Mai 2007:100.

22. Inspection Générale des Affaires Sociales 2005:14.

23. Fassin 2005:382.

24. Association Nationale d'Assistance aux Frontières pour les Etrangers 2003:37–38; Fassin 2005:376.

25. Anafe 2003:28.

26. Ticktin 2006.

27. The state's detention of unaccompanied children in fenced zones has been denounced by human rights activists and NGOs and has generated fierce debates on the right to defend borders versus the obligation to protect endangered children.

28. Only the OFPRA and the Commission of Refugee Recourse are competent to assign refugee status and accord protective assistance to undocumented migrants. But in order to apply the asylum seeker must be on French soil and obtain an application and temporary resident card from a local prefecture office. In 2001, 94 percent of the unaccompanied minors who sought asylum and were held in detention zones were admitted to the country; in 2002, 79 percent were admitted (Anafe 2003:41–44). Admittance was only the first step toward legalization and asylum. In the second and crucial stage of the process, only a third of the minor applicants were recognized as refugees and granted asylum.

29. This test was problematic for a number of reasons. There was no reference sample for youth of foreign ancestry or for the French population. It had a margin of error estimated to be between eighteen months and two years because of different rates of maturation as well as the nutritional deficiencies that young minors experienced in situations of war and economic deprivation. After conducting interviews at courts throughout the nation, inspectors concluded that only those departments with the highest numbers of unaccompanied minors used the test to determine age, predicating assistance and protection on minority status. Furthermore, this "scientific" measure of age quickly became a substitute for the more comprehensive and time-intensive social inquiries customarily used to establish family background, personality development, and current circumstances (Inspection Générale des Affaires Sociales 2005:23–25).

30. Appadurai 1996.

31. To gain some sense of a complicated phenomenon, I include portions of judicial proceedings, excerpts from judges' meetings, formal interviews, and informal conversations with court personnel, and internal documents that the president of the juvenile court permitted me to study from the Justice Ministry's Protection Judiciaire de la Jeunesse and the Justice Ministry 2003 inspection of the Paris juvenile court, as well as media coverage of undocumented migrants.

32. Council of Europe, European Committee for the Prevention of Torture and Inhuman or Degrading Treatment or Punishment, 1991, 1996, 2003, 2006.

33. Dalrymple 2002.

34. Inspection Générale des Services Judiciaires 2004, fiche 21:5.

35. Landrieu 2003:6–7.

36. See Dalrymple's diatribe on "The Barbarians at the Gates of Paris" (2002).

37. See the reports in *Agence France Presse*, 4 May 2001, 15 May 2001, 25 August 2001, 4 October 2002; *Agence France Presse*, 29 August 2002; *Le Figaro*, 28 August 2001, 2 August 2002, 4 October 2002; *Libération*, 23 August 2001, 1 September 2001; *Le Monde*, 15 November 2001, 16 November 2001, 30 June 2002, 31 July 2002, 11 August 2002, 30 August 2002.

38. *Agence France Presse*, 4 May 2001.

39. *Libération*, 1 September 2001.

40. *Agence France Presse Magazine*, 30 August 2002.

41. *Le Monde*, 6 September 2002.

42. Plantet 2003:2.

43. *Agence France Presse*, 25 August 2001.

44. Donzelot [1977] 1997:81. See *Agence France Presse*, 15 May 2001; *Romanian Business Journal*, 30 April 2001; *Rompres News Agency*, 5 October 2002.

45. Barrow 2003.

46. Prime Minister Jospin's speech, entitled "Romania and France in an Enlarged Europe," was made during a 23–24 July 2001 trip to Romania.

47. Barrow 2003:10.

48. *Le Monde*, 15 November 2001, 16 November 2001. Until 2002 when sexual majority was set at eighteen years of age, it was not possible to prosecute the adult clients of underage male prostitutes. The head of the Brigade de la Protection des Mineurs affirmed that prostitution among Romanian boys "had taken the Paris police and court by surprise." In interviews, boys like Marius denied being homosexual despite engaging in sexual acts for money. They distinguished between anal penetration, which they refused, and fellatio, which they allowed. In their view the former was a marker of homosexuality in contrast to oral sex, particularly when performed *on* them but not *by* them.

49. Following the collapse of socialist economies in eastern Europe, Romanian families developed new migration strategies, seeing themselves as temporary rather than permanent migrants in France (Diminescu 2003). Their children often resisted this project and developed alternate subjectivities and future plans.

50. The Paris ASE was particularly affected by the numbers of unaccompanied foreign minors in France receiving 53 percent of the national total. Of the five departments in the Paris region, the agency in the city proper had 34 percent of the total number of unaccompanied minors in 1999, 30 percent in 2000, and 27 percent in 2001 (Etiemble 2002:3–5).

51. Cf. Landrieu 2003:10.

52. Diminescu 2003.

53. Interviews with caseworker Manuela Neagu at the NGO Parada, 11 December 2003, and Police Chief Bertrand at the Brigade de la Protection des Mineurs headquarters, 12 March 2004; see also *News Press*, 17 June 2002.

54. *Agence France Presse Magazine*, 30 August 2002.

55. *Le Figaro*, 2 August 2002.

56. *Le Monde*, 10 January 2003.

57. *Le Monde* 27 May 2002.

58. *Le Monde*, 6 June 2002.

59. Report of the Défense des Enfants International–France 2003.

60. Interview, 12 March 2004. These were primarily Bulgarian, Moldavian, Latvian, and Romanian women over the age of eighteen and Romanian minor girls between the ages of sixteen and eighteen.

61. Given the limited afternoon hours of Court L, 2:00 to 6:00 P.M., and the legal mandate that suspects see a judge within twenty-four hours of arrest, the hearings scheduled on weekends and holidays were heard by other judges during their monthly rotations on call.

62. *New York Times*, 5 October 2003.

63. This NGO Parada changed its name to Hors La Rue, or Off the Street.

64. Interview, 3 December 2003.

65. Hepatitis B is a chronic viral infection that causes inflammation of the liver and can result in carcinoma. It can be managed medically but is not curable.

66. Fassin 2005; Ticktin 2006.

67. *Antenne 2 Broadcast*, 22 September 2003.

Chapter 9

1. *Le Monde*, 8 December 1999.

2. Fassin 2005; Ticktin 2006. This shift also occurred in Great Britain.

3. Wacquant 2004:124.

4. In the last five years there has been a reassertion of executive power over judicial authority and repeated attacks by ministers of Interior on magistrats (*Le Monde*, 18 May 2007).

5. Wacquant 2004:120–121.

6. Ibid.:129.

7. Mucchielli 2004.

8. Duprez and Kokoreff 2000.

9. Rosen 2006.

10. She began her career in business management before turning to the law and training as a judge at the Ecole Nationale de la Magistrature. She worked briefly as a deputy prosecutor at the Evry court before accepting a position in civil law (*Le Monde*, 18 May 2007).

11. See question 16 at www.sitoyen.fr/mon-vote-a-moi/mon-vote-a-moi.php. I would like to thank my 2007 research assistant, Chloe Asselin, for bringing this Web site to my attention.

12. Quoted in the *New York Times*, 21 October 2006.

13. Ryan and Ziedenberg 2007:14; Bishop, Frazier, Lanza-Kaduce, and White 1999; Fagan 2006.

14. Quoted in Ryan and Ziedenberg 2007:9.

15. See the editorial in the *New York Times* bearing this title on 11 May 2007.

16. Woolard 2005.

17. As a result of the 2005 Supreme Court Roper *v.* Simmons decision, those who committed crimes when they were under eighteen are no longer eligible for the death penalty. Roper *v.* Simmons, U.S. Supreme Court, no.03-633, 13 October 2004.

18. Hartney 2006.

19. Former Princeton professor and Bush administration appointee John Dilulio predicted a crime wave of unprecedented proportions based on the arrival of "tens of thousands of severely morally impoverished juvenile superpredators" (quoted in Ryan and Ziedenberg 2007:3). He recanted these doom-and-gloom forecasts, but despite the new data, the public perception that juvenile crime rate continues to rise remains as strong as ever.

20. Ryan and Ziedenberg 2007:11.

21. See the debates over the prosecution of Omar Ahmed Khadr in "A Legal Debate Develops in Guantánamo over the Prosecution of Boy Fighters," *New York Times,* 3 June 2007.

22. Bouakra 2006.

23. "France is not so rich in children that it can afford to neglect doing what is required to help them become normal adults . . . juvenile delinquency is one of the most pressing issues of our time" (Protection Judiciaire de la Jeunesse 2001:18).

24. French judges' position, 5 July 2007, http://www.justicedesmineurs.com/article -11193931.html.

REFERENCES

Abu-Lughod, J. 1980. *Rabat: Urban Apartheid in Morocco*. Princeton, NJ: Princeton University Press.

Agence pour le Développement des Relations Interculturelles. 2002. *Les mineurs étrangers isolés: Les réponses des professionnels sur Paris-Ile-de-France*. Paris: Author.

Allaix, M. 1995. La spécialisation des magistrats de la jeunesse: Une garantie pour les mineurs de justice. In *Justice des mineurs: Évolution d'un modèle*, edited by A. Garapon and D. Salas, pp. 73–80. Paris: Librairie Générale du Droit et de Jurisprudence.

Alleg, H. [1958] 2006. *The Question*. Lincoln: University of Nebraska Press.

Allen, F. 1964. The Juvenile Court and the Limits of Juvenile Justice. In *The Borderland of Criminal Justice: Essays in Law and Criminology*, pp. 43–61. Chicago: University of Chicago Press.

American Psychiatric Association. 1994. *Diagnostic and Statistical Manual of Mental Disorders*. 4th ed. Washington, DC: American Psychiatric Association.

Ancel, M. 1960. Introduction. In *The French Penal Code*, edited by G. O. W. Mueller, pp. 1–13. South Hackensack, NJ: Fred B. Rothman and Co.

Appadurai, A. 1996. *Modernity at Large: Cultural Dimensions of Globalization*. Vol. 1. Minneapolis: University of Minnesota Press.

Ariès, P. 1962. *Centuries of Childhood: A Social History of Family Life*. New York: Knopf.

Association Française des Magistrats de la Jeunesse et de la Famille. 2002. *Les mineurs délinquants dans le monde commun: Un devoir de société. Vers une pédagogie de l'espoir*. Paris: Tribunal pour Enfants de Paris.

Association Nationale d'Assistance aux Frontières pour les Etrangers. 2003. La roulette russe de l'asile à la frontière: Zone d'attente: Qui détourne la procédure? www.anafe.org.

Aubin, A. 1996. Un problème de sécurité publique. *Etudes Tsiganes* 1:37–46.

Aubusson de Cavarlay, B. 1998. La réponse pénale à la délinquance des mineurs: Résultats statistiques. In *Réponses à la délinquance des mineurs: Mission interministérielle sur la prévention et le traitement de la délinquance des mineurs, Rapport au Premier Ministre* by C. Lazerges and J.-P. Balduyck, pp. 265–275. Paris: La documentation française.

———. 1999. France 1998: La justice des mineurs bousculée. *Criminologie* 32(2):83–99.

Augé, M. 1986. *Un ethnologue dans le métro*. Paris: Hachette.

Aussaresses, P. 2001. *The Battle of the Casbah: Terrorism and Counter-Terrorism in Algeria, 1955–1957*. New York: Enigma Books.

Bachman, C. 1992. Jeunes et banlieues. In *Intégration et exclusion dans la société française contemporaine*, edited by G. Ferréol, pp. 128–154. Lille: Presses Universitaires de Lille.

Bailleau, F. 1996. *Les jeunes face à la justice pénale: Analyse critique de l'application de l'ordonnance de 1945*. Paris: Syros.

———. 1998. La justice des mineurs: Des principes à la pratique. *Sauvegarde de l'enfance* 5:290–297.

Bailleau, F., and C. Gorgeon, eds. 2000. *Prévention et sécurité: Vers un nouvel ordre social?* Saint Denis La Plaine: Les éditions de la délégation interministérielle à la ville.

Balibar, E., and I. Wallerstein. 1991. *Race, Nation, Class: Ambiguous Identities*. New York: Verso.

Baranger, T., and B. Bougeneaux. 2005. Interview, Denis Salas. *Justice* 185:207.

Barrow, N. 2003. Études sur les mineurs roms roumains. *Etudes Tsiganes* 1:1–31.

Bataille, P. 1997. *Le racisme au travail*. Paris: La Découverte.

Baudouin, J. 1990. *Le juge des enfants: Punir ou protéger?* Paris: Broché.

Bauer, A., and X. Raufer. 1999. *Violences et insécurités urbaines*. 2nd ed. Paris: Presses Universitaires de France.

———. 2005. *Violences et insécurités urbaines*. 5th ed. Paris: Presses Universitaires de France.

Baulon, M.-A. 2000. *Chronique des "petits-riens": Des Enfants. Un Juge. Un Tribunal.* Paris: Plon.

Beaud, S. 1994. "L'école et le quartier. *Critiques sociales* 5–6:13–46.

———. 2002. *80% au bac. Et après? . . . Les enfants de la démocratisation scolaire*. Paris: La Découverte.

Beaumont, G. de, and A. de Tocqueville. 1833. *Origin and Outline of the Penitentiary System in the United States of North America*. London: J. and A. Arch.

Begag, A., and C. Delorme. 1994. *Quartiers sensibles*. Paris: Seuil.

Bell, J. 2006. *Judiciaires in Europe: A Comparative Review*. Cambridge: Cambridge University Press.

Bell, V. 1993. Governing Childhood: Neo-liberalism and the Law. *Economy and Society* 22(3):390–403.

Benec'h-Le Roux, P. 2004. A quoi sert l'avocat du mineur délinquant? *Questions Pénales* 17(3):1–5.

Benloulou, G. 2001. Interview with Jean-Pierre Rosenczveig. *Lien Social* 581. http://archive.linesocial.com/dossiers2001/581a590/581-1.htm.

Beriss, D. I. 2000. Culture-as-Race or Culture-as-Culture? Caribbean Ethnicity and the Ambiguity of Cultural Identity in France. *French Politics, Culture, and Society* 18(3):18–47.

———. 2004. *Black Skins, French Voices: Caribbean Ethnicity and Activism in Urban France.* Boulder, CO: Westview Press.

Bessin, M. 2004. Emergency Placements in Juvenile Justice: Abandoning the Time for Education. *Social Science Information* 43(3):371–387.

Bishop, D., C. Frazer, L. Lanza-Kaduce, and H. White. 1999. *Fact Sheet #113: A Study of Juvenile Transfers to Criminal Court in Florida.* Washington, DC: U.S. Department of Justice, Office of Justice Programs, Office of Juvenile Justice and Delinquency Prevention.

Blatier, C. 1999. Juvenile Justice in France: The Evolution of Sentencing for Children and Minor Delinquents. *British Journal of Criminology* 39(2):240–252.

Body-Gendrot, S. 2000. *The Social Control of Cities? A Comparative Perspective.* Oxford: Blackwell.

Body-Gendrot, S., N. Le Guennec, and M. Herrou. 1998. *Mission sur les violences urbaines.* Paris: La documentation française/IHESI.

Bonelli, L. 2007. Policing the Youth: Toward a Redefinition of Discipline and Social Control in French Working-Class Neighborhoods. In *Youth, Globalization, and the Law*, edited by S. A. Venkatesh and R. Kassimir, pp. 90–123. Stanford, CA: Stanford University Press.

Bonnemain, C. 2000. Les incivilités: Usages d'une nouvelle catégorie. In *Prévention et insécurité: Vers un nouvel ordre social?* edited by F. Bailleau and C. Gorgeon, pp. 55–66. Paris: Les éditions de la délégation interministérielle à la ville.

Bonnemaison, G. 1982. *Face à la délinquance: Prévention, répression, solidarité.* Rapport au Premier Ministre par la Commission des maires sur la sécurité. Paris: La documentation française.

Bordet, J. 1999. *Les jeunes de la cité.* Paris: Presses Universitaires de France.

Bouarkra, N. 2006. Mineurs "dangereux" et juges "laxistes." http://www.monde-diplomatique.fr/2006/11/BOUAKRA/14205.

Bourdieu, P. 1986. La force du droit. *Actes de la recherche en sciences sociales* 64:3–19.

Bourgois, P. 1995. *In Search of Respect: Selling Crack in El Barrio.* Cambridge: Cambridge University Press.

———. 2001. The Culture of Poverty. In *International Encyclopedia of the Social and Behavioral Sciences*, edited by N. J. Smelser and P. B. Baltes, pp. 11904–11907. Oxford: Pergamon.

Bousquet, R. 1998. *Insécurité: Nouveaux risques. Les quartiers de tous les dangers.* Paris: L'Harmattan.

Bowen, J. R. 2007. *Why the French Don't Like Headscarves: Islam, the State, and Public Space*. Princeton, NJ: Princeton University Press.

Boyer, H., and G. Lochard. 1998. *Scènes de télévision en banlieues: 1950–1994*. Paris: L'Harmattan.

Bridges, G., and S. Steen. 1998. Racial Disparities in Official Assessments of Juvenile Offenders: Attributional Stereotypes as Mediating Mechanisms. *American Sociological Review* 554(63):561–564.

Bruel, A. 1995a. Un bon juge et un bon débat. In *La justice des mineurs: Évolution d'un modèle*, edited by A. Garapon and D. Salas, pp. 65–72. Paris: Librairie Générale du Droit et de Jurisprudence.

———. 1995b. *Rapport d'activité du tribunal pour enfants de Paris*. Internal court document provided to the author.

———. 2000. Un itinéraire dans la justice des mineurs: Entretien avec Alain Bruel. *Esprit* (October):75–85.

Bui Trong, L. 1993. L'insécurité des quartiers sensibles: Une échelle d'évaluation. *Les Cahiers de la Sécurité Intérieure* 14.

———. 2000. *Violences urbaines: Des vérités qui dérangent*. Paris: Bayard.

Cabanel, G.-P. 2000. *Prisons: Une humiliation pour la république: Rapport de la commission d'enquête sur les conditions de détention dans les établissements pénitentiaires en France, 2000/07, no. 449*. Paris: Senate. www.senat.fr/rap/199-449/199-449.htm.

Caldeira, T. 2000. *City of Walls: Crime, Segregation, and Citizenship in São Paulo*. Berkeley: University of California Press.

Canivet, G. 2000. Amélioration du contrôle extérieur des établissements pénitentiaires: Rapport au garde des Sceaux, ministre de la justice. Paris: La documentation française. http://www.ladocumentationfrancaise.fr/rapports-publics/004001169/index.shtml.

Carle, J.-C., and J.-P. Schosteck. 2002. *La délinquance des mineurs: Rapport de la commission d'enquête du Sénat* [Carle and Schosteck Commission Report]. Paris: Journal Officiel.

Castel, R. 2003. *From Manual Workers to Wage Laborers: Transformation of the Social Question*. New Brunswick, NJ: Transaction Publishers.

Catta, E. 1988. *A quoi tu juges?* Paris: Flammarion.

Çelik, Z. 1997. *Urban Forms and Colonial Confrontations: Algiers Under French Rule*. Berkeley: University of California Press.

Chaillou, P. 1987. *Le juge et l'enfant*. Toulouse: Edouard Privat.

———. 1989. *Mon juge*. Belfond, Montréal: Editions du Pré aux Clercs.

———. 1995. *La violence des jeunes: L'autorité parentale en question*. Paris: Gallimard.

———. 1999. *La délinquance des mineurs*. Allocution au début de l'année judiciaire, Cour d'Appel de Paris. Unpublished speech, copy provided to the author.

Chazal, J. 1946. *Les enfants devant leurs juges*. La Chapelle–Montligeon: Éditions familiales de France.

Chouk, A., L. Gillet, A. Spire, and E. Terray. 2002. *Enquête sur les comportements policiers*. Syndicat des avocats de France, Ligue des droits de l'homme, and Syndicat de la magistrature. Paris: Syndicat de la magistrature.

Cicourel, A. V. [1967] 1995. *The Social Organization of Juvenile Justice*. New Brunswick, NJ: Transaction Publishers.

Cloward, R., and L. Ohlin. 1960. *Delinquency and Opportunity: A Theory of Delinquent Gangs*. London: Routledge and Kegan Paul.

Cohen, A. K. 1955. *Delinquent Boys: The Culture of the Gang*. Glencoe, IL: Free Press.

Cole, D. 2007. Why We Have Lost the War on Terror. The Brennan Lecture, Georgetown University, 18 January.

Cole, J., and D. Durham. 2007. Introduction: Age, Regeneration, and the Intimate Politics of Globalization. In *Generations and Globalization: Youth, Age, and Family in the New World Economy*, edited by J. Cole and D. Durham, pp. 1–28. Bloomington: Indiana University Press.

Collovald, A. 2000. Violence et délinquance dans la presse. In *Prévention et sécurité: Vers un nouvel ordre?* edited by F. Bailleau and C. Gorgeon, pp. 39–53. Saint-Denis la Plaine: Les éditions de la délégation interministérielle à la ville.

Comaroff, J., and J. L. Comaroff. 2006. Reflections on Youth, from the Past to the Postcolony. In *Frontiers of Capital: Ethnographic Reflections on the New Economy*, edited by M. S. Fisher and G. Downey, pp. 267–281. Durham, NC: Duke University Press.

Copfermann, E. 1962. *La génération des blousons noirs*. Paris: Maspéro.

Council of Europe, European Committee for the Prevention of Torture and Inhuman or Degrading Treatment or Punishment. 1991, 1996, 2003, 2006. *Report to the Government of the French Republic Concerning the Visit Undertaken by the European Committee on the Prevention of Torture*. www.cpt.coe.int/en/states/fra.htm.

Cour des Comptes. 2003. *La Protection Judiciaire de la Jeunesse*. Rapport au President de la République suivi des réponses des administrations et organismes intéressés.

Coutant, I. 2005. *Délit de jeunesse: La justice face aux quartiers*. Paris: La Découverte.

Coutin, S. B. 2000. *Legalizing Moves: Salvadoran Immigrants' Struggle for U.S. Residency*. Ann Arbor: University of Michigan Press.

Crenshaw, K. W. 1995. Race, Reform, and Retrenchment: Transformation and Legitimation in Anti-discrimination Law. In *Critical Race Theory: The Key Writings That Formed the Movement*, edited by K. Crenshaw, N. Gotanda, G. Peller, and K. Thomas, pp. 103–122. New York: The New Press.

Dalrymple, T. 2002. The Barbarians at the Gates of Paris. *City Journal* 12(4). www.city-journal.org/html/12_4_the_barbarians.html.

De Almeida, Z. 1975. Les perturbations mentales chez les migrants. *L'information psychiatrique* 51(3):249–281.

Debuyst, C. 1995. L'école française dite "du milieu social." In *Histoire des savoirs sur le crime et la peine*. Vol. 2, *La Rationalité pénale et la naissance de la criminologie*, edited by C. Debuyst, F. Digneffe, and A. P. Pires, pp. 303–356. Montréal: Les Presses Universitaires de Montréal et d'Ottawa.

Défense des Enfants International–France. Yearly reports. www.dei-france.org.

Devine, J. 1996. *Maximum Security: The Culture of Violence in Inner-City Schools*. Chicago: University of Chicago Press.

Diminescu, D. 2001. L'installation dans la mobilité: Les savoir-faire migratoires des Roumains. *Migrations Société* 13(74):107–116.

——. 2003. *Visibles mais peu nombreux: Les circulations migratoires roumaines*. Paris: Maison des Sciences de l'Homme.

Dirks, N. 2002. Annals of the Archive: Ethnographic Notes on the Sources of History. In *From the Margins: Historical Anthropology and Its Futures*, edited by B. K. Axel, pp. 47–65. Durham, NC: Duke University Press.

Doek, J. E. 2002. Modern Juvenile Justice in Europe. In *A Century of Juvenile Justice*, edited by M. K. Rosenheim, F. Zimring, D. S. Tanenhaus, and B. Dohrn, pp. 505–527. Chicago: University of Chicago Press.

Donzelot, J. [1977] 1997. *The Policing of Families*. Baltimore, MD: Johns Hopkins University Press.

Douglas, M. 1966. *Purity and Danger: An Analysis of the Concepts of Pollution and Taboo*. London: Routledge.

Dray, D. 1998. L'imaginaire de la sanction chez les victimes d'agression. *Esprit* 248:101–120.

Dray, J. 1999. *État de violence*. Paris: Editions No. 1.

——. 2002. *Rapport sur la proposition de loi renforçant la présomption d'innocence et les droits des victims*, no. 3647. Paris: Assemblée Nationale. www.assemblee
-nationale.fr/11/rapports/r3647.asp.

Dubet, F. 1987. *La Galère: Jeunes en survie*. Paris: Fayard.

Dubois, L. 2000. Republican Antiracism and Racism: A Caribbean Genealogy. *French Politics, Culture, and Society* 18(3):5–17.

——. 2004a. *A Colony of Citizens: Revolution and Slave Emancipation in the French Caribbean, 1787–1804*. Chapel Hill: University of North Carolina Press.

——. 2004b. *Avengers of the New World: The Story of the Haitian Revolution*. Cambridge, MA: Harvard University Press.

Duché, D.-J. 1983. *L'enfant au risque de la famille*. Paris: Paidos/Centurion.

Duprez, D., and M. Kokoreff. 2000. *Le monde des drogues: Usages et trafics dans les milieux populaires*. Paris: Éditions Odile Jacob.

Duret, P., and M. Augustini. 1995. *Anthropologie de la fraternité dans les cités*. Paris: Presses Universitaires de France.

Durham, D. 2004. Disappearing Youth. *American Ethnologist* 31(4):589–605.

——. 2007. Empowering Youth: Making Youth Citizens in Botswana. In *Generations and Globalization: Youth, Age and Family in the New World Economy*, edited by J. Cole and D. Durham, pp. 101–131. Bloomington: Indiana University Press.

Einaudi, J.-L., D. Colinet, and S. Pouget. 2002. Les mutations d'une loi. *TDC* 844 (15–30 November). www.cndp.fr/tice/teledoc/Mire/mire_cvo-tribunal.htm.

Emerson, R. M. 1969. *Judging Delinquents: Context and Process in Juvenile Court.* Chicago: Aldine.

Enloe, C. 1988. *Making Feminist Sense of International Politics: Bananas, Beaches, and Bases.* Berkeley: University of California Press.

Esmein, A. [1913] 1968. *A History of Continental Crime Procedure with Special Reference to France.* New York: Augustus M. Kelly.

Estrada, F. 2001. Juvenile Violence as a Social Problem: Trends, Media Attention, and Societal Response. *European Journal on Criminal Policy* 41(4):639–655.

Étiemble, A. 2002. Les mineurs isolés étrangers en France. *Migrations Études* 109:1–15.

Fagan, J. 2006. *The Changing Borders of Juvenile Justice: Transfers of Adolescents to the Adult Criminal Court.* MacArthur Issue Brief #5. New York: Author.

Fanon, F. [1952] 1967. *Black Skin, White Masks.* New York: Grove Press.

Fassin, D. 1999. L'ethnopsychiatrie et ses réseaux: L'influence qui grandit. *Genèse* 35:164–171.

———. 2005. Compassion and Repression: The Moral Economy of Immigration Policies in France. *Cultural Anthropology* 20(3):362–387.

Fassin, D., and R. Rechtman. 2005. An Anthropological Hybrid: The Pragmatic Arrangement of Universalism and Culturalism in French Mental Health. *Transcultural Psychiatry* 42:347–366.

Feeley, M., and J. Simon. 1992. The New Penology: Notes on the Emerging Strategy of Corrections and Its Implications. *Criminology* 30:449–474.

———. 1994. Actuarial Justice: The Emerging New Criminal Law. In *The Futures of Criminology,* edited by D. Nelken, pp. 173–201. London: Sage.

Ferguson, A. A. 2001. *Bad Boys: Public Schools in the Making of Black Masculinity.* Ann Arbor: University of Michigan Press.

Fisher, M. 2004. Wall Street Women Herstories. In *Constructing Corporate America: History, Politics, Culture,* edited by K. Lipartito and D. B. Sicilia, pp. 294–320. New York: Oxford University Press.

Fishman, S. 2002. *The Battle for Children: World War II, Youth Crime, and Juvenile Justice in Twentieth-Century France.* Cambridge, MA: Harvard University Press.

Floch, J. 2000. Rapport fait au nom de la Commission d'enquête sur la situation dans les prisons françaises. Tome 1 2000/07, no. 2521. Paris: Assemblée Nationale. www.assemblee-nationale.fr/rap-enq/r2521-1asp.

Foucault, M. 1977. *Discipline and Punish: The Birth of the Prison.* New York: Vintage.

———. 1991. Governmentality. In *The Foucault Effect: Studies in Governmentality,* edited by G. Burchell, C. Gordon, and P. Miller, pp. 87–105. London: Harvester Wheatsheaf.

Frontline. 2007. 8 May broadcast. *When Kids Get Life*. www.pbs.org/wgbh/pages/frontline/whenkidsgetlife/etc/synopsis.html.

Gans, H. J. 1962. *The Urban Villagers: Group and Class in the Life of Italian Americans*. New York: Free Press of Glencoe.

Garapon, A. 1985. *L'âne portant des reliques*. Paris: Le Centurion.

———. 1995. Justice rituelle, justice informelle, justice décentralisee. In *La Justice des Mineurs: Évolution d'un Modèle*, edited by A. Garapon and D. Salas, pp. 138–152. Paris: Librairie Générale du Droit et de Jurisprudence.

———. 1997. *Bien Juger: Essai sur le rituel judiciaire*. Paris: Éditions Odile Jacob.

Garapon, A., and D. Salas, eds. 1995. *La justice des mineurs: Évolution d'un modèle*. Paris: Librairie Générale du Droit et de Jurisprudence.

———. 1999. *La république pénalisée*. Paris: Hachette.

Garland, D. 1996. The Limits of the Sovereign State. *British Journal of Criminology* 36(4): 445–471.

———. 2001. *The Culture of Control: Crime and Social Order in Contemporary Society*. Oxford: Oxford University Press.

Gilbert, J. 1986. *A Cycle of Outrage: America's Reaction to Juvenile Delinquency in the 1950s*. New York: Oxford University Press.

Goldstein, D. 1998. Nothing Bad Intended: Child Discipline, Punishment, and Survival in a Shantytown in Rio de Janeiro, Brazil. In *Small Wars: The Cultural Politics of Childhood*, edited by N. Scheper-Hughes and C. Sargent, pp. 389–415. Berkeley: University of California Press.

Goldstein, J. 1987. *Console and Classify: The French Psychiatric Profession in the Nineteenth Century*. Cambridge: Cambridge University Press.

Grémy, J.-P. 1996. *Les violences urbaines*. Paris: Institut des Hautes Études de la Sécurité Intérieure.

Hajjar, L. 2005. *Courting Conflict: The Israeli Military Court System in the West Bank and Gaza*. Berkeley: University of California Press.

Hamon, H. 2001. La violence de la judiciarisation. Paper delivered at Conference of the Association Française des Magistrats de Jeunesse et de la Famille, Paris.

Hargreaves, A. G. 2000a. A Second Division? Post-Colonial Intellectuals in Contemporary France. *Contemporary French Civilization* 24(2):267–286.

———. 2000b. Half-Measures: Antidiscrimination Policy in France. *French Politics, Culture, and Society* 18(3):83–101.

Hartigan, J., Jr. 2005. *Odd Tribes: Toward a Cultural Analysis of White People*. Durham, NC: Duke University Press.

Hartney, C. 2006. *Fact Sheet: Youth Under Age 18 in the Adult Criminal Justice System*. Oakland, CA: National Council on Crime and Delinquency.

Herzog-Evans, M. 2000. *Procédure pénale*. Paris: Librairie Vuibert.

Heuyer, G. 1914. *Enfants anormaux et délinquants juveniles: Nécessité de l'examen psychiatrique des écoliers.* Thèse de doctorat en médecine. Paris: Steinheil.

———. 1942. *Enquête sur la délinquance juvénile: Étude de 400 dossiers.* Alençon: Imprimerie Corbière et Jugain.

Heuyer, G., and J. Dublineau. 1932. *Le vol généreux.* Congrès de médecine légale. Extrait de la Semaine des hôpitaux du 15 juillet 1932.

———. 1934. La réaction d'opposition chez l'enfant. *Revue médico-sociale de l'enfance* 2:92–102; 3:186–197.

Hirsch, S. F. 1998. *Pronouncing and Persevering: Gender and the Discourses of Disputing in an African Islamic Court.* Chicago: University of Chicago Press.

———. 2006. *In the Moment of Greatest Calamity: Terrorism, Grief, and a Victim's Quest for Justice.* Princeton, NJ: Princeton University Press.

Hodgson, J. 2005. *French Criminal Justice: A Comparative Account of the Investigation and Prosecution of Crime in France.* Portland, OR: Hart Publishing.

Horn, D. G. 1994. *Social Bodies: Science, Reproduction, and Italian Modernity.* Princeton, NJ: Princeton University Press.

Huyette, M. 1999. *Guide de la Protection judiciaire de l'enfant.* Paris: Dunod.

Ighilahriz, L. 2001. *L'Algérienne.* Paris: Fayard.

Inspection, rapport final, SEAT de Paris. 2003. Direction de la Protection Judiciaire de la Jeunesse. Inspection des Services, Inspection no. 1 SP 2002 (14 May). Paris: Ministère de la Justice.

Inspection Générale des Affaires Sociales. 2005. *Mission d'analyse et de proposition sur les conditions d'accueil des mineurs étrangers isolés en France.* Rapport no. 2005 010. Paris: Author.

Inspection Générale des Services Judiciaires. 2004. *Juridiction des Mineurs de Paris.* Le Tribunal pour Enfants (fiche 2–22), Le Parquet des Mineurs (fiche 23–41). Paris: Ministère de la Justice.

Inspection préliminaire, SEAT de Paris. 2003. Direction de la Protection Judiciaire de la Jeunesse. Inspection des Services, Inspection no. 1 SP 2002 (16 January). Paris: Ministère de la Justice.

James, A. 2007. Giving Voice to Children's Voices: Practices and Problems, Pitfalls and Potentials. *American Anthropologist* 109(2):261–272.

Jérez, C. 2001. *Le juge des enfants, entre assistance, répression et rééducation.* Paris: Sofiac.

Jobard, F. 2002. *Bavures policières: La force publique et ses usages.* Paris: La Découverte.

Jobard, F., and M. Zimolag. 2005. Quand les policiers vont au tribunal: Étude sur les outrages, rébellions et violences. *Questions Pénales* 18(2):1–4.

Katz, M. B. 1989. *The Undeserving Poor: From the War on Poverty to the War on Welfare.* New York: Pantheon Books.

Korbin, J. 1998. "Good Mothers," "Babykillers," and Fatal Child Maltreatment. In *Small Wars: The Cultural Politics of Childhood*, edited by N. Scheper-Hughes and C. Sargent, pp. 253–276. Berkeley: University of California Press.

Kwolek-Folland, A. 1994. *Engendering Business: Men and Women in the Corporate Office, 1870–1930*. Baltimore, MD: Johns Hopkins University Press.

Lacassagne, J-A. 1885. *Actes du 1er Congrès d'anthropologie criminelle*. Rome.

Lagrange, H. 2001. *De l'affrontement à l'esquive*. Paris: Syros.

Landrieu, B. 2003. *Rapport sur les mineurs étrangers*. Paris: La Préfecture de la région d'Ile-de-France.

Lazerges, C. 2001. *Rapport d'information, no. 3501*. Paris: Assemblée Nationale. www.assemblee-nationale.fr/rap-info/i3501.asp.

Lazerges, C., and J.-P. Balduyck. 1998. *Réponses à la délinquance des mineurs: Mission interministérielle sur la prévention et le traitement de la délinquance des mineurs, Rapport au Premier Ministre* [Lazerges and Balduyck Commission Report]. Paris: La documentation française.

Lebovici, S. 1951. Rapport sur les facteurs psychogènes de la délinquance juvénile. In *Actes du II Congrès International de Criminologie*. Vol. 1, pp. 119–128. Paris: Presses Universitaires de France.

———. 1993. Du côté de l'enfant. *Autrement: Série Mutations* 134 (January):114–125. (Special issue: Parents au singulier: Monoparentalité: Echec ou défi?)

Leder, D. 2007. Imprisoned Bodies: The Life-World of the Incarcerated. In *Prisons and Punishment: Reconsidering Global Penality*, edited by M. Nagel and S. N. Asumah, pp. 55–70. Trenton, NJ: Africa World Press.

Lefaucheur, N. 1989. *Dissociation familiale et délinquance juvenile: Les avatars scientifiques d'une représentation sociale, Association Marie Lambert. Rapport pour la Caisse Nationale d'Allocations Familiales*. Paris: Caisse Nationale d'Allocations Familiales.

———. 1993. Sur la scène de l'anormalité familiale. In *Les recompositions familiales aujourd'hui*, edited by M.-T. Meulders-Klein and I. Théry, pp. 123–136. Paris: Nathan.

Léger, R. 1990. *La Colonie agricole et pénitentiaire de Mettray: Souvenirs d'un colon, 1922–27*. Paris: L'Harmattan.

Le Gouaziou, V., and L. Mucchielli, eds. 2006. *Quand les banlieues brûlent . . . Retour sur les émeutes de novembre 2005*. Paris: La Découverte.

Lepoutre, D. 1997. *Coeur de banlieue: Codes, rites et langages*. Paris: Éditions Odile Jacob.

Lernout, Y. 1995. Vers une justice de réciprocité? In *La Justice des Mineurs: Évolution d'un Modèle*, edited by A. Garapon and D. Salas, pp. 81–88. Paris: Librairie Générale du Droit et de Jurisprudence.

Le Sueur, J. 2006. Introduction. In *The Question* by H. Alleg, pp. xiii–xxv. Lincoln: University of Nebraska Press.

Lewis, O. 1961. *The Children of Sanchez: Autobiography of a Mexican Family*. New York: Random House.

————. 1966a. *La Vida: A Puerto Rican Family in the Culture of Poverty—San Juan and New York.* New York: Random House.

————. 1966b. The Culture of Poverty. *Scientific American* 215:19–25.

Mack, J. W. 1909. The Juvenile Court. *Harvard Law Review* 23:104–122.

MacMaster, N. 1991. The "seuil de tolérance": The Uses of a "Scientific" Racist Concept. In *Race, Discourse, and Power in France*, edited by M. Silverman, pp. 14–28. Aldershot, UK: Avebury.

Mai, N. 2007. Errance, Migration, and Male Sex Work: On the Socio-Cultural Sustainability of a Third Space. In *Places We Share: Migration, Subjectivity, and Global Mobility*, edited by S. Ossman, pp. 97–120. New York: Lexington Books.

Mary, P. 2001. Pénalité et gestion des risques: Vers une justice actuarielle en Europe? *Déviance et Société* 25(1):33–51.

Masclet, O. 2002. Les parents immigrés pris au piège de la cité. *Cultures et conflits* 46:147–173.

Mauger, G. 1995. Le monde des bandes. *Neuropsychiatrie de l'Enfance* 43(3):99–102.

————. 1998. Bandes et valeurs de virilité. *Regards sur l'actualité* (July–August):29–39.

Maurer, Bill. 1997. *Recharting the Caribbean: Land, Law, and Citizenship in the British Virgin Islands.* Ann Arbor: University of Michigan Press.

Maximy, M. de, T. Baranger, and H. de Maximy. 2000. *L'enfant sorcier africain entre ses deux juges.* Paris: Odin Éditions.

Merry, S. E. 1990. *Getting Justice and Getting Even: Legal Consciousness Among Working-Class Americans.* Chicago: University of Chicago Press.

————. 2001. Spatial Governmentality and the New Urban Order: Controlling Gender Violence Through Law. *American Anthropologist* 103(1):16–29.

Merton, R. 1938. Social Structure and Anomie. *American Sociological Review* 3:672–682.

Meyer, P. [1977] 1983. *The Child and the State: The Intervention of the State in Family Life.* Cambridge: Cambridge University Press; Paris: Maison des Sciences de l'Homme.

Monjardet, D. 1996. *Ce que fait la police: Sociologie de la force publique.* Paris: La Découverte.

Morford, J. 1997. Social Indexicality in French Pronominal Address. *Journal of Linguistic Anthropology* 7(1):3–37.

Mouhanna, C. 2000. Les services publics and la question jeune: De la crainte au rejet. In *Prévention et insécurité: Vers un nouvel ordre social?* edited by F. Bailleau and C. Gorgeon, pp. 95–108. Paris: Les éditions de la délégation interministérielle à la ville.

Mucchielli, L., ed. 1994. *Histoire de la criminologie française.* Paris: L'Harmattan.

————. 1998. *La Découverte du social: La naissance de la sociologie en France (1870–1914).* Paris: La Découverte.

————. 2000a. Familles et délinquences: Un bilan des recherches francophones et anglophones. *Études et données pénales* 86:3–102.

————. 2000b. Review of *Violences et insécurité urbaines. Pénombre* 22:9–11.

————. 2002. *Violences et insécurité: Fantasmes et réalités dans le débat français.* Paris: La Découverte.

———. 2004. L'évolution de la délinquance juvénile en France (1980–2000). *Sociétés contemporaines* 53:101–134.

———. 2005. *Le scandale des "tournantes": Dérives médiatiques, contre-enquête sociologique.* Paris: La Découverte.

Muncie, J. 2007. Youth Justice and the Governance of Young People: Global, International, National, and Local Contexts. In *Youth, Globalization, and the Law*, edited by S. A. Venkatesh and R. Kassmir, pp. 17–56. Stanford, CA: Stanford University Press.

Murard, N. 2000. Autorité et amour: Éducation des enfants ou mise en condition? *Mouvements* 8 (March–April):16–22.

Nagel, M., and S. N. Asumah, eds. 2007. *Prisons and Punishment: Reconsidering Global Penality.* Trenton, NJ: Africa World Press.

Nathan, T. 2001. *L'influence qui guérit.* Paris: Éditions Odile Jacob.

Naves, P., and B. Cathala. 2000. Accueils provisoires et placements d'enfants et d'adolescents: Des décisions qui mettent à l'épreuve le système français de protection de l'enfance et de la famille. Inspection des services de la Protection Judiciaire de la Jeunesse. http://afmjf.free.fr/IMG/pdf/rapport_Naves_Cathala-3.pdf.

Nicolau, G. 1996. *Ethnologie en Herbe: Le Cabinet F1 117, 20e Sud. Approche ethnométhodologique.* Mémoire du DESS. Paris: Publications de l'université Paris 7–Denis Diderot.

Noiriel, G. 1992. Français et Étrangers. In *Les lieux de mémoire.* Part III, *La France.* Vol. 1, *Conflits et partages,* edited by P. Nora. Paris: Gallimard.

Nye, R. A. 1984. *Crime, Madness, and Politics in Modern France: The Medical Concept of National Decline.* Princeton, NJ: Princeton University Press.

O'Brien, P. 1982. *The Promise of Punishment: Prisons in Nineteenth-Century France.* Princeton, NJ: Princeton University Press.

Ossman, S., and S. J. Terrio. 2006. The French Riots: Questioning Spaces of Surveillance and Sovereignty. *International Migration* 44(2):5–21.

Panter-Brick, C. 2002. Street Children, Human Rights, and Public Health: A Critique and Future Directions. *Annual Review of Anthropology* 31:147–171.

Paperman, P. 2001. Les faits et les personnes: Impartialité et aveu dans la justice des mineurs. In *L'aveu,* edited by R. Dulong, pp. 232–240. Paris: Presses Universitaires de France.

Peyrefitte, A. 1977. *Réponses à la Violence.* Rapport à M. Président de la République présenté par le Comité d'études sur la Violence, la Criminalité, et la Délinquance. Paris: La documentation française. [State-commissioned report on delinquency.]

Philips, S. U. 1998. *Ideology in the Language of Judges: How Judges Practice Law, Politics, and Courtroom Control.* New York: Oxford University Press.

Plantet, J. 2003. Que faire des mineurs étrangers isolés? *Lien Social* 663:1–4.

Protection Judiciaire de la Jeunesse. 2001. Paris: Ministère de la Justice.

Pujadas, D., and A. Salam. 1995. *La tentation du jihad.* Paris: J. C. Lattès.

Pupavac, V. 2001. Misanthropy Without Borders: The International Children's Rights Regime. *Disasters* 259:95–112.

Rabinow, P. 1989. *French Modern: Norms and Forms of the Social Environment.* Cambridge, MA: MIT Press.

Rainwater, L., and W. L. Yancey, eds. 1967. *The Moynihan Report and the Politics of Controversy.* Cambridge, MA: MIT Press.

Rassat, M.-L. 1990. *Procédure pénale.* Paris: Presses Universitaires de France.

Raux, E. 1890a. L'enfance coupable. *Archives d'anthropologie criminelle* 5:221–258.

———. 1890b. *Nos jeunes détenus: Étude sur l'enfance coupable.* Lyon: A. Storck; Paris: Masson.

Rhodes, L. A. 2004. *Total Confinement: Madness and Reason in the Maximum Security Prison.* Berkeley: University of California Press.

———. 2005. Choosing the Subject: Conversation in Supermax. *Cultural Anthropology* 20(3):388–411.

Ricoeur, P. 1995. *Le juste.* Vol. 1. Paris: Editions Esprit.

Roché, S. 1993. *Le sentiment d'insécurité.* Paris: Presses Universitaires de France.

———. 1996. *La société incivile: Qu'est-ce que l'insécurité?* Paris: Seuil.

———. 1998. *Sociologie politique de l'insécurité: Violences urbaines, inégalités et globalisation.* Paris: Presses Universitaires de France.

———. 2000. La théorie de la "vitre cassée" en France: Incivilités et désordres en public. *Revue française de science politique* 50(3):387–412.

———. 2001. *La délinquance des jeunes: Les 13–19 ans racontent leurs délits.* Paris: Seuil.

———. 2002. *Tolérance zéro? Incivilités et insécurités.* Paris: Éditions Odile Jacob.

Rose, N. 1996. The Death of the Social? Refiguring the Territory of Government. *Economy and Society* 25(3):327–346.

———. 1999. *Powers of Freedom: Reframing Political Thought.* Cambridge: Cambridge University Press.

———. 2000. Government and Control. *British Journal of Criminology* 40:321–339.

Rosen, D. M. 2005. *Armies of the Young: Child Soldiers in War and Terrorism.* Piscataway, NJ: Rutgers University Press.

———. 2007. Child Soldiers, International Humanitarian Law, and the Globalization of Childhood. *American Anthropologist* 109(2):296–306.

Rosen, L. 2006. *Law as Culture: An Invitation.* Princeton, NJ: Princeton University Press.

Rosenczveig, J.-P. 1999. *Justice pour les enfants.* Paris: Robert Laffont.

———. 2002. *Justice, ta mère.* Paris: Robert Laffont.

Rudder, V. de, C. Poiret, and F. Vourc'h. 2000. *L'inégalité raciste: L'universalité républicaine à l'épreuve.* Paris: Presses Universitaires de France.

Rufin, M. 1996. *Protection de la jeunesse et délinquance juvénile.* Paris: La documentation française. [Rufin Commission Report.]

Ryan, L., and J. Ziedenberg. 2007. *The Consequences Aren't Minor: The Impact of Trying Youth as Adults and Strategies for Reform.* Washington, DC: Campaign for Youth Justice.

Salas, D. 1992. *Du procès pénal.* Paris: Presses Universitaires de France.

———. 1995. L'enfant paradoxal. In *La Justice des Mineurs: Évolution d'un modèle,* edited by A. Garapon and D. Salas, pp. 41–62. Paris: Librairie Générale du Droit et de Jurisprudence.

———. 1997. La délinquance d'exclusion. *Les Cahiers de la Sécurité Intérieure* 29:61–75.

———. 2005. *La volonté de punir, essai sur le populisme pénal.* Paris: Hachette Littératures.

Sarat, A. 2001. *When the State Kills: Capital Punishment and the American Condition.* Princeton, NJ: Princeton University Press.

Sarkozy, N. 2005a. Assemblée Nationale (speech), 15 November. http://www.interieur .gouv.fr/misill/sections/a_l_interieur/le_ministre/interventions/archives-sarkozy -2005-2007/15-11-2005-assemblee-nationale/view.

———. 2005b. Déplacement de M. Nicolas Sarkozy à Perpignan (speech), 13 October. http://www.interieur.gouv.fr/misill/sections/a_l_interieur/le_ministre/interventions/ archives-sarkozy-2005-2007/13-10-2005-perpignan/view.

———. 2007. Conférence de presse sur la sécurité, l'aménagement du territoire et l'immigration. www.interieur.gouv.fr/sections/a_la_une/toute_l_actualite/ministere/ archives/conference-presse-11-01-07/.

Savage, J. 2007. *Teenage: The Creation of Youth Culture.* New York: Viking Press.

Sayad, A. 1991. Les enfants illégitimes. In *L'immigration ou les paradoxes de l'altérité,* edited by A. Sayad, pp. 185–258. Bruxelles: De Boeck.

———. 1999. *La double absence: Des illusions de l'émigré aux souffrances de l'immigré.* Paris: Seuil.

Scheper-Hughes, N., and D. Hoffman. 1998. Brazilian Apartheid: Street Kids and the Struggle for Urban Space. In *Small Wars: The Cultural Politics of Childhood,* edited by N. Scheper-Hughes and C. Sargent, pp. 352–388. Berkeley: University of California Press.

Scheper-Hughes, N., and C. Sargent, eds. 1998. Introduction: The Cultural Politics of Childhood. In *Small Wars: The Cultural Politics of Childhood,* edited by N. Scheper-Hughes and C. Sargent, pp. 1–33. Berkeley: University of California Press.

Schouler, C. 2001. *Vos Papiers! Que faire face à la police?* Paris: L'esprit frappeur.

Scott, E., and L. Steinberg. 2003. Blaming Youth. *Texas Law Review* 81:799–840.

Scott, J. W. 1996. *Only Paradoxes to Offer: French Feminists and the Rights of Man.* Cambridge, MA: Harvard University Press.

———. 2007. *The Politics of the Veil.* Princeton, NJ: Princeton University Press.

Serre, D. 2001. La "judiciarisation" en actes: Le signalement d' "enfant en danger." *Actes de la recherche en sciences sociales* 136–137:70–82.

.

Shore, B. 1996. *Culture in Mind: Cognition, Culture and the Problem of Meaning.* Oxford: Oxford University Press.

Shweder, R. A., M. Minow, and H. R. Markus, eds. 2002. *Engaging Cultural Differences: The Multicultural Challenge in Liberal Democracies.* New York: Russell Sage Foundation.

Silverman, M. 1995. Rights and Differences: Questions of Citizenship in France. In *Racism, Ethnicity, and Politics in Contemporary Europe,* edited by A. G. Hargreaves and J. Leaman, pp. 253–263. London: Edward Elgar.

Silverstein, P. A. 2004. *Algeria in France: Transpolitics, Race, and Nation.* Bloomington: Indiana University Press.

———. 2006. New Martial Races: Rap and the Racialization of French Suburban Violence. Paper presented at the American Anthropological Association Annual Meetings, San José, CA.

Slyomovics, S. 2005. *The Performance of Human Rights in Morocco.* Philadelphia: University of Pennsylvania Press.

Smedley, A. 2006. *Race in North America: Origin and Evolution of a Worldview.* 3rd ed. Boulder, CO: Westview Press.

Soulez-Larivière, D. 1987. *Les juges dans la balance.* Paris: Seuil.

———. 1995. Psychologie du magistrat, institution judiciaire and fantasmes collectifs. *Pouvoirs* 74:41–54.

Stephens, S. 1995. Children and the Politics of Culture in "Late Capitalism." In *Children and the Politics of Culture,* edited by S. Stephens, pp. 3–48. Princeton, NJ: Princeton University Press.

Talbot, M. 2000. The Maximum Security Adolescent. *New York Times Magazine,* 10 September.

Terra, J.-L. 2003. Prévention du suicide des personnes détenues: Évaluation des actions mises en place et propositions pour développer un programme complet de prévention. Rapport de mission à la demande du garde des Sceaux, ministre de la Justice et du ministre de la Santé, de la Famille et des Personnes Handicappées. www.presse .justice.gouv.fr/art_pix/rapportterra.pdf.

Terrio, S. J. 2003. You'll Get Your Day in Court: Judging Delinquents at the Paris Palace of Justice. *Political and Legal Anthropology Review* 26(2):136–164.

———. 2007. Youth, (Im)migration and Juvenile Law at the Paris Palace of Justice. In *Youth, Globalization, and the Law,* edited by S. A. Venkatesh and R. Kassimir, pp. 163–191. Stanford, CA: Stanford University Press.

Terrio, S. J., and A. Sobanet. 2005. Silence in the Court and Testimony Behind Bars: Juvenile Defendants and the French Judicial System. *French Cultural Studies* 16:21–39.

Théry, I. 1993. *Le démariage: Justice et vie privée.* Paris: Éditions Odile Jacob.

———, ed. 1998. *Couple, filiation and parenté aujourd'hui.* Paris: Éditions Odile Jacob.

Thrasher, F. M. 1937. *The Gang: A Study of 1,313 Gangs in Chicago*. 2nd ed. Chicago: University of Chicago Press.

Ticktin, M. 2006. Where Ethics and Politics Meet: The Violence of Humanitarianism in France. *American Ethnologist* 33(1):33–49.

Tomel, G., and H. Rollet. 1892. *Les Enfants en prison: Études anecdotiques sur l'enfance criminelles*. Paris: Plon.

Touret-de-Coucy, F. 2004. Justice pénale des mineurs: Une théorie éprouvée par la pratique. Unpublished paper.

Tribalat, M. 1998. Intégration des jeunes d'origine étrangère. In *Couple, filiation and parenté aujourd'hui*, edited by I. Théry, pp. 271–303. Paris: Éditions Odile Jacob.

Vasseur, V. 2000. *Médecin-Chef: A la prison de la Santé*. Paris: Le cherche-midi éditeur.

Venkatesh, S. A. 2007. Policing Ourselves: Law and Order in the American Ghetto. In *Youth, Globalization, and the Law*, edited by S. A. Venkatesh and R. Kassimir, pp. 124–157. Stanford, CA: Stanford University Press.

Venkatesh, S. A., and R. Kassimir, eds. 2007. *Youth, Globalization, and the Law*. Stanford, CA: Stanford University Press.

Vieillard-Boyer, H. 1996. *Banlieue: Ghetto impossible?* Saint-Étienne: Éditions de l'Aube.

Villepinte, Les actes du colloque. 1997. *Des villes sûres pour des citoyens libres*. 24–25 October. Paris: Ministère de l'Intérieur. www.ladocumentationfrancaise.fr/rapports -publics/984000425/index.shtml.

Wacquant, L. 1992. Pour en finir avec le mythe des "cité-ghettos": Les différences entre la France et les États-Unis. *Annales de la recherché urbaine* 52 (septembre):20–30.

———. 1997a. Three Pernicious Premises in the Study of the American Ghetto. *International Journal of Urban and Regional Research* 21(2):341–353.

———. 1997b. For an Analytic of Racial Domination. *Political Power and Social Theory* 11:221–234.

———. 1999. *Les prisons de la misère*. Paris: Éditions Raisons d'Agir.

———. 2004. Comment sortir du piège sécuritaire? *Contradictions* 22:120–133.

———. 2005a. Les deux visages du ghetto. *Actes de la recherche en sciences sociales* 160:4–12.

———. 2005b. Burn Baby Burn, French Style? Webcast, 17 November, on "Roots of the Riots in the French City," Center on Institutions and Governance, University of California at Berkeley.

Wasserman, G. A., L. Miller, and L. Cothern. 2000. Prevention of Serious and Violent Juvenile Offending. *Juvenile Justice Bulletin* (May):1–14.

Weil, P. 2005. *La France et ses étrangers: L'aventure d'une politique de l'immigration*. Paris: Gallimard.

Whyte, W. F. 1955. *Street Corner Society: The Social Structure of an Italian Slum*. Chicago: University of Chicago Press.

Wilson, J. Q., and G. L. Kelling. 1994. Vitres cassées. *Les Cahiers de la Sécurité Intérieure* 14:163–180. [Translation of 1982 article.]

Wilson, W. J. 1987. *The Truly Disadvantaged: The Inner City, the Underclass, and Public Policy.* Chicago: University of Chicago Press.

Winter, B. 1994. Women, the Law, and Cultural Relativism in France: The Case of Excision. *Signs: The Journal of Women in Culture and Society* 19(4):939–974.

Woolard, J. 2005. Juveniles Within Adult and Correctional Settings: Legal Pathways and Developmental Considerations. *International Journal of Forensic Mental Health* 4(1):1–18.

Wright, G. 1991. *The Politics of Design in French Colonial Urbanism.* Chicago: University of Chicago Press.

Wyvekens, A. 2004. *The French Juvenile Justice System.* Working Group on Juvenile Justice. www.esc-eurocrim.org/files/french_juvenile_justice.doc.

Xuereb, J.-C. 1982. Les fondements et la pratique de l'intervention judiciaire. In *L'Enfant maltraité,* edited by P. Strauss and M. Manicaux. Paris: Fleurus.

Yngvesson, B. 1993. *Virtuous Citizens, Disruptive Subjects: Order and Complaint in a New England Court.* New York: Routledge.

Zilberg, E. 2007. Refugee Gang Youth: Zero Tolerance and the Security State in Contemporary U.S.–Salvadoran Relations. In *Youth, Globalization, and the Law,* edited by S. A. Venkatesh and R. Kassimir, pp. 61–89. Stanford, CA: Stanford University Press.

Cases, Circulars, Laws, and Rulings (www.legisfrance.gouv.fr)

Cases
Selmouni v. France (25803/94), 28 July 1999.
Tomasi v. France, 27 August 1992.

Circulars
Circular no. NOR JUS F 98 500 88C.

Laws
Law of 22 July 1912. www.textes.justice.gouv.fr/art_pix/loi1912.pdf.
Ordinance no. 58-13000 of 23 December 1958.
Law no. 80-1041 of 23 December 1980.
Law no. 93-2 of 4 January 1993.
Law no. 93-22 of 8 January 1993.
Law no. 93-1013 of 24 August 1993.
Law no. 96-585 of 1 July 1996.
Law no. 98-468 of 17 June 1998.

Law no. 2000-516 of 15 June 2000.

Law no. 2002-1138 of 9 September 2002.

Law no. 2003-239 of 18 March 2003.

Law no. 2003-19 of 26 November 2003.

Law no 2004-204 of 9 March 2004.

Law no. 2007-1198 of 10 August 2007.

Rulings

Conseil d'état, Décision du 27 juin 2008, no. 286798, Mme M. www.conseil-etat.fr/ce/jurispd/index-ac-ld0820.shtml.

INDEX